The Intentional Life

What legacy do you want to leave?

The Intentional Life: Crafting Your Legacy, One Day at a Time blends theories of positive psychology with individual testimonials from a diverse selection of contributors to help readers discover their personal answers to this important question.

Consisting of 365 letters organized around seven "Life Health Principles" – Optimism, Values, Self-Care, Relationships, Community, Nature, and Service – this book shares the wisdom and experiences of a wide range of individuals alongside reflection questions and vision worksheets. *The Intentional Life* helps you develop a broader and deeper perspective about your course in life. Chapters will enable you to solidify what gives you meaning and joy as you learn from the experiences and insights of over 300 authors at varying stages of their life.

Whether you are finishing high school, attending college, starting a career, or engaged in other pursuits, this book will serve as an essential foundation for moving forward with a rich and fulfilling life. And doing so, one day at a time.

David S. Anderson, Ph.D., is Professor Emeritus of Education and Human Development at George Mason University. He is a lifelong educator who has dedicated his life to the positive development of young adults, including health promotion and wellness, drug and alcohol misuse prevention, and engaged strategic planning and accountability. He remains active with research, writing, and consulting and has served in community leadership roles in Celebration, Florida.

The Intentional Life

Crafting Your Legacy, One Day at a Time

DAVID S. ANDERSON

Routledge
Taylor & Francis Group

NEW YORK AND LONDON

Designed cover image: Bruce MacPherson, 2025

First published 2026
by Routledge
605 Third Avenue, New York, NY 10158

and by Routledge
4 Park Square, Milton Park, Abingdon, Oxon, OX14 4RN

Routledge is an imprint of the Taylor & Francis Group, an informa business

© 2026 David S. Anderson

ISBN: 978-1-032-89074-6 (pbk)
ISBN: 978-1-003-54108-0 (ebk)

DOI: 10.4324/9781003541080

Typeset in Sabon
by Apex CoVantage, LLC

This book is dedicated to Sally Coleman and Gayle Hamilton.

Each of these beautiful women brought wisdom, foresight, humility, and grace. Each one, in their own way, believed in the future and the power of human potential to live their lives to the fullest. Their love, compassion and legend served so many, so well and for so long.

May we all be blessed and honored to be influenced by people with such a legacy.

TABLE OF CONTENTS

PREFACE

The Intentional Life is like the fulfillment of a dream. As I reflect on my years as a college student, so many years ago, I recall thinking, as a second-year student, "I wish I'd known that last year." Similarly, as a third- and fourth-year student, I thought, "Wow, I really know a lot now, but I thought I knew a lot last year!" And so it goes – as a very young professional, while I knew a lot, I also knew that I had a lot to learn. And as a midlife professional, I realized that I knew a lot but had a lot to learn. And now, as a seasoned professional of over one half of a century, I realize that although I know a lot, there is a lot more to learn.

What was it that I wish my earlier self would have known? What are some of the expectations that I had, and how accurate were they? Was I as prepared as I could have been? Would some additional or experience have been helpful with moving forward and moving ahead with life? Sure, we can always do better. And we always have some reflections and regrets. But perhaps, just perhaps, a bit more insight and advance preparation would have been both reasonable and appropriate.

Life, for each of us, is a matter of learning from life experiences. Our own experiences are vitally important – if we choose to learn from them. But others' experiences are also most helpful – to draw on and integrate (by affirming, by modifying, and by ignoring) into our own lives.

Here's an example. I recall a talk by a distinguished professor at a professional development conference. He talked about Bill W., one of the founders of Alcoholics Anonymous. And he talked about William Jellinek, author of *The Disease Concept of Alcoholism*. He told stories about experience with each of these pioneers in the field of the prevention of alcohol problems and substance use disorders. He then said, "I can tell these stories because I was there. But who is going to tell these stories when I'm gone?" The richness of those stories – and those experiences – is often something that is not captured in the writings prepared by or about these individuals. But that professor's comment touched an important nerve for me.

Here's another example. My grandfather was a pediatrician in Brooklyn, New York, and he practiced (and made house calls!) until he was 89½. He was the first trained pediatrician in Brooklyn and worked on many diseases and the smallpox epidemic. When we often gathered during holidays, we would ask him to tell us stories about his life growing up on a farm in Michigan, putting himself through college and medical school and experiences as a doctor. As grandchildren living vicariously through his eyes, we offered our pride and admiration for his dedication and his attention to the well-being of his patients. A humble man, he often said, "What's really important, however, is education." He said that – an emphasis on education – is what he wanted to be remembered for. That's why he put not only himself and his sister through college, but he also provided funding for one year of college for each of his 12 grandchildren. That's what he believed in, and the legacy he wanted to leave.

And a third example may help bring this home even more. Through the vision and courage of my direct supervisor, a unique and forward-thinking experience was initiated for new students at the university. At the time, I served as the director of a 670-student residence hall. The idea was to create an immersive experience for first-year students to better prepare them for their life career. At that time over a half century ago, the average person was estimated to have three different careers over their lifespan. So what can be done to prepare for this most effectively? That was all part of the Career Planning Center for about 75 students. Each student enrolled in a yearlong class, and they focused on thinking about careers. An early assignment was for students to prepare their résumé as they envision it when they graduated. They needed to "fill it in" to best position themselves for their desired career four years later, upon graduation from college. Students were puzzled with this but then realized that they needed to do some things during their first year so they would be best prepared to have their résumé look like they wanted it to years later.

FOUNDATIONS

With my work in health promotion and drug and alcohol misuse prevention, I began in the same decade that the two national research institutes on these issues were founded. So I learned from other people, and the body of literature and knowledge was growing and growing. Thus, about ten years ago and inspired by the conference professor's words, I decided it would be helpful to capture the experience and insights from many individuals, from many different professional backgrounds, each of whom had been involved for decades in the field. At this time, some colleagues with very rich experience had already died. So it became most timely and appropriate to interview numerous individuals, which I did. Then I had to determine how to put these comments together, which I did. The resulting publication, *Leadership in Drug and Alcohol Abuse Prevention* (Routledge, 2016), incorporated their various views within an organized conceptual framework. It also included short essays on various topics relevant to leadership at the local, state, and national levels. For that one topic, the book incorporated decades upon decades of wisdom and professional experience and included best practices based on current science. The intent for those entering or already immersed in that field of study and practice was to help these individuals be more competent, confident, and committed to quality implementation.

Through my journey of life, with more of my life obviously behind me than ahead of me, I have listened to and learned from others. Although I didn't always follow the advice or direction of others, I listened to it. And when I encountered tough situations or what I considered to be poor examples, I made the decision to do otherwise.

Some examples will help:

- I recall a supervisor who said he liked to sit behind a desk to look over it with others; he specifically stated that he liked the chairs for others to be lower than his so he could look down at them. What I learned from that is that the physical setting makes a difference. I also vowed that I would not do that and tried to arrange my future offices so there wasn't a barrier between myself and guests.
- Living in the Washington, D.C. area, I had the opportunity to attend some presidential inauguration ceremonies. No, I wasn't one of those who got tickets – I just showed up early. One time, we were in the front of the group of "regular" people, crowded at the fence line. I recall people passing to their reserved seats, and I would hear someone say, "There goes someone important." Well, the label of "important" is relative, as everyone has some importance for some others or some settings.
- In giving a speech, one of the key pieces of advice is as follows: "Tell them what you're going to tell them; then tell them; then tell them what you told them." In other words, have some "bookends," some content at the beginning and the end that wraps around the core content.
- In my years as a counselor at a new camp for boys, the founding director had one key word that he emphasized for the counselors and the campers – "unselfishness." That permeated his life and his leadership and was a key value that he instilled. That resonated well with me with my focus on nonprofit activities and the sharing of knowledge through research, writing, teaching and services.

BACKGROUND

My background had some key learning moments and opportunities. I was raised in the Virginia suburbs of Washington, D.C., and enjoyed the opportunity to take advantage of and visit museums and momentous occasions. I recall, sadly, the funeral processions of President John F. Kennedy – going to and coming from our nation's Capitol building. I recall, through my membership in the Boy Scouts, having the opportunity to serve as an usher for the governor's box at the 1965 presidential inauguration. I had the opportunity to be a guest on an early television show *Youth Want to Know* and also served on the leadership board that started a teen dance club on weekends. Each of these were growth opportunities, with limited preparation. But each of these activities provided a way to stretch my boundaries and experiences.

What these experiences did – of course with the support and encouragement of my parents, teachers, and other adults and mentors – was to prepare me for the next experience. They helped me stretch and grow. They helped make the "uncomfortable" a bit more comfortable – like breaking in a new pair of shoes. These experiences helped ground me with various values and commitments. These experiences were so formative, like building blocks, one on top of another. Was it like a Lego set, with the detailed instructions and pictures to prepare the perfect final outcome? Not at all. There was and is no manual to guide each of us. That is the challenge, and the joy, of life and living.

For me, what these experiences did was to endow me with the importance of service, of sharing, and of helping better prepare others for what lies ahead. That's what led me into the world of student development – with the vast majority of my professional career focusing on the growth and development of college students and young adults. My career then focused on the health and human potential of young adults – primarily in the college setting. My entire career was based in the nonprofit sector.

Did things all go according to plan? Was it all intentional? Whatever the plan was, did it work out? No, no and no. But yes, yes and yes also. The "no" response is that there wasn't a specific plan – it was fuzzy. Going to college, I joined the premed student organization, as I wanted to follow in my grandfather's footsteps as a medical doctor. What I learned from that and doing rounds with doctors while wearing a doctor's white jacket was that I did not want to devote my professional work with the bodies of humans; rather, I wanted to work with the hearts and minds of individuals to help them live more productive and joyful lives. And that led to seeking a master's degree in college student affairs and higher education administration.

With the internship and then full-time work that went with that academic degree, I learned a lot. I also had a budding interest in teaching and volunteered to be mentored with teaching a course; this led to teaching other courses while I served in my administrative role. I also had some interest in learning more about what other institutions are doing to address various issues; that led to local and national research projects. This compilation of experiences and the quest for greater knowledge and expertise led to pursing an advanced degree in public administration/public affairs and ultimately a faculty position. In that role, my focus was on teaching, research and service, with the earlier preparation serving as excellent foundations for that young-adult focus that emphasized human growth, potential and development.

So although the initial plan did not unfold as initially intended, what did unfold was the intention of listening to myself and honoring my own natural skills and interests with both people and organizations. I listened to my interests and competencies with human development and management, and with health promotion and systems change. These principles grounded me and guided me throughout my career and continue to sustain and nourish me.

Even though there were no magic answers in my own personal and professional development, what did exist was a thoughtful and planful process. And this was coupled with some serendipity along the way, including opportunities to participate and continue to learn and sharing. All of this helps serve as the foundation for this book – to provide some tools and some inspiration for you with your own journey.

THE BASIS FOR THIS BOOK

With *The Intentional Life*, this is an idea that has been bubbling for many years. And then it became time to pull it together. It had its seeds nearly 30 years ago. I recall vividly a telephone call from a professional counselor at the University of Notre Dame. I had met Sally briefly before. She was in charge of the implementation of a national drug and alcohol misuse prevention initiative, based on a bequest from an anonymous donor. She had an idea and asked for my advice. I responded by saying that her idea – of a national conference – was not what was needed. I clarified further by saying that this already existed, sponsored annually by the U.S. Department of Education. She asked what was needed, and I said what we needed was to have a type of "think tank" approach, whereby individuals would gather to envision the future that was needed and would be appropriate for best addressing current and emerging needs of young adults. When she asked what that would look like, I responded by saying that I didn't know but that an innovative approach could be developed. With that, she involved several people on campus and from elsewhere to create a creative and thoughtful learning environment. This became the Challenge 2000 conference, with over 200 people attending. With two dozen vision groups, participants discussed and crafted what they deemed appropriate to deal with the needs of young adults. While the focus was on reducing and preventing drug and alcohol misuse and problems, the emerging strategies actually served as a foundation for holistic health and personal well-being and positive development. At the end of the conference, each of the groups provided a brief report-out regarding their many hours of discussion and planning. Some common themes emerged, and those served as the foundation for a follow-on conference a year later, when seven thematic areas were discussed in detail. For each of these seven themes, specific ideas for implementation by individuals, groups, schools and communities were identified. Those discussions served as the foundation for a book prepared by Sally and me, *Charting Your Course: A Life-Long Guide to Health and Compassion*. With numerous essays and thought pieces, that book provided a framework for quality decision-making and healthy living. Not too long after the book's publication, Sally became ill. And I recall some of her last words to me: "David, it's up to you now to carry this forward."

Thus, it is based on the foundations laid by Sally and her team, and all those gathered during the Challenge 2000 conferences, that *The Intentional Life* book is grounded. The seven life health themes that emerged from those vision groups serve as the seven thematic areas around which the legacy letters in this book are organized. The focus on "beginning with the end in mind" (per Stephen Covey) is the basis of being more intentional.

APPLICATIONS OF THIS BOOK

For most of the readers, the overall vision about life is fuzzy at best. Sure, some individuals have a clear idea about the goals to which they aspire. Some of these goals will be more general in nature. Some visions will focus more on process. Some will focus on career, some will emphasize accomplishments, others will highlight family, and many will center on qualities of life. Some may even be aimless and just attend to the here and now.

The intent of this book is to equip the reader – the young adult – with more tools and perspectives that will be helpful as they move ahead. These are many lessons learned and "I wish I would have known" perspectives. So here they are! However, this book does not encompass all sorts of knowledge about important knowledge and skills. Consider, for example, the importance of sleep, nutrition and exercise, the important qualities of conflict mediation and time management, and the skills of healthy relationships and decision-making. Consider the various elements incorporated in the eight dimensions of well-being – Physical, Emotional, Intellectual, Financial, Spiritual, Relational, Environmental and Vocational. Even though many of these are incorporated in this book, based on the insights and experiences of the contributors, these are best addressed in other books. In this realm, I must note two books I edited – *Wellness Issues for Higher Education* and *Further Wellness Issues for Higher Education*. These were designed to provide college professionals – those working with college students – with the latest science and knowledge, as well as practical applications, on a wide range of wellness topics. While each topic could encompass an entire book or multiple books, the intent was to provide a succinct overview so these professionals would be better prepared to prevent, identify and address many of the current and emerging needs of college students. Although the focus was on the higher education setting, the same content (i.e., the same science) could be applied to other settings. In that way, those in business settings, or community leadership, or recreation and leisure, or transportation, or public office, or elsewhere could benefit from that latest science on numerous well-being issues. To not be so prepared can be viewed as missed opportunities to maximize human potential.

Based on all of this, the intent of this book is to help change the foundations and the commitment to broader, richer and deeper thinking among young adults as they embark on the lifelong journey – of life and of living. Ideally, the insights and recommendations of the contributors are helpful with individual planning and thinking. The aim is to help change the nature of the conversation among young adults. As individuals reflect on each Legacy Letter and talk about what it means to them, even deeper reflection and decisions will likely evolve. With the reflection and inspiration offered with each Legacy Letter, individuals can ponder the issues and, where appropriate, take action (or make plans to take action). And different individuals will respond differently to what is said or implied throughout the book. Particularly with conversation and sharing perspectives, each individual will be more likely to develop richer plans – each one different from the other. And that is the beauty of this and the process; it's like a patchwork quilt, made up of so many different patterns and colors.

It is my hope that these words throughout this book, the wisdom of those who have traveled similar or different paths, and the inspiration provided can be helpful toward the aim of a more productive and meaningful life. I hope it can help "move the needle" in some small way. Most important, I hope that individuals are more likely to achieve that which gives them meaning, joy and a legacy befitting their dreams.

David S. Anderson
January 24, 2025

Introduction

" Where to from here with my life?" "How do I become successful?" "What is the meaning of life?" "What is my unique place on this planet?" These are questions, among others, that are commonly found among young adults. Particularly true when reaching the age of adulthood, so many questions and issues arise. Typically, this is a time when high school graduation occurs and various opportunities await. Is it attending a local community college or perhaps a vocational-technical school? Is it attendance at a four-year college or university? Is it military service or some other work? Is it a gap year for travel or reflection? Or is it something else?

The important thing is that this time of life is a perfect opportunity to raise a series of questions. It is a wonderful time to reflect and make some decisions about the next phase of life. This time is one that affords the challenges surrounding the most appropriate pathways forward. Although these are important decisions, adjustments can be made after a decision is made. That is, ongoing "fine-tuning" is both desirable and is often necessary.

This book, *The Intentional Life: Crafting Your Legacy, One Day at a Time*, provides each reader with the opportunity to reflect and to plan. The book is designed to aid each reader think more deeply and broadly about their own lives. The hundreds of pages included here are meant to be savored and nurtured, slowly – thus, the emphasis on "One Day at a Time."

Importantly, this book is not designed as a road map for one's life. If that were the case, then an organized, logical approach for getting to the desired destination would be appropriate. Sure, back roads and alternative transportation routes may be useful. However, to have "one best approach" or "one size fits all" is not relevant for living one's life.

When looking at the phrase "the intentional life" as part of the book's title, the focus is on being more intentional with one's life. It's about focusing on specific qualities or skills to enhance whatever is sought. It's about gathering sage wisdom from different sources and making more deliberate choices along the way. It's about being more planful and organized, about being more deliberate and thoughtful. The intent is not one of preparing the "perfect road map" for one's life – that just doesn't exist. It's also important

DOI: 10.4324/9781003541080-1

to acknowledge that so many twists and turns, challenges and obstacles, ups and downs occur throughout one's life, and many of these, in spite of good planning, just couldn't be anticipated. The question then becomes one of how to deal with these mishaps and to determine what is next. Ultimately, the emphasis of this book is on a process that is grounded and by design.

The phase "crafting your legacy" is important as part of this book's title. The responsibility is placed on each individual's shoulders – whether they choose to accept it and do something about it – for helping to shape one's own future. This book, and the life experiences and recommendations from hundreds of contributors, is designed to provide some insight and specific tools for helping shape one's future. Thus, the word "crafting" is central, as it focuses on the design and organization of the end product (i.e., one's life) and the processes (i.e., the decisions along the way). And the use of the word "your" is such that each individual has this opportunity, to a large extent, and that what might work out well for one person will likely be different from the next person.

The use of the word "legacy" has an important place. As the reader thinks about their ancestors, consider great-grandparents or distant relatives, as well as grandparents, parents and even siblings. What is remembered about them? What was important to them? How did they live their lives? What did they accomplish, whether with their professional work, their community activities, their service, their relationships with others, their family or more? Those are all part of their legacy. The question is whether that legacy – how they are remembered – is something they sought. Is it what they intended? And if it's not what they intended, is their legacy something about which they are proud or satisfied? If it's not what they sought, why is their legacy different from what they intended? What happened? And what could have been done to help them achieve the legacy they wanted?

With this book, the focus is to assist the reader to think more deeply and broadly about their own lives and to do this with the "tools" of rich experience from hundreds of people. The reader is encouraged to use the various elements in this book as a foundation for charting their own future direction. It is believed that individuals typically have dreams for their lives – whether that is based in their professional work, their family, their community involvement or some other factor. With this personal vision, the book may have inspiration and resources that help them achieve that vision. That vision serves as the basis for the legacy to which a person aspires. With that vision, and with greater thoughtfulness and intention, it is believed that individuals will be more likely to achieve that desired legacy.

Overall, the purpose of this book is to help each reader be more intentional and more forward-thinking. It is to help readers have a vision or goal in mind for one's life and to take steps that are most helpful for achieving that end. Here are some common quotes, illustrating that same theme:

- "Begin with the end in mind." Stephen Covey
- "If you can dream it, you can do it." Walt Disney

- "If you are always trying to be normal, you will never know how amazing you can be." Maya Angelou
- "Those that fail to learn from history are doomed to repeat it." Winston Churchill
- "Be the type of person you want to meet." Zig Ziglar
- "If I have seen further, it is by standing on the shoulders of giants." Sir Isaac Newton
- "I love you because no two snowflakes are alike, and it is possible, if you stand tippy-toe, to walk between the raindrops." Nikki Giovanni

This book is different, as it is designed primarily for a youthful audience, although the messages and inspiration will be valuable for youth of all ages. In addition, it's not a traditional academic book with lots of references and logical explanations. It is designed to be applied and used on a regular basis. One's life journey is never completed until it is indeed over. The book takes the experiences of many individuals and shares their voices. These collectively provide a wide range of points of view and serve as inspirational guidance and lessons learned. How often have people said, "I wish I would have known that before"? This is designed to try to offset that. And it's designed to be manageable ("one day at a time") and fun.

For context, consider the following:

> *Imagine there is a bank account that credits your account each morning with $86,400. It carries over no balance from day to day. Every evening the bank deletes whatever part of the balance you failed to use during the day. What would you do? Draw out every cent, of course? Each of us has such a bank, its name is time. Every morning, it credits you 86,400 seconds. Every night it writes off at a lost, whatever of this you failed to invest to a good purpose. It carries over no balance. It allows no overdraft. Each day it opens a new account for you. Each night it burns the remains of the day. If you fail to use the day's deposits, the loss is yours. There is no drawing against "tomorrow." You must live in the present on today's deposits. Invest it so as to get from it the utmost in health, happiness, and health. The clock is running. Make the most of today.*
> *— Marc Levy, If Only It Were True*

With this perspective, each individual has choices about their lives – how they spend their time, how they spend their money, what friendships are wanted, the nature of activities and free time, having a family and so much more. Certainly, each of us has constraints, such as how to make a living, how to pay the rent and various obligations. The ultimate aim is to help individuals live their lives, to the greatest extent, in ways that are fulfilling, enriching and rewarding in the mind of each person.

The messages throughout the book are designed to meet young adults where they are in various settings. Some young adults are in college or have plans to go to college. Others are those who decide to enlist in the military, have family obligations, attend vocational or trade school, work full- or part-time or follow some other path. Many of the issues are common across settings, and some will have different applications based on the particular setting. In all, the variety of themes and messages embedded in this book are designed to inspire, motivate and further ground the reader at this important junction of their life.

BACKGROUND

The Intentional Life comes from multiple foundations. The underpinnings for this book are based on both theory and practice. Theoretically, the book is based on positive psychology and human motivation. Also, theoretical foundations are seen with the theory of planned change, including force field analysis. Practically, the book is based on the traditions found in self-help groups such as Alcoholics Anonymous (AA) and Narcotics Anonymous (NA), with the phrase "one day at a time." Further, organizationally the book is based on seven thematic areas surrounding one's life and healthy living that evolved from a think tank process several decades ago.

The chapter will also highlight briefly the theoretical constructs on which the book is based.

A central foundation for this book is the theory of positive psychology. Much of the professional literature is based on the work of Martin Seligman, who emphasized resilience and well-being. Rooted in his research on the theory of learned helplessness, Dr. Seligman's work promotes resilience and emphasizes the value of quality relationships in one's growth and development. Related to that is human motivation theory, classically ascribed to the work of Abraham Maslow and the hierarchy of needs. With that construct, the basic needs, such as those physiological in nature as well as safety needs, take priority before psychological needs (such as belonging and self-esteem) and can be addressed in a meaningful way. And all of these are important foundations for the ultimate aim of self-actualizing or self-fulfillment. The blend of these two theoretical foundations provides the aspirational focus of the contents of this book – thinking about what the future of one's life might look like.

Related to this foundation is the attention to making plans and ultimately taking action to achieve that dream or desired outcome. Organization theory is used with the personal applications found throughout this book. Within that, a helpful framework is the theory of planned change, whereby individuals take more deliberate action to achieve the desired state of affairs with their lives. With this, attention is provided to both driving forces and restraining forces. With force field analysis, the first step is to identify as clearly as possible the desired state of affairs as well as the current state of affairs. Then, with attention to the current state of affairs, examine what types of forces would be helpful for providing movement toward the desired state of affairs; similarly, what forces are in the way (or restraining) movement in that desired direction. Then identify what will strengthen or enhance the driving forces and what will weaken, reduce or eliminate the restraining forces. That clearer understanding helps provide guidance with action steps that can be used to make progress toward that desired state of affairs – what specifically can be done to enhance the driving forces and weaken the restraining forces.

The application of this principle to individuals is straightforward. When thinking about something desired, such as a high academic grade, what are the forces that help to get there (e.g., doing the assigned readings, gaining good comprehension of the content, getting good rest, preparing assignments ahead of time, following instructions for papers or tests, seeking feedback for improvement, staying mentally sharp through exercise and good nutrition, and good time management). And for the restraining forces, these can include things such as spending minimal time studying or preparing, listening to others who minimize academic performance, succumbing to temptations to party, procrastinating, becoming too stressed and not seeking assistance when desiring it. Further, each of these individual factors that contribute to the driving and restraining forces can be examined to assess what can enhance or reduce their individual impact (i.e., do that same process at a more micro level). While this sounds cumbersome – and it can be – a mindset of this nature can be helpful in more effective and helpful planning and thus better outcomes that are desired.

Another practical foundation for this book is the "one day at a time" foundation, found commonly with the self-help approach of AA and also with so many other self-help approaches. This approach is implicit with the recovery from a substance use disorder (SUD), as the commonly accepted view is that an individual with a SUD is never "cured" and that recovery from the SUD is a lifelong process. While the individual may want to put the SUD in their distant past, many professionals in the field believe that the most helpful approach is to keep a clear focus on what is most manageable – that is, today. The recommendation is to attend to the immediate situation and manage it well. Certainly, individuals are encouraged to gain numerous life skills to help offset many of the stressors that may have contributed to the SUD. And difficult situations and life challenges will continue to occur; however, keep these manageable. By focusing on "the today" and the "here and now," greater success for managing day-to-day activities and situations is much more feasible. And as these days add up to weeks, months and years, that pattern of success becomes more natural.

With this book, *The Intentional Life*, the focus is on small steps. The focus is on "today" while making plans and taking steps for a more productive "tomorrow." As highlighted in the section "Using This Book," individuals are encouraged to look at a single reading for a day. Each one is on a separate page and provides a specific focus or area of emphasis. So the emphasis is on a type of "Morning Watch" or "First Watch" – making a commitment to grow personally and to take the time to read one Legacy Letter each day. In addition, the reader is encouraged to use the Inspiration provided by the contributors to reflect on oneself and even make plans for personal improvement, as offered by the contributor.

The other practical foundation for this book and the basis of the framework for the following seven chapters comes from the Challenge 2000 conference held in 1994. Spearheaded by Sally Coleman, a counselor at the University of Notre Dame, this several-day event brought together over 200 interested individuals from across the nation. The ultimate questions addressed in that setting was one of envisioning a healthy future for individuals and communities and to identify strategies to achieve that future. The conference attendees attended keynote sessions, focused workshops, and vision groups. It was these vision groups that were the heart and soul of the conference, as attendees, in groups of eight to ten individuals, participated in facilitated small-group discussions, totaling about ten hours over the three-day conference period. When a spokesperson from each of the 23 groups reported out at the conference's closing session, some common themes emerged. It is these themes that were organized into seven thematic clusters. A focus on each theme was believed to result in greater health and success among young adults. By attending to each of the seven themes and by attending to them as an entire group, the belief is that young adults would be more productive, achieve maximum health and life balance, be less harmfully involved with drugs or alcohol and be more likely to achieve their own desired outcomes with their lives. Following this conference, each vision group leader prepared a summary of their group's discussion and findings. That document and the seven themes surrounding life health planning served as the basis of a follow-on invitational conference in 1995, where each of the seven themes were examined more closely from a practical perspective. And then emerging from that conference was the development of a book, *Charting Your Course: A Life-Long Guide to Health and Compassion* (University of Notre Dame Press, 1998). *Charting Your Course* included short essays on each of the seven themes, as well as Legacy Letters from a variety of individuals with advice to young adults.

It is thus this foundation of positive psychology, the organization planning approach, a day-to-day emphasis found with self-help groups, the approach of self-directed planning grounded in seven thematic areas, and legacy conceptualization on which *The Intentional Life* is based. The aim is to focus on the future, and use the classic "7 Ps" approach: Proper prior planning prevents pathetically poor performance. Readers are encouraged to have an overall or specific vision, engage in quality, informed planning and to make and then follow through on plans to achieve that vision. With the approach found in this book, having confidence is important, and a key foundation for this personal confidence is the engagement of the insights and wisdom found from so many people, from many walks of life, who have gone before. It is also one of attempting to avoid the "Monday morning quarterbacking" when individuals dissect all that went wrong with the previous day's game. Again, focusing on proper prior planning is important for minimizing negative consequences of a proximate or distant nature and to promote the desired outcomes.

THE FRAMEWORK

The organizing framework for the book is the seven thematic areas, with a chapter devoted to each of these. As cited with the background, these seven thematic areas emerged from a think tank process that examined how young adults can live more healthy and productive lives. Noteworthy, however, is that these seven thematic areas do not stand alone – they are all interconnected.

Helpful for this chapter is a brief overview of each of the seven thematic areas. More detail about each of these is provided in the individual chapters. However, gaining some brief insight into the seven thematic areas, in a logical order to be specified, can be must instructive. While each of these seven thematic areas is interconnected and the grouping of these seven could be envisioned in a circular arrangement, the focus is instead on a process from the inward to a more expansive view. Specifically, the first principle is that of Optimism, because without some sense of a positive view, paralysis or lack of inertia or energy may exist. Built on that modicum of optimism is the Values principle, serving as a type of central focus or North Star. This is followed by Self-Care, providing specific tools organized around health promotion and wellness. Relationships (interactions with self and others) and Community follows, showing how the focus extends from inside oneself toward the external view. Connectedness with Nature and the natural world follows, and the process ends with Service or giving back. With that very brief overview, additional insights about each of these seven thematic areas helps anchor the reader and the development of a personal legacy.

The first thematic area, found in Chapter 2, "Setting the Stage: Optimism," serves as the foundation for the remaining six thematic areas. Essentially, without some sense of optimism, any progress is hampered. There must be some basic optimism that attention to anything is worthwhile – whether it is a life planning process, engagement with exercise or diet, skills development for work, practice of a hobby or craft, or relationships. Attention is provided to issues such as self-esteem, attitude, creativity and self-responsibility. Following a brief content overview, dozens of Legacy Letters offer experiences, insights and recommendations from the contributors. Chapter 3 is titled "Anchoring Your Life: Values" and highlights the importance of individuals listening to, clarifying and articulating more clearly their own values. Attention is provided to honor and respecting one's core beliefs, and how they address competing values. Attention is also provided to how to deal with situations when another person has different values.

Chapter 4 focuses on "Skills and Tools: Self-Care." The contents of this chapter and its Legacy Letters builds on the first two thematic areas. The contents within self-care incorporate numerous areas that encompass healthy living, such as, among other topics, mental health, time management, stress management, exercise, nutrition, drug and alcohol issues, financial management, body image, sleep and personal safety. The contributors' Legacy Letters will highlight their observations and recommendations, with direct application to the reader's life.

Chapters 5 and 6 complement each other and continue the building process toward a healthier and more planful life. The first of these, "Bonding: Relationships," emphasizes healthy relationships with family, friends, acquaintances, neighbors and even strangers. Key elements for promoting healthy relationships are highlighted throughout the chapter. Also important in this chapter is attention to having a healthy relationship with oneself. The second of these chapters, "Connections: Community" attends to the range of community settings and helps identify ways in which community can flourish. Communities abound in one's life, including the setting where one lives (like a neighborhood) as well as the school or classroom setting, an athletic group, club or organization, a worksite or faith-based setting. Community can be short term in nature (such as a traveling group or conference) or much longer term in scope (such as a membership organization or extended family group). Issues within community include communication, decision-making, organization, activities and functions.

The final two chapters with the thematic areas help round out the seven areas of emphasis for building a productive and meaningful life. In Chapter 7, "Nurturing Yourself: Nature," the emphasis is on an individual's connectedness with the natural world. This includes helping individuals participating in the natural world, from spending time outdoors to enjoying the sights, sounds and smells that surround them in different settings. It includes respect for all that nature brings, including being environmentally engaged with behaviors such as recycling and sustainability. Chapter 8 is titled "Giving Back: Service." The focus of the chapter's contents is on giving back, with the theoretical underpinning that much is gained by those who give. Whether it is through volunteer or paid work in an organized way, or an attitude of helping others and giving, service encompasses themes of "servant leadership," the "helper therapy principle."

The book ends with Chapter 9, titled "Reflection, Review and Action: Conclusion." This chapter helps wrap up the entire book with attention to each of the seven thematic areas and the 365 Legacy Letters incorporated within these areas. While the theme of legacy development is never complete, attention to this process at the earliest possible time is emphasized throughout this book. Being reflective, building on others' insights and experiences and being planful and deliberative can aid individuals to achieve their goals.

While no guarantees exist that just because someone sets out a goal it means they will achieve it, they are more likely to do so if they are thoughtful and grounded. The alternative is to be aimless and without direction, focusing more on the here and now and on immediate gratification. The longer-term planning process, grounded with dreams and aspirations, can help individuals achieve greater heights than would have been possible otherwise. This chapter pulls together the seven thematic areas and highlights the importance of taking specific action steps toward making their own future better and brighter.

CONTRIBUTORS

The insights and wisdom provided in this book are based on the contributions of over 300 different people. These include colleagues and friends, who collectively cover a broad and diverse group and come with two degrees of separation from the author. An intentional decision was made to not include family members; although siblings, cousins and other relatives had extremely insightful life experiences and were most influential in various ways throughout life, that potential bias was reduced from the beginning. Specifically, through the author's long career, contributors were identified who had had some positive influence on his life and its direction. Because this career was primarily college and university based and because the focus was on wellness, health promotion, and drug and alcohol misuse prevention, greater representation in those professional areas were necessarily included. Further, because over one-half of the professional career was at one institution of higher education (George Mason University), a greater representation from individuals from that setting is likely. So the first degree of separation for individual contributors was those with whom the author had direct contact. This could be another educator or policymaker, a student or a researcher, a community leader or a campus administrator. Some contributors were former students or staff members from over a half century ago, and others are more recent contacts and colleagues. Based on the author's research, publications, advocacy, advisory groups and public presence, invitations were made throughout the United States and abroad. The second degree of separation focused on individuals by whom an invited contributor had been inspired or was believed to have positive, inspirational comments for young adults. Contributions overall were sought from individuals from numerous walks of life, whether in education or government, in sports or theater, in blue-collar and white-collar jobs, and parents and youth. The reach for these contributors was facilitated by the commitment to provide as many experiences and inspiration to young adults as possible. Many other points of view and experiences from varied settings around the world was sought, and contributions were reviewed for diversity of viewpoints, variety of backgrounds and life experiences, and overall perspectives. Further, balance among the seven thematic areas was sought.

Instructions for contributors were straightforward. Acknowledging space limitations, contributors were asked to provide a Legacy Letter suitable for young adults, based on their own life experiences and insights.

They were asked to provide their best possible guidance to "their younger young-adult self" based on their own worldview. Although they were introduced to the seven thematic areas, no additional guidance was provided regarding specific topics or issues to address. They were also asked to summarize their contribution with a single declarative sentence and conclude with some reflection or task-oriented recommendations to the reader. Their biographies emphasize what they chose to highlight, although briefly. Noteworthy is that the stories, insights and recommendations in each of these Legacy Letters come from the rich experience of the contributor and are offered in their own words.

By drawing on the experiences and insights of hundreds of contributors, the reader will gain collective wisdom that can help guide them with their own decision-making. With a framework of seven thematic areas and reflective questions to help guide the reader, the aim is that readers will be more planful and be more deliberate with living their lives.

USING THIS BOOK

The Intentional Life can be used in a variety of different ways. Initially intended as a daily inspirational guide, the book can be used in various other ways.

The primary way the book can be used is as a daily inspirational or motivational guide. As the book's title suggests – "One Day at a Time" – a single Legacy Letter would be appropriate for each day of the year. Since the book is organized by the seven thematic areas, each Legacy Letter could be read sequentially; however, that would result in all contributions around a specific theme (e.g., Optimism) being read together over a single period. The recommended approach is to balance Legacy Letters from different thematic areas. To help with that, a proposed schedule of topics is provided at the back of the book, with each date having an identified Legacy Letter. This organization provides diverse topics, intertwining topics from the seven thematic areas to varied coverage of each area within each week and month. Each reader may wish to generate their own sequencing of Legacy Letters using a random number generator based on specific dates.

With this approach, it is recommended that individuals make a commitment to engaging with the contents and suggestions with this book. This may be like a type of reflection time, perhaps at the same time of each day (similar to a "Morning Watch" activity).

Another approach may be more of a response to a current situation facing the reader. For example, if a person is feeling less hopeful or "down," they may wish to read several Legacy Letters in the Optimism chapter. Similarly, if they want to deepen a relationship or are having problems with an existing relationship, they may want to read several contributions in the Relationships chapter.

A related approach is to make arrangements with one or more other people to follow the same process. If a small or larger group of individuals are reading the same Legacy Letter each day (or a set of Legacy Letters over a given time), they can meet or engage with one another online to discuss their respective views about the contents of the letter as well as their own thoughts about the inspiration statement at the end. This could be a type of "book club" approach with individuals committing to the same reading and then sharing their varied perspectives about what they read and thought.

When reading a Legacy Letter, each one has some inspiration at the end; this is a type of reflection question or suggested activity for the reader. These are designed to help stimulate the reader with the importance of engaging in a thoughtful and grounded process regarding the pathways for their lives. It will essentially focus on their commitment to engaging in a regular process of reflection and planning. With these, the reader is strongly encouraged to take that seriously and to do some active thinking and determine any appropriate application for that recommendation from the contributor. The reader may write some notes in the book or have a separate notebook with comments and ideas incorporated. By keeping it separate, the same Legacy Letter and inspiration can be reviewed a year later, and the reader can review the notes made previously and see how the current state of affairs is similar or different. Also of consideration is a separate journal, whereby the reader writes reflections and observations periodically.

Also incorporated throughout the book are Legacy Worksheets. These are found at the end of each chapter and provide a framework for processing the chapter's contents. They are also found with the Conclusion chapter, with some insights about how to pull together the varied content and insights for crafting one's own legacy and future. With these Legacy Worksheets, readers are encouraged to write notes to themselves to help sort through much of the content. Readers may wish to prepare their own version of each of the seven thematic area worksheets, in both print and electronic form, to help keep track of the various thoughts and insights gleaned through the process of reading and digesting the content.

Whatever the approach, the aim is to have the reader be more thoughtful and planful with their lives. Thus, each reader benefits from determining what approach works best based on their personal style and interest. Plus, if one approach isn't as appealing, then it is recommended that another approach be tried.

With all of this, it is important that the reader be mindful of a key part of the title: "One Day at a Time." That is, while someone may be particularly interested in enhancing their self-care habits or improving their relationship skills, what is important is to be mindful of personal growth in small, incremental steps. While some of the Legacy Letters may be transformational for the reader (as was their preparation as cited by some of the contributors), having only one Legacy Letter a day can be quite appropriate. Even more important is that the attention to, and the diligence provided to, doing this type of personal growth is essential for personal growth. Will that be challenging? Certainly. Does this appear urgent? Probably not. But will it be helpful? Yes, it's only as helpful based on the effort put into it. It's like a financial consideration – investing a little, every day, can accumulate to reap lifelong rewards. Said differently, if an individual is concerned about how their own life is going to turn out, some investment today (and every day) is essential for helping shape one's own personal legacy.

IN SUMMARY

This introductory and foundational chapter provides the framework for the book and the sources used with the voices found in the Legacy Letters. The introduction is organized around the core message of helping individuals – the young adult – be more intentional and planful with their lives.

In review, readers are encouraged to ask themselves the following questions:

- What is your life story?
- How do you want it to unfold? How do you expect it will unfold?
- As you are constructing your life story, what tools do you need?
- As you move forward, who will help you with the nature and direction of your journey? Who are your allies, your supporters, your cheerleaders, your advocates?
- How can you be more planful as you move ahead and to avoid waking up with regrets?
- What can you do today and tomorrow so that you are able to say, "This was a life well lived"?

The road forward is often daunting and unclear. Although engagement with *The Intentional Life* is not a clear road map or a guarantee about achieving the desired outcomes, the incorporation of the ideas, the intentions, the lessons learned, and the advice from decades and decades of experience can help each individual be more likely to achieve their own desired outcomes and thus their own legacy.

Optimism

Setting the Stage

The essential starting point for a healthy and productive life is optimism. There must be some basis for movement, for change, for enhancing one's life and for a different future. Even if this optimism is minimal, some must be present. There must be a vision, however undeveloped, of a future that is better in some ways than what currently exists.

The theme of optimism is essential as an individual considers a better tomorrow. That is, optimism is an integral part for the belief that individuals can envision, plan, develop, promote and sustain change and healthier living. While perfection can never be achieved with individual lives, improvement with productivity, outcomes, processes, satisfaction and overall worldviews is reasonable and can be attained. Through all of this must exist some sense of hope, whether large or small.

Why is optimism important? Simply put, this is because without some sense of positivity or some basis for moving forward, nothing changes. If one doesn't have some sense of hope, even a modicum of inspiration, then a fatalistic "why bother" attitude is likely. Essentially, without some sense of optimism, any movement progress is hampered. There must be some basic optimism that attention to anything is worthwhile–whether it is a life-planning process, engagement with personal health, skills development for work, practice of a hobby or craft, relationships or something else.

Optimism is all about setting the stage for improvement, for enhancement, for a better tomorrow. It is valuable when envisioning a major change as well as when addressing minor adjustments or tweaks.

With everyone's life, challenges exist, obstacles appear daunting, disappointments occur and lack of success is present. When these not-so-desired results or processes occur, how one views and addresses them can be most revealing and even rewarding. These challenges may appear to be insurmountable. But are they? Perhaps a careful assessment and an identification of ways to deal with them, will result in some "chinks in the armor" of them.

Concurrently, opportunities present themselves, and opportunities are discovered or uncovered. Optimism helps move things forward, from the onset of a new initiative or during the process to help sustain the effort.

DOI: 10.4324/9781003541080-2

THE CONTEXT OF OPTIMISM

As a contextual matter, the emphasis on optimism first is vital. It is the foundation on which the remaining six themes are based. Without some sense of optimism–again, whether large or small–individuals may not consider how their values align with their activities, or whether to examine their own values or key guiding concepts. Without some optimism, attention to the various elements of self-care, whether diet or exercise, time management or drug/alcohol use or other well-being issue, may appear to be useless. Optimism helps with both relationships and community, as it provides the basis for some belief in improvement and with investing in healthier individual and group interactions. With the areas of nature and service, having some positive outlook about becoming involved in those areas, whether through appreciation of the natural world, environmental respect, giving back or serving others, can help offset the view of "Why bother?" or "Is this really necessary?"

Many people will view optimism is a type of "Pollyanna" approach. They may see having an optimist view as naive or as unrealistic. In fact, optimism is essential for any movement. Plus, the emphasis on optimism is not simplistic–such as a view of "Well, I'll just be hopeful that things will work out, so I don't have to do anything more about it." That approach is not appropriate. Some effort is important and will be exemplified with careful thinking, planning, collaboration, resiliency and reflection. Underlying all of this is some positive worldview, and these efforts can indeed make a difference.

Optimism is much more than "whether the glass is half-full or half-empty of water." It incorporates a larger life perspective about yourself, about how you view yourself within the context of the world around you. It incorporates a can-do spirit; while not blindly enthusiastic, optimism is the necessary hope and belief that your decisions do make a difference. Important is that that optimism can be modified for specific situations, large and small, and even modified over time.

THE ROLE OF OPTIMISM

With the foundational place of an optimistic outlook for proceeding with becoming more intentional with life planning, it is helpful to have some reflection time. For example, envision a world or a community where greater attention to thoughtful planning exists. Consider periodic reflection about where one is, where one is heading and basing this on individualized settings as well as with families, school and work groups, community settings and larger settings. Consider the envisioning of a "wouldn't it be nice" setting where goals are set, reviewed, revised and renewed. Consider reasonable self-assessments of individuals and groups that also include external assessments. Consider even greater anticipation of and preparation for challenging situations, and gathering the tools and resources that help address them.

How does optimism fit within the concept of a life that is more intentional and that has more intentionality within its unfolding? The essence of this is that individuals are constantly faced with opportunities as well as challenges; the question is one of how these are dealt with. Does one adopt psychological paralysis when faced with a challenge? Similarly, does one stop reaching and striving when achieving a hard-earned and well-deserved (or even without such effort) honor or outcome? With a life that is filled with more intentionality, the emphasis is on becoming more deliberate and planful with overall vision and aims, and keeping focused on the achievement of personal and professional desires. Optimism–again, whether broad based or more focused–is an essential ingredient for moving on and moving forward.

OPTIMISM AND PLANNED CHANGE

Embedded within the thematic area of Optimism is the area of study called "planned change," highlighted in detail in the Introduction of this book. As note, this process helps individuals and groups guide their activities and their decisions toward some specified and desired results. Planned change can incorporate various other frameworks and structures. Consider the SWOT analysis, where one looks at strengths, weaknesses, opportunities and threats. Consider the Eisenhower matrix, with attention to which is urgent and what is important (noting these may be different). Also of value is the force field analysis (Lewin, 1951), where thought is given to the desired state of affairs and the current state of affairs; then, to help move the current situation toward the desired results, examine what might be driving forces (moving things toward the desired outcome) and what might be restraining forces (holding things back from making progress).

Central to planned change efforts is attention to various challenges and obstacles one faces. While individuals and organizations may resist change, whether due to uncertainty, lack of trust, limited resources, lack of preparedness or varied visions, the important emphasis is that of thinking more deliberatively and in a planful way with moving forward with life.

LINKAGE WITH OTHER THEMATIC AREAS

Optimism plays a vitally important role with each of the other six thematic areas. Consider the area of Values; for one to better understand what is important to them and to reflect on where they want to be, optimism must be present in order to believe that change is possible. Similarly, for one to feel confident to stand true to their own values and not be unnecessarily swayed by others' values (perhaps to gain their acceptance), optimism is critical for maintaining the course. Self-Care also requires the incorporation of optimism. Consider one's efforts with diet and exercise, consider individual efforts to improve conflict skills or anger, as well as time and stress management. Individuals must have some underlying optimism so that their efforts will sustain themselves over time, particularly as challenges or even a perception of lack of progress occur.

With the theme of Relationships, optimism is important for initiating, cultivating and nourishing a relationship. One has to believe that their efforts–their investment of time and energy–will be fruitful and result in positive outcomes. Individuals must believe their efforts are, in fact, worth it; that's optimism. The same is true with Community, with individuals having a positive orientation regarding their own investment (whether time, energy, money support or otherwise) is meaningful and appropriate. Further, do one's efforts help with the community, and its own positive well-being.

The thematic area of Nature also blends nicely with optimism. With the aims of maintaining, protecting and even restoring many of the natural resources, one must believe that the efforts with which they involve themselves make a difference. With the aim of being nourished by the woods, the rivers, the oceans and the sky, one must believe that the investment of time will be beneficial as a healing as well as a proactive approach. Finally, Service incorporates optimism, as one thinks of the various things they do to help and service others. Again, they must feel a sense of affirmation that their efforts are timely and appropriate; otherwise, they may have a "why bother" or "who cares" approach. Optimism is central to remaining engaged with these important undertakings.

CONCLUSION

The messages and insights embedded in the over 50 Legacy Letters in this chapter provide rich perspectives from numerous walks of life. The theme of Optimism permeates the contributors' emotional and heartfelt experience. From attention to an attitude of possibility, to overcoming and learning from challenges, to dealing with uncertainty, to perseverance, the Legacy Letters provide rich insights and perspectives from individuals with varied backgrounds. The attention to optimism as the first of seven thematic areas is critical, as it sets the stage for all that is to come. With this, an underlying theme is that one's attitude is a choice. This is the case for emotions, such as happiness and love; it is also the case for how individuals interact with one another, such as with respect, compassion and kindness. And central to this chapter, optimism is a choice. How individuals choose to proceed is up to them; the perspectives and motivations in this chapter provide a helpful foundation for moving forward.

Messages What are key points or themes highlighted in the Legacy Letters within the Optimism area?	
Reflections What are your thoughts and feelings about what is shared and recommended regarding Optimism?	
Resources What individuals, groups, organizations or other information would help you better understand and apply recommendations in the Optimism area?	
Commitments What are you willing to commit yourself to doing regarding the Optimism theme, both in the near term and in the more distant future?	

FIGURE 2.1
Legacy Worksheet for Optimism

A LONG LIFE
Peter Stearns

Habits like resilience, curiosity and hope are known to be key components of happiness, and they are essential in preparing for the inevitable unexpected turns in any interesting life.

Life today–on average–is longer than we sometimes imagine, and this means it is important to think about the long haul, amid all the other concerns of young adulthood, and be open to the unexpected.

When I was in high school, I was convinced that life was short. In fact, it was shorter back then than it is today–longevity has improved considerably. But my conviction was wrong even so: I simply did not know what real adulthood would mean, as it stretched over several decades.

My confusion had two results. First, I was in a hurry, and that has been true for me all my life. I had to get things done just in case there was no tomorrow. For the most part, this has not been a bad thing, though I have probably rushed some stuff that would have benefited from more patience. But my main blind spot was in not realizing how many different challenges and opportunities a long life involves. I assumed that if I marched as quickly as I could into a suitable work and family framework, my personal definition would be pretty well fixed.

And that was simply not the case. After about a decade of settling in, it turned out that most of my work projects would involve issues that I could barely have imagined when I was starting out. And the best single job of my life, in university administration, was a target I could not have identified for myself a few decades before.

My example is hardly unique: most people now hold three or more different jobs during their lifetimes, and they have to adjust to other basic life changes as well.

So what does this mean? To my mind, it means that life is going to be more interesting–and sometimes challenging–than one might predict. Preparing to take advantage of the unexpected, to remain curious and flexible, is a vital component of a full, long life. It also means thinking about education less as a first-job license and more a chance to learn how to learn. Facing a long life that will be partly unexpected is an invitation for hope and flexibility and a really great ride.

Imagine challenges or opportunities that might occur down the line, and think about how resiliency and hope would help shape a response.

Peter Stearns has taught history at the University of Chicago, Rutgers University, Carnegie Mellon University and George Mason University and won a distinguished lifetime research award from the American Historical Association. He served as Provost at George Mason for over 14 years.

THREE KEY LESSONS
Angie Hattery

Work hard, strive for excellence and, above all, strive to find the humanity in everyone you meet.

My dad died in February 2023. I was invited to deliver remarks at his memorial service a few months later. My dad was a giant in the field of diagnostic radiology and led a major medical center, and I knew I would be speaking to an audience of hundreds, including dozens and dozens of radiologists he had mentored, not to mention his four grandchildren. I was nervous. What would I say? I decided to reflect on three lessons he and my mom imparted to me growing up. Perhaps these lessons will inspire you!

Work hard. No matter what you decide to do in life professionally and in relationships, work hard at it. Even the most successful athletes, with all their "natural" talent, credit their hard work for their success; they are the first to the gym and the last to leave. Invest in the things that matter to you, and you'll reach your personal and professional goals.

Strive for excellence. Whatever you decide to pursue in life, strive to be the best you can be. That doesn't mean everything has to be excellent. Maybe the grilled cheese sandwich you made for lunch is only okay. Decide what matters to you and prioritize it. Don't settle for less than the best in yourself or in others. Your excellence will inspire those around you!

Strive to see the humanity in *everyone* you meet. In my own life, I have friends who are different from me but also friends who have had very different life experiences; two of my good friends spent more than 20 years each in prison. By choosing to see them for *who they are* and not one bad thing they have done, I've gained a whole new perspective on the world and been inspired to work for social justice!

Every day, try to find one thing you can work hard at, perform that task with excellence and see the humanity in everyone you meet along the way. Your life will be richer for it.

How would you rate yourself on each of these three items? What, specifically, can you do to maintain or improve your rating?

Angie Hattery, Ph.D., is a sociologist who studies some of the most pressing social issues, including mass incarceration and gender-based violence. She has written 12 books, including *Way Down in the Hole: Race, Intimacy and the Reproduction of Racial Ideologies in Solitary Confinement*. She is a partner, mother and grandmother who tries every single day to live by the values she learned growing up.

CALLIOPE'S WHISPERS
Paul J. Kachoris

Do more of what makes your heart happy!

Whisperings . . . Inaudible, Silent
Whispers . . . constantly
bending the inner ear of your
heart.

Barely, barely, barely hearing
Calliope's faint Callings as
they tumble out,
somewhat, half-alive, gasping for
Life. Are they even there?

Straining to apprehend them,
trying to resurrect them.
Perhaps some encrypted
messages begging to be heard.
Is there something there for you?

Yet betraying them; denying
them.
Unable to legitimize them
Turning a deaf ear to them.
Fearing to be led astray by
believing in YOU.

But Listen! Listen! Listen:
Calliope is Calling!
Make them fit YOUR Name.
There IS something here for
YOUR Life!

Have courage! Hold them!
Possess them! Self-actualize
your OWN golden legacy.
Your kernel has been incubating
since your birth when YOUR
Karma was given wings.

Revere Calliope. Unplug your
ears!
Allow Her to usher in your
Karma's flutterings.
Hear them beating on your heart
Let them in!

Finally, finally, finally allowing
the blossoming of your Lotus
Destiny.
Unleashing your unfettered Self to
claim your Cosmic Legacy!

During my freshman year, my inner drummer, "Calliope," called me into premedicine. At precisely the same moment, I "happened" serendipitously to meet my best college friend, Bob Hattery. He too had his own "Calliope" going. Our dual heart whispers immediately joined us together into a deep, interpersonal brotherly love: a mutually respectful, purposeful, full-of-love friendship. We kept each other on track for many years to become physicians. We helped each other to "do what made our hearts most happy!" It was our best friendship relationship that made our "Calliopes" proud. We listened to her inner whispers and self-actualized.

> Pick and meditate on a specific stanza in the "Calliope's Whispers" poem that speaks to you. What jump-starts your "heart"? Write a "heart" poem for yourself.

Paul J. Kachoris, M.D., is a child, adolescent, adult psychiatrist in active clinical practice for 60 years. He has held clinical, educational, academic and administrative positions in inpatient and outpatient psychiatric settings, and masculine psychological studies.

MIND THE MAGIC
Tamir Sammy Diab

When aligned with your passions, magical synchronistic moments will guide you.

After earning my bachelor's degree, I started a career in public health research, driven by my interest in epidemiology. After a few months, my subconscious mind began wandering toward childhood memories of nature and art. Day in, day out, it was as though a dormant creative voice was awakening within me, calling me toward another path.

One weekend, while watching a behind-the-scenes feature on a visual effects–heavy film, I was captivated by the artists' passion for their craft. They drew inspiration from nature, which resonated deeply with me. Motivated, I enrolled in an introductory 3D class. My instructor recognized my enthusiasm and urged me to explore better-funded programs. A turning point came when I attended a discussion on the visual effects for *Stuart Little* (a live-action/animated film) in Washington, D.C. The meticulous detail involved in animating the computer-generated mouse fascinated me, and I realized this was my calling. I found an academic program in Vancouver that aligned perfectly with my goals.

Confiding in my boss about my career change was daunting, but his response was transformative. He encouraged me to follow my passion, even if it meant embracing the unknown. His belief in me reframed the fear of failure into an experience of growth. I began to view this new path as a journey toward my true calling rather than as a destination.

Since then, I've worked on commercials and Oscar-winning films and am now developing virtual reality experiences that address mental health. I've learned that following your passion can unlock extraordinary opportunities, where diverse knowledge finds common ground. It is vitally important to do as much legwork as possible; however, don't forget to ask the Universe to help guide you along the way. When she begins speaking with you, you'll know. Happy travels.

Be patient with change. Be kind to yourself, and look for the silver lining in any initially perceived failure. Read The Alchemist *by Paulo Coelho.*

Tamir Sammy Diab is an Egyptian American work in progress. He is a father, son, husband, sibling, fisherman and music lover. He is immensely proud of the sacrifices his parents made in order to give him and his siblings more opportunities. He was born in Maryland to Alexandrians, Sammy Diab and Moushira Elshafei.

PERFECTION DOES NOT EXIST
Chris Cole

Stop pursuing the ideal and start living a fulfilled life!

In a world that constantly bombards us with images of flawless beauty, ideal success, unblemished lives and finding the ideal mate, it's easy to fall into the trap of believing that perfection is not only attainable but necessary. The truth, however, is that perfection does not exist. This may sound discouraging at first, but it's actually incredibly liberating. Understanding that perfection is an illusion frees you from the unrealistic expectations that can lead to disappointment, frustration and even self-loathing.

I spent so much of the first half of my life striving for perfection. I'll hold off until I find the perfect job. I need to find the ideal person for me. I have to have the perfect home. My grades or my annual evaluation need to be perfect. It seems like today there is an even greater drive for perfection than ever before.

The pursuit of perfection often comes at the cost of your happiness and mental well-being. You might find yourself constantly comparing your achievements, looks or skills to others, believing that you must match or surpass them to be worthy. But this mindset overlooks the beauty of imperfection–the unique qualities, experiences and perspectives that make you who you are.

It's your imperfections that shape your character, build resilience and allow you to connect with others on a genuine level. You are perfectly imperfect just as you are.

Instead of striving for perfection, focus on growth and progress. Embrace the idea that making mistakes is not only okay but essential for learning and development. Celebrate the small victories, learn from setbacks and understand that every step you take is valuable. Be grateful for who you are and what you have. Gratitude turns what we have into enough and so much more. By shifting your focus from an unattainable ideal to a journey of continuous improvement, you'll find more joy, fulfillment and authenticity in your life. Your idea of ideal is a made-up fantasy, and that's not reality. Remember, perfection does not exist, but you are enough just as you are!

What can you do to shift your mindset toward growth and progress, rather than striving for perfection?

Chris Cole is the CEO of APNH: A Place to Nourish your Health, a health center providing services to those who face stigma or challenges in receiving culturally competent care. Previously, Chris was the Director of AIDS/LifeCycle and the National Director of the AIDS Rides. Chris is in the process of becoming an ordained minister in the United Church of Christ.

MAKE LEMONADE OUT OF LEMONS
Jill S. Tietjen

Prepare for the worst; hope for the best!

You might think someone was born with a silver spoon in their mouth and everything in their life is perfect. Or you might see someone in the lower socioeconomic rungs and think everything in their life is bad. You would be wrong in both cases–you can't tell by looking at someone what their life experiences have been. But you can be sure of one thing–everyone faces obstacles in their lives. Absolutely everyone. And the difference in how people deal with their obstacles can be summarized in one word–attitude.

As you look at any situation you are facing, don't become immobilized. Try and imagine what you think is the worst outcome and then envision what steps you would take to deal with that outcome. Don't dwell on them; take any steps that you can take now. And know that you will be ready. In fact, you will probably be overprepared. Now hope for the best!

The advice I give about attitude and preparation is based on my personal experience. When my first husband and I were newly married and each 22 years old, his parents died in a murder-suicide. His younger brothers, 14 and 18 years old, came to live with us. We got them through high school and college and one through law school. The worst had happened.

But my case and this situation are unusual. However, obstacles are everywhere, for all of us. And rather than become paralyzed, we can address and overcome them in reasonable ways. Whether you believe it or not, you already have the tools to deal with any situation that you will face in your life. You will be able to make lemonade out of the lemons that life gives you. It takes a good attitude–one that will sustain you through your journey.

FIGURE 2.2
Jill Tietjen at the White House Rose Garden accepting Admiral Grace Murray Hopper's National Medal of Technology from President George H.W. Bush and Commerce Secretary Robert Mossbacher in September 1991.

How will you face the next difficult situation in your life? Would envisioning making lemonade out of lemons help with your attitude and problem-solving approach?

Jill S. Tietjen, P.E., is an author, international speaker and electrical engineer who has spent her career in the electric utility industry. She has been inducted into the Colorado Women's Hall of Fame and the Colorado Authors Hall of Fame.

WHAT HOLDS YOU BACK?

Penny Rue

Individuals often have fears that keep them from achieving their dreams.

I have enjoyed a career that allowed me to be good company for the journey to thousands of emerging adults. I love working with these young people, as they are filled with dreams and aspirations. They want to make the world a better place, or make their parents proud, or build the next great company, or cure a terrible disease. One of the most important questions I've learned to ask and explore is, "What holds you back?"

It turns out that a common impediment is an unvoiced fear. We avoid looking fear in the eye for some very good reasons. Most of us struggle to identify what's in the way, confused by the quicksand we're mired in. What *is* holding us back? Often it is a voice in our head, planted early on, that speaks to some deep insecurity. It turns out, though, that facing fear with curiosity can really work.

Having an eager and inquisitive approach may result in the next question: "What might go wrong here?" Because when you really dig in, the fear is often something like, "I'll look stupid"; "They won't like me"; "I might fail"; "The earth will open up and swallow me."

And after getting those answers to your own questioning, you might then explore, "What would be so bad about that?"

The fear might be covering pain, or providing an excuse not to try, or confirming an old script about our not being good enough. Confronting our fears helps build resilience, the ability to get back up again after getting knocked down. Resilience lets us take a calculated risk, to apply for that scholarship or try out for that play, or tell our parents we've changed our major. And being good company to others is about helping them to learn resilience and to learn to overcome obstacles and hurdles in pursuit of a dream.

What is holding you back? What fears can you identify? What can you do to explore and overcome these restraints?

Penny Rue is an executive leadership coach with over 40 years of experience helping college students achieve their dreams.

FEARFUL OR FIERCE? OVERCOMING PHOBIAS
Connie Revell

If you overcome your fears, you can turn them into strengths.

Growing up in rural Montana, where "showing off" was frowned upon, I developed a morbid fear of public speaking. I avoided all audiences and dodged class assignments that would have put me in front of roomfuls all the way through graduate school. I chose the path of newspaper reporter as the likeliest way to avoid public speeches. I was hardly alone–glossophobia is the most common of phobias, affecting three out of four of us.

But careers branch and spread, and eventually I accepted a job directing communications at a state public health agency. In the first week, I was asked to introduce myself in a speech to all 400 agency employees, and I panicked. Somehow, sweating and squeaking, I stayed upright for the full half hour, pledging to avoid such trauma in the future.

Still, unable to avoid public speeches entirely, I grudgingly accepted the fact that practicing could help alleviate some of the stress. My family bore the brunt as I rehearsed each speech the night before, usually more than once.

Then came the invitation to join a federal, state and local team that devised ways to improve performance in the public, private and nonprofit sectors, producing results that affect people's lives. My teammates were dazzlingly talented and the work stunningly gratifying as we designed a model called Performance Partnerships that actually succeeded. Falling thoroughly in love with the subject matter made it easy to join my teammates presenting to audiences from Vermont to Hawai'i. Soon the World Bank sent me to West Africa. Other countries invited me to share our method of producing better results. I learned that if you care enough about a topic, you can spread the news anywhere.

FIGURE 2.3

This eagle, on my property, exemplifies the fierceness I call on young people to use to overcome their fears.

> Identify some of your greatest fears, and explore ways to tackle and overcome them using causes you truly care about. Start small and build confidence.

Connie Revell worked in newspapers before becoming involved in performance improvement in government and nonprofit agencies. She focused on topics ranging from public health to simplifying rules and regulations.

IT'S NOT ABOUT AN EASY TOMORROW
Craig PoVey

Embrace the challenges of today.

I remember so clearly the multiple times I just couldn't wait to get out of a situation, or I just couldn't wait to finish a task. There were moments when I thought, "If only my body would quit hurting, I could accomplish so much more."

Now, looking back at all those experiences, I've realized that it was during the difficult times that I grew the most, learned the most and strengthened my armor for the unforeseen challenges that I would later cherish. I wouldn't wish some of my challenging, "bad" experiences on my worst enemy. However, I would never wish for my loved ones and fellow beings a life free of challenges, pain or difficult times. Perseverance comes from the rewards of battles won. Love, care, kindness, tolerance and understanding come from perseverance.

As an avid cyclist, I know that whereas it's a fun adrenaline rush to speed downhill, the long, arduous climb up brings a different kind of feel-good experience. Combining the challenging climbs with the fast, fun downhill screamers makes for the best rides!

When you come to a fork, choose the path that goes uphill!

Think of a recent challenging situation. How can you turn that into a learning experience and even something rewarding?

Craig PoVey has been married 36 years, raised three children and never had a job he didn't love. Most of his career has been devoted to developing systems that help young people choose healthy lifestyles.

THE GLASS IS HALF-FULL
Scott Evertz

View what you see, and do each day optimistically and as an opportunity, regardless of what it might be, and act on it.

Every day, we are bombarded with experiences that can seem daunting or overwhelming. It's part of being human. What we observe and are expected to do can seem to be simply too much, pointless or downright scary. It's sometimes hard to approach our days and what we experience during them with any sense of optimism.

However, I swear to you, if you will try your best to be the "eternal optimist," you will see opportunities for learning and growth and accomplishment. Simply stated, look your day in the face and say, "I will experience and learn many things today. I will do something good with those experiences and learning regardless of what is challenging me."

By many measures, my life has been pretty amazing. However, it is not the spectacular things I've experienced (like being appointed to a job in the White House, climbing mountains in Rwanda or being invited to Elton John's home) that has made it so. It's because I have lived with a sense of optimism in all I have experienced.

And lest you think mine has been a life of privilege in which nothing truly bad has happened which makes it easy for me to say that, let me disavow you of that. Rather, it is because of how I view my life. I see my life as a collection of experiences–good and bad–that I have approached with a measure of optimism.

It can be very hard at times to keep that optimism in cases of real serious adversity. However, if you can do it, you will view your life as awfully amazing whether you've spent 22 years on this planet or 62 as have I.

How do you view your life in terms of a glass of water - half-full? What can you do, today, to help reshape your views with more optimism?

Scott Evertz's career journey exemplifies a profound dedication to social justice and the pursuit of global impact. In 2001, he was appointed Director of the White House Office of National AIDS Policy under President George W. Bush, a role that included efforts to safeguard domestic funding for HIV/AIDS initiatives while spearheading the development of international funding mechanisms, including the landmark creation of the Global Fund to Fight AIDS, Tuberculosis and Malaria.

YES, YOU CAN DO IT!
Rita Chi-Ying Chung

Believe in yourself, and have the courage to go for your dreams.

I am a woman of color and a first-generation college student. As a child, I was led to believe I would be a failure. My first day of school, teachers told my parents, who were refugees with minimal English, that I was retarded since I didn't speak English and did not fit the stereotype of a model Asian student. As I struggled to learn English as a second language, I became so nervous that I developed a severe stutter. Kids at schools, family members and others laughed at my stuttering. Being made fun of was amplified by wearing thick glasses and being Chinese. I was labeled and called a "retarded stuttering four-eyes Chink." I was placed in the "slow learner" classes throughout my school years and did not graduate from high school. My personal and career path were predetermined by being branded as retarded. So I was doomed to fail! More insidious was that I passively accepted my fate and internalized that message.

Yet, I am now a retired university professor. How can that be? How did I moved from being labeled as a "retarded failure" to a Professor Emerita status, an invited speaker to the United Nations and recipient of numerous state and national awards and commendations? "What happened?" you may wonder.

As you can imagine, my journey was not easy; it was filled with disparaging, demeaning disappointments, ridicules, failures and harsh criticisms. No one believed in me; I was alone, by myself. For many years, I too believed in what others thought of me.

But instead of going into details of my journey, I will focus on a key value and belief that propelled me from a highly toxic, negative and painful situation to who I proudly am today. The key to breaking the shackles of being labeled as a failure is COURAGE: courage to believe and have faith in yourself, courage to stand up and speak out, courage to dream and to pursue your dreams, courage to learn from your failures and courage to seek out unconditional social support.

How can you find courage? How can you stop listening and internalizing the negativity around you? What, specifically, gives you the strength and resiliency to fight negative comments and have the courage to believe in yourself?

Rita Chi-Ying Chung is a Professor Emerita at George Mason University, Counseling Program. She has received multiple national and international awards for her work in social justice and human rights, been an expert witness in major national court cases and has worked throughout the world as an invited speaker and consultant.

BA-DA-BOOM, CRASH!
Tim Kuchta

Defining success for yourself is an important part of your life journey.

Ba-Da-Boom, Crash! If you do not know what that is, it is "drumspeak." It gives you the aural/verbal experience for a very popular drum pattern. It acts like punctuation to a sentence. Sometimes it means "Oh yeah!" and sometimes it's the icing that drummers play after a vaudeville punchline is delivered. I cannot remember for sure when I first heard it, and I do not think it was when I started drumming at the age of eight. But 53 years later, I have not only said it countless times, but I have also played this riff thousands of times.

Music and drumming have taken me to wonderful places–not just geographically but spiritually as well. Drumming has been foundational to my life's journey and has been involved with many of my successes in life.

Ah, but what is SUCCESS? you may ask. That is only for you to answer. As you go on *your* journey through life trying to achieve "success," please realize there are a multitude of variables that interact in many ways with your success. But first, you must define your true meaning of success; you need know what success is to you. Then you can sprinkle in some passion, commitment, hard work and then more hard work.

Nonetheless, there will probably come a time when you realize you did not reach your definition of success and BA-DA-BOOM, CRASH! Now what? You always have choices! Pick yourself up and keep going, maybe redefine what success is to you. But please, realize that this is quite normal. Setbacks do happen! Try not to concern yourself with someone else's definition of success. You define yours! Everyone else can define theirs. Also, when these setbacks occur, please realize this is life, and *do not* stop being kind to yourself.

Then, at some point, you will hear it (or maybe it's just me): BA-DA-BOOM, CRASH! And you will realize, Aha, I have found SUCCESS!

Take a moment to think about success, and define what it means to you.

Tim Kuchta is a drummer, percussionist and music educator. He holds a B.A. in music from Duquesne University and a master of music from the University of Miami. He is currently teaching elementary music in Boca Raton, Florida and performs music throughout South Florida.

FEELING COMFORTABLE BEING UNCOMFORTABLE
Maggie Mac Neil

Sometimes, to reach your goals, you have to stretch your boundaries.

As a former elite athlete, one of my all-time favorite quotes (author unknown) is, "The comfort zone is a beautiful place, but nothing ever grows there." When my club coach wrote it on the whiteboard before morning practice one day, it really resonated with me and inspires what I do and how I do it. Over the course of my life and athletic career, I have been faced with challenges beyond what I would have ever thought possible; this quote always reminded me that if you're not uncomfortable, you're not growing to your full potential.

To achieve at the highest level possible, there were times where I had to step out of my comfort zone to improve and reach my goals. Although this is an important part of growing and evolving, this also must happen at the right time and place. For example, I was invited to move away from home and pursue my Olympic dream with a high-performance group at the age of 14. However, this was not something my family or I were interested in at that age. There were other opportunities, more suited to the time and place I was in my life to step out of my comfort zone, for me to feel comfortable being uncomfortable.

My most "out of my comfort zone" was when I left what I had known for 22 years and enrolled at Louisiana State University. Having grown up in Canada and completing my undergraduate degree in Michigan, it was a huge leap of faith to pick up my life and move to the American South to follow a coach, having never set foot in the state and not knowing what the city, facilities or people were like. Despite this, I knew this was the right move for me and my career heading into the Paris Olympics, reuniting with the coach who was able to bring out my best and coached me to every accomplishment there is for a swimmer.

After two years in the bayou, I can say it transformed me completely. I was extremely happy with my training and atmosphere and also learning about and embracing different pieces of southern culture. I am now heavily invested in women's college basketball, and I can eat a whole king cake in one sitting. I learned more about who Maggie Mac Neil is outside of swimming and will likely include these traditions and experiences in my life forever.

Thinking about your own life journey, where can you step outside your comfort zone and grow?

Maggie Mac Neil, OLY, Canada, MSc, Olympic Champion 100m butterfly, Tokyo Olympics 2020/1.

ORANGES?

Lawrence D. Czarda

Only one person can truly determine your life—you.

Growing up as the only boy in a first-generation Hungarian family during the culturally turbulent time of the 1960s, assassinations, civil rights, Vietnam, Nixon and more, I lost my father in an accident caused by a drunk driver.

We all have 20/20 hindsight, and I do know why family and friends worried about my future. But somehow, a random critical comment from a former football coach was a catalyst for me. Coach M, in a health class, called me out and said that I should start practicing my life's work—namely, stacking oranges in the fruit section of the local supermarket since that was all I could ever become. Not that that work is not honorable, but really?

I now reflect on a long career serving on and chairing boards in the not-for-profit world of health care, the arts, K–12 education and more. Public service in my local government and more than four decades in executive-level management in higher education. And a large, diverse family of so many interesting people.

And more than a handful of critically important mentors and guides who helped me see that only I could limit my potential. Not to become wealthy or famous but to become who I was meant to be here in this beautiful and troubled world.

Only you are truly in charge of you. None of us can be limited by anything your own Coach M can say or do. You are in charge of your life.

FIGURE 2.4

From a regular podcast, "Dialogues From the President's Corner." As the host says, "Only you can tell your story."

What do you see as your own potential? What seems to hold you back, and what can you do to limit those constraints?

Lawrence D. Czarda holds bachelor's, master's and doctoral degrees. He is a lifelong educator and administrator and has been President of Greensboro College in North Carolina since 2010.

YOUR VALUE
Mitchell Moore

It is vitally important to remember, cherish and value your unique self.

We place value on things that are rare like gold or diamonds. We say they are worth a lot because they are rare. Have you considered how rare you are?

Since this world started spinning, there has never been, nor will there ever be, another YOU. That makes you priceless. You are rarer than gold, more valuable than diamonds. Oh, there may be people who look like you or talk like you, but they do not see the world through your eyes or speak your words.

Others may have hands and fingers, but they do not have your touch. You are as unique as your fingerprints, you are rare . . . you are valuable . . . more valuable than you know.

Now, I do not know why you were born here, at this time and place. I do not know what your purpose is—that is for you to discover. I do believe that you were born on purpose and for a purpose and that somewhere, someone is waiting for what you uniquely have to give.

For centuries, ships have been carrying valuable cargo through treacherous seas to people waiting on distant shores. Now ships in harbor are safe, but that's not what ships are built for.

Today, I am going to encourage you to get out of your safe comfort zone, keep sailing across those rough seas because someone is desperately waiting for the unique rare gift that only you can deliver.

I thank you for being you and doing what you do. Please keep investing in people; it's the best investment you can make. And remember, "there has never been, nor will there ever be another

YOU!" That makes you priceless.

Thanks for being you and doing what you do.

What, specifically, are your unique traits that make you valuable for others?

Mitchell Moore is a valuable member of the helping profession as a licensed chemical dependency counselor and internationally certified prevention specialist. He is also a husband, grandfather and beekeeper.

PARADIGM SHIFT IN MY LIFE
Kenji Matsumoto

With the unpredictability of life, it's important to have dreams and pursue them actively.

My volunteer experience at a slum in Kenya defined my passion to help improve the health of people in need. In Tanzania, in addition to conducting research studies there, I raised funds to send orphans to school and donated meals at underserved communities. I established a pen pal cultural exchange program between middle and high schools in Tanzania and the United States. It was an exciting time; I was living my dream.

My life took a significant turn while working in Dar es Salaam, Tanzania for two years. I started experiencing persistent headaches. I initially dismissed them as minor illnesses, common in developing countries. However, after persistent recommendations from friends, I sought medical attention. The MRI–the only MRI machine in the country then–revealed a tumor the size of a golf ball in the right frontal lobe of my brain. I was medically evacuated to the United States.

The initial diagnosis provided a prognosis of two to three months of life remaining. How is this possible at age 27? Seeking a second opinion led to a new and better diagnosis. My doctor informed me that no similar cases had been reported, making me potentially the first case ever documented.

Exactly four years after my mother's passing, I completed my final cancer treatment. The support of friends and family worldwide was the core to my recovery–a kind of medicine no doctor could provide. I emerged from this ordeal with a renewed sense of purpose: to use my skills and talents to help those in need.

Just three months after finishing treatment, I joined Doctors Without Borders, tackling the dual epidemic of HIV/AIDS and tuberculosis in Swaziland. I then climbed Mt. Kilimanjaro to prove to myself that I was still capable of achieving my dreams. Another dream came true in Uganda, where I helped improve the treatment program for pediatric cancer at the country's only cancer hospital.

Life is unpredictable, and setbacks are inevitable, but our response and perseverance are within our control. Dreams are not just for dreaming–they're meant to be achieved. Pursue with passion and grit. Let's continue to chase goals and dreams and inspire and support others along the way.

What can you do today to turn adversity into a stepping stone for achieving your dreams?

Kenji Matsumoto is an infectious disease epidemiologist with a passion for global health. When not tackling public health challenges, you can find him playing tennis, volleyball, surfing or exploring new world destinations.

TAKE THE RISK
John Bauer

To grow and truly embrace life, you must be willing to take some risks.

"President Kennedy has been shot!" roared radio and television to a stunned America in November 1963. In my first semester of graduate school, I was comfortable as always in my safe school setting in sunny California. But as the reports came in, suddenly something stirred inside me. Was this all there was to my life? Get another degree, land a teaching job and, well, play it safe? Avoid discomfort? What about Kennedy? Wasn't he a wounded navy war hero, having saved the lives of PT boatmates in the Pacific during World War II? What had stirred inside him to be the man he became?

It was time to shake up my life, so I soon joined the Kennedy-inspired Peace Corps. I would leave my comfort zone behind by spending two years in West Africa. I took the risk. Success in teaching aside, the Peace Corps experience opened the door to other opportunities: a boat trip down the coast of West Africa, a safari in East Africa, doing a bit of Europe before heading home.

Home, sweet home, until I got drafted into the Vietnam War mess. I said to myself, "Well, this is the war of my generation and I don't want to miss it." And I didn't. Recalling Kennedy's war experience, I took a big risk and signed up for Infantry Officer Candidate School. I knew where that was headed. And I was right. A year after coming home from serving the country as a Peace Corps volunteer, I was in Vietnam leading an infantry platoon engaging in combat operations.

One night, a listening post (three men outside the main area) came under intense fire and all were severely wounded, needing a rescue team. I chose not to order any of my men into certain danger, so I decided to lead a volunteer squad myself. Perhaps by divine providence, the enemy had pulled back, and we retrieved all three wounded men successfully.

The old basketball saying holds true: "Don't be afraid to miss. Take the shot. You can't score if you don't shoot."

Wishing you all the best as you navigate your future.

Write a short summary examining why you were glad you took a risk to do something you didn't have to. Then write another short summary about a risk you didn't take but were sorry you didn't.

John F. Bauer, Ed.D., retired high school English teacher and college professor. Author of *West of Pleiku, the Infantryman's Novel*. Military awards: Silver Star, Purple Heart (x 2) and Combat Infantryman's Badge.

EMBRACING UNKNOWN OPPORTUNITIES
Angie Asa-Lovstad

Sometimes the doors and windows we don't see right away are the ones that lead us to the most profound growth.

Transitions are an inevitable part of life, and often, they arrive when we least expect them. My own life has been a series of shifts–from personal losses to professional changes. Through it all, I've held on to a deep belief: there is always another door or window open, even when the opportunity seems hidden or nonexistent in the moment.

Sometimes we face choices that seem unclear or paths that don't make sense at first glance. It's only in hindsight, after we've walked through that door or window, that we can connect the dots and understand why it was the right step. I've learned to trust the unknown, to take the leap even when the outcome is unclear. In these moments of uncertainty, courage becomes your greatest ally, allowing you to embrace new opportunities that shape your future in ways you can't yet comprehend.

For young adults stepping into the next phases of life, it's easy to feel overwhelmed by the pressure to have everything figured out. But I want to encourage you to lean into the unknown and remain optimistic. Not everything needs to make sense immediately. One thing you can do is to take a small step toward an uncertain opportunity that feels uncomfortable; after you do that, reflect on how it might fit into the bigger picture of your life, even if the outcome isn't immediately clear.

Trust in your resilience, stay curious and give yourself permission to explore new paths–even when they seem to lead somewhere unexpected. Over time, you'll come to see that each transition was part of a larger, more beautiful journey.

Think of a time when something unexpected led to growth in your life. What lesson did you learn?

Angie Asa-Lovstad is a master connector, coach and facilitator with ASA Facilitation who helps people discover their potential and embrace change. She specializes in fostering connections that ignite personal growth, helping others navigate their paths with optimism and courage.

GRATITUDE

Charles Eberly

Having gratitude for so much that life has to offer provides rewards for yourself and others.

When I was younger, I had lots of idealism (which I still have). I believed then and now that young people hold the keys to the future. After all, I was young! I had lots of ideas, lots of ambition and lots of commitment. I wanted a strong professional career, I wanted a family and I wanted to do things in my life that made a difference with those around me. I was grateful for the opportunities that came forward and for the support of so many others around me–in both my personal and professional lives.

Now I am 83 and with limited mobility that makes moving about a struggle. It would be easy to list all of the activities I used to do and complain about all the daily tasks that are now very difficult.

One day last year, three words came to me: "I am grateful!" Beginning with "I am grateful to be alive." I started to say "I am grateful" at the start of many thoughts I shared with others, and it was not long until I found my entire outlook on life was elevated. More than that, other people responded more positively to me. Instead of "I'm okay" or "Not bad" or many other phrases that start with a negative thought, things were very different when I began with "I am grateful"; specifically, the altitude of my attitude increased remarkably, and others responded in far more positive ways to me. As stated in Psalm 118:24, "This is the day the Lord has made" that we should be happy with the present moment, we should be grateful with present circumstances.

Now each morning when I wake up from my sleep, the first thought in my head is, "This is the day the Lord has made. Let us rejoice and be glad in it."

How would you describe your gratitude today? In what ways do you show it?

Charles Eberly is Emeritus Professor of Counseling and Student Development at Eastern Illinois University and a higher education consultant.

VALUES IN CHARACTER TO BE CHERISHED
Paul A. Kinser

Embrace these values and seek them in others.

I am the product of a low-income, single-parent family from the Midwest. I earned degrees in philosophy, economics and education. I finished a 40-year career as Professor and Provost (CEO) of a 13,000 student college campus in Central Florida.

Looking back on that career, my advice to young adults is, be honest, be trustworthy, work hard and have courage.

Be truthful in all that you do. Use diplomacy rather than coercion. Being honest, caring and diplomatic in your communication builds trust.

Trust is earned when you do what you say you are going to do. In so doing, you will be appreciated and respected by others and, more important, by yourself. Trust builds teamwork and productivity.

Embrace hard work. Spend time preparing yourself to accomplish a worthy goal. Few students, employees or leaders are successful without working hard to get the job done.

I needed courage hiking in Nepal in the Himalayas. I came upon an excessively high, swinging foot bridge across a raging river. I was scared to death. Eventually, my group crossed, and I was left alone on the wrong side. I became angry with the fear in myself. The anger overcame the fear and gave me the courage to finally cross.

It took courage to interview for the position of Provost. The college president told me that after a national search, he would hire me only if I received 100% committee support. My chances were not promising. I worked many hours preparing for the interview. Finally, I was the only candidate recommended and finally got the job.

As I reflect on my career and personal life, I realize the importance of these values. I still think of these events when honesty, trust, hard work and courage are called for.

In what ways do these values resonate for you? What other values are most central for your life today?

Paul Kinser is a retired Provost Emeritus from Valencia College in Orlando, Florida. While there, he taught economics, developed a new campus in Osceola County and served in several other administrative capacities. He and his wife, Mary Ann, have enjoyed a life of world travel and family time with their son, an attorney, and two grandchildren, both in college. Paul and Mary Ann exercise avidly and enjoy long-distance bike riding.

HOW A REFUGEE MAY CHANGE THE WORLD
Nguyen Dinh Thang

Change the way you see yourself, then set your lifelong goals and work very unflinchingly to achieve them.

One day in December 1978, at the age of 20, I fled the Communist regime in Vietnam with my parents and two younger siblings on a boat, heading into the vast ocean and an unknown future. We arrived in Malaysia and were taken to a refugee camp. While there, my dad asked me, "Son, what's your plan for your future?" "Fight against social injustice for people of all races and all creeds," I replied without hesitation. After a long pause, my dad found his voice: "Be realistic, son. We are only refugees."

Like all refugees who had lost everything, my parents worried first and foremost about rebuilding our lives in a new country. Quietly, I pursued my dream, though. Three weeks after arriving in northern Virginia, I rallied former high school friends to champion for the voice of Vietnamese refugees in mainstream politics.

Fast forward ten years, in 1988, governments in Hong Kong and Southeast Asia declared Vietnamese boat people no longer refugees but economic migrants to be pushed back to sea. While working as a research engineer at a navy lab in Maryland, I volunteered with Boat People SOS and traveled to Asia to find ways to save my unfortunate compatriots from forced repatriation to Communist persecution.

In 2001, I left my 15-year engineering career to join the nonprofit sector full time. I have since worked with colleagues and volunteers at Boat People SOS to assist tens of thousands of refugees, immigrants, victims of violence and victims of labor and sex exploitation in America and some 30 other countries. For the past 20 years, every day has been a fulfilling day. "Being a refugee" has not precluded me from pursuing my dream.

FIGURE 2.5
Dr. Thang's visit to a Hong Kong "closed" camp for Vietnamese boat people in December 1988.

Ask yourself, "30 years from now and looking back, what would I wish I could and should have done with my life?" Then come up with a plan to do exactly that.

Nguyen Dinh Thang is CEO and President of Boat People SOS, one of the longest-serving nonprofit organizations established and run by former Vietnamese refugees. He obtained a Ph.D. in Mechanical Engineering at Virginia Tech.

RED SQUARE
Cedric Rucker

It's important and helpful to be prepared for life's journey.

Sometimes it is hard to reach back to those moments of realizing a turn in one's life course, especially as the passage of time mountainously accumulates. Today, I am scratching my head to fathom how this journey has been realized. As a "government cheese" kid, I got free lunches in a segregated public school. Prospects were uncertain, a future undiagrammed. The world I was born into was hardly limitless. There were strict boundaries connected to race, class and gender. A formidable landscape.

So how, how did the walls built around me, the box that restricted options, get demolished? People whom I did not think needed to care about me actually did. As a kid growing up in a housing project in a southern urban town, this was not to be expected. Ministers inspired community members to fight through the last apparent elements of "massive resistance" to open doors of access. I remember messages of inspiration and hope shared with the congregants, challenging us to no longer settle. Suddenly, pathways were revealed out of the shadows.

What stands out the most for me was a high school teacher, Sarah Davydovna. After President Nixon's return from the Soviet Union, Russian-language programs were seeded in urban high schools across the country. Deciding to be adventurous, I selected Russian for my foreign language. In one defiant moment, I remember confronting my teacher, "I will never get this. It makes no sense, and a kid like me will never go to Russia anyway, or any other foreign country for that matter." Sarah Davydovna's response: "You never know where life's journey will take you. You will always want to be prepared." I just couldn't see that possibility.

Boy, was I wrong. Years later, I will never forget the first time that I found myself standing in Red Square. Taking it in–the Kremlin, St. Basil's, the Gum Department store encircling me. I just started crying, not able to stop. I was taken back to my teacher and her message, challenging me to be open to possibilities unknown. Here I stood, in a place so far away from those restrictions of my birth. In a land, speaking a language that initially seemed so out of reach. That moment ever speaks to me. Davydovna's message has prepared me for each new adventure. I have now traveled to over 100 nations, loving the journey, ever open to possibilities.

Identify some things you can do in the near future to prepare for your own life journey.

Cedric Bernard Rucker serves as Senior Vice President for Student Affairs and Dean of Students at the University of Virginia.

COURAGE: LISTEN! WATCH! PRACTICE!
Edward Spencer

*Listen to and watch others who can and will teach you about courage;
the lessons learned will help you so much as your life goes on.*

Looking back on my formative years, I so remember the many times when my father would talk about courage and the importance of being courageous. Now in my senior years, I can appreciate what he meant as I recall personal crises which, in retrospect, I had to face:

Losing my biological mother when I was just three years old; a compound break of my right arm at age eight; Dad transferred three times in a five-year period resulting in my attending nine schools before graduating from high school; my high school and college girlfriend killed in an airplane crash just one week after our college graduations; dropping out of medical school to pursue a career in higher education; seeking postgraduate school jobs for my wife and myself in an era of strong anti-nepotism; adopting a seven-year-old boy; surviving prostate cancer in 2004; being one of the prime Virginia Tech administrators having to deal with all aspects of the aftermath of the killing of 32 students and faculty on our campus on April 16, 2007; losing my wife to metastasized breast cancer in 2009 after an 11½-year struggle; losing my only son to aerosol substance abuse in 2014; being left to serve as both grandfather and surrogate father to two young grandchildren; and now being recently diagnosed with Parkinson's disease.

I share these challenges as real examples of what just one person has faced in his life. Although each one of these was challenging, what helped me through was honoring my father's priority on being courageous.

Think about how you might respond if you were faced with these or similar crises. What lessons in courage might you call on? How will you maintain your optimism when faced with such situations?

Edward Spencer, Ph.D., spent 42 years (1970–2012) in higher education administration, retiring as the Vice President for Student Affairs at Virginia Tech.

BUILDING A SUCCESSFUL LIFE
ONE MISTAKE AT A TIME

Eileen Crawford

"Wrong" decisions can lead to ultimate success and happiness if you believe in your ability to learn and grow from them.

There is not much scarier than waking up the day after you leave high school or college for the final time, realizing you are an unemployed young person with adulthood staring straight at you. Until then, your life path is neatly laid out before you: Be a baby, play in your sandbox, learn to read and write, survive middle school, try to find something relevant in high school and, finally, make your parents proud as you head off for . . . what? It is finally your turn to decide what comes next. What if you make the WRONG choice?

What if I accept that new job and end up hating it? What if I move to Denmark and can't survive the winters? What if I flunk out of law school? Here's the good news: You *can't* make the wrong choice. No matter what path you follow, you will gain something important from it. You will learn what you like or can't tolerate, what you need in your life and what you don't. Once confronted with crafting your own life-work balance, you will discover your real talents, abilities and values. Careers are built job by job, experience by experience. You might make it halfway up the ladder only to discover you no longer care about reaching the top, or you might find someone or something unexpected has yanked that ladder right out from under you.

What matters more than "making the right choice" is nurturing the belief in yourself that no matter what life throws in your face, you will find your way through it. When transitioning to "responsible adult," your most important call is to *do something*. That something will lead to something else, and you will be off and running. Trust yourself to figure it out.

Work to build the skills of resilience in yourself by trying things where the outcome is not certain and then working through it. Take a drive to a new place, follow random roads and find your way back (without GPS). Keep tackling new challenges, living out of your comfort zone and learn you can survive.

What choices do you have in your not-too-distant future? How can you build your confidence to make needed decisions and walk confidently toward what lies ahead?

Eileen Crawford is a mother, grandmother, and Licensed Mental Health Counselor in private practice in Ponte Vedra, Florida. Her research area of interest is resilience, and she writes, speaks and teaches on building strength-based resilience individually and in families.

YOU CAN DO IT–YOU ARE GOOD
Manny Borja

You are a good and loving person.

Please imagine that you are the only person in the world. Now think of four things you would like to do or wish you could do. *(You may continue reading after you have come up with the four things.)*

May we ask, "Is it true that whatever those four things may be, you would like to do them because you feel and think that they were *good* for you?" This proves that you are, by nature, a *good* person. Therefore, no matter what others may think of you, *you* know you are a good person.

Why, then, may some people think otherwise of others? Is it because they may forget that we are all the same as human beings? Is it because we do not understand them, and may we say that once we understand, we will see/find the goodness in them?

It has been said that the goal of education is to be able to understand, because once we understand, we can truly love and be happy. May we also say that the ultimate goal of education is to love all so that we can understand all, and to understand all so that we can love all?

A Chinese proverb says, "A journey of a thousand miles begins with a single step." You have taken the first step in finding and understanding goodness/love in the world because you have found the goodness/love in yourself. May we say that to better understand and love others, it is best to first understand and love yourself?

The English word "education" comes from the Latin words *educare*, meaning "to bring up," and *educere*, meaning "to bring forth." May we say that a true education is the pulling out and bringing forth from ourselves the good that we already have, given by Source?

Source has also given us free will. Having choices in life is a wonderful opportunity to be able to bring out our goodness.

When you find yourself in a situation that is most challenging, you may ask, "How may I show my goodness, my best, in this situation?"

Having choices in life is a wonderful opportunity to be able to bring out our goodness.

As you reflect on this, what changes do you have for the four things you noted at the beginning of this? What can you do to help achieve these?

Manuel/Manny Flores Borja was born and still lives on the island of Saipan, Mariana Islands, Micronesia and is a Chamorro author.

ADAPTABILITY IN THE FACE OF ADVERSITY
Carol Filak

Prepare to adjust to change, whether positive or negative, in a thoughtful and respectful manner.

Everyone messes up! What is important is how you respond. When you are faced with a disappointment or adversity, experience the emotion and then refocus on an appropriate solution. You need to process the emotion to make a clear, thoughtful and ultimately a better decision.

Resist the impulse to drink or take drugs to ease the pain; these will only make a bad situation worse, not bringing any clarity or meaningful resolution. Don't overreact, but also don't ignore adversity; respond to the problem you face. Give it time before you come to any final decision. If the challenge is too overwhelming, don't be afraid to reach out to someone who has your best interests at heart. Whether it's not being able to get a critical class, receiving a DUI or having a health-related illness, discuss your options with an appropriate adult to help you arrive at the best solution.

As an example, a student came to the health center complaining of fatigue, fever, headache, sore throat and body aches. When it was determined he had mono, he had to take off the entire semester; he was also worried about how it would affect his scholarship. He was referred to me; the primary focus was his health and complete recovery, but other concerns were valid and impactful.

I spoke with his parents, met with his adviser and helped him develop a plan to create a schedule of classes, secure his financial aid, established regular check-ins at Student Health and engaged Counseling Services for him when he became overwhelmed. He did well, but it took a lot of hard work and perseverance. The point is that there are educators, administrators, counselors and others who care about you! Although some challenges may seem insurmountable, there is help out there if you need and seek it.

Some potential action steps include being realistic of your expectations, not expecting perfection, establishing a support system, developing a rapport with professors and advisers, keeping your cool when disappointments occur and not being afraid to ask for help.

As you reflect on current challenges, which of these action steps can you do now? What can you do to get these functional for future challenges?

Carol Filak, RN, Ph.D., is a retired Nurse Administrator with over 40 years of experience in the neonatal intensive care unit, home health nursing, hospital clinical settings and teaching. Her management skills were successfully utilized while working in George Mason University's Student Health Services.

THE STRENGTH WE WEAVE: VULNERABILITY, RESPECT AND THE LUMINOUS JOURNEY

Peter Poeck

True strength is the courage to acknowledge our vulnerabilities and weave them into the tapestry of unwavering respect that defines who we are.

We all begin our journey of life with a personal backpack filled with dreams. Sometimes the seemingly strong person who pushes themselves too hard ends up collapsing under the weight they carry, your breaking point. Remember, respect is key regardless of someone's appearance or mood. Don't become the bully, because the hand that bullies today may be the one that seeks help tomorrow.

Even if you hit a wall (burnout), recovery takes time. Be aware of the impact it has on those around you. They might offer help, but they might also choose to distance themselves, run away or ignore you.

So choose strength, but don't be afraid to show vulnerability. Be the one who shows respect; true strength lies in both resilience and compassion.

As your journey of life goes further, remember that true strength lies in the harmonious balance of resilience and vulnerability. Carry your burdens with purpose, but don't be afraid to throw away some weight along the way. Be the embodiment of respect, because in your kindness lies the power to inspire and uplift all those around you. Be kind to yourself and smile, because you only have one life and everyone else is taken.

True strength isn't a heavy load but a tapestry woven with resilience, vulnerability and respect. It's in embracing our journey, not just the destination, that we truly shine.

In my own work, I am guided by the RAVE (respect, appreciate, value everyone) and COACH (care, observe, act, communicate, help) methodologies.

FIGURE 2.6
Be kind to yourself and smile, because you only have one life and everyone else is taken.

In what ways do you show resilience and compassion? In what situations might you do better with both of these?

Peter Poeck lives in Belgium. He has juggled the balls of resilience, vulnerability and respect to new heights. He works for a global IT integrator as a global event manager with a twist.

TOUCHING LIVES THROUGH LEADERSHIP
Sandy Spavone

Embrace opportunities beyond your comfort zone to shape a meaningful legacy.

Early in my career, I was a teacher, eager to educate and guide students to absorb the content I was assigned to teach. One day, a student challenged me to not just teach but to touch others' lives through leadership. That moment shifted my perspective and planted the seed for a career beyond the classroom.

Over the years, I began to take on roles that were outside my comfort zone, moving from the familiar environment of education into nonprofit work. Volunteering for tasks that weren't "mine to do" and building lasting relationships with leaders in related fields were pivotal in this transition. These experiences led me to grow from a program assistant at Family, Career and Community Leaders of America, Inc. (FCCLA) to eventually become its Director of Programs. I then stepped up and out of my comfort zone to take on the role of Executive Director of a new nonprofit National Organizations for Youth Safety (NOYS). When I first took that uncomfortable step forward, I would wake up thinking, "What have I done?" but diligently worked to grow NOYS from a home office and one employee (me) to a team of employees and impactful work.

Then the opportunity to apply to serve as CEO of FCCLA was available, and so, I took another risky step to leave what I had built at NOYS and loved doing to pursue another growth opportunity. While I had good and long hard days, some days I hung on to the quote to not undo in doubt what you did in faith and have seen FCCLA grow in membership, content and financial security. It wasn't always "comfortable," but it has been worth every moment to continue to offer more opportunities for more youth every day.

Through all of this, I learned that sometimes the best career moves are unexpected. It's about saying yes to opportunities, even when you're unsure, and recognizing that failures can be stepping stones to success. My life embodies the philosophy that when you find something you love to do, you'll never "work" a day in your life. My journey wasn't linear, but it was intentional. It was driven by a commitment to leadership, a willingness to grow and a passion for making an impact.

> *Identify one opportunity today that feels outside your comfort zone and explore it. Reflect on how embracing this challenge could help shape your legacy.*

Sandy Spavone is CEO of FCCLA, with over two decades of experience in youth leadership and nonprofit work. She believes in touching lives through leadership and embracing opportunities to create a meaningful career.

THE JOURNEY THROUGH LIFE
Sandra Tull

Embracing change is an important part of becoming.

Each and every one of us is on a lifelong journey. Included here are clues to help you on your journey, giving you a sense of purpose to move ahead and not give up.

Because you have picked up this book to read, congratulations. This book is full of wisdom and ideas to assist you on your life's journey. It is a journey, and as a young adult, you have many life roads to explore and travel.

There is a saying, "You are made for more." Please hold that thought, not only for today but throughout your whole life's journey.

To move toward "being more" on your journey, please recognize there is always change, around you and in you. Some change we all create by what we do and speak, yet some change seems to just happen. The change that we do have control over, we must address in a timely manner. Not being aware of or not paying attention to change has a negative effect and you will feel "dissed" and dismissed.

Change brings choices. The worst misnomer is that we have no choice or that there are only two choices: this way or that way. Not so! Be encouraged to seek alternatives to what is placed before you as a choice. For instance, if you and friends are going for a meal, is there only one place to go? What about distance, cost, menu? The choices are many.

Always contribute to an overall group decision. Make your choice known. This decision-making may be new to you. Continue to be empowered to make decisions for changes and choices based on your needs, desires and dreams.

Are you considering employment, college or a trade school? What job/ profession gets your attention? Firsthand knowledge is so important before you make a decision. Change happens. Be in charge of the change that you have control over. The choices are yours.

Work toward decision-making becoming an "art form" in you. Too many people see only black and white. When this happens, life choices are limited. People who experience this narrow vision become bitter, angry and disheartened. They give up with knowing and believing they are "made for more."

What sort of change strategies can help you on your journey to become "more"?

Sandra Tull is an RN, BSPA and holds a master's in counseling psychology and is an ordained priest in the Episcopal Church.

TURNING REJECTION INTO A REVOLUTIONARY ARRIVAL TO ONE'S TRUE PURPOSE

Alicia D. Justice

Take unsuccessful events in your life and transform them into something positive.

In 2008, I was a semester away from graduating with a master's in public health (MPH) degree. I began applying to fellowships in hopes of landing a dream opportunity. I applied for a fellowship at Johns Hopkins Medicine, and although I was a finalist, I was ultimately not selected.

While I continued to apply to other fellowships and full-time job opportunities, I quietly believed that I did not get it because I reached too high and wasn't good enough for such a distinguished opportunity.

It wasn't until 2017 that I revisited this limiting belief when a colleague said, "Alicia, I just looked at the DrPH health equity and social justice program at Hopkins. You should apply–you'd definitely get in!" While I appreciated the sentiment, I brushed it off and decided not to apply. After being waitlisted at another university, I reflected on what rejection means for me.

In the fall of 2019, I applied to the Johns Hopkins Bloomberg School of Public Health DrPH Health Equity and Social Justice Program and soon learned I was accepted. With the support of the best adviser and dissertation committee chair, I introduced a novel topic to understand how public health entities design a culture of equity within their organizational infrastructure and explore how leaders facilitate psychological safety for their teams. Four years later, I successfully defended my dissertation and became a doctor of public health from the same institution for which, a decade prior, I had told myself I wasn't good enough.

I encourage you to challenge any limiting beliefs that ruminate after you experience an undesirable outcome. My so-called rejection wasn't that at all–it was a redirect. What may feel like a rejection in the moment could very well be a revolutionary setup toward something bigger–better. Practice self-reflective exercises to train your mind to reframe rejection into redirection. The path toward success isn't void of failures or redirections. Find balance in the redirection by committing to moving forward mindfully.

Think of a recent situation that didn't have the result you wanted. What are several interpretations of this for you?

Alicia D. Justice, DrPH, MPH, is a public health doctor and national health equity strategist contributing to various public health initiatives. Originally from the Gulf Coast she is a big sister, auntie, fur mama, self-proclaimed retired comic book kid and a '90s R & B and hip-hop music connoisseur who enjoys Pilates, trail running, tasting new foods, and traveling.

WHAT'S NEXT?
Jason Anderson

In our eagerness to get to the next stage in our lives, we can overlook the joys of where we currently stand.

Have you ever noticed how eager we all seem to be to get to the next part of our lives? This realization first occurred to me when I was in high school. I would hear friends at school talking about how much they were looking forward to "finally being done with this place," and I found myself wondering if they'd really thought that through. Sure, I was balancing school with a part-time job and there was never really enough time to just go fishing with my buddies. Yet life on the whole was pretty good. Yet I fed into it a bit and found myself also yearning to get onto the next chapter.

When the next chapter arrived (serving in the army for three years), it didn't take long before I started longing for my enlistment to end so I could finally get to college. On the first day of college, I couldn't help but start wondering how long this would take before I could start my career.

While it's one thing to work hard for a goal and to look forward to achieving it (i.e., graduation), it's another to be wishing our lives away. Looking back, I'd give just about anything to relive my relatively carefree years of high school. The army? Same answer. Although maybe not as carefree, I created friendships and made memories in the service that I wouldn't trade for anything. College was a time to be exposed to so many different people, perspectives and content. I wish I had allowed myself to be more present rather than so distracted by my eagerness to get it over with.

This dynamic is not limited to young adulthood. In the 30 years of my career, I have encountered countless people whose longing for a promotion or retirement spares them the appreciation of their current situation. Set goals, work hard to achieve them, yet don't allow your desire to achieve cloud your ability to really appreciate where you are now. Think about what you could do to more regularly lean into the blessings of your current situation.

What are the circumstances of your current situation (relationships, opportunities) you will likely miss some day?

Jason Anderson is an army veteran, husband and father of two grown boys and resides in northern Minnesota. After a 25-year career in probation/parole, he currently supports organizations across the country as a professional development trainer. His passions include all things outdoors and his faith, and he dabbles in community theater.

AN UNPLANNED CAREER JOURNEY
John Chappell

It's wonderful when there's a match between your heart and your professional skills.

I had a number of notions and interests growing up, and I set my professional sights on becoming an engineer. Although I am degreed, I've barely worked as an engineer because another interest overtook that one.

With more exposure over time to the working world and the nascent spread of personal computers in the 1980s, I became enamored of computers' information processing capabilities at the desktop. At the same time, I realized my first employer was inefficient and marginally effective at getting its core business operations executed owing partly to tedious manual work processes and inefficient information-sharing methods. When it became clear there was going to be a huge wave of adoption of computers into every business in the country, I matched my interests and energy with another employer who wanted a technically adept individual to deliver functional, effective results from their novel investment in computer technology in their offices.

That hiring supervisor, an exceptional naval officer, first assigned me to build an inventory control application from scratch. That was not something my engineering degree prepared me for directly, but I got to it. And I fell in love with the exercise of creating applications. I'd found a new passion. And the more programming I did, the better I got at it. These initial systems were transformational for the organization, to the point of appearing almost magical. That's how potent the initial technology wave was.

Those two factors together engendered personal gratification and professional satisfaction and have sustained me since. I eventually realized I'd found a sweet spot that not everyone does–loving my career and being good at what I do.

Think about what you are good at, whether natural skills and/or learned. How do these match with your planned career path?

John Chappell has been a constant fan of science in general and especially of our space programs and of science fiction and fantasy stories. Outside of the left-brained exercise of writing software, he's learning how to write fiction.

YOU ARE ALREADY A WINNER
Bob Lynn

Life's challenges are your opportunities to find your way.

My name is Bob Lynn, and my story is one that began with many challenges that, rather than knocking me down, brought me to achieving so much to include a doctorate degree and the privilege to work with challenged communities around the globe.

Of course, we don't have the opportunity to choose the hand life thrusts on us. In my case, I grew up in Brooklyn, New York with the constant message that I was limited and success only meant survival. With an emotionally detached family system, the future looked bleak from the start.

This is where it begins and sadly ends for too many. The lesson learned from my experience is that whatever anyone else can do, so can I. This is not to trivialize the many barriers caused by economic and social challenges; importantly, within each of us is the ability to have a winning hand even when we have been dealt a poor set of cards.

Once you accept that your success has no limits, you can then take advantage of the opportunities often masked by doubts. So what does it take to be a winner?

First, begin with a can-do attitude focusing on your strengths and resources. With this in mind, develop goals as to where you want to be and then make a plan. Thinking outside the box requires knocking on doors you might otherwise view as closed.

Seeking mentors and asking for guidance expands your opportunities and possibilities for success. Always look forward while building your future.

You will find along the way that a positive winning attitude grounded in kindness and humility can be the key to a quality life. Success begets success, and as one's foundation becomes stronger, perceived limits fade. There may be setbacks on your journey, which can become lessons learned and which should not be defined as failures.

At the end of the day, you need to build a semipermeable membrane around yourself that screens out doubts and naysayers. Embrace your journey, face your challenges and enjoy the ride.

How can you be a winner, as you define it? What tips and strategies can you use and follow?

Bob Lynn, Ph.D., is an internationally recognized lecturer, researcher and clinician in Counseling Psychology and Substance Use Disorders. He is a Licensed Professional Counselor and Senior Fellow in Neurofeedback and a recognized expert in Family Therapy and Behavioral Therapy.

BEYOND THE BURNOUT–NEVER TOO LATE TO DREAM

Sally Pauwels

Focus your energy on goals that will bring you not just success but also fulfillment.

Three decades of my corporate business life and the last years in a toxic company had taken their toll. Burnout, a thief of passion, creativity and energy, slammed me to a halt for five long years. Even though I was burned out, a tiny part of me just wouldn't give up. I really wanted to try something new, something that would make me feel excited and happy again. The path forward wasn't an easy one. It was a heavy climb, with moments of ups and downs.

After three struggling years, like a sunrise after a long night full of nightmares and dreams, I found the perfect coach at the perfect moment. Together with her, we went on a challenging adventure. Eventually, my goal was to start a small creative business of my own, a world away from my corporate past. This wasn't just a new career; it was a way for finding my passion again, a chance to write a new chapter filled with happiness and joy.

During my solo climb, people and organizations tried to help but also disrupted my path to getting better. According to the possibilities and laws, I made decisions that straightened my path to success. This meant I've lost friends but also gained new friendships that understood my situation and believed in me.

Remember, the weight of your backpack of life can be a heavy burden, but always take time to process things you're carrying so that your backpack of life gets lighter.

It's never too late to ignite a new dream. Your potential is boundless, and you have the ability to regain feelings of control and confidence in your life. But it takes the support of people who love and believe in you.

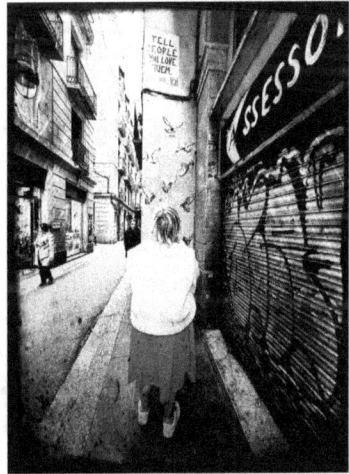

FIGURE 2.7
It's never too late to ignite a new dream.

What are some specific things you can do to lighten your backpack? Who can provide support to you during this journey?

Sally Pauwels has called Belgium home throughout her life. After starting her career in information technology in 1990, burnout forced a shift in 2019. She launched Me My Story, a small business that provides her energy and strength.

OPTIMISM FROM THE INSIDE OUT
Kimberley Timpf

Get an inside view of the power of optimism.

In the animated movie *Inside Out 2*, Joy is one of five emotions inhabiting the mind of 13-year-old Riley, alongside Sadness, Anger, Fear and Disgust. As Riley matures, a new set of emotions–Anxiety, Envy, Embarrassment and Ennui–show up to complicate her life. The same angst and confusion you may remember experiencing is similar to what Riley faces when Anxiety fills her mind with worst-case scenarios and self-doubt. Joy counters Anxiety's negative projections with scenes of hope and positivity from Riley's memory bank, guiding her through the uncertainty.

Although we may not have an animated character to guide us, we do have *optimism*–a powerful tool we can employ all on our own. Optimism allows us to look beyond difficulties and see potential and possibility. Optimism doesn't ignore problems or pretend they don't exist but shifts the focus to hope, solutions and the potential for positive outcomes. One effective strategy for doing this is to call on "moments that matter"–those meaningful life experiences filled with happiness, connection and accomplishment. Recalling past successes and positive outcomes can strengthen sense of self by helping build resilience to face difficulties with a more hopeful mindset.

Like Riley, we all face moments when anxiety, fear or doubt try to take control. But by embracing optimism, we can navigate adversity by calling on hope and possibility. Optimism isn't about dismissing life's difficulties; it is about trusting in our ability to overcome them. Remembering the times we've succeeded, felt joy or found connection with others–our "moments that matter"–can be a counterbalance to our fear, empowering us to push through uncertainty. Optimism helps shift our focus from dwelling on what could go wrong to imagining what can go right, reminding us that good things can still happen, even in the face of life's challenges.

Important note: Sometimes, normal emotions like sadness, stress or anxiety can persist and optimism alone can't help us push through. If that happens, don't be afraid to reach out for help–from a counselor, adviser, mentor or trusted friend. Getting help is not a sign of weakness but a true act of optimism and a courageous step toward regaining balance in your life.

What are your key "moments that matter"? How can you be intentional about creating new moments moving forward?

For over 25 years, Kimberley Timpf has worked with colleges, universities and the e-learning industry to create environments and online learning tools that promote student safety, well-being and belonging.

LIVING IN POSSIBILITY
Denny Roberts

Explore, declare and develop your unique talents and stay open to living your truest and best self in unexpected ways.

From the age of five, I was obsessed with learning how to play the piano, and by middle school, I was in community competitions. By high school, I was winning awards and beginning to see music as a viable career. College scholarship awards cinched it–I would be a concert pianist!

But what I didn't know was that being a performing artist required access to exceptional mentors, dogged dedication and privileged access I never knew was part of the proposition. As the reality sank in that my career aspiration was out of reach, I looked at ways to continue my dedication to music but not depend on it to put a roof over my head and food on the table. The "artist's way" I viewed the world, connecting and integrating insights and inspiration from encounters with others, resulted in my pursuing a career in higher education. The gift of combining the artist in me with a commitment to innovation in education allowed me to be who I was meant to be while serving others and making a living. Looking back, living in possibility was essential for me to more deeply know myself, turning my insights into life purpose and experiences far exceeding my wildest imaginings as a youth.

Fulfilling the vision I had for myself was tempered by realizing that some of my life experiences limited but others expanded my opportunity, leading to a path that was deeply fulfilling but adjacent to what I first believed I was called and prepared to do.

FIGURE 2.8
Piano has been my life companion - a constant source of insight and inspiration.

What draws out your best efforts, and how are you nurturing your gifts to full excellence? How can your gifts align with work or contribute to an affirming and fulfilling life?

Denny Roberts writes and consults on human development, leadership and internationalization. He practices piano every day, participates in choral groups and is a faithful music patron for multiple ensembles.

WHAT YOU SEE IS WHAT YOU GET
Jamie E. Washington

Where we focus will impact how we move through life's moments.

Life presents us with an ever-changing landscape of joys and struggles, opportunities and challenges. Acknowledging both is essential for personal growth and emotional balance. While challenges often demand our attention, developing an attitude of gratitude allows us to shift focus from what is lacking to what is abundant. This perspective fosters resilience, contentment and a deeper appreciation for the blessings life offers.

One effective way to cultivate gratitude is through a *daily practice of reflection*. Setting aside a few minutes each day to identify and write down what we are grateful for can create a profound shift in mindset. Whether it's the warmth of the morning sun, a kind gesture from a friend or simply the ability to breathe deeply, recognizing these moments transforms ordinary occurrences into extraordinary gifts. Over time, this habit rewires the brain to seek positivity, even amid adversity.

Another meaningful approach is to *create a physical reminder* of life's blessings. This could be a gratitude jar, where small notes about things we appreciate are deposited, or a photo album featuring cherished memories and loved ones. These serve as visual anchors, reminding us to focus on the good even during challenging times. Revisiting these symbols of positivity reinforces a mindset of abundance and appreciation.

Finally, *sharing gratitude stories* with others can amplify its effects. Narrating moments of thankfulness–such as a teacher who changed our life or a friend who supported us–helps us relive those uplifting experiences. Sharing these stories not only spreads positivity but also inspires others to reflect on their blessings. This collective practice of gratitude strengthens relationships, builds empathy and fosters a supportive community.

Acknowledging life's "blessings" is not about ignoring hardships or struggles; it's about giving greater weight to life's gifts. When we develop an attitude of gratitude, we invite a perspective that highlights the silver linings and reminds us of the abundance around us. We can cultivate a life enriched by appreciation, resilience and joy. What we choose to see becomes the lens through which we experience life–and gratitude transforms that lens into one of beauty and hope.

Identify specific ways you can shift your focus to the blessings of life.

Rev. Dr. Jamie E. Washington is a dynamic and visionary leader with over 41 years of experience in education, administration and consulting. He is President and Founder of the Washington Consulting Group.

DETOURS AND DEAD ENDS CAN BE USEFUL
Sarah K. Fields

Try new things even if they aren't directly on your career path.

Students often tell me they feel tremendous pressure to have a career plan when they start college. I don't think that is ideal. When I was seven, I planned to sell shoes. I tried that, but it was harder than I expected. When I was 17, I thought I'd be a forest ranger, but there was more science in forestry classes than I enjoyed. Then I gave up on career plans. My parents, fortunately, kept telling me that everything I learned would come in handy someday–that all knowledge was fuel for life's journey. Life isn't a straight line.

The best advice I got during my first year of college was to take academic risks and to take one random class a term to see what windows it opened. Decades later, some of those random classes are still the most memorable–that ethics class still makes me think.

And one random class as a graduate student, a class on the history of women and sport, changed my whole career path. I've loved sports my whole life, both as a participant and as a spectator. I'm a mediocre athlete, so I never dreamed that I could make a living in sport. However, it turns out that all those random classes I took, all those random teams that I played on, all those hours I spent watching and talking about sports prepared me for a career as a sports studies scholar. I don't sell shoes, but I know the importance of footwear in sports. I'm not a forest ranger, but I know that outdoor activities are critical to our mental and physical health. I have even taught sport ethics.

So don't be afraid to take a risk with your academic studies or other learning and growth opportunities. That class, that activity, that workshop or that training might not seem relevant to the path you think you are on, but it could pay off in interesting ways later. Or maybe you just learned something fun.

All knowledge is fuel for your life's journey. You need as much fuel, as much knowledge, as you can gather on your path. Because it is okay if your path isn't a direct one. Detours and dead ends are not bad things in education or life.

What is a topic that you think might be fun to learn about–through a class or self-education–but doesn't have any direct connection to your career plans?

Sarah K. Fields is a professor at the University of Colorado Denver who enjoys hanging out with her pets.

A JOURNEY OF BELIEF AND SUPPORT
Eileen M. Vélez-Vega

It is vitally important to dream big and never give up.

Growing up in a home with limited financial resources, my parents instilled in me a powerful belief: I could achieve anything as long as I worked hard. They never imposed limits on my potential, and this unwavering faith in me became the foundation of my self-worth. Despite our family's challenges, I never felt restricted by our circumstances; instead, I saw opportunities in every obstacle.

This mindset fueled my determination to excel academically and immerse myself in extracurricular activities like dance and science, technology, engineering and mathematics (STEM) camps. To fund my dreams, I sold chocolates for school fundraisers and worked in my uncle's extermination business. These experiences, along with prayers, taught me not only the value of hard work but also the power of perseverance and independence.

I wanted to be an astronaut, so I went to Space Camp and then pursued engineering, becoming the first engineer in my family. I once told my mom that someday I would like to be Puerto Rico's Transportation Secretary, a goal I couldn't fully grasp at the time or even understand. I didn't know the steps to make it happen, and my mom never even laughed at my idea. She always reminded me that there were no limits to what I could achieve.

I traveled the world and grew as an engineer. I returned to Puerto Rico and then, one day, I received an unexpected call that would change everything. After years of hard work, perseverance and unwavering belief in myself, I made history as the first woman to become Puerto Rico's Secretary of the Department of Transportation and Public Works.

My journey stands as a testament to the power of believing in your dreams, having the support and love from parents and teachers and working relentlessly. Today, they call me "Madam Secretary"; I have become a role model for young girls everywhere, showing them that no dream is too big and there is no challenge we cannot overcome. Every setback, frustration and challenge were simply stepping stones to a brighter future.

FIGURE 2.9
This 2011 and 2019 survivor timeline shows my 3-week old daughter and me after I had just restarted chemotherapy. While I was losing all my hair, my miracle baby had plenty for both of us!

Identify your dreams, as broad or specific as you can.

Eileen M. Vélez-Vega is a civil engineer, public servant and the first woman to become the Secretary of Transportation and Public Works in Puerto Rico.

UNCHARTED PATHS
Chia-Liang Dai

Find ways to integrate your mind, body and community.

As an Associate Professor in Health and Physical Education, my journey is shaped by an interdisciplinary background that blends education, counseling psychology and public health. Born and raised in Taiwan, I began my career teaching and providing counseling to elementary school children, where I developed a deep passion for guiding young people toward healthier behaviors and lifestyles. I also coached school sports teams, which further fueled my enthusiasm for physical activity and holistic well-being promotion.

However, it was my role as a school psychologist that significantly changed my career trajectory. Working with children facing mental health challenges, combined with my academic interest in counseling psychology, deepened my understanding of the mind-body connection. This insight led me to pursue a Ph.D. in health promotion and education, with a focus on counselor education. I came to view health not just as the absence of disease but as a multifaceted journey encompassing mental, physical and emotional well-being.

My research focuses on health behavior change, particularly through mind-body practices like yoga and mindfulness meditation. My studies explore the connections between physical activity, mental health and substance use prevention, as well as how family and cultural factors influence risky behaviors. I am dedicated to making a tangible impact on underserved children. For me, my sports-related services are not just about promoting physical fitness; they are about teaching life skills, resilience and emotional intelligence, especially for children facing difficult home circumstances.

My work reflects my belief that true health comes from the integration of mind, body and environment. I see health promotion and education not just as a way to reduce risky behaviors but also an opportunity to empower individuals, families and communities to live healthier, more fulfilling lives. Whether through research or community engagement, I am committed to helping others navigate the complex journey toward whole-person health.

With this background, my core recommendations for you are to stick to what you are passionate about, stay connected to what you love and find ways to nurture your mind and body in the challenging journey of your life.

What are some specific habits you can incorporate into your daily life to nurture your mind and body as you navigate the challenges you face?

Chia-Liang Dai, Ph.D., is an associate professor of health and physical education. With a background including elementary school teacher, sports coach, school psychologist and military mental health counselor in Taiwan, his research focuses on holistic well-being promotion and health behavior change.

EMBRACE THE POWER OF POSSIBILITY
Nicole M. Augustine

Optimism isn't just a feeling; it's a decision to see the possibilities in every situation, creating momentum for a brighter future.

Optimism isn't just about wearing rose-colored glasses. It's a conscious decision to believe that things can and will improve, no matter the current circumstances. Choosing optimism is choosing to focus on the possibilities rather than the problems. It's the understanding that even in the most difficult times, there's room for growth and positive change.

I remember a time when things felt like they weren't going my way. It would have been easy to spiral into negativity, but I made a choice to shift my mindset. I began using the affirmation, "Things are always working out for me." This wasn't just wishful thinking; it was a reminder to look for opportunities in the challenges faced. Over time, I began to see my reality shift, not because my circumstances changed but because my perspective did.

Young adulthood is full of transitions, challenges and unknowns. It can feel overwhelming at times, but here's the truth: Optimism is a tool you can use to guide yourself through these transitions. When you choose to see challenges as opportunities, you unlock a deeper level of resilience. You're no longer waiting for life to happen to you; you're shaping your future.

Optimism isn't about denying reality. It's about choosing where to place your focus. As Napoleon Hill famously said, "Whatever the mind can conceive and believe, it can achieve." So conceive a future where things are working out for you. Believe in your own power to shape your life, and watch as optimism becomes the engine that propels you.

Here are three specific ways that you can bring this perspective to fruition:

- **Reframe a challenge:** Think of a challenge you are currently facing. How can you reframe this situation through an optimistic lens? What opportunities might be hidden within it?
- **Create your affirmation:** Write down one affirmation that reflects your belief in the possibilities that life holds. Repeat it daily and notice how it shifts your mindset.
- **Gratitude practice:** Each day, write down one thing you are looking forward to. Focus on the positive moments ahead, no matter how small.

Reflect on your life right now. What can you start doing today to shift your perspective toward one of possibility?

Nicole M. Augustine is a public health innovator, author, speaker, and project director dedicated to inspiring others to reframe challenges through optimism and positive language and promoting meaningful community change.

"DON'T STOP BELIEVIN'"[1]

Jason Kilmer

Musical lyrics have the power to reassure us, guide us, calm us and provide joy.

As a huge fan of music (and quoting song lyrics), I decided to pass on my advice with excerpts from a number of my favorite songs or artists. I hope it is helpful, but "it's your thing, do what you wanna do."[2]

"Don't try to live your life in one day."[3]
You might tell yourself, "I want it all"[4] and take on too much. Instead, "you have to learn to pace yourself."[5]
Remember that "everything counts in large amounts."[6]
"And isn't it ironic?"[7] We're expected to do a lot.
But "don't be discouraged–oh, I realize, it's hard to take courage."[8]
Go ahead and do what puts a smile on your face.
"Be good to yourself because nobody else has the power to make you happy."[9]
In fact, "you can dance if you want to."[10]
In conclusion, "I couldn't really put it much plainer"[11]
"Be yourself, no matter what they say."[12]

---

1. "Don't Stop Believin'," Journey
2. "It's Your Thing," the Isley Brothers
3. "Life in One Day," Howard Jones
4. "I Want It All," Queen
5. "Pressure," Billy Joel
6. "Everything Counts," Depeche Mode
7. "Ironic," Alanis Morissette
8. "True Colors," Cyndi Lauper
9. "Heal the Pain," George Michael
10. "The Safety Dance," Men Without Hats
11. "New Moon on Monday," Duran Duran
12. "Englishman in New York," Sting

As you think about your own journey, what song lyrics come to mind when you need to motivate yourself? Which ones make you laugh? Which ones make you think? Consider what soundtrack best tells and supports your story.

Jason Kilmer, Ph.D., is a Professor in Psychiatry and Behavioral Sciences and an Adjunct Professor in Psychology at the University of Washington in Seattle.

MOVING ON, MOVING UP
Fred Bemak

Think about how to move on and move up in your personal and professional development and your life.

It was a complicated world when I was a young adult, and it is a complicated world now. However, my work path was accidental–I had few plans and vague interests and ideas about what I wanted and where I was going. In retrospect, the driving force behind my young adult journey and successful life expedition was based on three qualities that developed as I grew.

First, courage involved not being afraid to take risks and having the strength and initiative to pursue dreams. Speaking up for ideas and beliefs, speaking up for what is just and fair, speaking up for human dignity and human rights–all of this was developed as I experimented. I challenged myself to go above and beyond, allowed myself to dream and embraced the discomfort to reach for the dreams. By cultivating courage, it has become my lifelong friend.

I also found inquisitiveness, openness and exploration to be essential. I was always hungry to understand and to know the whys and hows. This requires an openness to differences and changes, to others, to ideas and to personal discomfort. The thirst, curiosity and imagination to breathe in the beauty and richness in the world can change your life as it did mine.

A third quality is freedom from social norms and expectation. With your many pressures about how to move forward and how to move up, some may help you grow and develop more fully, and others may be a hindrance. Standing up for issues like civil and equal rights, and freedom of expression may result in criticism, antagonism and rejection even though you know you are on the right path.

FIGURE 2.10
Courage to bring one's skills to new and different environments: Contributing to a better world.

How do you make the choice for a richer, more meaningful life that brings happiness as you move on and move up to help and support yourself and others?

Fred Bemak is a Professor Emeritus at George Mason University, Adjunct Professor at Victoria University of Wellington and Affiliate Professor at the University of Malta. He has received multiple national and international awards for his work in social justice and human rights.

THE LONG AND WINDING ROAD
Allison Macfarlane

Keep your eyes open and seek advice to create your own future.

You just never know, nor can you predict, where you will end up in your career. Right now, you may have some fixed ideas–or no clue–about what you'll be doing in 10 or 20 years. I'm here to tell you to keep an open mind because you may surprise yourself.

When I was young, I knew I wanted to be a scientist, but that was all. I ended up a geology major in college and then in graduate school. I thought I would be a professor at a university, teach classes and spend my summers collecting rock samples in mountains.

In graduate school, I got stuck in a war zone while doing fieldwork in Nepal, which made me realize that rocks (or the study of rocks) wasn't worth dying for. So I started searching for other topics that interested me by talking with folks who worked in fields I was interested in. Most told me to give a new field a try and were very encouraging. A few were not. But it helped to hear them out.

I ended up studying nuclear waste disposal. And from there, over a period of years, I became a newcomer expert in the field. Nuclear waste is both a technical and a political issue, and the political side of it led some members of Congress, particularly interested in preventing nuclear waste from being left in their district, to seek out my advice.

After some years, I was asked to sit on a national commission on nuclear waste management–one of the best experiences of my career during which we spent two years studying the issues in detail. Most surprising was what happened after the commission ended: I was asked by the leader of the U.S. Senate and President Barack Obama to be the next chair of the U.S. Nuclear Regulatory Commission, a 4,000-person independent government agency. Who knew, when I was a kid, that I would end up in a Senate-confirmed position ensuring that the country's nuclear materials and nuclear reactors are kept safe and secure?

After some years, I returned to academia, enriched by my experience in government–and knowing that you just never know where your path will take you.

With the forks in the road or big life decisions, identify a variety of folks with experience whom you can seek out for advice.

Allison Macfarlane is Professor and Director of the School of Public Policy and Global Affairs at the University of British Columbia in Vancouver, Canada. She has taught at a number of universities and was the first geologist ever to be a commissioner at the U.S. Nuclear Regulatory Commission.

EMBRACE CHANGE AND TRUST YOURSELF
Walter P. Parrish III

Life's unpredictability demands resilience, self-trust and a willingness to embrace change.

As a child, I learned early that life is unexpected and can feel unwieldy. After my father died when I was nine, my mom and I had to navigate our new realities. As an only child, I spent a lot of time observing and listening, which I believe helped me to develop emotional intelligence–understanding and managing my own emotions while being acutely aware of others' emotions.

I grew up a child musician and originally went to college to study music education. To support my mom and myself, I worked several jobs in high school and college. Despite taking on these responsibilities and other challenges, including financial pressures and racism from faculty, I tried to remain committed to my passion for music.

Those challenges also helped me to realize that perhaps music was not my only passion in life.

Using my resilience, emotional intelligence and instincts, I uncovered a new passion that allowed me to have a significant impact on people's lives and career trajectories. I obtained a master's degree and eventually earned my Ph.D. in education. With 17 years of experience, I have worked to support and inspire students, educators and administrators, while driving systemic change in higher education.

Overcoming hardships, adapting to change and being consistent in the face of challenges taught me the value of resilience and trusting yourself.

Embrace your individuality, trust your unique strengths and be adaptive in the face of adversity. By doing so, you'll not only overcome obstacles but also unlock your full, authentic potential.

What is holding you back from fully trusting yourself in uncertain times?

Walter P. Parrish III, Ph.D., is an experienced academic leader and advocate for diversity, equity and inclusion in higher education, specializing in pathway programs, faculty development and institutional transformation.

TRUST SERENDIPITY
Gerardo M. González

Having goals is important for achieving personal aspirations, but staying alert to serendipitous opportunities can open a world of unimaginable possibilities.

Our society puts a premium on setting goals for ourselves and our future. Many feel that setting goals gives shape and direction to their lives. Some people know from a young age exactly what they want to do; others, like me, have found it more difficult to formulate long-term plans.

I am a first-generation college graduate. My family and I came to the United States as refugees from Cuba. My father was an automobile mechanic and my mother a factory worker. Going to college had never occurred to me until, in a moment of uncertainty, a friend made a chance remark: "Gerardo, why don't you go to college?" This was fate sending me a message. Going to college led to a variety of unexpected study and work experiences that ultimately turned into a long, successful career in academia. What characterizes all the opportunities I had is that in every case, I threw myself wholeheartedly into my work. If I failed at something, I was motivated to try harder. I believe that if you put your heart into whatever passion you pursue, one thing can lead to another, and as you discover more about your talents and interests, your path can grow organically.

When I faced going to college, I wondered, "What if I fail?" It can be easy to slip into believing you can't do something. Instead of worrying, however, I just took the next step and watched where it took me. Those new experiences provided me with information, clues, answers and even opportunities to learn and discover something about myself. I trusted that by staying present in the moment and alert to opportunities, I would find my path. Any conversation, random meeting, or relationship has the potential to impact your dreams and open doors to opportunity. While goals are important, trust serendipity.

As you reflect on this writing, think about ways in which serendipitous encounters or events have influenced your life. What did you learn from them?

Gerardo González is Professor and Dean Emeritus of Education at Indiana University. Recognized as a leading founder of the peer education movement in America, in 2018, Indiana University Press published his memoir titled, *A Cuban Refugee's Journey to the American Dream: The Power of Education.*

NO STONE LEFT UNTURNED
Joaquin Flores Borja

Prepare yourself to have a wonderful life.

How wonderful this world would be,
If each one of us treated it as it should be.
We start from home to learn respect,
And the kind of community we'd love to expect.
Healthy, strong, educated, and civilized,
Not until it is too late to be realized.
The phrase "better late than never,"
Shouldn't happen, now or ever.
When each of us connects as a link,
We will bond and adhere to success without a wink.
We build and mold our life like an architect,
From lessons instilled, and from our intellect.
Precise, perfected, interior and exterior,
To each of us be equal and no one superior.
In harmony, understanding, and direction,
In perfection that nothing needs correction,
Because early in life we learned from our parents and teachers,
Who helped us to be doctors, scientists, judges, and good leaders,
Who instill in our life the value that makes us precious,
Humble, wise, focused, refined, as we display dignity by being gracious.
We fear no adversity, challenge, or any obstacle,
And we solve with solution that we say it's not impossible.
When certificates, diplomas, or degrees are presented,
And each of us with joy and happiness represented,
We each open a new chapter and pages added,
As we sit on a chair with a seat that is padded.

What are some ideas in the poem that point to how you may have a wonderful life?

Joaquin Flores Borja, also known as Jack, was born and raised on the island of Saipan in the Mariana Islands. He lived in Chicago, Illinois for 30 years and is now residing in San Diego, California. Jack has written numerous poems, both in English and in Chamorro (his native language), and his poems have been published in several books and have also been studied in the academic field.

THE TROUBLE WITH OPTIMISM
Rick Davis

Optimism can get you in trouble–but it's good trouble.

In the middle of a muddle, when everyone around you is imagining the worst, the optimist may seem a bit delusional. "How is this ever going to work out?" "There's nothing we can do." And then, "Look at the optimist over there, smiling like nothing's wrong." It can be an uncomfortable way to stand out from the crowd, as I know all too well.

Except that I'm usually not pretending that nothing's wrong. I'm drawing on my experience that optimism is justified more often than not if we tackle the problem together. It's a callback to all those instances when the thing, whatever it was, *did* work out because I and the folks around me kept at it.

I don't think I am a "born optimist," and I'm not sure that type of person actually exists. But I learned over the years that a belief in good outcomes seems to help make them come true, while a persistent pessimism has the opposite effect–with only one benefit: the chance to say, "I told you so" when something goes wrong.

A number of these optimism-building experiences come from my life in the theater. I've been thrown on stage with an hour's–sometimes minutes'– notice when a performer got sick or, on one memorable occasion, fell out of a tree while hiking in the Rocky Mountains. I've been the director of huge productions where everything went wrong at dress rehearsal. My optimism that things would work out helped to give my fellow travelers a tiny boost in their own confidence. And come opening night, things worked out!

That's not to say that optimism *alone* guarantees a good outcome. Optimism without a plan of action won't get you very far. But it can give you, and those around you, the space and the energy to keep going, trying new things, moving ahead.

So after many years of practice (and more than a few setbacks), my optimism is now baked in. I'll smile when things start to go wrong because I think they're most likely on the way to going right.

Try it next time you're in the middle of a muddle, and never mind the doubters casting gloomy looks your way. They'll come around!

In what ways have you found your belief in positive outcomes helped with actually achieving those results? What else helped, and what else could have helped?

Rick Davis is Dean of the College of Visual and Performing Arts and Professor of Theater at George Mason University and is active as a director, translator, librettist and performer.

INSIGHTS FROM INSIDE
Justin Harmon

Everyone should strive to be a lifelong learner.

One of the more rewarding moments of teaching is when the tables get turned and you learn something from your students. I was giving a lecture on understanding the experiences of others to a group of new students, and I wanted them to think about—and draw—the happy memories from their past and their enjoyable daily activities. The goal was to get them thinking about enjoying life now and in the future.

Oh, I should probably mention this took place inside a federal prison and these "students" were prisoners.

Responding to the everyday experience that he looks forward to most, one gentleman said that it's when the guards open the cells in the morning, and he gets a taste of "freedom" to do what he wants for the day. Of course, I was forced to consider just what freedom really means, but nonetheless, I was heartened by his statement because he chose to make the most of his time behind bars and to make decisions about how to live his life despite the condition of his circumstances.

Another student referred to his first time snow skiing with his daughter, and how nervous he was compared to her, yet how that shared activity was so important to their father-daughter bonding and her being able to trust him to keep her safe. This is something he thinks about to this day and something he reflects on to help him ward off unhealthy temptations that might keep him from reuniting with his daughter in the future.

Another student chose not a single memory but recurring experiences he shared with his parents as a child: that of sitting on their front porch swing and talking. He indicated that his parents meant so much to him, and although they're no longer alive, those memories continue to give him inspiration.

It's easy for us to dismiss those who have trespassed against society. It's easy to assume they're bad people, somehow beneath us. But as I was reminded, these folks are not all bad; most of them simply made bad decisions. They're trying to change, to become better versions of themselves.

And that was a lesson worth learning.

How has a rush to judgment proven you wrong in your life? What did you learn from that experience?

Justin Harmon, Ph.D., is an associate professor at University of North Carolina at Greensboro. He likes getting lost in the forest, among the crowds at concerts and in good books.

AGAINST ALL ODDS
Aish Ravi

Optimism and perseverance are essential for addressing life's challenges.

As an Indian athlete in Australian Rules Football, I faced cultural and racial challenges, advocated for policy change on racial vilification and achieved success on and off the field through perseverance and passion. Playing Australian Rules Football–a sport dominated by white Australians–was a journey of resilience for me. As an Indian person with brown skin, I was always up against the odds. From the beginning, no one believed in my abilities, and I was often the only person of color on the field. Racist remarks and subtle forms of exclusion were regular parts of my experience, and the cultural norms of the sport didn't align with my own.

Games were frequently scheduled during the day, conflicting with my cultural commitments, and the standard uniform was not culturally inclusive. To maintain my values, I had to modify my uniform by wearing skins to cover my arms and legs, ensuring that I felt both respectful of my culture and safe on the field. Along the way, I also advocated for policy change to address racial vilification, fighting for a more inclusive environment in the sport.

Despite these obstacles, my passion for the sport never wavered. I knew I might not be the most physically athletic player, but I focused on honing my skills and developing a deep understanding of the game to outsmart my opponents. This dedication paid off. Our team won a premiership, and I was honored with the best and fairest athlete award.

My experience taught me that perseverance, belief in oneself and optimism are essential when navigating challenging paths. It is vital to take time to reflect on what can be learned from personal struggles and remember that persistence often leads to breakthroughs. It is helpful to challenge yourself to identify areas in life where self-doubt has held you back. Take the first step toward overcoming it with an optimistic mindset. Push through challenges with a sense of optimism and focus on what you love.

Identify at least one area in your own life where self-doubt has held you back. How can you challenge yourself to apply optimism to address this now and in the future?

Aish Ravi is a business and economics teacher, sports coach and board member with a deep passion for sport and learning. Her passion lies in learning and making change. Her hopes to continue creating opportunities for others like her to thrive.

JUST AROUND THE CORNER
Daniel Torres

Life can take some interesting turns as you pursue your own destiny.

Six years ago, I made one of the most important decisions in my life: to emigrate. Since I was a child, I imagined what it would be like to live in a different place than the one I was used to, with completely unknown people. I imagined myself walking through the streets of some European city or looking up at the sky from some exotic island. But as I grew up, this idea faded away. I finished high school, started university and started working more and more. The idea of looking up at the stars in the sky from an exotic island became just a distant and unlikely dream.

However, one person would change this forever; it was a fleeting love but one of those that makes you tremble and turns your world upside down. To such an extent that when he decided to spend some time in the United States, I didn't hesitate to go with him and leave my house, job, friends and family.

The important thing wasn't our relationship; the important thing was everything that came after.

Finding a country with different customs, another language and a million possibilities helped show me the person I wanted to be and the possibility of building my future at will. At first, this was with a lot of anxiety and always missing everything I had left behind. The days passed and then months and years. People who were introduced to me during this time became family; those crazy customs that I saw at the beginning became my daily life.

FIGURE 2.11
The possibilities always take amazing directions. Photo Credit: Christian Cordoba.

While Florida is not an exotic island, it has a sky full of stars that light up my nights. Here, I found my true vocation, which I practice with passion every day.

Emigrating has many nuances, good and bad aspects. The good thing is everything is initially unknown, and you are able to see, with your own eyes, what no one can show you. The bad thing is always having to explain the joke.

Life always has something good in store for us, sometimes not how we dreamed but always with a mysterious and at the same time great power. Go for it! Your destiny is just around the corner.

What is it that you dream about? What is right around your corner?

Daniel Torres, 35 years old, was born in Buenos Aires, Argentina.

GROWING MY LIFE WITHOUT BEING COMFORTABLE
Mari

Take the time to listen, grow and be challenged.

As an only child growing up, I was always surrounded by adults. These adults gathered at our home every weekend to play cards, or we would go on excursions around the island with one another. We would all cram into my father's bucket seat Plymouth Fury car to visit new sites, open homes, eat shaved ice and other local delectables and pick the wild guava so my mom could make her homemade guava jelly. Those were the days.

Those were my humble beginnings, and as the years went by, exposure to life as a college student, worker and community leader began to shape me even more. I think I began to blossom when I came into my job. Through travel and work, I was able to build connections with many different people and cultures from the community–representatives in business, government, service providers, community coalitions, cultural and age. I began to understand people and how our early life experiences can dictate how we see others and if we connect or not connect with them.

You can spiral down that deep dark tunnel or choose to stand up against the turbulent waters. I choose to surround myself with those with positive energies and those who will support, teach and continue to nurture my self-growth. My son once told me, if you are comfortable, that is when you stop growing as a person, so being uncomfortable from time to time helps one continue to grow and be the best one can be.

Was this all intentional or merely me just being lucky enough to be surrounded with the right people in my life? Let me be clear: life wasn't all peachy keen, but isn't that how we learn? Take the good with the bad, becoming resilient to overcome the hardships while keeping those foundations you learned early on in life. For me, it was having good character, caring for others and making those elders (and my ancestors) proud. I will continue to take one day at a time.

What are some areas of your life where you would consider stepping outside your comfort zone to help grow and thrive? What would help you actually do that?

Mari claims her right as a senior but keeps her youthful energy. She enjoys her work with the community and collaborative partners with whom she has a strong relationship.

LÂCHE PAS LA PATATE (NEVER GIVE UP)
John Nauright

Keep your eye on your long-term goals and persevere.

In Louisiana, we have a saying from our Louisiana French heritage that says, "Don't drop the potato." However, it is used to encourage someone to never give up and persevere. Perseverance is key to meeting the day-to-day challenges of life. It is important to keep long-term goals in mind.

I am a dual Australian and American citizen and that I have lived and worked in many countries. But my career goal was always to get back to the state of my birth, which is Louisiana, and particularly to Louisiana State University.

I faced a number of challenges along the way, including having my job at one university eliminated due to a merger. As I picked up leadership skills and experience, I was in a position for a right place, right time moment–and I ended up at LSU 20 years after I thought I might get here, but I never gave up on the possibility.

How did I do this, and can you keep your chin up when you get knocked down? It is easier than it might seem. It means not getting too lost in the noise of day-to-day life but enjoy the ride while mapping what you are doing against your long-term goals. Twists and turns will happen. The mistake I finally learned from–which I hope you can avoid–is to roll with the tide and realize that each challenge is an opportunity to build for the ultimate goal.

FIGURE 2.12
This is me in one of my happy places at Piha Beach in Aotearoa/ New Zealand.

Now, your goals may change as you adapt to life and develop new skills. All my degrees were in history, yet I ended up as dean of a college of business and spent nearly all of my career in kinesiology (human movement) departments. I never thought that would be my path when I first set out after completing my Ph.D. As opportunities arose that were interesting, I took them on. This led me around the world, picking up skills, connections and opportunities along the way. But I never dropped the potato, and 30 years after my professional journey began, I have arrived at my dream destination! Geaux, Tigers, and geaux, you!

What are your long-term goals in your work, family, community, society and otherwise? What will help you persevere to help you achieve these goals?

John Nauright is Director of the School of Kinesiology and Karen Wax Schmitt and Family Endowed Professor at Louisiana State University.

POSSIBILITY THINKING
Robert Chapman

Possibility thinking is to discovery as absolute thinking is to inflexibility.

My grandfather used to say, "You know what you learn and learn what's taught, but never forget, that's not all there is to know."

When you recognize that there is always something new to learn, you automatically embrace possibility thinking. An adage suggests that if you always do what you've always done, you will always get what you've always gotten. Challenging the limits of an existing body of knowledge fosters an environment that welcomes questions and celebrates curiosity, leading to deeper thinking and a broader perspective.

Consider every invention or innovative procedure we take for granted today. These advances were once nothing more than ideas, the product of someone's curious imagination that asked, "What if?" However, an idea remains just a concept, a notion until one decides to act on and pursue it to answer the what-if question. This action is the transformative power of possibility thinking.

As a thought experiment, imagine you work in a hospital pathology lab. When cleaning beakers and slides for reuse, you discover a strain of bacteria with a unique property: they can survive extremely high temperatures in sterilization. Although the "obvious" question is how to remove these bacteria from the lab equipment and solve the problem, what opportunity or opportunities might these heat-resistant bacteria present to someone who engages in possibility thinking? *What if* the heat-resistant properties of these bacteria could lead to the discovery of chemicals, products or devices that could revolutionize medicine or space travel or whatever?

Never forget that "discovery consists in seeing what everybody has seen and thinking what nobody has thought" (Albert von Szent-Gyorgyi).

> *Given your work or studies, how might "possibility thinking" energize you? What situation facing you, now or in your recent past, could benefit from engaging in "possibility thinking"?*

Robert Chapman is a retired professor of behavioral health counseling from Drexel University. With 50 years of experience in behavioral health, he is particularly interested in preventing high-risk collegiate drinking.

THE OTHER SIDE OF FAILURE
David K. Wiggins

Failures provide opportunities for learning.

I have always been inspired by the work of the famous Black poet Maya Angelou. A major force in the world of literature with a legion of admirers, she was well known for dispensing advice often based on her difficult early years that included sexual abuse, a variety of different jobs and unsuccessful relationships. One piece of advice offered by Angelou that has always made a difference in my approach to life has to do with the potentially powerful effects of transcending failure. In Angelou's moving and optimistic words, "Failure is only a temporary change in direction to set you straight for your next success."

Angelou was seemingly working from the premise when offering her advice that everyone experiences failures in their lives that test their resolve and, in some cases, are excruciatingly painful and disheartening. She was also making the point that it was important for people to recognize the transitory yet beneficial nature of failure. With Angelou's advice as a backdrop, I would suggest that you should, if not necessarily embracing failure, recognize its redemptive power. Furthermore, acknowledge that it can potentially lead to changes in approach that will improve your life and make you that much more effective and impactful.

The most successful people I know have turned failure on its head, using it, learning from it, energized and motivated by it rather than being crippled by it. Basketball star Michael Jordan was cut from his high school's basketball team as a sophomore; J. K. Rowling of Harry Potter fame was told by her editor at Bloomsbury to find a day job because she would never be a successful writer of children's books; Thomas Edison was told by his teachers he was too stupid to learn anything; Albert Einstein suffered from dyslexia but became a famous physicist; Walt Disney was fired by the *Kansas City Star* newspaper because his editor believed he lacked imagination and had no good ideas; and Academy Award–winning director Steven Spielberg was rejected several times by the University of Southern California's School of Cinematic Arts.

Think about some failures in your own life. What have you learned from them, and what can you do with those experiences to make you stronger?

David K. Wiggins is professor emeritus of sport studies at George Mason University. He is the editor or author of 20 books and past president of the North American Society for Sport History.

Values

Anchoring Your Life

When constructing a house, the builder prepares the ground with a strong foundation. Before the footers are poured, plans are drawn. And before the plans are developed, some concepts serve as the basis for the construction. These broad and specific concepts may include the overall look and design, type of materials, size, cost, views, accessibility elements and more. Similarly, with an individual's life, some foundations as well as an overall framework are important for moving forward. The focus on values is all about gaining greater understanding of what is of greatest importance to oneself.

At the outset, it is important to acknowledge several things about values. First is that this is often a difficult subject for understanding and for clarification. Values are somewhat amorphous, unlike many mechanical structures or chemical reactions. Values tend to be difficult for many people to describe or even to acknowledge for themselves. Second, values are something that individuals need to discover, understand and own for themselves, even though it is often quite difficult to articulate clearly and discuss with others. They are not like blueprints or information that can be taken off the shelf and applied. Third, values come from various sources along one's life journey. They are drawn from one's upbringing, particularly one's family, family values and family culture. They also are based on varied life experiences, challenges and interactions with influential others. Fourth, values can be understood through careful observation and assimilation individually. They can be better understood with periodic and systematic reflection. These are personal and individualized. They may be drawn from positive experiences as well as negative examples that one may seek to avoid. Fifth, values may be shared with others, such as with family members, work settings, organizations, faith communities and more. Finally, values may change over time. Whereas general constructs of values for an individual will likely remain the same, often the specifics or varying circumstances may change.

Values may include issues such as spirituality, cultural competence, human respect, dignity and understanding. Values may also include conflict and understanding of self and others. Values are a central and often overlooked

DOI: 10.4324/9781003541080-3

core element in the determination of one's life plan and ultimately about the specification of one's legacy.

UNDERSTANDING VALUES

What are values? How are values different from ethics? And where do morals fit in? In short, values are what is important to the individual. Values help guide decisions and actions. Morals incorporate the principles for individual or group actions and an assessment of right and wrong. An individual's or group's moral compass is often cited, again in the determination of what might be appropriate or inappropriate actions. From an overall perspective, ethics are very similar to morals and constitute the translation into behaviors and actions. Ethics may include the standards of behavior and may be exemplified in codes of conduct for organizations or professions.

Values represent the core foundations for so much. It is the core beliefs, the basis for decisions and the overarching guidance for one's actions. It may be reflected with priorities on honesty, or health, or quality relationships. It may include something like dependability or perseverance. Values could also be about financial wealth, achievement and success. The morals emerge from one's values and help constitute the rules or standards as well as guiding principles.

With young adults, values have been instilled from numerous sources. Initially, it is with parents, guardians and family members. Community members, friends, school, faith settings, mentors and others have consistent influences as individuals grow and develop. There may be situations involving behavioral standards and even the law or organizational policies that help influence one's values. Examples in one's life, both desirable and less favorable, are influencers on one's values; these include individual based as well as those from group settings, observing situations and even media reports. As such, values are continuously evolving and being refined. Many, and perhaps most, core values will remain the same throughout one's life; others will get modified or altered.

What is important, for young adults in particular, is to become clear with one's own values. This can be a challenge, particularly when faced with peer and adult influences. As one reaches the legal age of majority, 18 in the United States, new responsibilities and opportunities emerge. Similarly, when faced with new situations, individuals need to determine what course of action is most appropriate. One may be faced with competing values or values that appear to be in contradiction with one another.

Also of consideration is how to reconcile different points of view about what is important, as individuals determine and understand their own values. For example, if a parent values one thing, but a faith community leader values something else, and a close friend or a mentor value something different, how is one to decide what to do? That's the process of determining and developing values. Sidney Simon, decades ago, wrote extensively about values clarification; he clearly understood that so many people, particularly young adults, were in the process of developing greater awareness and understanding of their own values. He said, "Do everything you can to find out what it is you really,

really, really want." Sometimes these disagreements generate conflict among individuals or groups; the field of conflict or dispute resolution helps to find some common ground and seek some way forward. As part of this, the focus on core values, including clarification of what is most important individually and collectively, is central.

Beyond that individual understanding of values, also important is articulating these so that others know what is important. As individuals become friends, shared values often serve as the foundation for this developing relationship; these may be identical, similar or at least complementary ones and may also include respect for differences. Some individuals will succumb to others' values, so they will be accepted or respected, yet without honoring their own core values. What is important with values is to become clear with what is important to oneself, and then be clear with others about that. That may help determine what types of relationships are wanted, what type of professional position is desired, whether to pursue a certain hobby or activity, or how to manage various aspects of life. Affiliation groups, such as clubs or organizations, whether formal or ad hoc, are often based on some shared values. Although every individual in such a group will not have 100% identical values, these groupings are typically based, to some extent, on shared values.

As specific situations occur, values may get more formally developed or infused with individual or group behavior. This may be in the form of guiding principles as to what is important. With the recent COVID-19 pandemic, some guiding principles about staying safe or, at a minimum, not dying helped with individual health and community well-being. Similarly, one may have a guiding principle about not driving an automobile, vehicle or boat while impaired. Or one may have a guiding principle about not making important decisions on the spur of the moment but allowing for some time to pass, or to seek the advice and counsel of key individuals in one's life. Whatever it is, these guiding principles help anchor discussions and decision-making.

THE ROLE OF VALUES

Values play an important role in an individual's life. They are helpful in shaping one's decisions and behavior. They are instrumental in determining choices and pathways. They are essential for developing relationships that matter, whether for a short term or a longer term. Values can guide one toward a specific outcome or set of outcomes; furthermore, values are quite helpful in determining the processes to be used in achieving those outcomes.

Whether articulated clearly or fuzzier in nature, values permeate one's life on a regular basis, whether hourly or daily. Values can help individuals understand situations and their surroundings; they often are used in the ongoing decisions that are faced regularly. Values also are useful in understanding and making sense of what others are saying or doing.

Consider, for example, the role of terms such as healthy or unhealthy, good or bad, safe or unsafe, legal or illegal, responsible or irresponsible, wise or unwise, and important or unimportant. These are all infused with values and will be helpful in guiding, supporting, reviewing and making decisions. When faced with a situation, whether a dilemma or not, and whether urgent or not, a review of core foundations – or values – will be useful in moving forward.

Often, values may compete with one another. Although something may be healthy, it may also be unwise; this distinction could be based on a situation or environmental condition. Similarly, something may be legal, yet unsafe. And something else may be healthy, yet inappropriate. In moving forward with decision-making, consider how different values can be incorporated, such as is found with making a quilt or doing some baking. For example, the Eisenhower matrix incorporates distinctions between something being urgent/not urgent and important/not important; this puts things in four quadrants. For personal applications with so many decisions, it is important to examine the wide range of constructs with how different values can blend together or compete with one another in various situations. Beyond that, different values may have higher or lower priority than others, helping to guide decisions.

Another way in which values can be helpful is with the determination of how important it is to become involved with a situation, an issue or a cause. When faced with an occurrence in life, individuals first become aware and then decide if – and then how – they might become involved. A situation may occur that appears to be of no interest or importance to someone. Another situation may occur when the individual feels the desire or need to become involved. Consider, for example, an incident where someone may be in harm's way or is being abused physically or emotionally by someone else. Different individuals may make varied responses to that. Consider also a situation where a person appears to be in need (e.g., stranded on a roadway, unable to swim in a lake, panhandling); personal values help determine the appropriate response for that person and that situation.

Extending beyond the individual level, values are also helpful with interpersonal relationships, including one-on-one situations as well as groups. An understanding of what is important to oneself is helpful when establishing a relationship with someone else, whether this is for friendship purposes, collegial work, recreation or leisure activities, romantic life or other purpose. Even though all values on all dimensions do not need to line up perfectly for a quality relationship, some core ones do need to do so. And the specific core ones will vary from person to person. That is, honesty may be most important to one person for any relationship, and respect may be most important to another person for any relationship they have.

Group interactions take the interpersonal factor one step further, as some values are central for groups to be functional and productive. Again, the specific values that would be important and thus shared among group members will vary from group to group. Consider groups such as those in the work setting, classes and schools, recreation, personal growth, exercise, self-help or mutual aid group, faith community or other intact or ad hoc groups.

Furthermore and typically in a work or community setting, leaders have a special role to play. This can be with helping the group members honor the established values of the organization or place, as well as review their attainment and ongoing appropriateness. A leader may have responsibilities for helping shape the values as well as to articulate these values both inside and outside the group setting. As noted earlier, setting priorities is needed very often, and different values may need to be examined and reviewed both as part of the process of setting priorities as well as influential for understanding the priorities. Particularly with the presence of limited resources, whether in terms of people, time, materials and skills, priorities need to be set within the construct of the values.

Finally, the important role of values is based on a core belief inherent in this book. Specifically, that is the value of human potential and the belief that individuals can continue to improve and do better. The value is one of positivity, and that is that all individuals ultimately do want to do the best they can do, as defined by themselves. The value is one of self-determination, and that is that individuals have both the right and the responsibility to make grounded decisions for themselves regarding how they want to shape and live their life. Coupled with this is the view that individuals are worthy of the investment of effort to achieve improvement and greater success, as defined by the individual themselves. Values play an important role as individual lives unfold – and hopefully in ways that result in a more productive and meaningful life.

LINKAGE WITH OTHER THEMATIC AREAS

Just as this book is based on the value of human potential, the link to the first section of this book – Optimism – is clear. That is, values are helpful in moving one's life forward (in contrast to stagnation or regression). Although setbacks do occur, the positive outlook represents an important value for individuals with themselves and others and for individual and collective growth. Through the incorporation of many of the insights from the next section of this book – Self-Care – knowledge, attitudes and skills are forthcoming for better managing a life of health and safety. Self-care highlights decisions surrounding one's physical, emotional and mental well-being, with so many topics and issues competing for the time and attention – the prioritization – for inclusion in one's value system. Values are integral for quality relationships; as highlighted in that section of the book, relationships include those with others and, importantly, with oneself. Community is founded on values, as much is written about the ways in which a community spirit can be developed and enhanced. Having shared values with others in a work, school, community, religious or other setting helps with the important role of community – and the feeling of community among individuals. Similarly, having a value on the importance of respect for the natural world and its resources is important. This includes engaging with nature for grounding, nourishment, relaxation, reflection and inspiration. Service as a thematic area is imbued with values, as it is based on the centrality of unselfishness and love, both key values. Service is about helping others, having sacrifice, mentoring, volunteering and sharing of time and talent.

CONCLUSION

The over five dozen Legacy Letters in this chapter focus on values – what was important to the authors based on their upbringing or experiences, and what suggestions they have for the reader. Building on the theme of optimism found in the previous chapter, attention is provided to consider what is important in one's own life and the importance of listening to oneself. Themes about how one's values are shaped, the importance of moving forward, following dreams and the proverbial question about the meaning of life emerge throughout these contributions. A core message revolves around the importance of learning what values are important to oneself and to help keep various life activities and responsibilities as consistent as possible with one's own values. With the reflection elements found with these Legacy Letters, opportunities for exploring and sharing abound. The experiences of the contributors shared in this chapter are helpful for shaping conversations with others, who will have different views about personal applications. Collectively, these topics can be helpful in starting to clarify and refine and ultimately live one's own values.

Messages What are key points or themes highlighted in the Legacy Letters within the Values area?	
Reflections What are your thoughts and feelings about what is shared and recommended regarding Values?	
Resources What individuals, groups, organizations or other information would help you better understand and apply recommendations in the Values area?	
Commitments What are you willing to commit yourself to doing regarding the Values theme, both in the near term and in the more distant future?	

FIGURE 3.1
Legacy Worksheet for Values

CONSIDERING CAREER OPTIONS?
Beth Brock

Make plans, recognize they might change and stay true to your long-term goals.

Don't settle for trying to do something you like. Find something you think you'd be good at or that comes easily to you, and you'll be more successful. Take an aptitude test to learn which career areas would be a good match for you. Do your research to learn which fields are forecast to be in demand when you're ready to apply for full-time employment and go there if possible. Danny Kaye, an actor and humanitarian, said, "Money isn't everything, unless you don't have any."

I loved being outdoors and being with all the world's creatures. I tried to find a career that would be a good match for my skills and my love of nature, but I realized it wouldn't work out for me at that time. The jobs that were a match were scarce and didn't pay very well. I decided to become a trial lawyer so I could make enough money to enjoy nature in my free time. I chose accounting for my undergraduate degree because I was good at it. Both fields – law and accounting – were in demand.

FIGURE 3.2
Accounting skills are used by volunteering to save African wildlife. Meeting a wild bull elephant in Mana Pools, Zimbabwe, that shares a special bond with the nonprofit organization's president.

When I entered my fourth year of college, I was exhausted from going to school full time and working part time. I considered dropping out but recognized my student loans would begin to come due, and I wouldn't achieve my financial goals. Knowing I was close to qualifying for a good career in accounting, I stuck it out and passed the Certified Public Accountant exam.

Following college graduation, I worked with a public accounting firm before becoming a financial administrator at a university. I made enough money while working that I could save for retirement, donate to conservation and vacation in nature around the world. I loved my job in higher education, but I retired in my mid-50s. Now I use my accounting skills to volunteer with an African wildlife conservation organization. I am truly living the dream.

Write down two or three things that come easily to you or that you think you'd be good at and would be a way to make money.

Beth Brock was senior manager, National Tax Department of Ernst & Young and Vice President, Fiscal and Auxiliary Services at George Mason University.

EXPLORING YOUR LIFE PURPOSE
Anthony Arciero

Authentic goals and service to others create the path to our life purpose.

At almost any age, we might wonder why we are here, and what purpose our lives serve. This is especially true during times of transition, when the world seems laid out in front of us. It's easy to become overwhelmed and fall back to what society tells us is the most lucrative or status-filled career. Yet it is often true that when people pursue and achieve those "standard" goals, they do not feel the sense of meaning and purpose they had expected. They think to themselves, "I've done everything I was supposed to. Why do I feel so empty?"

To explore your life purpose, begin with the understanding that it is not somewhere "out there." It is based on your core values, beliefs, interests and strengths – the foundation of who you are. The great news is that it is inside you already! Instead of looking for it, create your life purpose. Imbue everything you do – your job, your relationships and hobbies – with purpose. You can't go wrong! You cannot pick the wrong career. Whichever direction you take, bring your values, interests and strengths – your authentic self – and proceed with purpose.

The hidden secret to living a life of purpose, in addition to living authentically in accordance with your values, is service to others. Could you set aside time to tutor a child or mentor a high school student? If you can find a way to serve others that is also consistent with your strengths and interests, that is even more powerful! You gain a sense of significance when you help someone else pursue their life goals. That significance tells you that you are creating your unique life purpose.

So don't go out searching for the meaning of life. Start within and know that you are already there. Incorporate your core values and strengths into the activities and relationships that are most interesting to you. And importantly, serve others as an integral part of your purpose pursuit.

Remember, using these simple principles, you cannot fail. So go out and create your life purpose and live it every day.

What are your core values? Your strengths? Your interests? How might you use these elements of your character to serve your community and the world around you?

Anthony Arciero earned his Ph.D. in educational psychology and is the director of research for the Pursuit of Happiness.org. His research focuses on overall well-being and the exploration of life purpose at all ages.

CREATING YOUR OWN LIFE WORTH LIVING
Nell Davidson

Finding your own purpose in life in an important and evolving opportunity.

What makes a life worth living? Will the answers be the same for you as for all the people around you? Will your answers remain the same throughout your life?

Finding your purpose in life is not accomplished once; you answer "what makes life worth living" multiple times over many years. Your parents, your family and your community may have provided some possible answers, but they can't choose the right answer for you. The important thing is to be the decision-maker in your own life.

It can be difficult to find your own voice and choose what *you* want after years of being told what you should want. No one else's answers will be as good as yours on this "test." To succeed, you must be your own person, be mindful of your own strengths, never give up trying to be the real you.

So that means you may have to struggle with feeling good about who and what you are. People say, "Just be yourself." But it starts out being a bit difficult as a task. It also probably means learning the difference between what you can make people believe about who you are and who you really are. Does it only matter to you to succeed in having people believe an image of who you are?

Early in my training as a physician, I went to the funeral of a patient I admired. I had never been to a funeral in an African American church before. They sang a hymn I have remembered to this day, which began, "Let the life I have lived speak for me."

If you live a life of purpose and service to others, you won't be disappointed by what your life says about you.

> *Do you have a role model or mentor? If you can't identify one now, be open to finding one in the future, a task you can rush or force.*

Eleanor Davidson is a physician who trained in traditional academic medicine (internal medicine and nephrology). It took a while for her to find her true passion, which was the primary care of students in college and university settings, where she focused on mental health within the primary care arena.

CONQUER

Elena Enache

Reflections on your life journey help with finding your own worth.

I remember the first time I told someone I wanted to conquer the world. I was seven, sitting on the playground, my legs dangling from the monkey bars as other kids shared their dreams. One wanted to be a doctor, another an astronaut, but I, with all the certainty a child could muster, declared, "I'm going to conquer the world." My friends laughed, thinking I was joking, but I wasn't.

Even at that young age, something inside me burned to be more, to do more. As the years passed, that childhood declaration grew into a relentless drive: I wanted to be the best in everything. With my jobs, the cycle repeated – early mornings, late nights, endless ambition. I climbed the corporate ladder quickly, each promotion a step closer to the world I wanted to conquer. But with every step up, I knew I wanted something else.

After years of relentlessness, it hit me: I wasn't chasing the world; I was chasing a version of myself I hadn't yet become. And so began the hardest journey of all – the journey to conquer myself. It wasn't about the awards or the promotions anymore. It was about understanding who I was, facing my fears and finding peace within. It was about learning to silence the doubts that told me I wasn't enough, to stop seeking validation from others and to start listening to my own heart. That journey was far from easy. It meant unraveling years of striving and ambition, confronting buried insecurities and redefining what success truly meant. But slowly, as I peeled back the layers, I found a new kind of strength – a strength that wasn't tied to achievements or external praise but to a quiet confidence in who I was becoming.

Now, when I think back to that little girl on the playground, I realize she wasn't wrong. I did conquer the world, just not in the way I expected. The world I conquered was the one within me, the one that mattered most. And in doing so, I found something far greater than any worldly success – I found myself.

As I reflect on this journey, I encourage you to consider your own path. Start by embracing your imperfections, facing your fears and recognizing your inherent worth, independent of what you accomplish. The real battle often lies within, and the most meaningful victories are those we win over ourselves.

What truly drives you? Where are you finding your worth?

Elena Enache is a tech executive, public speaker and business adviser and mentor. She has a great life balance and enjoys innovation in everything.

POWER OF CHOICE
Catherine Malloy

Decisions are yours to make!

You wake every morning and it begins. What will I wear? What will I eat for breakfast? What route will I take to work? To stop at Starbucks or not? Choices, choices, choices. The question is, are these "real" choices or merely a matter of rote? Are they preprogrammed responses to the rhythms of everyday living? Comfortable routines? Do these choices rise to the level of biological imperative? Probably not, but it is situational. Of course, eating is a biological imperative. Twinkies and Ho Hos and coffee for breakfast do not serve this biological imperative, but eating healthy does! All this is to say, choices are impactful; they have power and importance.

Let's explore choices a little more. The first thing to remember is that just like feelings, choices are real. Meaning, they exist and are inescapable in this life. What is important is the act of choosing; it is where your real power lies. I hear you saying, "Choosing what to wear gives me real power. . . . Give me break!" I grant you a break, but if you're in the military, you've pretty much given up that choice of what to wear.

Viktor Frankl, a Holocaust survivor and renowned psychologist and neurologist, in his book *Man's Search for Meaning*, states, "What man actually needs is not a tensionless state but rather the striving and struggling for some goal worthy of him." Another way to say this is that one must choose a worthy goal and strive and struggle to attain it; this is in contrast to not choosing (a choice nonetheless) and living in a "tensionless state." I suggest that living in this tensionless state is the source of today's anxiety crisis, as it is the result of choosing not to choose. But to me, Frankl's most important insight is, "Everything can be taken from a man but one thing: the last of the human freedoms – to choose one's attitude in any given set of circumstances, to choose one's own way." This is the true power of choice!

So, what if the fear of being wrong or of making a mistake paralyzes you from making a decision from choosing? What then? Choose, and get comfortable with making mistakes. The only mistake anyone really makes is choosing not to fix a mistake!

What are the habits you have developed to help you make choices? Are you choosing "worthy" goals for yourself?

Catherine Malloy, B.S.N., M.P.H., Dr.PH., is Professor Emeritus of Health, Fitness and Recreation Resources at George Mason University. She continues to be actively involved with her coastal community and the League of Women Voters.

MARCHING ORDERS
Craig McConnell

Have a life inspired by four key words: live, love, laugh and learn.

People encourage me to "move on." And I know they wonder why, four-plus years out, I am still struggling with the loss of my soulmate. They just don't get it, and I hope they never get it, because if they do, that means they too have lost an integral part of who they are as a person – a spouse, a partner, a soulmate.

People can never grasp how, after so many years, how intertwined our lives had become. All the inside jokes. All the memories. Most of her. So many of us. Everywhere I look. There we are. She and I – and it is overwhelming to grasp that I have become the sole keeper of those memories. The only one on the planet who has lived them all. The heartbreaks. The laughs. The magical adventures.

And then one day, she was gone.

And then what? Do you just move on? Do you expect the life we had built together to just unravel? After all that time, we were "one," and you cannot just cease to love someone. You can't split your life into a before and after – it just doesn't work that way.

Because to this day, four-plus years after she commenced what she called her next grand adventure, she is still an integral part of who I am as a person. Forget the one who is in all most treasured photos and all my best memories? Impossible. Forget the one whose smile could literally light up a room who brought me joy daily? Impossible. My wins were her wins. Hers were mine.

Losing her has devastated me. It has worn me down. But I got to love her, not for as long as I had hoped, but I got to love her. I got to love her kind, generous and compassionate heart. I got to love her sense of humor and the joy of hearing her laugh. I got to love her, and for that, I am eternally grateful. And every day, I do my best to follow her final marching orders: LIVE, LOVE, LAUGH and LEARN.

Bottom line? I got to love her, and for that, I am eternally grateful.

Write down the marching orders you follow in your daily life. To what extent do you live them?

Craig McConnell is a father and grandfather who continues to share the light that his wife of 45 years, B. J. McConnell, carried throughout her life and career. In her life, she inspired young people, parents, neighbors, community leaders, elected officials, government and national agencies and countless others with her practical, grounded and no-nonsense approaches for healthy, safe and fulfilling lives.

DELAYED YET NOT DETERRED
Bryan E. Porter

Finding your passion will help with your purpose.

I grew up wanting to be a university professor – with an aim of teaching the next generation of young people and to bring forward ideas for my community's health and well-being. My first college major to that end was biology; my intent was to study genetic engineering to ultimately save lives from disease. However, I was terrible in the lab and reading about biology put me to sleep (not a promising start to a hopeful career in the academy).

Then I took a psychology course out of an interest that began when I was in high school; that early interest was buried when an older friend warned such a major required "a lot of reading and writing," not my favorite tasks then. And to be honest, these are not my easiest responsibilities now. However, the professor created an energy I had not felt before; that also opened a door to a passion I had not fully imagined because I had abandoned the topic earlier out of fear.

As fate would have it, within weeks I was a psychology major. This was despite my hesitation about working harder at skills not wholly comfortable to me. Plus, my career and goal to help the community and teach were changed for the good.

In my nearly 30 years of being a psychology professor, I have studied ways to reinforce and support safe and healthy behaviors and shared this impact with students. Several of my former students have also become professors or government leaders, allowing me to realize my dream of training the next generation who will teach and reach ever more others.

Each of us has many paths to professional happiness. The key is to pay attention to your interests and not discount any of them outright and certainly not out of fear. It is easier to find your way by following that pull from your heart. You will learn what you need to learn and turn your weaknesses into strengths – if you have passion for your purpose. In the end, I laid fear aside and became what I was meant to be – delayed but not deterred. I hope you do the same.

Write down three to five key things that constitute your passion. Now identify some ways you might bring these to life.

Bryan Porter is associate dean of the graduate school and professor of psychology at Old Dominion University in Norfolk, Virginia. He enjoys sharing a passion for improving community health with undergraduate and graduate students at all levels in their careers, and revels in watching the impact they make on the world upon graduation.

BROCCOLI VERSUS SPARKLE?

Betty Waters Straub

Thriving with one's health requires a plan, some guidance and a commitment.

What does it mean to be "healthy"? Dimensions of health often include surprises: the acronym SPICES that students helped me develop may help you remember them: social, physical, intellectual, career, emotional and spiritual. And yes, we used a big chili pepper in its logo.

The following quick reference offers specific actions you can take, which provides examples of using mindfulness – for example, to find broccoli's benefits and the sparkle (energy, optimism, gratitude) it adds to your health.

Social: willing and able to develop relationships, particularly among different cultures. Make friends with a classmate who doesn't seem to quite fit in. Attend an event that highlights people from different countries.

Physical: exercising, sleeping, using foods and drinks for optimal performance. Take an exercise class to learn new ways of keeping your body moving. Dare to take a nutrition class, to know what you'll be eating the rest of your life. Find ways to deeply relax.

Intellectual: pursuing knowledge, applying learned lessons, sharing information with others. Create or join a study group where you can share your knowledge – the best way to retain complex information.

Career: researching various professions, pursuing service-learning opportunities to test the waters of interest, completing coursework and early employment in a few chosen fields.

Emotional: finding comfort in being who you are, seeking help with trauma or major disruptions in life, practicing daily moments of gratitude. Talk to a counselor at school or on campus about buried issues that can sabotage your best efforts.

Spiritual: deliberately seeking purpose for your life, celebrating the development of the Real You, helping others understand the importance of being authentic.

Each of these ideas allows you to pursue thriving while living your best life. Choosing broccoli (a food powerhouse) can add sparkle anytime you need it.

How do you define healthy? How can you stay true to SPICES or your own framework?

Betty Waters Straub, Ed.D., a research scientist and a former university faculty member, develops community-based efforts to improve healthy outcomes.

IDENTIFYING CORE VALUES TO HELP YOU NAVIGATE LIFE

Kimberley Timpf

Identify your core values to create a framework for living a purposeful, authentic life.

Michelle Obama said, "I have learned that as long as I hold fast to my beliefs and values . . . then the only expectations I need to live up to are my own." Her words highlight why a core set of values is essential to navigating life's complexities. And believe me, there will be complexities! When our values are unclear, we may make choices that cause inner conflict. But when we identify and understand our core values, they can serve as a personal compass to shape our decisions and life direction.

Think of someone you admire. The principles you appreciate most in that individual likely reflect much of the person you aspire to be. Respect, for instance, is a value that guides effective interactions with everyone, from peers to parents to instructors, helping you appreciate diverse opinions and perspectives and fostering positive relationships. Perseverance can help you push through to overcome challenges, while dependability means that you place a high degree of importance on being trustworthy and reliable. But values can sometimes conflict – for example, overextending yourself to be dependable could undermine your perseverance, thus achieving neither. Maintaining a healthy balance between your values requires self-awareness, flexibility and prioritizing what matters most.

Social media can often complicate the process of identifying your values. Although it can inspire and connect, it can also create unrealistic standards, shaping your values in subtle ways that may challenge your beliefs. The pressure to follow trends can sometimes lead people to compromise their values in exchange for social approval, prioritizing material success over qualities like honesty, empathy or hard work. Remember that trends don't always align with what's meaningful.

Finally, stay mindful of how easy it can be to compromise your values. Making decisions that go against your beliefs can erode your sense of identity and trust in yourself, leading to regret and a loss of self-respect. Over time, that can damage relationships, reputation and opportunities.

Staying true to your values, even when hard, builds character and confidence. It ensures you're making choices that reflect who you are, what matters most and that the expectations you're living up to are your own.

When you've felt the most fulfilled or satisfied in your life, what personal values or beliefs were you honoring in that moment?

For over 25 years, Kimberley Timpf has worked with colleges and the e-learning industry to promote safety, well-being and belonging.

JUST DO IT

Matt Sanders

Think about doing something you love with your life.

I often get asked how I got into acting, and the truth is, I just did it. Growing up, I loved making films, and that's how I spent my free time in high school and college. After college, I had a few months before my air force active-duty service began, so some friends and I spent all our time making videos and actually became some of the first YouTube revenue partners ever. In 2009/2010, this was a new concept, and it made all those childhood dreams seem doable.

But then, duty called.

While I was serving, I witnessed my friends give up on their dreams for various obligations – kids, finances, societal expectations. I swore that if I had the opportunity, I wouldn't squander my dream if I didn't absolutely have to.

Well, when I got out of the military, I started doing corporate jobs I thought I was "supposed" to do or felt that I needed to even though I hated what I was doing. Suddenly, I was miserable and mad that I was doing the very thing I said I wouldn't.

So one day, fed up with it all, I decided to see if "I still had it." After about ten minutes of research, I went to an open call at a nearby talent agency. By the next week, I had an agent, auditions and booked my first commercial.

Today, seven years later, I just watched one of my films airing on TV.

Don't get me wrong, it's not easy. Like

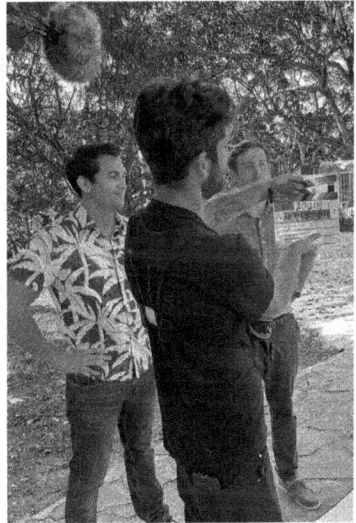

FIGURE 3.3
A production assistant slates as Matt Sanders prepares to shoot a scene for a movie.

anything, it takes hard work, education and a ton of rejection. But I LOVE IT. It's my passion and I'm finally living it. All I had to do was go and actually do it.

Life is going to be challenging no matter what, but it might as well be challenging doing something you love. So go DO IT.

What are the first practical steps to live your passion? Can you do those today?

Matt Sanders is a Screen Actors Guild–Eligible actor, with agents in all the major markets across the nation and has booked dozens of commercials with multiple films streaming internationally.

VALUES SERVE AS OUR NORTH STAR
Katy McQuaid

Identify your core values and use them to guide you.

Values are the things that matter the most to us. My core values are honesty, integrity and teamwork. They were the reason I said no when asked by the executive director (EXDIR) of the large government agency where I worked to do something illegal.

The EXDIR was a very charismatic and influential leader. He was relentless in pressuring my boss and me to pursue a very large contract to a specific company for the movement of *all* air cargo for the agency. This contract activity was worth *millions* of dollars. With each phone call came a veiled threat that if we didn't do it his way, we would suffer the consequences. We felt the pressure, and we owed the EXDIR an answer. My boss and I stayed in alignment with our values and made the decision to not sole source the movement of air cargo to one specific company.

I thought, *This is it. My career is over.* I repeated, "I have to wake up and be able to look at myself in the mirror every morning." It was also about the workforce; we needed to model integrity to them.

The last time I saw the EXDIR was on my way to work in Afghanistan. While I was there, he was removed from the agency's headquarters building while the FBI searched his office and helicopters flew over headquarters and his home not far down the road. He was eventually convicted of honest services fraud, conspiracy and money laundering and sentenced to 37 months in federal prison. The EXDIR's fall reinforced my decision to say no to his vendor.

This experience taught me how important it is to live in alignment with my values. There was no promotion or position that was more important to me than my integrity and doing the right thing. When we know our values and live into them, we are far more likely to be led to success within our activities in an empowering way.

I encourage you to reflect, identify your top three core values and write them down. Take time to understand what drives you and stay in alignment with it. Use your values as your North Star. It's as simple as asking yourself, "Is this decision in alignment with my values?" If not, make a decision that *is* in alignment with your values.

What are your core values? Can you think of a time when you made a decision that was not aligned with your values, and what the outcome was and how you felt? How can you use your values to help stay true to yourself?

Katy McQuaid, former Deputy Director of Logistics in the Central Intelligence Agency, spent more than three decades in the CIA.

MY STORY
Melissa Grimm

Listen to your dreams and then get the preparation and skills to follow them.

Hi, everyone. I'm a barber, and I just wanted to tell you a short story about myself. I have been a cosmetologist/barber for the last 25 years, but it all started at a very young age for me.

I've wanted to do hair since I was a little girl – probably five years old. I had 112 Barbies and every one of them had a different hairdo. I was cutting it, styling it or using markers to give them highlights.

I also cut my mom's best friend's daughter's hair a couple of times; she was not very happy. LOL. But over the years, when I was younger, I taught myself how to do pretty much everything with hair. My mom's best friend also was a hairdresser, so I would ask her to position me a certain way when she did my hair so that I could see what she was doing, and I could figure it out and mock it when I wanted to do it for myself.

Around the time I was in the sixth grade, I started doing my own hair – whether cutting, coloring or other things. When I was in high school, I started doing my friends' hair; this was for boys and for girls and included cutting and coloring.

When I was 19, I found a newspaper ad for a full apprenticeship through Great Clips. It was then, when my son was about five months old, that I started my apprenticeship. As a young, single mother, putting myself through school and working full time, the struggle was real. However, I knew the minute I started cutting hair in a salon that it was what I wanted to do forever.

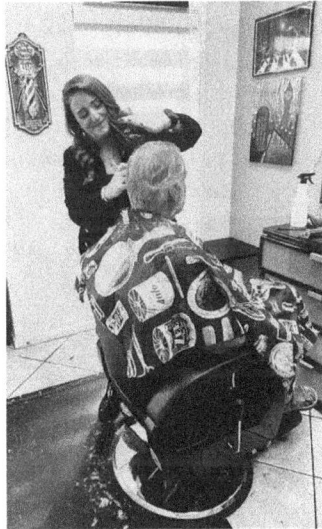

FIGURE 3.4
I take great pride in my work, and strive to make each customer happy – both with my limited time with them and with the final result!

I am eternally grateful to be one of the few people who knew what I wanted to do for a living as a very young girl. I am so grateful to say that after 25 years, I still love what I do and I will continue to do it until the day I retire.

What were your dreams as a child as well as later? How do those work for you today? What can you do to help achieve those early dreams?

Melissa Grimm is a 44-year-old barber who is following her childhood dream.

THE FIRE IN THE BELLY
Chawky Frenn

The "fire in the belly" is the thirst that fuels your passion and guides you on the path to fulfilling your purpose.

I often ask students to reflect on what gives their journey purpose and meaning, encouraging them to look inward for insights. One of my students, a finance major on track for a career in her uncle's New York stock market firm, enrolled in my Painting I course to fulfill her core requirements. Discovering a passion for painting, she decided to pursue a minor in art when she joined my Painting II course. After graduation, while working at her uncle's firm, she asked me for a recommendation to pursue a master's in architecture at Columbia University, citing the "fire in the belly" as her driving force. She left family expectations and followed her dream to create low-income housing to help underprivileged communities in her native country.

Another student, struggling with depression, was driven to use her art as a platform to address mental health and trauma. She found healing through her creative expression and encouraged others to channel their energy in similar ways. With dedication and faith in her purpose, she participated in numerous exhibits, received a university grant and authored and published a book titled *Resurrection: Returning to Roots From Trauma*.

Their stories illustrate the transformative strength of recognizing and honoring one's inner passion, the "fire in the belly," the innate yearning for a meaningful and fulfilling life, a driving force that transforms obstacles into ladders toward one's highest self, illuminating each step along the way.

What is the fire in your belly? In what ways has this changed over time? What are things that help give your life purpose and meaning?

Born in Lebanon, Chawky Frenn emigrated to the United States in 1981. He completed his B.F.A. from Massachusetts College of Art in 1985 and his M.F.A. from Temple University in 1988. He is a professor of art at George Mason University in Fairfax, Virginia. Frenn participated in numerous exhibits and received critical acclaim nationally and internationally. He was awarded the Fulbright-Nehru Academic and Professional Excellence in 2017 and 2024, and Mason's Teaching Excellence Award in 2009. Frenn authored two books, *100 Boston Artists* and *100 Boston Painters*. His work appeared in *100 Artists of Washington, D.C.*, *Male Nude Now* and a monograph, *Art for Life's Sake*.

USING VALUES AND STRENGTHS TO FLOURISH
Julie Edwards

Identify what values are most important to you so you may craft the life you want, live intentionally and flourish.

At this stage of my life, I've come to realize the importance of values and aligning my life with them. Through intentional effort, I have found my purpose and have had opportunities to make a significant impact in my work, personal relationships and community. I have been able to celebrate successes, identify lessons learned in failures and continue to pursue what is meaningful to me. This has come from not only identifying my values but also recognizing the inherent strengths I possess to use them to craft the life I want to live.

Values are at the core of what is important to you. There is so much power in identifying them early on so they can help guide your decisions, develop relationships and choose a career that will bring meaning to your life. One of my prominent values is integrity. I strive to be a person of my word, to have my actions align with what I say I am going to do. I also live by the golden rule: to treat others as I want to be treated. This has allowed me to build strong relationships by treating others with respect and to maintain those relationships. Other values important are empathy, equity and community service.

At times, I experienced doubts and imposter fears, wondering if I was "good enough." I learned that I was not alone in these feelings and that many people experience similar feelings every day. The antidote for me is to use my strengths on a daily basis, coming from a place of authenticity, aligning with what I value most. Gratitude is my top strength and I cultivate it daily by thanking colleagues for the work that they do, showing sincere appreciation to family and friends and identifying three things I'm grateful for every night.

FIGURE 3.5
Our family volunteering to pack food to be sent to families in other countries.

I encourage you to identify your strengths by listing what you value most. Once your values are clear, determine how you can use the strengths inherent to you to pursue what is meaningful so you can live the life you want and flourish.

Identify specific steps you can take to clarify your own values and your own strengths.

Julie Edwards, Ed.D., is the Assistant Vice President of Student Health and Wellbeing at Cornell University with experience in public and community health.

A FULFILLING LIFE
Tabatha Curtis

A rich career and many accomplishments tell part of the story.

Tabatha Curtis is the former Director of the Franklin County Prevention Coalition in Tennessee. She has over 20 years of experience working in the field of prevention and over 33 years of experience in working with youth and families. Tabatha has extensive knowledge and experience as a trainer in the outcomes-based Strategic Prevention Framework planning process and was a coalition coach for the Partnership for Success grant for the state of Tennessee. Ms. Curtis also was responsible for mentoring coalition development within the state of Tennessee and has served as a grant peer reviewer.

Five years ago, Ms. Curtis embarked on developing Drug Endangered Children Response Communities within established prevention coalitions. Ms. Curtis had the insight of how both programs – Drug Endangered Children and Prevention Coalitions – were utilizing the same multisector/discipline model. Tennessee developed 6 response communities in 2020 and now has grown to 12 response communities in 2024 under her leadership as the Tennessee Bureau of Investigation–Drug Endangered Children Alliance statewide coordinator. Tennessee has now become a promising practice utilizing this model. The programs Ms. Curtis oversees provides a multifaceted approach to meeting the needs of children and families by implementing prevention and intervention programs in schools and extracurricular settings; ongoing community mobilization integrating law enforcement into community organizations; parent engagement opportunities and/or referral to services related to substance use prevention.

Ms. Curtis is a graduate of Middle Tennessee State University, a graduate of the Community Anti-Drug Coalitions Academy, a National Drug Endangered Children certified trainer, a National Drug Endangered Children Alliance board member, a graduate of the Tennessee Bureau of Investigation Director's Leadership Academy and a Level II Certified Prevention Specialist.

Many of you will read this and think, why has this lady submitted her bio or vitae? I wanted to share what many years of hard work and sacrifice looks like at the professional level. You may say, what a great legacy. However, in reality all those contributions and accolades are only superficial. We spend so much of our time in life trying to accomplish goals that we believe define who we are. My legacy is not defined by professional accomplishments; it is defined by my faith in God, my marriage and my children.

What does this professional journey and its reflection say to you about your own pathways forward?

Tabatha Curtis has a long and rich career of accomplishments and a legacy that goes beyond that.

CORE PERSONAL GOALS
Martin Ford

When people invest themselves in activities and relationships that are aligned with their core personal goals, they experience greater effectiveness, an enhanced sense of life meaning and improved health outcomes.

When I was in high school trying to decide what academic and career pathway to follow, my father (a counseling psychologist) gave me some advice that proved to be useful throughout my life: "Keep as many options open as you can for as long as you can." And yet, that advice begs the question of where do these potentially promising options come from. Fundamentally, they flow from efforts to *learn about yourself and how you fit in with the broader "world out there,"* beyond your immediate surroundings. Translation:

1. You need to continuously *explore* and actively try out new ideas and activities in a quest to find life experiences that energize you and make you feel like "this is what I was meant to do" and "this is who I was meant to be."
2. You need to *connect* with lots of different people in many different settings so that you can learn about (and sometimes create!) new life opportunities – opportunities that often come to us via chance encounters or by just "being in the right place at the right time."
3. From these experiences, you can then *identify your core personal goals* – the things in life that fascinate you, that arouse your passions and that feel particularly authentic and satisfying to you. When you align your choices and daily activities with your core personal goals, life will feel empowering and meaningful. Conversely, when things start to feel "out of whack," you can use the guiding light of your core personal goals to search for new pathways to personal and professional fulfillment.

See https://apg.gmu.edu as a starting point for identifying themes most likely to lead you to your core personal goals. There, you will also find a tool for connecting promising core goal themes to your unique, real-life choices and circumstances.

What specific steps can you commit to taking in the near future to help clarify your core personal goals?

Martin Ford is Professor Emeritus in the College of Education and Human Development at George Mason University. Martin is the creator of motivational systems theory and, with Peyton Smith, author of *Motivating Self and Others: Thriving With Social Purpose, Life Meaning, and the Pursuit of Core Personal Goals* (Cambridge University Press, 2020).

BLENDING YOUR PASSION WITH YOUR CURRENCY
Doug Everhart

It is important that you, as a young adult, identify the things you value most in life and also how to be paid to do what you love to do.

Your college/developmental years are meant to explore everything you possibly can. Find out who you are, what you value, what you believe in . . . what makes up your true and authentic identity? What are your spiritual beliefs? What are the things you most enjoy doing? By getting involved in as much as you can, giving thought and consideration to everything possible, you will begin to filter what you like and what you don't like. At some point, it will become clear what it is you truly value and what you are truly passionate about. At that point, the question becomes, "How can I get paid to do THAT – the thing I most enjoy doing?"

But the next question is, "What is the 'currency' that carries the most value for me? Is it money?" If it is, that's fine. But maybe it's time. Maybe it's giving back to the community. Maybe it's making a difference in the world or in someone's life. If you can match your ideal currency as a way to get "paid" to do what you love to do, you've "won" in the game of life.

When I entered college in the mid-1980s as an engineering major, I definitely had my sights set on a high-paying career for the lifestyle I thought I wanted (money, cars, nice house, etc.). But by the time I was done with undergraduate school, I had my degree in engineering, but through my various experiences as a student leader on campus, I had determined that my passion was health education (specifically alcohol education) and my "currency" was to make a difference in students' lives and make the world a better place (neither was centered on money). Now nearing the end of my career, I wouldn't do it any differently. To this day, my passion and currency, in perfect alignment, have provided a successful career and a fulfilling life.

Answer two important questions: What's your passion? What's your currency?

Doug Everhart has been in collegiate health education/promotion for 35 years, spending 10-plus years at three different campuses (University of Redlands, University of California, Riverside, and University of California, Irvine). He has had volunteer/leadership roles with several national organizations, including national organizations dealing with college athletics, bystander roles, healthy campuses and peer education.

UPLIFTING ALL OF YOU
Michelle J. Curtis Park

Remember your background of culture, spirituality, positivity and gratitude.

When my son graduated high school and joined the Air Force Reserves, I wrote this letter as to offer some guidance. Alex is Indigenous – Pueblo of Laguna and Diné (Navajo) Nation – and Asian – Japanese and Korean.

Dear Son:

I write you now as you are stepping out on your own. As you exist from an ethnic background, you are expected to live and survive in a different society than the one in which you have been raised. You have been taught to take care of the land and nature, to respect your elders and to always offer help. You were raised with the values to treasure family, to work hard at anything you do and to not be foolish with your decisions (including finances).

I have tried my best to raise you with the belief that what *you* think of yourself matters most and not what an app says, not what others say or a stereotype of your cultural backgrounds. If you are happy with yourself, you will project so much positive into the world and that positivity will come back to you. So please take care and protect yourself, physically, emotionally, spiritually and socially.

I think about our values of family, spirituality and working hard – if those have purpose in your life *(ikigai)*, you will always be surrounded with positive. I have no doubt there is negative and evil out there; however, with your strong foundation in a spiritual existence, you can overcome that negative energy. Spirituality is just as important as your values. That spirituality takes many different forms, and you can practice your spirituality anywhere. So please practice a spiritual existence even if it's not at a church.

Lastly, be grateful every day; that will set the tone for your routine existence. If you can master having gratitude, you will value every situation, person, experience and life that you encounter. Know that the Creator has put that in your path for a reason. *Hushja mei (Keresan*: be strong, stay focused on what needs to get done).

Mom

As you reflect on this letter what are the main messages that resonate for you?

Michelle J. Curtis Park is Pueblo of Laguna – Corn Clan – and Diné (Navajo) – Big Water Clan.

FOLLOW YOUR HEART

Louie Roccato

Happiness is something we are all looking to attain and can be achieved by doing what you love.

It is the process of life to figure out why you were put on this earth, what you can contribute to society and who you are as a person at your core. I believe that if you follow the things that have brought you joy, passion and intrigue in your life, it will bring you down the path that you were meant to end up on. You will be doing not only what you love, but you will also be able to share that joy with the rest of the world and inspire others to do the same.

For me, this central purpose is dance. From a young age, I was exposed to the arts: music, martial arts, paintings, sports, cultural festivals and more. I always danced through life, even when I didn't have any training. It was something inside of me that took over and gave me joy. Growing up, many of us hear that boys shouldn't dance, that you can't make a living from being a dancer and that the career span of a dancer is so limited. Even though those words were coming from people outside of my circle, I took them to heart.

While continuing to dance, I started off college as a premed student. I always was interested in the human body and how it worked; however, in my mind, I was only having that as my major because I thought it was more respectable and I could make a good living with it. The only problem was that my heart wasn't in it. Without that key aspect, I felt lost and uninspired in my studies. That's when a professor asked me, "Why are you doing this? Is this really what you want?" that I came to the realization that I was doing what others wanted me to do.

I ultimately decided to switch to a dance major after three years in school, and it was the best decision of my life. I now dance professionally all around the nation – I am doing what I love and am able to support myself doing it. I am now able to spread the joy and love I have within myself to others, and there is nothing better.

What brings you joy and love? What is your passion? What is the core of your purpose?

Louie Roccato has been dancing professionally for over 15 years. His mission is to spread love and light into people's lives through his performances.

NO EASY MILES
Earl Smith

There is no such thing as an easy mile.

It was in the early 1980s, and I had just started my career as an assistant professor at the State University of New York at Brockport. In the new faculty and staff orientation, we were asked to introduce ourselves and share one "fun fact" about ourselves. I had competed in track and cross-country in high school and in the military, and despite being in my 30s, I was still in good physical shape, consistently running the mile in six to seven minutes. It was my identity. Sharing this one fact opened up a new door for me!

Shortly thereafter, I was invited to be one of the first faculty to serve as a special adviser and counselor to incoming students. I was given an office in the dorm and not only held my office hours there, but I even slept over twice a month to facilitate the late-night conversations (and snacking) students like to have!

I remember our first meeting like it was yesterday! I told my personal story of **no easy miles** . . . of growing up on Long Island, going to Vietnam, attending college at SUNY, going to graduate school at UCONN and arriving at Brockport after marriage, starting a family and my graduate training at UCONN.

This one simple statement helped dozens of students reflect on their own personal journeys, what it was like to live away from home for the first time and navigate college. It also provided a road map for them to consider what they wanted their college "miles" to look like.

Soon after that, our group started a weekly two- to-three-mile jog. No racing, just a fun jog each week noting the last mile. Most of the group stuck with it, even through the cold winter months.

Together we came up with a set of mottos:

- Don't give up. Don't ever quit on yourself.
- Eventually – if not soon then later – you will find success.
- Remember, you must do the work.
- You can't make excuses for not trying.
- There are no shortcuts to gaining excellence.
- There is no such thing as an easy mile.

These mottos guided our running, our time in college and our lives.

The title of this chapter is my motto. What is your motto? What keeps you grounded?

Earl Smith, Ph.D., is a sociologist teaching and researching in the areas of racial stratification, urbanization and mass incarceration. He has written several books and is currently revising *The Social Dynamics of Family Violence,* which becomes a fourth edition. He is currently a professor at the University of Delaware.

THE VALUE OF DISCERNMENT
Norman Whitmire Jr.

Discernment is an important resource for life decisions.

Don't you seek happiness? Are you satisfied with your life right now? What does success look like for you? What is your purpose in life? Are you struggling to find the answers to these questions? Perhaps you ought to consider doing some form of discernment.

Discernment has several definitions, but in a nutshell, it is the ability to judge something difficult or obscure. In a practical sense, it is an important exercise when trying to figure out what to do with your life and discovering what your purpose might be. Everyone has a purpose; everyone is here on this earth for a reason. Discernment can help you think about what your purpose might be. It can provide some direction in your life. People whom we admire as being "successful" have identified their purpose, set goals and met them. If they have discerned well, they may even feel a sense of accomplishment.

How did they do it? How can you do it? Well, for starters, think about your passions. What do you enjoy doing? What brings you pleasure, and what gives you joy inside? I mean that kind of joy that you feel in your gut! That's where you can start. Actually, keep that gut feeling in the back of your mind because at some point in your discernment, you will need to make a choice; your gut will be invaluable in making it. But at this point, you're just getting started. You may not have enough information to allow you to make a decision that will bring you the happiness or satisfaction you seek . . . or deserve.

Try talking to someone close, a person whom you trust: your spouse, a close friend, your priest or clergyperson, someone who does what you think you'd like to do. Let them brainstorm with you because lots of ideas may emerge. As you contemplate what your purpose might be or what might bring you joy, imagine. Imagine yourself doing it, living it, being it from day to day . . . and in 20 years. Can you see it? If you can, great! You're on the right track. If not, consider your other options, or go back and do some more discerning. Then think about how that could lead to a transformation in your life, your family, your community or the world.

Write down some key elements of your purpose. Consider including your life overall, relationships, career, community, volunteer work, personal well-being and whatever else is important to you.

Norman Whitmire Jr. practiced internal medicine for nearly ten years in northern Virginia. Then in his midlife, he discerned a call to ordained ministry. He is now an Episcopal priest in New York City.

DISCOVERING MY PASSION
Kathi Townsend

Identifying individual passions is central to living a rich life.

Our passion is what allows us to work tirelessly, lose track of time when engaged in an activity, give to those around us and receive the gift of positivity and energy back from others. It motivates us, pushes us on, fuels faith and evaporates obstacles.

We choose to feel love, hate, anger, serenity. When we are unhappy, we have little sense of humor left to give to others. When we feel good inside, others are drawn to us because they want to borrow a spark of positive energy. That spark comes from passion for life and our ability to see how remarkable and special we really are. That spark is the silver bullet that destroys ego and self-centeredness. Underneath the stress and chaos of daily life are new adventures, new ways of thinking, relating, loving and receiving. When we allow ourselves to see our power and follow our passions, we find union of body, mind and spirit and the ability to feel at peace, loving and loved.

Here are some questions that will help you discover *your* passion. With these, be as descriptive as you'd like.

- What ideas, things, places and/or people am I most inspired by?
- What about *me* I am most proud of?
- What am I most often complimented on?
- What do I most often give to others in my relationships?
- What would the people closest to me say my passions are?
- How do I use my passion each day to inspire myself? Inspire others?

By adding to our passions lists, we focus on what's going right, and we begin to see the world through a collaborative lens where opportunity, kindness, positivity and victory are natural and everyday occurrences.

Take the questions here and write down your responses (and put a date on it). Also consider coming back to these same questions on a periodic basis.

Kathi Townsend has worked in the field of mental health, trauma and addictions since 1972. She has been immersed in and taught several forms of Eastern arts since 1969. A renowned and innovative lecturer and educator, she gives a hope-filled perspective on the vulnerabilities of being human, keeping our heads above water when surrounded by stress and change.

ON SERENDIPITY
Cathy McCandless

Opportunity doesn't always come knocking; sometimes it's just wandering around out there, hiding in a cloud of chaos, waiting for you to invite it in.

"Psst! Wanna buy a lottery ticket?" If that's not practical, pursuing any unlikely possibility will do, just so it's beyond wonderful.

There's not much chance at all that you'll actually win the lottery. Buy a ticket anyway to remind yourself to stay open to totally unexpected, totally unearned, totally outrageous good fortune. Don't think of this as advice, by the way; consider it a life hack.

This doesn't mean that you shouldn't bother to plan meticulously, work hard toward your goals and prepare yourself for the life you want to live. You definitely should. You owe it to yourself, and the quality of your future life depends on it. Just be sure to leave a little room for the unexpected because that's where life's magic resides.

So many wonderful things have come to me out of the clear blue: loves of a lifetime, forever friends, amazing adventures, my entire career.

Hopefully, life is very long, and for that reason, good planning is essential to get from one end of it to the other. But life is also not always orderly or predictable, and in the disorder there are often amazing opportunities. The important thing is having the vision to recognize them and the courage to embrace them wholeheartedly.

So go out and buy that lottery ticket or pursue the impossible dream, just to remind yourself of all the outrageously unlikely good fortune and the totally unexpected opportunities you're likely to encounter in the years to come. To win the actual lottery, you need to buy a ticket. In the lottery of life, though, no ticket is required. All you really need is an open mind – and an equally open heart – and a willingness to embrace the unexpected.

Serendipity isn't always as dramatic as winning the lottery. As you look around you, do you see anything unexpected going on that might turn out to be really wonderful? Are there any interesting opportunities you didn't notice before?

Born in 1949, Cathy McCandless grew up in Southern California and northern Virginia and, after a number of interesting pit stops, ended up in New York City, much to her delight. (Talk about serendipity!) "One of the things I love about 'the City' (as New Yorkers provincially call it)," she says, "is the pixie dust: You never know what you'll encounter on any given day."

TRUE LOVE: A JOURNEY THROUGH THE TUNNEL
Ching-Chen Chen

Fighting for your "true love" is a journey that demands resilience, hope and self-discovery.

Pursuing my "true love" in the counseling profession has been a lifelong journey filled with both "sour and sweet" moments. Growing up in a typical Asian Tiger family with high academic expectations, I chose to rebel against my parents' career expectations. Instead, I listened to my inner voice and followed my "true love." In my 20s, counseling and psychotherapy were still stigmatized in Taiwan, and there were no licensed counselors or psychologists at the time. I challenged systemic barriers and privilege, pivoting my career to advocate for the counseling profession and to make a greater impact. This journey then led me to study abroad, where I became a counselor educator, training future counselors to make a difference in the field.

Fighting for my "true love" has been like going through a tunnel filled with fear, anger, uncertainty and frustration. When I moved to a new country, I faced the identity shock of transitioning from being "somebody" in my home country to becoming "nobody" as an international student and later as a first-generation immigrant. Despite these challenges and moments of darkness, I always believed that light would be waiting at the end of each tunnel. Today, I am proud to be the first foreign-born counselor educator elected president of a national professional organization, continuing to inspire international students and faculty to pursue their dreams.

Even as a national leader, I continue to fight for my "true love" every day. However, I do not regret the challenges I have faced because I have come to realize that all the hardships are like diamonds hidden in the tunnel, shaping me and making my journey worthwhile.

I encourage you to listen to your inner voice, discover your "true love," fight for it, embrace the challenges and trust that light awaits you.

Reflect on a dream or goal about which you are passionate. What challenges are you willing to face to achieve it? Write down three action steps you can take today to move closer to your "true love."

Ching-Chen Chen, Ed.D., is an Associate Professor at the University of Nevada, Las Vegas, with research interests of cross-cultural measurement, evaluation, parent-child relationships, substance abuse counseling, multicultural counseling, and developmental psychology. She is the first foreign-born counselor educator elected president of a national professional organization – the Association for Assessment and Research in Counseling – and is committed to advancing the counseling profession globally.

SHAPING OUR VALUES
Vonnie Veltri Clement

What shapes our values determines who we are and where we want to go with our lives.

Our values change over time. They are shaped by our nuclear family growing up. Our school friends and social media (for good or for ill) shape our values in middle and high school. If we go on to college, our values are once again reshaped by what we read and study, our professors and the campus environment. As we move out into the world, our spouses or significant others, children and extended family impact who we are and what is important to us.

What is the string of pearls that ties this all together? What fills in the gaps as we move from one stage of life to another? It is not always seamless. There are successes and failures, happy times and lonely times, seasons of loss and seasons of gain. I have experienced all of these seasons in my life, and my faith has been the one constant that has enabled me to live a life intent on glorifying God. If you don't share this faith or believe in God, what is central to your life, and what is in your core and is your constant?

This leads me to the question, "What is the constant in your life that shapes your values and motivates you to do what you are called to do?" This is a core question, whether what you do is as a philosopher, pipe fitter, computer scientist, educator or artist, to name a few. How will this have an impact on how you define who you are and what is important to you? What shapes your values?

I encourage you to think about your core and most central values. Where did they come from? How will they shape your decisions about school, work, relationships and religious convictions as you move through life? How will your values impact the city and country you choose to live in, and for how long? In other words, how do you plan to live your life based on the values that you hold?

Write down what you believe are your five most central values. Then, in six months, do it again and compare them.

Vonnie Veltri Clement was a Senior Associate at the U.S. Department of Education and coordinator of Drug and Alcohol Prevention Efforts on college campuses. Prior to that, she was the Assistant Dean and an Associate Professor of Psychology at Grove City College in Pennsylvania. Presently, she is employed part time with Howard County Schools as a home instruction reviewer.

YOU HAVE CHOICES
Chesley Kennedy

Having clarity about what has an impact on our choices can help guide decisions.

I remember hearing the statement, "Child, you don't have to be afraid unless you want to be afraid," during a challenging time in my life when everything I had worked for felt like it was crashing around me. I've searched for its origin but haven't found it, yet the thought has stayed with me.

In my early 20s, I dropped out of college, convincing myself that this pursuit of a degree wasn't for me. My nights were filled with dancing, drugs and drinking until I could barely feel my legs. Despite the partying, I managed to start a successful business. However, I eventually realized that I could not drink and party like others; I didn't know when or how to stop. Seeking help, I embraced sobriety, which became a transformative gift that led me back to college and a career in counseling.

The day I closed my business was filled with excitement and hope for my new path of returning to college. I looked forward to a career where I could serve others, even if it meant earning less money. But as I locked the door of my business for the last time, a wave of terror washed over me. "What have I done?" I wondered, questioning my decision to leave behind a successful venture.

That is when I heard it: "Child, you don't have to be afraid unless you want to be afraid." This comforting thought resonated deeply within me.

Over the years, I've found that my career and happiness are not defined by financial success; rather, they are defined by the impact I can make as a counselor. Each day, I choose not to be afraid, embracing the opportunity to help others. This choice has become a guiding principle in my life, reminding me that fear is optional, and I can choose a path of hope and service.

Simply put, if you could choose to be afraid or not, wouldn't you choose to be fearless? Fear or fearlessness is a choice we can make.

Identify one or two choices you have in your life right now. How can this perspective about fear be helpful in your decision-making?

Chesley Kennedy, M.Div., LCAS, leads Spartan Recovery @UNCG at the University of North Carolina at Greensboro, a program for students in recovery from alcohol and other drugs.

ARE YOU PAYING ATTENTION?

Giang T. Nguyen

Take in the view, wherever you may be in life. It may lead you in directions you never before imagined.

I love to travel. It lets me see unfamiliar places and appreciate new perspectives. I also love to take *lots* of photos along the way. On our many vacations, my husband reminds me to be "in the moment" rather than simply to record each stop on our itinerary, to pay careful attention *while I'm there*.

This advice holds true in our day-to-day lives. At each point in my life, it's been valuable to stop and reflect on where I am (physically and metaphorically) at that given moment. The view in front of me evolves, and so do the things I see on the horizon. If I compare my life journey to a hike in the woods, I can envision hills and valleys, moments when some goals are clearly visible in the distance and other moments when goals that once were obvious might no longer seem logical or desirable. Taking stock of what's currently in front of us and possible destinations from our current vantage point lets us envision futures we might never consider if we wear blinders and simply march forward to a predetermined goal.

FIGURE 3.6
I took this photo of my husband and my mother walking on a winding dirt road with some local people in rural northern Vietnam.

In high school and college, I had a vague idea of what I wished for in life. I wanted to be a doctor, but my concept of that was based on the little exposure I had in my first two decades of life, and I couldn't have imagined the things that I've been able to do (as a doctor) since then. I can safely say that if I had not been "in the moment" and paid attention to the new potential "destinations" appearing on the horizon with each new step, my life would be much less interesting (and likely less fulfilling) than it is today.

Consider what brought you to the place where you are now. Who has helped you along the way? Write down their names and why you are grateful for them.

Giang T. Nguyen is a family physician, public health professional and college administrator. Giang immigrated from Vietnam as a refugee, and is immensely grateful to all who walked before him and who have helped to shape his beautiful journey through life. He lives in New England with his husband, Sean.

VALUE YOUR VALUES
Joe Gieck

Your values are central to your current and future life and beyond.

As a young person who is maturing, it is vital to embrace education in your values and future plans. You should begin to think about your future and what you want your legacy to be. Look to role models in your development of values and become a role model yourself.

Education should be at the forefront of this endeavor. Education is the engine that drives equality, social mobility and opportunity whether the individual choses an academic or a vocational path in the trades. The brain doesn't totally develop until the mid-20s, but the decision to include education is vital in the development of values in the individual. So many of my opportunities have come about as a result of my academic path and not necessarily because of my abilities or talents. With education, the individual gains self-confidence, structure, discipline and adaptability in personal values and goals. It also can open the door to the opportunity to aid in the good of one's self and others. Think about people and the good of society in your development of your values. Without good values in citizens, our country will not go forward positively.

This route can lead to leadership opportunities that are so necessary in your development and the good of society. Embrace and challenge the opportunity to become a leader, whether in academics, your work environment or in society. Leadership is the desire to make something better. Ninety percent of leadership is simply showing up and doing what's right versus what is popular. It's doing what you will say you will do in a timely fashion and being accountable with positive enthusiasm in your area of interest and values.

Your values will make a difference in how you live your life, so begin today in thinking of values and what you want your legacy to be.

Identify the top core values that guide you with your decision-making and your life overall.

Joe Gieck, Ed.D., ATR, PT, was Director of Sports Medicine at the University of Virginia for 43 years where he served as head athletic trainer, founder of the athletics life skills program, and professor in the Curry School of Education where he developed an undergraduate, master's and doctoral program in sports medicine/athletic training. He also cofounded the NCAA APPLE program for substance abuse education. He currently is professor emeritus in the School of Education and Clinical Orthopedics.

ACT IMMEDIATELY
Daniel Donovan

Do what you love today. Putting it on a list for later will undermine your journey to achieving your dreams.

My time in law enforcement taught me a critical skill that was not easy to translate to my personal goals, aspirations and daily habits. Law enforcement officers are often directed to respond quickly to evolving circumstances where little necessary information is available to make important decisions. Everything breaks down into minute-by-minute action steps that must be properly completed, otherwise your response is useless. The first, most crucial step is to arrive safely at your destination quickly. Whereas this was instinctual in law enforcement, it was not similarly applied in my personal life.

I lived a life completely detached from the training I received. My writing, my marriage, my goals to be an entrepreneur – all of them were reduced to aspirations instead of executions. As long as your dream is just a dream, nobody can take it from you. As soon as you act on it, other people may influence the level of success or the reputation with which you accomplish that success. You might be telling yourself, "If it is only in my head, no one can take it from me." You would be correct.

Unfortunately, no one can give it to you either . . . except for you.

If you want to be an author, start writing NOW! If you want to lose weight, get on the floor and do some pushups NOW! Not later. If you want to help people in your community, find an organization that shares your goals and call them NOW! Do NOT put these things on a to-do list. These are things you must live daily, starting right now. Make the lifestyle the goal, not the number on the scale or the words on the page or the ideal way you would like your community to thrive.

Stop reading right here, put a bookmark on this page, and spend ten minutes working on the dream or goal you have wasting away. You are a writer when you write, not when you publish. You are healthier when you make healthy decisions now, not when the scale reaches the magic number. Your community needs you now, not later. The journey begins with a single step, not with the first milestone. Act immediately.

Spend ten minutes writing your dream or goal. Then write some steps that can help you achieve that.

Daniel Donovan is a Christian, husband, father, former law enforcement officer, author of *Memoirs of a Death Row Inmate* and host of the *American Recovery Podcast*. He published his book in 2023 when he stopped dreaming of becoming an author but went out and made it happen.

FINDING AND LISTENING TO YOUR INNER VOICE
John McLaughlin

Taking on social problems you care deeply about enables you to make a difference for others and live an exciting, rewarding life.

Setting goals and intentions is crucial, but for the bigger questions about life, it's important to listen to others and find your own "inner voice." In high school, I had two amazing English teachers who taught classes on existentialism, the search for meaning and utopian visions. I was an idealistic Catholic youth who wanted to understand and help solve humanity's problems. I enjoyed all subjects, but I was good at math, and my parents encouraged me to major in math or science.

In college, my political, social and religious views changed a lot, and I switched majors multiple times. I kept getting pulled by my inner voice and followed it. The increasing homelessness in the United States during the 1980s, especially in New York City near where I grew up, felt like an urgent problem that needed my attention, so I decided to get involved. I must say, however, that listening to your inner voice isn't easy and you will encounter resistance!

Through my advocacy work in college, I met my wife. We worked in youth and adult shelters for a while after graduation and then pursued careers in teaching English as an additional language.

As job opportunities opened up, stalled or ended in the United States or Japan, I also did a lot of labor organizing to improve job security for contract and part-time teachers. Following my heart, I left a tenured university job in Japan to join my wife in Michigan, restart a migrant farmworker education program and start a family.

As an educator, I got involved in creating service learning programs, starting an immigrant workers center and consulting on bilingual correctional education programs. Eventually, I found a rewarding job that allowed me to make a difference for youth experiencing homelessness, other cross-systems youth and the educators and others who support them.

Remember, setting goals and listening to your inner voice can lead you to amazing places. Stay true to yourself and take action to make a positive impact in the world!

> *What does your inner voice say to you when you listen to it, about ways you are uniquely positioned to take action for a positive impact?*

John McLaughlin works for the U.S. federal government as team leader for homeless education programs. He practices Zen meditation, tries to garden and volunteers for a lot of Japan-related organizations and activities in the Washington, D.C. area.

TEACHING AND REACHING FOR JUSTICE WITH INTENTIONALITY

Shaun Harper

Pursue the justice you wish to see in the world.

For most of my adult life, I have intentionally raised public consciousness about structures and systems that cyclically disadvantage people of color, women, poor people, LGBTQ+ persons, and others whom injustice harms. While the majority of my career has been spent teaching at private universities, I unapologetically embrace my civic duty as a public intellectual.

As a Black gay man who grew up poor in a small, racially segregated Georgia town, the problems to which I am devoted to solving are familiar to me – I have either experienced them firsthand or been disturbingly proximal to their devastating effects on others whom I know and love. These experiences compel me to not only teach but also leverage numerous platforms to disrupt and dismantle sexism, racism, homophobia, transphobia and myriad other forms of human suffering every place they occur.

Intentionality is evidenced through my work at the University of Southern California Race and Equity Center, an organization I created 14 years ago that designs and delivers high-quality diversity, equity and inclusion learning experiences for professionals in hundreds of K–12 schools and districts, colleges and universities, government agencies, businesses and other organizations spanning a multitude of industries. Intentionality has also shown up in my independent consulting work with the military, global corporations, tech companies, professional sports teams and leagues and hundreds of other companies and institutions. More than 3 million Americans have read articles I have written for major newspapers, magazines and other media outlets. Reaching and teaching so many people via these vehicles has been intentional.

"He taught me much" is the highest praise gifted to me from students in my classrooms, professionals in my audiences and readers who access my written perspectives and advice. Justice deserves the intentionality and multidimensional strategies I bring to its daily pursuit.

Which injustices aggravate you? What can you do today to eradicate them?

Shaun Harper is Provost Professor of Education, Business and Public Policy at the University of Southern California, where he holds the Clifford and Betty Allen Chair in Urban Leadership. He also is the USC Race and Equity Center's founder and a past president of the American Educational Research Association.

FOLLOW YOUR DREAMS
Katrin Wesner-Harts

Helpful for life's journey is to identify your passion and work hard to achieve it.

One of the most influential people in my life has no idea about the impact that they had. It was a beautiful August day as the new freshman class was sitting on the campus lawn, waiting for convocation to begin. One of the speakers was the provost and he said, "You will work harder than you ever have before; but when you are done, you can do anything."

The first part makes sense. Middle school was harder than grade school, high school was harder than middle school, so college should be harder than high school. Otherwise, we didn't pick the right school. Education is designed to build on what we have learned in the past and to challenge ourselves to learn, grow and try new things in a (reasonably) safe environment.

The second part didn't make as much sense. Could I really do anything I dreamed of? What did that look like? What did I dream of doing? And was I willing to work that hard?

I knew I wanted to study psychology and that I wanted to help people. As an 18-year-old, I wasn't sure what that totally looked like, but that was okay. With the provost's words of encouragement in the background, I spent my college years learning to problem solve, try new things, explore new topics, take advantage of every opportunity that I could and build my confidence. I didn't always succeed, but I was in a place where it was okay to learn from failure or even mistakes. I also learned it was okay to take risks and try new things when feeling safe and supported.

Along the way, I learned I was passionate about prevention of drug and alcohol misuse – how can we and do we infuse prevention in all that we do. I learned the value of networking and have built a network of colleagues with whom I still, to this day, consult, collaborate and create. I have had amazing opportunities along the way. I can't help but thank the provost for some of that.

Identify ways you can find your passion, work hard and follow your dreams. And along the way, be kind.

Katrin Wesner-Harts, Ed.D., FACHA, is the director of the University of North Carolina Wilmington Student Health Center and remains involved in the prevention field. She was the 2019–2020 President of the American College Health Association, a true dream come true.

CULTIVATING SERENDIPITY
David K. Wiggins

It is important to cultivate serendipity.

I remember the moment very vividly. One evening, close friends of my parents came over to play cards, a regular occurrence that always involved engaging conversation and good-natured banter. About halfway through the evening, my mother's best friend noted how lucky I was to have a satisfying academic position that afforded me a daily schedule full of ample leisure time. My mother responded that my good fortune had nothing to do with luck but that "I had planned it that way."

My mother's retort reminded me that my life, while not devoid of luck as she suggested, has been full of serendipity – the word originally coined in 1754 by British writer Horace Walpole to describe discoveries and pleasant experiences that occur unexpectedly or by accident. I have experienced many serendipitous moments in my life, from meeting famous people without specifically intending to do so or engaging in impactful research projects that only came about after casually looking through the books in my local library or discovering unforeseen opportunities (and talents) after failing to achieve a desired goal.

I am convinced that these meaningful moments have occurred in my life because I have purposely cultivated serendipity in a variety of ways that can be duplicated by anyone interested in living more fully. The secret to cultivating serendipity is to be positive regardless of the circumstances and search for new opportunities with regularity while at once being receptive to the liberating feeling often resulting from change. The secret to cultivating serendipity also has to do with embracing randomness and adventure by seeking out different experiences, visiting different places and intentionally meeting and getting to know different people. Last but certainly not least, cultivating serendipity is more likely to occur if you attach real value to openness, take seriously the importance of being kind and generous with others without expecting anything in return and enthusiastically welcome the unexpected.

How has serendipity impacted your life as well as your friends and family?

David K. Wiggins is professor emeritus of sport studies at George Mason University. He is the editor or author of 20 books and past president of the North American Society for Sport History.

WHAT'S NEXT?
John Noltner

It's how you respond to the difficult thing that matters.

I've spent my career talking to people. Interviewing people and photographing them for an ongoing project called *A Peace of My Mind*, exploring ways in a divided world that we can remember what connects us.

During the pandemic, my wife and I sold our home, bought a van and spent two and a half years living full time on the road gathering stories of hope, healing and transformation. We drove across the country connecting with people who are looking for creative solutions to some of our most challenging issues. Immigration, race, class, gender, politics, faith. As a country, we are struggling with some challenging topics and a persistent sense of division. But do you know what else is true? We are surrounded by good people doing good things.

The stories that inspire me the most are the people who are faced with difficult circumstances and choose to make something good from it. The ones who choose love when hate would come easy. The ones who choose healing in spite of their wounds. The ones who find themselves at a crossroad and choose connection, compassion and courage in the face of impossible odds.

One of the stories that sticks with me is from Angela Bates, whom I met in Nicodemus, Kansas. The small town was founded by freed slaves in 1877 in the wake of the Civil War and the Emancipation Proclamation. Angela talked about some of the frustrations she had experienced in her life: misunderstanding, mistrust and discrimination. At one point, she realized that she couldn't control the things that happened to her, but she could control the way she responded to them.

FIGURE 3.7
The entire town of Nicodemus, Kansas, settled by freed slaves after the civil war. All of the current residents are direct descendants of the freed slaves who settled the town.

And I think that's the key right there. Things happen to us, and some are difficult. Some devastating. Others unforgivable. But that's not the end of the story. The single biggest question we can ask ourselves is, "What's next?" How are we going to respond to that thing, and how are we going to choose to move forward? Don't tell me why it's hard. Show me how it's possible.

When have you found strength in the midst of struggle?

John Noltner is a photographer and storyteller. He is the founder and executive director for *A Peace of My Mind*.

SPIRITUALITY MADE SIMPLE
Thomas E. Legere

You may be just a wave in the ocean, but you are on the earth for a specific purpose!

Spirituality is something about which a countless number of books have been written, about which many leaders of different faiths have spoken and about which much confusion and mystique exists. My experience with understanding spirituality can be summarized in the following items that I call "simple truths" to be read and reviewed in order. I also offer some sources for further reading.

1. It was 13.8 billion years ago that life burst forth and eventually set our world on a long journey to the present day and beyond. (Carl Sagan)
2. Since matter is neither created nor destroyed, we are all made up of star stuff, and everything has been here from the sub-atomic level since the beginning of time. (Albert Einstein)
3. There is no "God" who exists as a separate, discrete entity who looks like an old man in the sky with a beard. (Any respectable theologian)
4. "God," however, exists! The word "God" is a name for the guiding energies that are the basis of all creation: beauty, truth, goodness and love. (St. Thomas Aquinas)
5. To say that we believe in "God" means that we exist to make these energies manifest in our lives. (Teilhard de Chardin)
6. The only thing that holds us back from joining in this divine process is a stubborn ego. (All mystics)
7. Thinking that our ego is king is as crazy as a cell that thinks that it lives independent from its organism.
8. Spirituality is about waking up to the fact that we humans are like fish swimming around in the ocean looking for the ocean.
9. Such an awakening scares most people because it threatens the illusory independence of the ego.
10. Once free from this illusion, we are free to be ourselves and to serve "God" at the same time.
11. When the pain of living a shallow life is too much, let go of the ego (the "pretender to the throne") and "soar with eagles' wings."

Learning the above simple truths takes time and lots of mistakes along the way. But this is the key to living a healthy and joyous life! Every day, remember that you are stardust and that "God" is in your DNA!

What can you do, specifically, to increase your understanding of spirituality and your "stardust" qualities?

Thomas Legere, Ph.D., is a born teacher whose greatest joy is to remind people of the "pearl of great price" that lies within all of us.

MY FAVORITE DECISION METHOD
Darlind Davis

Have a good process for making life's decisions.

Our lives are peppered with lists of rules we are taught from childhood. Parents and mentors have continuously added interpretations to this basic guidance. We seek advice and absorb input as much as possible throughout our experiences. It is part of being human to want to be fulfilled and productive – while also being happy in the process.

I learned a quick method of determining the issues/people/items that are most essential to me. Imagine a jar and place a large stone in it to represent your life's highest priority (e.g., family, job, children). Now put smaller stones in the jar to represent other important, yet less critical things (e.g., recreation, hobbies, social life). Then fill the rest of your imaginary jar with sand; although a sizable quantity, this represents the least important parts of your life. Doing this encourages you to reflect and select the parts of your life that most need your focus and loyalty and helps to put everything in perspective visually. What is your big stone? What are you filling up your life doing? Do you change it sometimes?

When you're confronted with a decision, this organizing process can become very valuable. But there is a hidden challenge: how do you figure out if you have enough information to make a good choice, or do you keep searching for more information? We know it is often unwise to jump into a decision. However, you can also sense the answer from within. Getting to the answer is the crux of life. Just learn how to choose the large stone or the pebble.

Once, I was saddled with a difficult career situation and was very unhappy. I sought advice and the difficult choice was made easier because I went back to my big stone to evaluate my options. My little jar method gave me my answer, and a rainbow appeared over my desktop. I had to leave a frustrating and unfulfilling career situation (though very lucrative) to start the new chapter in my life. My family stone was bigger.

Listen to your inner soul and you will be content.

What are some reference points that can remind you of your priorities?

Darlind Davis's life's work involved 40 years in challenging positions at the local, state and national levels in the field of education, health and drug/alcohol misuse prevention. Currently, through writing and advocacy, she inspires people to reach their full potential.

TRUSTING YOURSELF
Susie Bruce

Listen to your inner voice as you make decisions.

When I was a teenager, and even in my 20s, it would make me crazy when I would ask my dad for advice on something and he wouldn't give me an answer. He would just say something along the lines of "*You* know what you should do." I would respond with, "But Dad, what do *you* think I should do?" This never worked, and he would tell me, "You have got to figure that out. You know the right answer." This annoyed me to no end at the time, but of course, my dad was right. I knew what I should do or needed to do, but I just didn't want to do it for some reason. Maybe because the task was hard, or it was an uncomfortable conversation to have, or just something I would rather not do.

A sense of duty and thinking beyond yourself was a big part of how I grew up, as my dad had enlisted in the U.S. Navy at age 17 and retired as a master chief, and my mom was a registered nurse. I didn't realize it at the time, but my dad's practice of rarely giving me direct advice was a huge gift. It made me trust my instincts and take the more challenging but also more rewarding path. Whenever I took the easy path, the one that wasn't what my "gut" said I really should do, I regretted it later. Sometimes I felt guilt, knowing that I could have helped someone or taken the initiative to mend a relationship but I didn't.

I use that feeling to motivate myself to do better in the future. If I have a challenging decision to make, my dad's words come back to me now, and I remember that I *do* know the answer that's in line with who I want to be.

Find some time when you're not distracted and think about a decision you need to make – it could be about a relationship, a school assignment or something at work. What does your inner voice suggest is the best response, not just in the moment but in the long term?

Susie Bruce has 30 years' experience in collegiate health promotion, focusing on substance misuse and hazing prevention. The best part of her job is building relationships with students, assisting them through challenges and cheering them on to reach their potential.

KNOW WHO YOU ARE
Jerry Rehm

Learning who you are is an important and lifelong process.

One of the best gifts you can give yourself is truly knowing who you are. Unfortunately, this is not as easy as it first appears. Our families, friends and school and work environments give us a long list of things we "should" be if we want to conform to assumed expectations. In addition, we have all our experiences that shape us. Successes, failures, struggles, exposure, relationships and much more teach us who we are. We notice we have preferences or values that are not shared in whole or in part by everyone in our social circle. This kind of personal development, choosing to keep some long-held traits and adopting others, is good as long as we come up with an integrated whole that works for us. It makes us unique.

Discovering who we are takes time. As if we were trying on different hats, we try different behaviors. We challenge established values. We may associate with people who are different than our closest carbon copies. We spend a lot of time inside our own head paying attention to all these different inputs. What first looked valid may be discarded eventually as "not me." Guide this process with purposeful introspection and thoughtful analysis. Be prepared for some surprises. For example, long-held career expectations may need to be discarded in the face of new information, or dating experiences may be important indicators of who gets more time with you.

Challenge yourself to not limit your analysis to friends and family; dig down deep into your gut to determine what you want to do, think, replicate or how to spend your time. You are in the process of discovering yourself. Don't be satisfied with a discovery that everyone else wants you to do unless it truly fits who you determine you are. It is healthy to test your discoveries by revealing them to trusted associates; however, remember that those folks are not you. Keep checking in with your inner self; keep what makes sense and discard the rest. You will continue to incorporate additional discoveries your entire life. Celebrate your unique self and live it accordingly.

Write down at least ten key traits or elements that best describe you from your point of view.

Jerry Rehm spent years working in four environments before finding the right fit for his values, skills and aptitudes. Also, he took years to accept his innate self to enable him to live in authentic relationships. He is a happy man living in Arlington, Virginia.

THE JOURNEY
Diane Rullo

Your previous circumstances do not need to determine your journey.

Education was not the focus in my family. "Get yourself through high school, then go get a job" was the message my three siblings heard. By the time it came to me, there was no need to repeat it; it was already ingrained. I barely made it through high school, not having any parental support. I attended school only four days a week, believing five days was unnecessary. I would sign my name on my report cards, with no one being the wiser. This independence had its advantages throughout my life, though it also created barriers stemming from my high school experience.

High school and the years that follow – whether you're headed to college, the military, the workforce or pursuing other paths – are crucial periods for acquiring skills that will advance your life both academically and personally. It's when you learn a range of skills and knowledge crucial for both academic and personal development. These years mark the beginning of your journey into developing essential abilities like critical literary analysis, effective writing, expanding your vocabulary, while also deepening your appreciation for the richness of language and literature – an exploration that will continue to grow through further studies. Reflecting on my own experiences, I realize that my skills in these areas were deficient during my advanced academic career. Trust me, investing energy in ongoing learning truly pays off for the rest of your life.

Despite the early messages of my childhood, I eventually pursued several degrees in higher education through sheer determination, refusing to let my past circumstances dictate my future. In pursuing higher education, I realized the disadvantages I faced from my earlier choices. There were moments when I doubted my path, especially when I faced setbacks. One pivotal moment was when I received my first college degree, but the most meaningful moment was standing on stage to receive my Ph.D. It was a reminder that my hard work and determination paid off. I learned that perseverance and a positive mindset can overcome even the most challenging obstacles. Making the early years count can really help avoid limitations and set yourself on a path to achieving your future goals.

How can you harness the lessons from your past experiences to overcome current obstacles and invest in your future success?

Diane Rullo is a faculty member at Walden University, Barbara Solomon School of Social Work. Her degrees are a B.A. in psychology, M.A. in counseling, M.S.W., and a Ph.D. in social work. She has been teaching graduate-level social workers for 30 years and has been in private practice since 1992.

FINDING MY CENTER
Karie Terhark

Take responsibility for your joy – it starts with knowing yourself.

A year ago, I faced a life-altering moment. I'd achieved career success and appeared to be living my dream, yet I couldn't recognize the woman staring back at me in the mirror. I felt lost, disconnected and unsure of who I was. It wasn't the toxic environment I had left behind that was to blame; it was me. My values no longer aligned with my life, and I needed to rediscover myself.

This journey began with a hard question: "Who is Karie Terhark?" My spiritual coach, Mary, asked me this during our first session on a paddleboard in the middle of a pond. I didn't have an answer. Over months of meditation, reflection and deep work, I unearthed the core of who I am.

I discovered five values – harmony, integrity, fun, collaboration and growth – that guide me as a leader and person. Living these values meant confronting my fears, letting go of resentment and committing to my well-being. Through yoga, journaling and self-discovery, I learned to lead from within, prioritizing my health and growth.

The biggest lesson? Leadership isn't just what you do for others; it's how you show up for yourself. When I healed and aligned my life with my values, my business thrived and I nearly doubled my sales goal in my first year. But more important, I found joy, self-love and clarity.

Carl Jung once said, "The world will ask who you are, and if you don't know, the world will tell you." I stopped letting the world define me. I am passionate, confident, fierce, kind and curious. I am centered.

As you tackle this for yourself, I believe it is important to start small – meditate, journal or read a book that sparks your growth. This will help with your journey.

Take time to ask yourself, "Who am I?" by reflecting on your values and the life you want to lead.

Karie Terhark is the founder of KT Facilitation, helping groups navigate change and collaboration. Based in Iowa, she inspires individuals who are looking to align with their values and lead authentically.

PLAYING SMALL FOR TOO LONG
Colber Prosper

Believing in yourself and your capabilities is critical for moving forward.

I have taught in K–12 and in higher education and currently own a consulting firm. I've worked in over ten counties, and I'm passionate about education, spirituality, social justice and people.

It was a cool spring morning and I'd just finished a panel interview for a management position at an Ivy League university. I had another interview at the top of the hour and I felt my anxiety rising. I asked if I had time to run to the restroom before the next round. I went into a bathroom stall and called my roommate, also one of my best friends. I told him, "I think I'm over my head," and he said something to the effect of you've experienced harder things, so you got this! He reminded me of the range of my capabilities. I decided to stop playing small and show up in my confidence, training and experience.

That interview was over ten years ago, but the lesson stuck. I'm currently the CEO of Prosper & Partners International Consulting Firm, LLC and author of *No Entry: Examining the Powers That Undermine Our Full Potential.*

I played small as a teenager and young adult because I wanted to appease others. But playing small bears some cost. I learned when you've played small for years, you don't fully know yourself. You're not fully aware of your capabilities and the emotions associated with self-growth. Second, you start believing that playing small is your true nature. You can lose some of your curiosity about all the amazing things you have within yourself and what you could potentially accomplish.

In the end, I didn't get that job. But in that moment, I exerted my freedom to witness what I was capable at "true size" or exemplifying the true depths of my skills and knowledge. Such a freedom, which I mentioned in my book, is what we owe ourselves and we're the only ones who can give it to ourselves. You got this!

FIGURE 3.8
My niece Lelle who is 6 and nephew Kálmi who is 4 drew pictures of love. They may not know the full definition of love but from an innate standpoint they know their position to it.

Take a moment and write down five key attributes or strengths that you possess.

Colber Prosper, M.S., is the CEO of Prosper & Partners International Consulting Firm, LLC and author of *No Entry: Examining the Powers That Undermine Our Full Potential.*

WORK-LIFE VALUES
Jim Moore

Every job has value, but how *you do it distinguishes you from others.*

From my experience, the following values contribute to a more meaningful life.

- **Show respect:** Believe in the worth of others and yourself. Treat each person (and yourself) with dignity and a belief that they (and you) have gifts that are important for the greater good. Help them (and yourself) discover, develop and share those talents. Your actions convey respect more than words.
- **Be curious:** Be inquisitive about life and open to the wonders of the world around you. Notice the beauty of nature, the magic of the arts and special moments in human interactions. Go beyond. Strive to learn. Do more than just the minimum of what is expected. Volunteer for projects outside your comfort zone.
- **Celebrate accomplishments:** Pay attention to the work of others, and acknowledge when a person or a team achieves a goal. Celebrate it in unique and meaningful ways. Affirm individuals who experience personal growth.
- **Acknowledge others:** Give credit to others when they identify a solution or share a good idea. It affirms that person and the entire team.
- **Seek to understand:** Before judging someone or a failed idea, first strive to understand that person or the reason that idea was advanced.
- **Ask "why" questions:** In problem-solving and in planning scenarios, strive to understand an issue and clarify desired outcomes before you settle on solutions or conclusions. If others are focused on demands, clarify what led to the demands and then focus on those issues.
- **Empower others:** Contribute to a work environment that values creativity and collective wisdom where individuals are expected to be a part of solution seeking and brainstorming sessions. Encourage new folks to ask the innocent "why" questions, to reexamine established policies and practices.
- **Change happens:** Look ahead and don't expect your field to remain static. Learn from areas outside of your profession. Develop a forward-focused mindset as you strive to discern factors that will impact your field.

Assess where you currently are on each value, and begin developing the others to create a more meaningful work life.

Jim Moore has worked in a machine shop, been a busboy in several restaurants, served as a night watchman and held multiple positions in the administration of higher education, including Vice President for Student Affairs/Dean of Students at three universities.

THE REAL QUESTION
Karen Kodzik

Let this question guide your path.

It's common that we look for answers to guide our paths, our future, our choices. But it is a question that is our guide. This question is the key, not just to career choices but also to our life's work. The common questions that misguide many of us is, "What's in it for me?" or "What advances my ambitions, my bank account, my life?"

Instead, I believe it is more important to start by looking in the mirror and asking yourself, "What am I going to give myself to?" as well as "What will I give my time, my talents, my heart to?" Then ask yourself the *real* question: "To whom is my time and talents in service?" Or said a bit differently, "Whose life will I advance; whose life will I make better?" This is the real question that guides our life, living, choices and path.

I have coached and counseled thousands of professionals over the years, helping them navigate the various crossroads in their careers. They are recognized as well as emerging leaders who often come to me because they have lost their purpose, their passion and their path. They are caught in the swirl of the ever-changing world of work. They have lost sight of the real question. When we bring that question back into focus and to the forefront, it is amazing how empowered they feel to forge forward.

As you reflect on your life to date as well as your future plans, write your response to the question, "To whom is my time and talents in service?"

Karen Kodzik, M.S., is a coach, counselor and consultant helping professionals realize rewarding careers. She is the founder of Cultivating Careers and author of *Navigating Through Now What?*

THE POWER OF NO AND THE VALUE OF FAILURE
Shawnte Elbert

Embrace failure and the courage to say no as essential steps toward growth and success.

Early in my career, I found it difficult to accept failure. I saw it as a personal shortcoming, a sign that I wasn't good enough. It took time and reflection to realize that every failure and every no I received was a lesson guiding me toward better decisions and deeper understanding. Similarly, learning to say no was a challenging yet liberating experience. Like many, I equated saying yes to every opportunity with being capable and successful. But I soon realized that overcommitting and spreading myself too thin only led to burnout and diminished the quality of my work, and how many used me for my talents and gifts.

One story that stands out is when I was offered a role that would have doubled my salary and moved me and my family closer to our home state. While it was exciting, during the on-campus interview, I knew I could easily do the role, but the difficulty would be working under the person who would have been my supervisor. The interview had red flags throughout; I literally felt like I was in the movie *Get Out*, being warned to get far away from there. Withdrawing from the search and saying no when asked to reconsider was one of the hardest decisions I made, but it was also one of the most empowering. That decision allowed me to focus on opportunities and settings that aligned with my values, leading to greater fulfillment.

The ability to recognize that failure is not the end but often a beginning gives us a chance to learn, pivot and grow stronger. For young adults navigating the complex journey to adulthood, I want you to know this: Your strength isn't measured by how much you can take on, or by how flawless your journey appears. It's found in the wisdom to say no when something doesn't align with your truth and in the courage to embrace failure as a stepping stone rather than a stumbling block. No is *not* a sign of weakness but of self-respect and clarity. Both failure and the power of no are vital in shaping a life of intention and authenticity.

Reflect on a time when you faced failure or had to say no. What did you learn from that experience, and how did it shape who you are today?

Shawnte Elbert, Ed.D., MCHES, CWHC, TTS, is a public health leader and wellness coach committed to helping individuals embrace their full potential through resilience and self-care. She is the founder of Elbert Innovative Solutions and co-CEO of Sister W.E.L.L.S., PLLC.

ALWAYS STAY TRUE TO YOUR CONSCIENCE
Benedict Rogers

Know your values and beliefs, be open to engage respectfully with others about their beliefs and be willing to defend your beliefs.

For all my adult life, I have lived a calling to defend human rights, particularly in some of the world's most closed and repressed places, such as North Korea, China and Myanmar, and in places of religious intolerance, such as Pakistan and Indonesia, or in countries emerging from conflict, such as East Timor. I have promoted religious freedom for people of all religions and none.

This has not been without risk. Two of my friends were assassinated, and I once missed a bomb by five minutes in Islamabad. I have been chased by police in China and deported from Myanmar twice. In Hong Kong, I was denied entry, threatened with a jail sentence and named as a collaborator in the trial of pro-democracy activist Jimmy Lai. I have also received dozens of threatening letters and emails from anonymous sources in Hong Kong, as have my neighbors and my mother. But I know that all of this is intended to try to silence me, and therefore I am determined not to be silenced but to redouble my efforts.

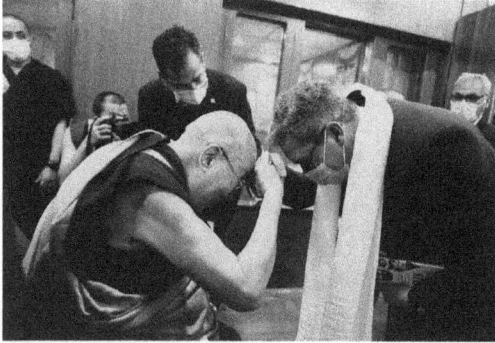

FIGURE 3.9
In 2023 I had the great privilege of meeting the Tibetan spiritual leader, His Holiness the Dalai Lama, at his residence in Dharamsala, India. The moment we both bowed to each other and our foreheads touched was a moment of both profound respect, deep spiritual connection and surprising intimacy between me and one of the world's greatest and most inspiring spiritual leaders.

If a set of values and beliefs are worth holding, they are worth defending, whatever the risks. And despite the risks, this work has been profoundly rewarding, working alongside far more courageous people who have risked far more than me. So don't give up, and never surrender your conscience, but always stay true to it.

Write down the values, beliefs or issues that are most central for you.

Benedict Rogers is a writer and human rights activist specializing in Asia and is the author of seven books including *The China Nexus: Thirty Years in and around the Chinese Communist Party's Tyranny* and *Burma: A Nation at the Crossroads.*

CHOCOLATE CAKE
Mary Ann Sprouse

Who do you want to be when you grow up?

It is fall and kids are preparing to go back to school. I'm watching a segment on the news of a father who has video recorded his daughter on the first day of school – each year – since kindergarten and asked her, "What do you want to be when you grow up?" This year is her senior year of high school, and she announces she wants to be a physical therapist. My neighbor also shared a video of her three-year-old niece being asked the same question; without hesitation, she declared she wants to be chocolate cake.

Asking "What do you want to be when you grow up?" is a popular question with young people. Although this question can help you navigate a path to a certain profession or career, asking about "who" you want to be when you grow up can open a broader path. This question invites you to consider your values, character traits and the impact you want to have on the world. This distinction between "what" and "who" invites deeper reflection. Developing a sense of identity and personal values shifts our focus from external titles to internal qualities and sets us up for creating a meaningful life.

While my neighbor's niece might not literally want to become a dessert, her comical aspiration reveals her desire to be something that brings joy and celebration. It's a reminder that the essence of identity is about how we impact the world and the people around us. Perhaps she sees being a chocolate cake as symbolizing happiness, sweetness and the ability to bring joy to others.

I was confronted by this deeper question while volunteering for a political campaign. Reading the material I was stuffing into envelopes caused me to examine my own values and what is important. I found this exploration more helpful overall than just focusing on a future career or building a résumé. Understanding who I wanted to be, how I wanted to show up in the world, was important for my whole life and not just my work life.

Perhaps my neighbor's niece will grow up to spread sweetness and joy in her own way – chocolate cake or not. Take a break from deciding what to be and explore who you want to be – to discover your version of chocolate cake.

Talk with friends and family about their values and how their values influence their decision-making.

Mary Ann Sprouse is a Licensed Clinical Social Worker and Certified Substance Abuse Counselor working in a variety of settings helping people explore who they are and live a purposeful life.

THE POWER OF INTEGRITY
Stephanie Ahles

Integrity is the compass guiding our actions and aligning our behavior with our beliefs.

It started innocently enough. One morning, I was late to work, and when my coworker asked why, I said, "Traffic was terrible," though I had simply hit snooze too many times. It felt harmless, a small lie to save face, especially since my coworker had to stay late because of me.

Over time, these small lies became a habit. Whenever something went wrong, it was easier to offer an excuse than face accountability.

Then one day, I was on the receiving end of a lie. My shift was over, and I had plans, but my coworker didn't show up on time. Frustrated, I stayed late. When she arrived and explained her tardiness, I recognized my own familiar excuses. In that moment, I realized how these "harmless" lies had eroded our trust. Hers in me and now mine in her.

That day, I learned that small lies lead to bigger problems. Each one had chipped away at my integrity and the trust others placed in me. Rebuilding that trust was humbling but taught me an invaluable lesson that integrity is nonnegotiable.

Integrity is our compass, guiding us to align actions with beliefs. Choosing honesty builds trust and authenticity. Even small lies can steer us far from who we aspire to be. Every time we choose dishonesty, even for a seemingly minor reason, we erode our moral compass. These little compromises can lead to bigger ones, and before we know it, we've lost sight of what truly matters.

Authenticity is the foundation of strong relationships. When we're honest with ourselves and others, we build trust and foster deeper connections. It's not always easy, but the rewards are immeasurable. By choosing honesty, we empower ourselves and inspire others to do the same.

Let your integrity shine! Let it light the way to a life you can be proud of.

Reflect on the person you aspire to be. Are you prepared to make the choices that will align your actions with your core values and let your integrity shine?

Stephanie Ahles, cofounder and owner of EmpoweringYOU, LLC, is an advocate dedicated to amplifying voices and empowering people to lead with confidence. Drawing on her expertise in participatory engagement, she creates inclusive spaces where diverse perspectives are heard and valued. Stephanie's work reflects her passion for fostering equity, building leadership capacity and driving meaningful change within communities and organizations.

THE MOST IMPORTANT QUESTION
Thomas Workman

Determining what you really want is central to achieving your own desired outcomes.

Every action you take is a choice, and every choice you make has an outcome. The goal is to make intentional choices that lead you closer to the outcomes you want. The most important question you can ask, then, is, "What do I want?"

Adult life is an endless parade of choices that only you can make: what to eat, when to sleep, where to live and work, what to do for relaxation, exercise, and entertainment, whom to choose as friends and lovers. Some choices you'll make daily, even hourly. Others you'll make only a few times throughout your life.

You've already seen how many people try to influence or dictate these choices. Parents. Teachers. School administrators. Friends. Police. Doctors. Bosses. Coworkers. There are laws or rules and a lot of opinions. There are many times it won't feel as if you have much of a choice at all, but you always do.

Every choice has an outcome of some kind. You can spend a great deal of energy trying to pretend that the choice you made has nothing to do with the outcomes you got, but doing that won't help you very much. You'll hear many opinions about what choices are right and what choices are wrong. But deciding whether a choice is right or wrong also won't help you much. The more important question to ask is whether the choice you are making is resulting in the outcome that you want.

The catch, of course, is knowing what you really want. That's not always very clear for most of us. What we want can shift a good deal throughout life or even in a single day or night. The trick, then, is to ask yourself what you want in any given moment and to connect the choices you've made to the outcomes you're getting. In that way, you can make different choices the next time and see if that gets you closer to what you really want. It's not easy, but if you are intentional about it, you'll get better at it every day.

Think of a choice you are now facing. What do the outcomes of previous choices tell you about your current choice?

Thomas Workman, Ph.D., lives on a small ranch in Phoenix, Arizona, with his husband and two cats. He currently works remotely as a principal researcher at the American Institutes for Research but soon plans to retire and run a small spiritual coaching business with his husband – another choice!

LIVING INTO INTENTIONS
Marcia Hyatt

Having a snapshot of your future can become your reality.

I was sorting through photos when I found a picture of my apartment. The amazing part was that the photo was taken three years earlier dreamed about my future after college. On spring break in my senior year of college, I traveled halfway across the country to visit my sister. She showed me where she practiced social work. I thought, "I would love to use my sociology degree here." We toured a community and saw an open house for a new apartment complex. I took a picture, thinking I'd like to live in a place like this.

Three years later, I found that old photo. I realized I was now living in an identical apartment and working where my sister worked. It wasn't magic. I took the social work civil service exam. But finding that photo reminded me of the power of intentions. I've had other experiences like this – imagining something clearly and then finding myself living into the intention. It is not as if I made it happen; I just took the next right step, mindful of my intention.

What does it truly mean to live intentionally? It begins with a conscious choice to pick up the pen and become coauthors of our lives, collaborating with our ever-changing circumstances. While this path isn't easy – our brains are wired to cling to familiar habits and patterns that ensure safety, acceptance and control – it offers the promise of a life filled with greater purpose and potential. The journey starts with awareness of what brings us joy. From there, we must dedicate time to understanding our unique gifts and how they can contribute meaningfully to the world. Finally, we must embrace the courage to align our actions with this newfound clarity, learning to live in a way that reflects our deepest values and aspirations. We do not "make" it happen, but one day, you may live what you had imagined.

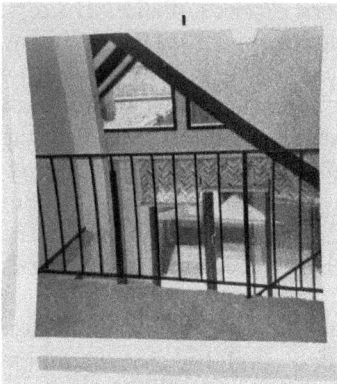

FIGURE 3.10
When I captured this photo, I envisioned myself living in a place like this and working at the same organization as my sister. That vision became my reality.

When have you felt the most alive, as if you were genuinely using you gifts? What would having a bit more of that look like in your life?

Marcia Hyatt is a leadership and life coach who has worked in higher education, corporate, nonprofit and entrepreneurial settings. Cofounder of the Center for Emerging Leadership, she is the creator of *The Best of Ourselves*.

R & R: RECOGNITION AND REFLECTION
Mike Jackson

Recognition and reflection are invaluable life skills to make you a better person.

These two attributes or skills can have significant impact in both your personal and work life. Your work-life balance will become increasingly more difficult as you move up in your career and volunteer in your community. Employing these skills will make you far more impactful and effective.

As a leader, you have a responsibility for the self-esteem of the organization. The greatest power you have to impact this is with recognition. This includes calling out a positive contribution by an associate or simply using their name to say hello! It could be a constructive situation that helps to mentor the individual in their role. The point is, you need to have consciousness in this area to have influence. When you raise the self-esteem of the individual, you raise the overall self-esteem and pride of the organization. The act of recognition enables motivation and promotes tenure in your company or organization.

You also have a duty as a leader to "work on the business while working in the business." This alludes to those transformational opportunities that typically arise out of the practice of taking time for reflection. Clearing your head, finding a quiet spot and just thinking about the larger picture in the organization can lead to innovative thoughts. This exercise will allow you to achieve things beyond your normal responsibilities. Simply put, it gets you out of the box when you practice reflection.

I learned these skills during my various roles in a Fortune 50 company, moving from an entry-level position to the president/COO. I kept two rocks on my desk, one with the word "Reflection" and the other with "Recognition." They served as a reminder for me and as a conversation starter with countless people. Often, these discussions would weave between the individual's personal and professional roles.

How will you practice recognition and reflection in your life?

Mike Jackson practiced and refined these skills during his 31-year career with a Fortune 50 company in the Food Industry. His total experience spans 54 years that currently involves board work with several companies. He is also active in community governance and a number of nonprofit organizations and is married to his high school sweetheart for 52 years.

SMALL WORDS OF ENCOURAGEMENT
Natalie Benson

Destiny isn't something that is found; it is created.

It's easier to remember the *ifs, ands* and *buts.* The *could haves, should haves, would haves* of a life lived longer than our teenage years. A perspective brought about by a fully developed frontal lobe in our mid-20s. Pondering the question of what I would have done differently if I knew. But that's just the thing – we don't know.

When we are young, we are waiting on a predetermined destiny handed to us in a yellow envelope of laminated papers, only to realize they are all blank. Left up to us to write the story of who and how we became the person we are when looking backward. Lessons etched into the fine lines of our aging skin, staring back at us in the mirror telling us that we have succeeded despite our failures. And while we may take some pages out of the books of our mentors, we ultimately compose the plotline of our own lives.

Yes, it's not uncommon to be afraid of what lies ahead. But the difference between a life well lived and just surviving is taking that fear and using it to forge a path into the greatness we all hold within us. Like nature, we must go through a rainy period to enjoy the bright blossom of the fruit of our labor. A balance of bitter and sweet. A cacophony of war drums plays as we defy all expectations and soar like an eagle high above the crowds of cynics who believed we would not make it this far, for we will not let the defeat of our past define the outcome of our future.

It all lies within our hands, and it is up to you. So, grasp at the reins of fate and charge forward into the sun. The future is waiting.

How do you view your life – past, present and future? What can be done to make your life one that is well lived?

Natalie Benson is a young poet and artist from New York. She is the author of *All Quiet on That Front: A Collection of Poems.* When she is not writing, she is working on her paintings inspired by everyday life, culture and the human form. You can find more of her poetry on Instagram *@allquiet_poetry.*

SEARCHING FOR YOUR PATH?

Joanne Bevins

Try following your heart and see where it leads you.

When I was a senior in high school in Baltimore, Maryland, I thought I wanted to be a first-grade teacher. At my school, there was a program for students who had met graduation requirements to attend school in the mornings and then spend the afternoons in some sort of work experience, either a paid job or a volunteer placement. I had hoped to be placed in an elementary school; however, I ended up in a middle school special education classroom with an incredible teacher. This was in the "dark ages" of special ed when students were segregated from their peers and basically warehoused until graduation. That experience changed my life.

I ended up going to one of only a few colleges in Maryland that had special education as a major. After graduation, my first job was identifying and teaching learning disabled children in an elementary school. My special ed teaching career spanned many years in four different states, ending in California. Along the way, I got a master's degree in learning disabilities, a second master's in reading instruction and an English Language Development certificate to teach in California.

After years in special education, I thought I had dealt with every type of childhood behavior. That was until a close family member was diagnosed with a mental health condition. Now I am an expert in my own lived experience with mental health. Looking for support, my husband and I found the National Alliance on Mental Illness (NAMI). We began by taking a class for loved ones and joined a support group for families. My family member is doing well and managing their life. I vowed that once I had the time, I would find a way to give back to NAMI.

My path has taken me a long way from my original intentions. However, my heart has always been with children and families. Fifty years after I graduated from high school, I am still helping special ed students – only now as a mentor to a new generation of teachers. As a volunteer, I teach the NAMI class that we took, lead a support group for families and do presentations for teachers about the warning signs for mental health conditions.

Research areas of interest that may have volunteer opportunities because they may help to shape your career path.

Joanne Bevins currently lives in Davis, California, is a field supervisor for Yolo-Solano Teacher Credentialing Center and volunteers for the National Alliance on Mental Illness Yolo.

AN EARLY AND LASTING LESSON
Justin Harmon

Sometimes everything you need to know really can be learned in kindergarten.

I believe that thinking critically is the pathway to changing one's world, something I learned in kindergarten from my grade school librarian. She taught all her students a short phrase that helped us to better understand how to recognize injustices in the world, the importance of appreciating differences among people, and the value of systematic thinking in creating a life that is well rounded: "Life is short. Therefore, I shall be a crusader in the fight against ignorance and fear, beginning with myself." I have carried this lesson with me ever since.

FIGURE 3.11
This is a painting of Dorothy Vickers-Shelley, on the right; the other woman is Vashti McCollum, best known from the 1948 McCollum vs. Board of Education decision striking down religion in public schools. Two powerful women!

That's not to say I haven't stumbled along the way or that I have always lived up to this pledge and ideal. Far from it.

When our librarian had us recite this statement, we always put our thumb to our chest when we got to the "beginning with myself" closing. I believe that's what she meant with the end of the phrase – that it's okay to fall short of our best sometimes, as long as we acknowledge having done so and strive to be better in the future. What that looks like for a six-year-old and what it looks like for a young or older adult may be categorically different but certainly not in its essence.

There are a lot of lessons I didn't learn as a kid, including some I refused to learn out of obstinacy and arrogance – and ignorance. I don't worry about those missed opportunities, though. Life is too short, after all. Instead, I'm just thankful that I was able to be positively affected by this woman who instilled this creed in me, one that is never far from my heart and mind, connecting me to my past and guiding me into the future.

What were some of the most compelling words of wisdom you ever received as a child? How have you applied them in your life as an adult?

Justin Harmon, Ph.D., is an associate professor at the University of North Carolina Greensboro. He likes getting lost in the forest and in good books.

DON'T MISS YOUR LIFE!
Joseph Bullock

Owning your truth helps with claiming your authenticity and moving forward.

Right now, as you read this, you may feel stagnant. Are you feeling like nothing you try will shake the stagnation and that nothing is changing? Are you feeling a lack of movement in this season of your life? In this moment, right now, maybe you are feeling that you should be much further along than you are currently, but you've been holding on to some people, places and things that you can't carry with you to your next level. You either must settle for your current circumstance or come to understand that some things must drop off for you to move forward.

At this point in time in your life, knowing YOUR TRUTH is critical to what happens next. There is power in knowing your truth. Deciding to LIVE in a place of TRUTH will defeat stagnation, indecision and move you forward. By stopping the lies of self-deceit, you also eliminate the possibility of living in a fantasy, creating stories with no opportunity to move you forward, or at worst, risk becoming a person living in a dual reality. You must first stop deceiving yourself!

Living a life of truth means that you have achieved a level of authenticity and clarity by knowing your truth: knowing who you are, knowing where you are and knowing where you want to go. You can now start gaining momentum by working toward living the perfect day.

The perfect day requires remaining disciplined to your truth. Divide your day into three segments: morning, afternoon and evening. Decide what is important to remain mindful of about your truth throughout your day to stay on target. Last, know and be compliant with your newly created "rule of law" for your life. Yes, treat your life rules like laws. Free your mind of limiting beliefs and be stubborn with tolerating mistakes. Do not allow yourself to stop/quit because of mistakes by developing and mastering a teachable, learnable mindset. Watch yourself become conscious about your beliefs, habits, actions and inactions.

You will find that you are either investing in your forward movement or compounding liabilities. Moving forward toward your truth will have no more meaning than what you give to your truth. OWN YOUR TRUTH!

What steps can you take to know, and then live, your own truth? Who can you engage to help you with this process?

Joseph Bullock has over 30 years of combined experience as an executive, professional therapist and clinical preceptor. Dr. Bullock is a member of the Federal Coach Network and Coachville. He provides coaching services to federal employees, executives, athletes and health-care professionals.

WHY

Anne Atkins

To help find your why, explore and identify your values, your goals, the impact you want to make on others and the world around you.

Hi, my name is Anne Atkins. I am retired after nearly 40 years in Virginia state government. I began my employment at the bottom of the ladder, only one grade above the lowest ranked clerical worker. In high school, I wanted to major in biology. But back in the day, many colleges required a foreign language for admission. A D in Latin and an F in French derailed the biology major idea. I tried majoring in business because there was no foreign language requirement. But my heart wasn't in it, and I started racking up low grades. Eventually, I found my footing in English, the one subject where I excelled.

I was floundering. I didn't have clear goals or a sense of who I was. The only thing I wanted was a college degree. I thought it was a magic key that would open employment doors for me. But I didn't know what the doors looked like or what was behind them.

I lived day to day without direction, tired and frustrated. Then one day, I came across a quote from Martin Luther King Jr.:

> If a man is called to be a street sweeper, he should sweep streets even as Michelangelo painted, or Beethoven composed music or Shakespeare wrote poetry. He should sweep streets so well that all the hosts of heaven and earth will pause to say, "Here lived a great street sweeper who did his job well."

This quote changed everything for me. It became my guiding principle, pushing me to define my values and goals. Over time, I clarified my purpose, which matured into a rich source of guidance and experience. Following Dr. King's advice, I earned my B.A. in English and an M.P.A. in public administration. I advanced through various professional positions until I retired as a public relations director and an executive staff member.

I encourage you to find your why. Discover who you are, your values and the impact you want to make on the world. Figure it out now. Your why will light the way for you.

What steps can you take today and in the coming weeks to help you find your why?

Anne Atkins began her career as a clerical worker and worked her way up into public relations and executive leadership. She volunteers as Communications Chair for Friends of Dragon Run.

A LEGACY TOUCHSTONE
Jim Westfall

Endearing legacies reflect the totality of one's being.

Life goes by so quickly. Crafting a legacy isn't something just for one's senior years. Legacies accumulate over a lifetime, representing far more than whatever a will and last testament might convey to one's beneficiaries.

- Finding and committing to a loving relationship is paramount. Doing something nice for your partner every day is an endearing practice. Also saying "I love you" often and expressing public pride in your partner strengthens that bond and demonstrates your affection.
- Children are one's lasting legacy. Their personalities and values will largely be a reflection of you. Don't neglect the time and attention kids deserve, especially during their formative years. One can't later backfill that missed opportunity.
- Forging strong family relationships provides a bedrock of support for those inevitable tough times in life. Although it is comforting to know family members have your back, your more defining imprint comes when you are the one who lends a hand. Family memories and earned affection endure.
- Friends are a joy and responsibility. Don't take them for granted. Treasure those you hold dear. Look for opportunities to demonstrate your appreciation openly.
- Develop the skills and personal discipline necessary to earn enough to provide for yourself and your dependents. It's both a responsibility and reflection on your person to become financially secure.
- Career demands and the lure of greater reward increasingly compete for time and attention. Take pride in quality workmanship, professional achievements and how those accomplishments enable one to be a more generous provider. Work with your partner to decide work-life balance priorities.
- Citizenship is one's responsibility to the community at large. It can be expressed through responsible behavior, consideration for others, charity and, if it moves you, more formally through organized public service.

There are few absolutely right and wrong choices in life but certainly lots of better and worse alternatives. The hope is the above perspectives are worth pondering as you make your decisions.

As you reflect on the seven perspectives, which ones seem to be the highest priority for you now? What can you do in the near future to help strengthen it?

Jim Westfall is married and lives in Sonoma County, California. He is mostly retired now after working 40 years in the financial services industry.

GRIT

Victoria M. Larsen

Grit is all about having courage and resolve, and strength of character.

Growing up, my father was a men's college basketball coach. It was never a matter of if I was going to college but where I would go with the expectation that I would compete as a student athlete. Although I understood the college recruiting landscape quite well, the journey to get there was filled with many more noes than yeses.

Challenges mounted as an 18-year-old navigating team dynamics, playing time, my academic pathway and life away from my family. Self-doubt and anxiety made a comfortable home in my thoughts. Keeping my eye on the prize, I packed in extra credits, played two sports and worked several internships and jobs to graduate in three years. I walked away with my diploma knowing grit was the greatest skill I was taking to graduate school.

Just as I completed my master's degree, COVID-19 broke out and industries went dark and hiring froze. I applied to dozens of jobs and was told no more than ever before. Nonetheless, I refused to allow the hard, diligent work and gritty attitude fall by the wayside. It was up to me to chart my own path forward and take baby steps, even if my final destination was not yet feasible and I wasn't where I wanted to be or where I thought I deserved to be. My journey of noes eventually led me to an opportunity of a lifetime working with our country's leaders at the White House, U.S. Capitol and newsrooms – places I never thought I would be. I began to be grateful for all of the noes.

Persisting and waiting my turn meant something much larger was around the corner. In our social media age, it is only human to compare ourselves to those on our screens. It is easy to fall into the trap of admiring someone else's successes and wonder why your efforts aren't reaping fruit. We often expect immediate success but fail to realize that the journey is often the greatest lesson. It is courage and character – grit – that will take you to the places you are meant to be with the people you are meant to be with.

Think of the noes in your life not as closed doors but as opportunities for better doors to open. Do not allow someone else's inability to recognize your strengths and talents to shake your confidence or define the imprint you get to make in the world. Your grit is one of your greatest superpowers.

In what ways can you incorporate grit into your life?

Victoria Larsen works for the Urban Institute in the Justice Policy Center and is entering the sport management program at Louisiana State University as a Ph.D. student.

KNOW THYSELF
Christopher C. Delatorre

To find your purpose, get to know yourself first.

Our heroes say a lot about the people we want to be. As a boy, I wanted to be Han Solo, a rough and tough rebel exploring the stars, fighting bad guys with a Wookie at my side. As I got older and my own story began to unfold, I felt more like Frodo in J. R. R. Tolkien's *The Fellowship of the Ring*, a halfling living in a world of giants where every encounter became a reminder of how I had yet to find my own sense of purpose. As time passed, I increasingly felt I didn't belong. Eventually, like Frodo, I learned that living my own life meant leaving those insecurities behind. To find my purpose, I would have to find myself first.

American philosopher Henry David Thoreau said, "Not until we are lost do we begin to understand ourselves." This reminds me of the Greek maxim "Know thyself," an ancient principle that affirms the importance of character, the unique traits that allow us to reach our individual potential – the qualities we gift to the world. This is why our heroes mean so much – we see ourselves in them; they remind us of who we are and want to be. Like our heroes, we find our strength in the forge of life's challenges.

Star Wars, The Lord of the Rings, Harry Potter, The Wizard of Oz – these stories follow the hero's journey, a narrative structure popularized by American writer Joseph Campbell. Here, the reluctant hero leaves the confines of ordinary life to embark on a perilous quest where they confront their fear and, as a result, return stronger, enlightened and with renewed purpose.

This is also illustrated in Paulo Coelho's *The Alchemist*, a story of a boy who upends his life in search of treasure, only to realize at the end of his journey that what he was looking for was back where he started all along. In learning this, he sees how everything in the world connects. He finds his purpose – he becomes a better person, the individual he is meant to be. And as Coelho writes, "When we strive to become better than we are, everything around us becomes better, too." Only when you know yourself will you find your purpose. When you do, you will discover the best life has to offer.

How well do you know yourself? Where do you see yourself on your life journey?

Christopher C. Delatorre is a team builder, facilitator and cultural strategist working toward a graduate degree in mental health counseling. His podcast explores toxic relationships – what they look like, why they happen and how to let go.

SELF-ACCEPTANCE
Marguerite Phillips

You have every right to be here.

If every young adult was sent off to college with a copy of the poem "Desiderata" by Max Ehrmann, their college years and possibly their whole lives would have meaning from the day they ventured into the chaotic unknown.

There is so much fear and self-doubting in a young person's life – fear of the unknown, of meeting new people, of falling in love and of being judged by others. Sometimes these judgments make a person feel less than whole.

Ehrmann wrote, "If you compare yourself with others . . . you may become vain or bitter . . . for always there will be greater and lesser persons than yourself."

Whether a person wants to become an artist, a writer, a musician or a teacher, they will be judged. So what?

People find their own path. Many start out to become chemical engineers and wind up being linemen for utility companies or valuable plumbers. Idealistic students want to be the next fashionista but instead become a successful speech pathologist. And some people love and enjoy being homemakers, fueling their need for success through providing a safe, loving home for their children. These homemakers, also known as domestic engineers, are tutors, artists, food bank volunteers, Parent-Teacher Association leaders and gourmet chefs.

Reading the 100-year-old poem of wisdom will reveal so much that has not changed in a century. There is still war, crime, hunger and political strife. What has changed is that every disaster, every unkind word, every weather event and much more flashes on your cell phone news constantly. This reminds a young person that the world is a very scary, unpredictable place to live. It sometimes makes them worry, get depressed and feel hopeless for the future.

Stop panicking and feeling powerless about the world's events. It's okay to turn off TikTok and Instagram and replace the chatter with music, reading and napping.

As Ehrmann said, "You are a child of the Universe. You have the right to be here."

How does the poem "Desiderata" resonate for you? What other poem, writing or saying best provides you with grounding and inspiration?

Marguerite Phillips is a grandmother of five young adults, all finding their way in life. Her kind husband and she have been married 58 years. She is a writer, artist and a good Samaritan.

WHAT IS SUCCESS?
Sally Sagen Lorentson

Understand your impact deepen your worth.

From my earliest years, I sought to understand success. Whether in crafting perfect chocolate chip cookies, writing essays for publication or breaking records in the swimming pool, I pursued excellence, striving for recognition on score sheets and critiques. Yet, over time, I realized success isn't merely about accolades or records that fade.

Through age, reflection and several fumbles along the way, I learned that maybe I'd been using the wrong measuring stick. Reflecting on life's journey, I've shifted focus. No longer fixated on grades or fleeting achievements (though still trying to perfect the chocolate chip cookie), I measure success by two measures: impact and worth. **Impact** is the splash – the fingerprints, the traces that I've been there and improved (or not) the lived experience of another. **Worth** is the value – the depth of that impact for me and for others. It's about the ripple effect of my actions – how deeply they touch others and enhance their lives.

Whether through work projects or family roles, I now ask, "Who benefits from what I do? How profound is that change?" In my work at a university, we often speak about "legacy" – seeking each day to ensure our legacy has an impact on the students we serve each day. Have you thought about what your legacy will be?

American writer Ralph Waldo Emerson perhaps said it best: "To leave the world a bit better, whether by a healthy child, a garden patch, or a redeemed social condition; to know even one life has breathed easier because you lived. This is to have succeeded."

Success is not defined by personal milestones alone. It's about making a meaningful difference, nurturing impact and embracing worth beyond superficial measures.

> *So, today, ask yourself, how are you making an impact? How are you deepening your worth? What specific steps are you able to take to reach this objective?*

Sally Sagen Lorentson, Ed.D., is a parent, a spouse, an exquisite baker and a higher education administrator. She enjoys the thrills and wonder of Disney theme parks, the joy of a baseball game and escaping in a great book.

IKIGAI

Fabian Pesci

Engage planning, patience and perseverance to find your life purpose.

The meaning of *ikigai*, in Japanese culture, is the concept that encourages people to discover what truly matters to them and to live a life filled with purpose and joy. I base my life on this concept all the time.

Find your purpose. Work on what you like, or work on what you are good at. Someone who is good at video games could become a designer of video games. If you love to cook, become a chef. If you love to entertain, become an event coordinator or event planner.

Life goes so fast, and it's not good to do a job and then not be happy. So, find your career, find the right person for you and have a hobby. When you have clarification on what you like or love, you will become successful.

Practice planning, patience, perseverance – these are the three big keys. I have worked for more than 20 years doing professional organizing. I have met so many families over the years. The majority are doing great from a financial and material situation. However, the majority are not happy. They fight with family or friends to get more or be more in control. They have lost their *ikigai*.

Money, power and fame will not bring happiness. When we die, the only thing we take with us is our memories of life. In the end, what is happiness? Happiness to me is sharing a meal with somebody you love, having a few great friends, taking a trip to a foreign country and having a furry pet.

Be happy with your achievements. Do not compare your life with others'. Practice with your life to be humble and kind. Be grateful about your life and health, and do not take that for granted.

FIGURE 3.12
This is me in my element - teaching a pottery class! This is what I love to do, and enjoy sharing this gift with others to help them create something of their own.

Never stop learning. In my 53 years of life, I have made so many mistakes and so many good decisions. They all make me who I am today. Do not be afraid to try. Think always positive about you, and never lose your *ikigai*.

What is the core of your "ikigai"? What will help strengthen this?

Fabian Pesci, born and raised in Argentina, worked as a sign language interpreter and then a professional organizer, created Fabu Pottery where he combines traditional textures on modern vessels and trays.

LOVING THE WORK YOU DO
Alison Wrynn

*Blending what you love to do with
your work and career is an ideal scenario.*

I have been incredibly fortunate to merge my two greatest joys – reading and sports – into a successful career. I'm not going to tell you I love going to work every day, but my work has allowed me to read about, participate in and watch sports, and it has been incredibly fulfilling!

My love of reading was fostered by my mother and my passion for sports by my father. My parents did not earn college degrees; my mother only took a few college courses, and my father, the child of immigrants, nearly completed an associate degree. He chose to enter the work world at a time when someone could still succeed without a college degree in engineering. Even though my parents did not have college degrees, they were clear that they wanted their children to go to college and find a career.

Even before I started kindergarten, my mother would take me to the elementary school library where she volunteered. I was put in the middle of all the bookshelves, given a book and told to "keep busy!" This encouraged me to learn to read at a young age.

I grew up loving sports and have been so fortunate to have the opportunity to have a career that has been focused on sport. My love of sport also taught me some tough lessons about equity as a little girl, as I was unable to play organized sport like my brothers (I grew up in the pre–Title IX era). But my dad still bought me baseball gloves and hockey sticks so I could play with the other kids in the neighborhood.

I became a high school physical education teacher and coach and then earned a Ph.D. with a focus on sport history. This allowed me to spend my days reading and teaching about sports. What a great way to make a living.

As you think about what you want to do with your future, think about how you can find a career that will allow you (as much as possible) to do something you love. These could be hobbies or classes in school.

What are the activities that bring you the greatest joy right now?

Alison Wrynn began her academic career with a B.S. in Physical Education from Springfield (MA) College, an M.A. in Physical Education from California State University, Long Beach and a Ph.D. in Human Biodynamics from the University of California, Berkeley. She served 17 years as a university faculty member and since 2016 has been a full-time university administrator focused on Academic and Student Affairs.

I DIDN'T WAKE UP TODAY TO BE AVERAGE
Nancy Hunter Denney

A daily personal mantra can change how you approach the time you've been given.

Average. Do you wake up every morning and say to yourself, "Today, I am striving to be a 'not out of the ordinary' human being," or are you among those of us with a powerful secret, a personal mantra that inspires effort, self-management and an optimistic outlook on life? Every day you get to make a choice. Every day you get to decide how to fulfill the external approximations of your capabilities or how to unleash a force found within the statement, "I didn't wake up today to be average!"

I've often been accused of having unrealistic expectations for myself and those I meet. I admit to wanting people to be more than they think they can be. I admit to suggesting that raising our expectations of others encourages their growth. I confess to believing when you strive for excellence, you honor those with less opportunity. You are demonstrating self-worth. You are trusting effort over making excuses. Average didn't put a man on the moon. Average won't find a cure for autism.

Ready to strive (or continue to strive) for excellence? Incorporate these five habits into your every day:

- Make a daily to-do list (i.e., prioritize actions and cross off items when completed).
- Pay attention to who is in your immediate environment and acknowledge them.
- Actively engage in ONLY productive behaviors that move you toward your goals.
- Follow a healthy routine (i.e., exercise, eat three meals a day at the same time and get at least seven hours of sleep).
- Check in with individuals who give you energy or insight.

Where will you be next year? Next week? Tomorrow? Include the simple mantra, "I didn't wake up today to be average!" to your morning thoughts and own the power it unleashes for the remainder of the day.

Nancy Hunter Denney has been sharing her original life and leadership strategies for over four decades in a variety of capacities, including higher education student affairs, professional speaking, authorship, publishing and directing a national leadership conference. She currently teaches public speaking at a college in Boston.

I ALWAYS FELT LIKE A MISFIT
Marian Stahl

Finding your own way, even as a misfit, can bring intense joy and meaning.

I remember being three years old, in a car, or maybe it was a truck, and "Vincent" by Don McLean came on the radio. I listened to that song and I cried, which earned me a punch in the arm and unkind words from my sibling. After that, when that song was on the radio, I would turn my head and look out at the stars as we drove and I would let the tears silently fall down my face. I didn't really know why I cried, but I did.

As I grew older, I tried to wear the right clothes, have the right hair. It seemed like the popular kids had everything figured out, so of course you wanted to be like them.

It took way too many years for me to look around and realize that it was okay to be the person I am. I finally realized that being a unique individual was so much better than fitting in. Plus, I have my adult life way more together than most people I know. Oh, I have my own issues, but then again, we all do.

I have learned to embrace that free-spirited artistic soul that I am. I am supposed to see things differently. I am supposed to see things that the average person does not. I have always felt deeply, had a strong sense of empathy and my brain works constantly. I am so grateful I am a misfit.

Being a creative person causes one to feel joy more intensely and sorrow more deeply. Successes are amplified, as are the hard times and failures. Our creative spirits are meant to use all of these moments to help the world see the depth of being and how that is a reflection of humanity. Not everyone will see, and many will not understand, but it is the job of the artist to be the messenger.

I am proud to be the person I am, the soul that I am and the misfit that I am. I am an artist. I am a messenger for humanity. Because I am a doer, I have become a leader in my community.

Identify ways in which you fit and don't fit with various parts of your life.

Marian Stahl Chamberlain is an artist. She is also a woodturner and carver, as well as a pastelist and printmaker with an intense love of art history.

REPLACING REACTION TRAPS WITH RESPONSE STRATEGIES

James Wilkinson

Authentic leaders know what they don't know AND own it.

As leaders, we are often asked questions we do not know the answer to. Not surprisingly, in these moments we still feel obliged to provide an answer. It's a natural transaction – question, answer, follow-up question, answer. But you need to understand that when you are unsure but still deliver a reactive answer, there are often negative impacts. This is why a *response strategy* is needed.

Here are some common reaction traps I've experienced:

- The shotgun approach – spewing out several answers in rapid succession, hoping one is correct (frustrating to listen to and folks quickly see through it)
- Pivoting to related topics where I'm more confident but not answering the actual question (again, frustrating and folks see through it)
- Using big words to impress with heightened vocabulary (demeaning)
- It's not my department (not taking ownership, evasive)

Eventually, I realized that not every question requires a full and complete answer in the moment. Today, I pause and consider each question and try to deliver intentional, thoughtful responses. I admit if I don't have a firm answer, but this doesn't cause me my credibility because I take ownership while showing respect and empathy.

Here are some go-to response strategies:

- Ask for clarity. (It sounds like you're asking about X; is that right?)
- Acknowledge their emotion. (You sound really upset. What happened?)
- Dig deeper. (That's a great question. Tell me more.)
- I don't know, but we'll find out. (My staff will follow up.)

Next, let them know next steps, and be sure what you say gets done:

- I'd like to help if I can.
- Let me see what I can do/what I can find out.
- Give me your contact information; I'll have my team get back to you.

Think of a time when you were asked a question and weren't satisfied with your response. How might your response have been better? What will you do differently?

James Wilkinson, M.A., CAE, has served for over 20 years as the chief executive at several nonprofit organizations and on the boards of several others. He is a contributing author to the upcoming anthology *Leadership DNA*.

Self-Care

Skills and Tools

In the journey of living, a common aim or goal is to have a long and healthy life. Although the proverbial "fountain of youth" does not really exist, many decisions about lifestyle are made on a regular basis. Faced with decisions about diet, exercise, sleep, relaxation, stress, body image and so much more, individuals decide how they want to live their lives. Coupled with factors that are inherited as well as those that are based on the environment and earlier decisions, an individual's journey toward healthy living is an ongoing and often challenging one.

Self-care encompasses narrow and broad awareness and skills on a variety of healthy living issues. What does it take to have a quality life in terms of one's physical, mental and emotional well-being? What are the habits and traits essential for thriving ideally and surviving at a minimum?

Although not designed as a primer on wellness choices or well-being issues, this section does highlight some of the perspectives and reflections of contributors regarding what an individual can do to take care of themselves. Highlighted are considerations for a quality life – as determined by each individual.

As implied with the title "Self-Care," the focus of this thematic area is on oneself. That is, the assumption is that each individual has the primary responsibility for their own development and well-being. This is increasingly true as one grows and through an older age for most. That is, when one is an infant, basic human needs are provided by parents and caregivers; as one grows into childhood and adolescence, greater opportunities for self-determination and independence arise. Through young adulthood and adulthood, these responsibilities transfer to the individual. During the years – the majority years of most individuals' lives – each individual has tremendous influence over numerous decisions and ultimately behaviors. This does not mean that everything can or should be done alone; so much interdependence and reliance on others remains (perhaps excepting living alone in the woods). As one encounters critical incidents, whether acute or chronic, reliance on others may become needed. And as an individual enters an advanced age, increased support and dependence on others will be likely.

DOI: 10.4324/9781003541080-4   **145**

SELF-CARE WITHIN A WELLNESS CONSTRUCT

The focus of the thematic area of Self-Care is on the numerous wellness dimensions. With Abraham Maslow's hierarchy of needs, the first two foundational items – physiological needs and safety needs – serve to illustrate the essential nature of the numerous self-care considerations for individuals. Overall, the focus of self-care is well illustrated in the various constructs of wellness. The National Wellness Institute highlights six dimensions: emotional, occupational, physical, social, intellectual and spiritual. Another framework adds environmental and financial dimensions, and yet another adds a cultural dimension. Some frameworks have fewer elements, and some blend a couple of dimensions into one. However these are designed, the important thing is that self-care, when seen in a wellness construct, is much more than taking care of one's physical body.

Thinking about the various dimensions, the physical one is certainly important. This is exemplified by how well one's body and mind are operating. To accomplish this, exercise (including stretching and recovery) is important. Also central to the body is diet and good nutrition. Of course, how diet and exercise work with an individual's constitutional factors is important, often based on factors such as body type, metabolism, allergies or intolerance to certain substances and more. Also having an impact on one's physical and mental self are decisions about drugs and alcohol, whether for medically prescribed purposes or personal reasons (such as self-medication, escape, recreation or relaxation). The impact of these decisions about substance use can affect any of the dimensions of wellness, all factors associated with self-care.

Other elements often found with self-care include decisions about safety (often linked to drug or alcohol misuse), whether as a prevention-oriented behavior or cautious outlook. Another element is sleep, an important factor for physical and mental nourishment. Stress management is incorporated within this thematic area, and linkages to relaxation and exercise are noteworthy. Time management is vital also, as it links with the overall balance of life and the range of personal and societal responsibilities.

Integrated within this area is balance. That will be determined by individuals as they face their lives and various opportunities. Individuals will prioritize how they manage the various elements found within the wellness constructs of their lives. This may be based on personal values as well as items of greater urgency. It may also be based on expediency as well as cost factors. Whatever the focus, individuals seek a life that is overall of a quality and fulfilling nature as they define it.

SELF-CARE AS A LIFELONG FEATURE

To engage in meaningful and appropriate self-care, some additional considerations are important. First, self-care is a lifelong process and one for which needs and issues change over time. Considerations important for young adults are paramount, as this is the time of life when adulthood is reached. For most young adults, it is a time when they are venturing out on their own, whether that is with attendance at college, enlistment in the military, employment in a full-time or part-time job, volunteering for some initiative, caregiving others, travel or other undertaking. This is a time when most young adults are living on their own or with others, away from the oversight and support of parents or guardians. For college students, many will live in the residence halls and then transition to off-campus living. For military, this may mean living in barracks or other communal settings.

Whatever the setting or circumstances, the challenges with self-care for young adults also present multiple opportunities for growth and development. Whether it is learning to cook, to clean, to manage finances, to organize time, to plan activities or other life pursuits, it is a time of intense learning. As young adults transition to later adulthood, middle age, older adulthood and then a senior citizen, needs continue to evolve. Plus, many issues and needs change over time with the natural features associated with the aging process.

In addition to different needs and issues that occur with aging, changes are also occurring with the natural structure and environment surrounding one's life. With technology and cultural changes as well as new desires and understanding, the need for adaptation continues. The issues young adults are faced with today are different from those of 20 years ago; similarly, the issues faced by young adults two decades from now will undoubtedly be different from those of today. With the existence of computers for personal use only four decades old and the existence of smartphones only two decades old, the needs as well as the opportunities surrounding self-care have changed. The emergence of social media as an increasing phenomenon requires different understanding than was needed just ten years ago.

Similarly, the latest science and discoveries in the medical and mental health worlds result in new protocols and standards for earlier identification and treatment of diseases. Greater understanding of causal factors, whether genetic, constitutional, environmental or otherwise, has implications for the prevention of harm and the promotion of well-being.

The important takeaway for individuals is to stay current with the latest knowledge based on quality research. It is also important to hold broad and relevant perspectives to maximize the individual potential that is typically sought. For example, with traditional Western medicine, certain protocols and procedures are identified and continue to evolve. Emerging into greater acceptance over recent decades has been the use of complementary and alternative protocols, something that continues to evolve with understanding, acceptance and utilization.

LINKAGE WITH OTHER THEMATIC AREAS

Self-care is clearly linked to the other six thematic areas found in this book. For example, priority has been given to the importance of optimism and hope within the medical field. This includes the use of placebos in studies examining the efficacy of various treatments and medicines to assess the extent to which one's disposition and attitude affect desired healthful outcomes. Optimism is also linked clearly with mental health, as that speaks to self-esteem and personal perspectives about the future. Similarly, the role of values is central to how self-care is applied. If an individual doesn't place a priority on the future, nor with personal improvement or living a full life (however one defines that), then much of the knowledge and many of the strategies will be for naught. The value placed on good science, on staying current, on consideration of new viewpoints and perspectives and on the overall quality of life help guide decisions and actions surrounding the range of self-care issues.

Self-care is not a solo activity. Although the primary responsibility for one's physical and mental well-being is with that individual, involvement of others is also critical. One dimension of this is with those with whom one has a relationship, such as a spouse or significant other, children or parents, work or school colleagues or others in one's life. The decisions and actions around self-care may have implications for these other individuals or groups and for the relationships themselves. Another dimension of the relationship element is the input provided by or consultation received from those with whom an individual has a relationship. This collaboration is often vital for the health of the relationship. The same considerations are relevant for the communities within which individuals find themselves; these community settings may have standards or expectations as well as values that are helpful for consideration of self-care decisions. With both of these – the individual relationships and the community settings – it is helpful for individuals to speak up with constructive feedback and reinforcement of others' positive and growth behaviors; such reinforcement helps sustain positive change for the individual and also helps strengthen the relationship and community feeling.

Clearly, the attention to nature and how that affects self-care is valuable. As seen in that section of this book, many individuals suggest that immersing oneself, whether partly or totally, in the natural world can be quite restorative as well as nourishing for the body, mind and spirit. The respect one shows for the natural world, whether through environmental initiatives, recycling or renewable resources, demonstrates care for one's surroundings. Similarly, the interrelationship with the service theme is such that individuals often attain positive feelings from their volunteering, their outreach, and their engagement with others in selfless ways. The issue is one of giving back to help boost those in need.

Overall, the interrelationship among all seven thematic areas is exemplified especially in the Self-Care arena. Each of these seven thematic areas works in concert with the other thematic areas, such as is found in a spiraling manner of continuous growth and regeneration.

CONCLUSION

This chapter encompasses so many elements helpful for individuals as they seek to live healthy and productive lives. Although not a specific guide to healthy living and encompassing the various elements of a wellness and well-being model, the over 50 contributors provide insights and recommendations designed to help individuals stay balanced and healthy. While that can also be accomplished with the guidance found in other thematic areas of this book (see especially Relationships and Nature), the focus in this chapter is more on the individual and their own routine decisions. The authors attend to mental health and the importance of love, they emphasize balance and patience, and they highlight both self-compassion and perseverance. Also included are insights regarding thinking as well as one's spirit. With their various backgrounds and cultures and the recommended reflections and proposed action steps for consideration, the reader will face numerous opportunities for growth and enhancement.

Messages What are key points or themes highlighted in the Legacy Letters within the Self-Care area?	
Reflections What are your thoughts and feelings about what is shared and recommended regarding Self-Care?	
Resources What individuals, groups, organizations or other information would help you better understand and apply recommendations in the Self-Care area?	
Commitments What are you willing to commit yourself to doing regarding the Self-Care theme, both in the near term and in the more distant future?	

FIGURE 4.1
Legacy Worksheet for Self-Care

EIGHT DOMAINS OF WELL-BEING
Giang T. Nguyen

Many factors contribute to our personal well-being; consider the roles that each of these plays in your own life.

We often hear about "wellness" and "well-being" (I prefer the latter perhaps because it implies some active personal engagement through the process of "being" well). What do we mean when we say these words? Some folks say, "I need to prioritize my wellness" when they simply mean, "I want to minimize my emotional anxiety and stress." My work at Harvard focuses on health and well-being for students and professionals. My colleagues and I often talk about well-being through a wider lens.

In my work and in my personal life, I strive to incorporate a multidimensional framework acknowledging that many factors simultaneously contribute to or detract from our well-being. These things can be organized into eight broad domains, and keeping each of these in mind throughout all stages of our lives can make a real difference in our well-being: (1) **Physical:** care for your body, including nutrition, sleep, exercise and following expert medical advice; (2) **Emotional:** take care of your mental health and accept the full range of emotions that make us human; (3) **Relational:** build and maintain positive and supportive connections with other people; (4) **Spiritual:** understand your personal mission and purpose, prioritizing your values, faith and moral compass; (5) **Environmental:** place yourself in clean, healthy settings and take good care of the earth around us; (6) **Vocational:** engage in work that is enriching and aligns with your strengths and interests; (7) **Financial:** build your understanding of how money works and be a good steward of your resources through wise economic decisions; (8) **Intellectual:** engage in lifelong learning, remain curious and focus on things that stimulate your mind.

Here are some final thoughts. First, your energy cannot be focused on all eight factors simultaneously; you may need to prioritize at particular points in time. Second, while your energy may largely focus on a particular domain, no other domains should be completely ignored. Through this broad awareness, you can take greater control over a life of balance.

Consider one factor you neglected lately and one thing you can do to address it.

Giang T. Nguyen is a family physician, public health professional and higher education administrator who has been on faculty at two Ivy League universities. Giang immigrated from Vietnam as a refugee, and is immensely grateful to all the people who walked before him and who have helped to shape his beautiful journey through life. He now lives in New England with his husband, Sean.

REFLECTIONS AFTER HALF A CENTURY
Joel M. Wagoner

Attending to these six suggestions will enrich the quality of your life.

Through my long and continuing career as a general dentist, I offer the following suggestions to those at the other end of their career and life activities. I have found these to be true for myself and with my work with thousands of patients over five decades of professional and community work.

- You must invest yourself in your life. Each new day offers an opportunity for adding value to the next, which offers more opportunities, and on it goes.
- You will struggle. The pain of struggling teaches you patience and improves your judgment. I have learned that good judgment comes from bad judgment. You will be grateful for the benefits of your struggles.
- Relationships are the basis for the most important aspects of your life. We are social creatures and we thrive on interpersonal contact. Deeper communication happens when you are physically present with another person than through seeing their image on a computer screen.
- Respect the dignity of everyone you meet. Personally, the mechanics in my father's farm machinery business taught me as much about life as those whom I met during my years in college and dental school. Your value system and worldview need the broadest possible foundation.
- Share your knowledge every day. Helping others to benefit from your experiences can be very rewarding and will encourage them to do the same.
- Be gentle with everyone, especially with yourself as you create and nurture the path you are on, using your yesterdays as a foundation for all of your tomorrows.

I have enjoyed sharing these few thoughts with you and hope they help provide some guidance as you move forward with your life.

Of these six suggestions, which ones can you commit yourself to doing every day? For those you did not select, what steps could you take to actually doing them?

Joel M. Wagoner grew up in a town of around 2,000 people, graduated from Duke University with a degree in psychology, earned a DDS degree from the University of North Carolina and spent two years in the U.S. Army Dental Corps before entering private practice, where he has spent over one-half century and continues his career as a general dentist.

DEALING WITH LIFE'S CHALLENGES
Joan W. Quinlan

With life's challenges, numerous helpful strategies exist to help you overcome them.

In the words of C. S. Lewis, "You can't go back and change the beginning, but you can start where you are and change the ending."

On life's path, it is common to experience bumps, obstacles and roadblocks. As an experienced traveler on this path, I have had my share of them: early sexual abuse, deaths of my father and brother in my 20s, domestic abuse and becoming a single mother with two babies, a traumatic brain injury from a fall that ended my career, deaths of my mother and husband seven months apart, overcoming substance use disorder and a freak traumatic incident.

So, what have all these struggles taught me that I can pass on to you?

- Accept that sometimes life is difficult, face the problem(s) and avoid numbing the pain with substances or other destructive habits.
- Learn about and use techniques such as mindfulness – or what I call "bodyfullness" – and allow yourself to feel the pain and struggle you may be or are facing. Tamping down your emotions will only result with them surfacing later in emotional and/or physical issues.
- Be present – defined by Jon Kabat Zin as "paying attention, on purpose, in the present moment, nonjudgmentally." I call it living intentionally – not living a distracted life (being in the past or worrying about the future).
- Consider energy modalities such as yoga, meditation, breathwork, sound healing, Reiki, reflexology and so forth. Their effectiveness is well researched, and I can attest to their success.
- Finally, learn the lessons that can come from any setback or life event. I can honestly say that in looking back at my events, they shaped my life in a way I never expected. Furthermore, I learned some important lessons that helped me grow emotionally and spiritually.

For me, the pain from my life's struggles prompted me to seek remedies through various energy medicine modalities.

As you think about challenges or obstacles in your life, what strategies or tools do you use to address them? What lessons can you learn from them?

Joan W. Quinlan, M.A., CTLC, is a highly experienced advocate for public health problem prevention and holistic living having worked at the U.S. Public Health Service for 30 years. She now aids individuals in overcoming their pain and suffering, empowering them to move forward through her expertise as a speaker, transformation life coach, sound healing practitioner, Reiki master, educator and a breathwork, meditation and yoga instructor.

PAYING ATTENTION
Brian Duffy

How we know what we know?

Have you ever wondered how successful people become successful? Do you think it is just luck? Is it the schools they attended? Is it the parents they had? Is it the friends they cultivated? Or is just a roll of the dice? The answer is yes and no! Luck, schools, parents, friends as well as randomness play a role and offer both advantages and disadvantages. So what is the answer to this binary dilemma?

I suggest that the one trait shared by successful people is what I call "paying attention." What is it? Paying attention is a whole-body experience – engaging our eyes, ears, nose, tongue and skin giving us our senses: sight, sound, smell, taste and touch. Other words to describe the senses include looking, listening, sniffing, savoring and feeling. Successful people engage with their senses fully. Specifically, successful people focus and focus at will. Who of us have never experienced a teacher telling their class to pay attention? Or the sports coach yelling, "Look, look, look at what is happening around you!" Pretty good advice.

Did you ever wonder how Steph Curry and Caitlin Clark hit their three-point shots from 27 and 28 feet? Of course, practice is a major component, but during a game, I offer that they are paying attention (focusing) using the senses most important to the shot's success. The vision to see the court that allows the shot and the touch to execute it. Or how about musicians: symphony orchestra players or jazz band members? What makes them successful at their craft? Again, the obvious is practice, but what makes the performance/show/musician successful? The players are looking, listening and feeling, each a little differently but paying attention, nonetheless. For the orchestra players, they are looking at their conductor and their musical score, hearing their instrument and listening to the orchestra and feeling the vibrations of their instrument whether it is string, reed, brass or percussion. The jazz player is communicating – that is, looking at bandmates, listening to the music being created and of course feeling the vibrations of their instrument.

Paying attention links our mind with our senses to allow us to experience the universe intellectually and physically.

Take a moment to become aware of your senses, and let them lead you to come to know what you know.

Brian Duffy – successfully retired due to paying attention.

BE GOOD TO YOURSELF
Eric S. Davidson

Finding ways to be sure you are being honest and kind about your positive qualities helps make life experiences much better.

As we paddled across the lake, I held back the tears. I had been eagerly looking forward to this adventure with my best friends for months. A week with best friends, communing in nature and fishing some of the world's cleanest waters. A trip to bring joy, not tears.

My friends are an exceptional group of individuals. I could go on for hours about how great they are. Growing up, my low self-esteem led me to believe that I was never their equal, always second to everyone. Any mistake, any error I would make in front of them would be magnified in my mind.

As we paddled, my negative self-talk was unrestrained. My "should haves" were spiraling out of control. I was being verbally and mentally abusive to myself. I was the only person beating me up, and I was being very successful. I had allowed my insecurities and fears to get my best. As I beat myself up, I only further fueled the monster I had created, making my trip less fun. I only realized how bad it had gotten when my canoe mate expressed concern for how poorly I was talking to myself.

That forced me to pause and truly reflect on the situation. My friends had been encouraging me. We were all sharing the trip's work equally. No one had called me the trip's weakest link. No one else was leading to my misery. At that moment, I gave myself grace, telling myself that my fears and anxieties were unfounded – that many of my fears and insecurities were nowhere near being reality. I wasn't perfect; lifelong habits of being self-negative are hard to break. But as I started being good to myself, I started enjoying my trip and the company of my friends. The trip got better and was one of my best life adventures!

Take a look at your own self-talk. What do you find? How can you make sure that you are being good to yourself?

Eric S. Davidson is resilient and is so thankful to Steve Perry for writing such a wonderful song reminding us to treat ourselves with kindness.

THE SILVER STANDARD
Joseph J. Cicala

To have a friend, you must be a friend.

One of my childhood heroes was the Lone Ranger. Set in the fanciful, fictional American West of the 19th century that captured so many imaginations in the 20th century, his adventures were staples of early radio and television programming for kids. Shooting only to wound, never to kill, with bullets of purest silver, his quest for justice rather than vengeance helped form the core of many a youngster's emerging moral code.

Frankly, those simple stories of good over evil were also fairly simplistic. They glossed over or nodded only slightly toward the deepest injustices on the frontier and in the larger society of the time. Still, the quest for justice is one we all share, and humble sources often lead to larger lessons. One emerges, I think, from a lesser-known aspect of the Masked Man's legend. It's the first tenet of the Lone Ranger Creed, composed for positive impact on impressionable young fans by creator Fran Striker: To have a friend, you must be a friend.

Like the stories, the statement is simple, but its implications are formidable. Imagine a world in which you actively seek, every day, to be a friend. Imagine further that because a true friend prioritizes others' needs, you take that first step not as others do unto you or as you think they'll do unto you, and certainly not as someone else tells you they'll do unto you but *as you would have them do unto you* . . . period. Imagine how many fewer people will be alone if you ride, however figuratively, with the Lone Ranger . . . and, so, how much further we all might blaze the trail to justice.

The Lone Ranger remains one of my heroes, in part because that first tenet still rings true. Like those bullets that were never used to kill, it's a silver standard that amplifies the golden rule.

> How might taking the first step guide your life going forward? What impacts might that have on others and on you? How do your own heroes, fictional or real, inspire you each day?

An award-winning professional, Dr. Joseph J. Cicala has served and studied across the sectors of American higher education. He is most proud of the contributions his students make to our world.

OPPORTUNITIES AWAITING
Dianne M. Strong

Numerous strategies can help prepare you to meet opportunities.

At age 80, I review my life. I recall the events that made me the kind and giving person I believe I have become. Raised in Connecticut in the '50s and '60s, I was the daughter of two pharmacists. Pharmacists are kind and caring people.

My parents knew that the one thing no one can steal from you is your education. They sent me to an all-girls boarding school for four years where I learned how to learn and how to respect others. With a bachelor's degree in journalism, a door opened to a free two-year master's in journalism.

As a certified Red Cross water safety instructor, on a snowy night, I answered a shopping center sign in Pennsylvania to become a scuba diver. This dramatically changed the direction of my life. Quickly, I learned that my best friend, my dive buddy, was meant to be my husband, Ron. As wives often do, I followed mine to the University of Guam seeking his master's degree in marine biology. As scuba divers, together we explored the world and its rich cultures and peoples, below and above the seas.

When invited to teach writing, I discovered my life's passion. It was to foster in others the joy of writing. By writing, we discover who we are. Second, we discover the power of writing, a skill that opens both minds and opportunities. As Dean of Students, I continued writing grants for substance abuse prevention or Trio programs to expand opportunities for others in education. I felt like a fulfilled individual, giving to others embarking on unknown adventures.

My advice includes the following:

- Listen more than you talk.
- Use journaling as a way to understand yourself and others.
- Seek perfection by always reading aloud and editing your work.
- Revise, revise, revise!
- Never fail to request help, as it is not a sign of weakness.

FIGURE 4.2
Scuba diving changed the course of my life. When doors opened, I walked through them for the last 55 years.

Identify ways you can best prepare yourself to meet existing and future opportunities.

Dianne M. Strong, Ed.D., is author of *Witness to War: Truk Lagoon's Master Diver Kimiuo Aisek* (Kickstarter, 2013) and served as Associate Professor of English and Applied Linguistics, University of Guam (retired).

TAKE TIME FOR MENTAL PICTURES
Jen Jacobsen

Stopping to take some mental pictures of what surrounds you can help anchor you.

I am well aware that I am old enough to be a parent to those for whom this book is intended. In considering what advice would have been valuable for me a few decades ago that's still relevant today, I cite the immortal words of the "philosopher" Ferris Bueller: "Life moves pretty fast. If you don't stop and look around once in a while, you could miss it." While these days I might identify more with Ferris's risk-averse best friend Cameron, the advice is still spot-on. Sometimes people, particularly emerging adults, can be so focused on the pressures around them and preparing for "real life" that it can be easy to forget that real life is also what's happening right now.

Ferris Bueller's Day Off came out a lifetime ago, yet pop culture returns to this theme again and again. If you've watched reruns of *The Office*, you'll remember Jim and Pam following her aunt's advice on their wedding day, by stopping to take "mental pictures" to capture the most important parts, because everything goes by so quickly. The same is true of so many meaningful times in our lives, even if we don't think about their importance at the time. What might you stop and take mental pictures of? And then, even more important, what do you do with these mental pictures? Hopefully, they nourish you, they ground you, they excite you, and they give you helpful perspectives about your life today and what it can be tomorrow.

More recently, Taylor Swift has something to say on the topic: "Make the friendship bracelets, take the moment and taste it." So this advice isn't just from a cynical Gen Xer talking about "kids on their phones these days"; it's always been something that's important and always something we've needed to be reminded to do. Find for yourself whatever resonates with you that gives a nudge to be in the moment, because life does move pretty fast.

> On each of the next few days, step back once per day and take a mental picture of what you see or are experiencing – and, if you'd like, write it down as well.

Jen Jacobsen has technically never left college. Since graduating, she has been in a number of roles supporting student well-being, first as a collegiate track and field/cross-country coach, then working in student affairs and health promotion and currently serving as the Executive Director of Health & Well-Being at Macalester College in St. Paul, Minnesota. Jen is enrolled in a doctoral program in public health so she can be part of two colleges simultaneously!

THINK SPIRIT FIRST!
Jeffrey W. Linkenbach

Think spirit first for a life filled with meaning, service and joy.

"Spirit" represents your essence, sacredness and vitality. The word "spirit" comes from the Latin word *spiritus*, meaning "breath" – what gives us life. By grounding your efforts in a positive spirit, you breathe life into your work and decisions. Spirit encompasses both mystical aspects that connect us to something greater and the practical essence of our identities – our innermost selves, values and authentic being (Sharan Merriam and Lisa M. Baumgartner, *Learning in Adulthood: A Comprehensive* Guide, 4th ed. [Wiley, 2020]). Spirit includes elements such as imagination, inspiration, intuition, kinesthetic knowledge, ongoing quest for insight, aha experiences, and the collective unconscious. Whether religious, think of spirit as the place inside you that experiences aliveness. Spirit serves as your guide to thought, awareness and action.

Practicing and learning to pay attention to spirit as your aliveness ensures you follow your unique calling, not a script or set of expectations from others. Honoring and connecting with your positive energy provide inspiration, intrinsic motivation, vision and purpose – moving you toward your deepest calling and positivity.

Spirit isn't merely a philosophical concept; it's a tangible guide for understanding and action. In every situation, Spirit moves first. As Gretchen M. Spreitzer and colleagues describe, transformative leaders focus on engaging with others, facing challenges head-on and making the most of our relationships and surroundings grow and become our best selves. Spirit is associated with direct experiences that touch our hearts and souls with a strong sense of purpose or connection. These experiences can be jaw-dropping moments when we see something truly amazing, feel deeply moved and realize there's much more to life than our own desires; Dacher Keltner and Jonathan Haidt say more on this. As documented by Martin E. P. Seligman, evidence suggests that in moments of joy – when we're truly engaged and find deeper meaning in what we do – we tend to be happier and healthier.

This broader understanding of spirit is essential for fostering a positive attitude and welcoming growth and lifelong learning as it transcends the small ego self in the pursuit of living a bigger story. As you face decisions, follow what makes you feel most alive. Think spirit first; follow your aliveness.

How can you best engage spirit in your life? What can you commit to doing to gain a greater experience of aliveness?

Jeffrey W. Linkenbach, Ed.D., is the Director and Research Scientist at the Montana Institute and has developed national award-winning programs that change community norms based on the science of the positive.

OWN YOUR MORNINGS!
Stephanie McGencey

You will feel more prepared if you start your day with some focused time for yourself.

Like many overstressed folks, I know exercise can help reduce stress. I enjoy exercising, but I don't have time to exercise. Exercise is NOT invigorating, so I don't work out in the morning. After a long day, I only have the energy to eat dinner and fall into bed with my to-do list running over my head like a cartoon bubble.

But recently, I decided to try something I read in a book over 20 years ago. *How to Be Like Women of Influence* shares intimate insights from several women I admire. I bought the book to "crack the code" on how to be successful without killing myself from overworking. Ironically, I read the book while on an international vacation I hoped would make me "unavailable" to work. The one life lesson that all the women profiled shared was the importance of rising early to do things like pray, meditate or exercise. I recently read another article about the *Miracle Morning*, which made me reconsider how I start my day.

For a month now, I have OWNED MY MORNINGS! I adopted the Miracle Morning approach (silence, affirmations, visualization, exercise, reading and scribing) and find that I am more relaxed, focused and centered when I start my day. Before my family, work, life and community obligations demand ALL my time, I spend about 90 minutes "getting myself together."

I have noticed that owning my mornings has helped me put my days into perspective. I realized that rushing headlong into my day led to an entire day of frenetic activity that often found me exhausted and wholly unsatisfied at how little I accomplished. I also realized how important it is to connect to ground myself in the peace and comfort my faith provides me.

I wish I had tapped into how empowering, calming and liberating it is to OWN MY MORNING years ago. I wasted so much time giving myself to others and my life pursuits that I forgot how important it is to put my mask on first! If you find that daily life feels like a race to exhaustion, try OWNING YOUR MORNING and see if it can help equip you to conquer your day!

What can you commit to doing – starting now – to "own your morning"?

Stephanie McGencey, Ph.D., is a strategic and thoughtful leader with 26 years of progressive experience working to advance holistic, evidence-based and strategic approaches to public policy analysis and program implementation. She leads the Women's Equity Center and Action Network to activate women of color changemakers to create responsive policy and practice environments.

RESILIENCE FOR MY PATH FORWARD
Sherrine D. Peyton

A visceral connection to the past can help motivate future directions.

My connection to the American dream is a complex tapestry woven with threads of resilience, struggle and a deep-rooted sense of heritage. Unlike the traditional narratives of immigrants seeking a better life in the land of opportunity, my family's origin story is a mosaic of oral tradition, historical records and the painful legacy of slavery that shapes my identity.

Delving into my family history, I had to navigate through slave manifests, Colored Troops Muster Rolls, the wills of enslavers and census data that sometimes only listed the gender and ages of the enslaved. Instead of boarding a ship with hopes of a brighter future, my forebears endured the horrors of slavery, their lives entwined with those of their oppressors. Unraveling the web of ownership and exploitation, I uncovered the names of families who held dominion over my ancestors, determining their fates with callous indifference.

This journey led me and a group of cousins to Mississippi, where the echoes of the past reverberated through the cotton fields and former slave cabins that still stood as a haunting reminder of bygone atrocities.

My ancestors' legacy, marked by struggles against oppression and injustice, informs my understanding of the American dream as a testament to endurance in the face of adversity.

I carry with me the burden of remembrance and the hope of a future shaped by the resilience of my lineage. The American dream, for me, is not just a pursuit of prosperity and success but a solemn vow to never forget the nightmares that forged the path to where I stand today.

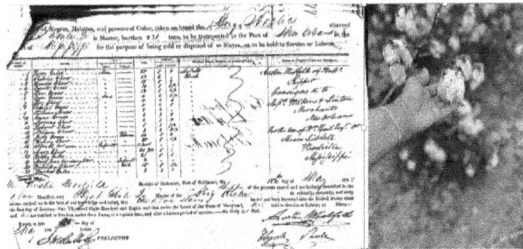

FIGURE 4.3

Two centuries separate these images: a manifest and me holding cotton from the same location of my ancestors in Mississippi.

Identify key features in your life, including your past and generations before, that ground, sustain and motivate you.

Sherrine D. Peyton is the founder of Peyton Consulting LLC, specializing in business development and innovative solutions for nonprofit organizations.

STOP, BREATHE AND TAKE TIME TO MAKE A PLAN
Tre Nelson

Take time to stop, breathe and make a strategic plan for your next steps in life.

In the rush of modern life, it's easy to make decisions on a whim, driven by immediate needs and pressures. However, some of the most critical choices in our lives require careful thought and strategic planning. Reflecting on my own journey, I've faced pivotal moments where taking the time to deliberate made all the difference. When I was working for Sigma Nu Fraternity, I spent six months weighing my post-job options: Should I return to Baton Rouge, Louisiana, to pursue a career in healthcare, or should I head to graduate school in Florida?

Fast forward. I have worked in Louisiana health care for five years and am close to finishing my MBA. I now look forward to another move to Baltimore for career and personal growth. I spent months considering a stay in Louisiana doing my current job or taking a risk to explore new opportunities. Five months of reflection allowed me to evaluate my desires, opportunities and the potential impact on my personal and professional growth. And the decision to move became clear to me.

For young adults, it's crucial to recognize the value of stopping, breathing and taking the time to plan. It's okay to be unsure about the future, but creating space to think deeply about your next steps can lead to more informed and fulfilling decisions. By making planning a deliberate part of your process, you can navigate life's transitions with greater clarity and confidence. Here are my suggested action steps that can help with personal planning:

1. Set aside dedicated time regularly to reflect on and write out your goals and decisions.
2. Break down your larger goals into manageable steps and create a timeline.
3. Seek advice and insights from mentors or trusted individuals who can provide different perspectives.

When you face decisions, what specific planning processes have you used in the past? How did they work for you? In the future, what will you actually use?

Tre Nelson is the Director of Economic Development and Community Initiatives at Ochsner Health. Recognized as part of the 2022 class of Forty Under 40 by the *Baton Rouge Business Report*, Tre focuses on driving economic growth and fostering community initiatives.

HEALTH, FUN AND MINDFULNESS
Betty Waters Straub

Being more mindful regarding your health will reap great rewards and can be fun too!

Can you see yourself five years from today? What will you be doing? Will someone be with you on your life path, a journey in finding your genuine purpose for living? How will you discover the authentic person living inside you? How can mindfulness be your best friend in discovering answers to these and other mind-boggling queries?

These questions provide a Harry Potter – like maze to explore. To help with the answers, Erik Erickson named multiple stages of development in his research (see *The Life Cycle Completed*) on the phases you might be in for a good while: Stage 5: Identity vs. Confusion, or Stage 6: Intimacy vs. Isolation. Understanding the common paths that you, friends and family are struggling with could be the very reason to use mindfulness, otherwise known as being deliberate in your thoughts and actions. Finding your identity requires support and encouragement; choosing to be with people who bolster your progress helps with self-confidence and pride in who you are, what you aspire to achieve, how you will focus on things that bring you joy and health.

Mindfulness requires a laser-sharp pathway to fully understand your current situation: a time of overwhelming stress, a decision that's driving you crazy, the coursework needed to complete your degree. Begin with a quiet place. Take deep, diaphragmatic breaths like singers do. Allow your gut instincts to assess consequences for your top three results. Notice how your body is reacting to each of these steps. One choice will emerge as a positive force that unites your emotions and intellect with your identity: who you are or who you want to be.

Being healthy, and having fun doing so, is a premise you can target to help with steps toward authenticity – being yourself, in all its glory, mistakes, sweet moments, failures and pure satisfaction. There will be many actions and intentions along your journey. Revel in each action you take, because you *will* find insight emerge every time you analyze the purpose you intend.

How can you practice more mindfulness with your own health? What or who can support you on this journey?

Betty Waters Straub, Ed.D., a former dean of student development, continues to engage with youth from infancy through college and early career stages. Her continued research in human behavior reveals lots of opportunities for students of all ages to identify their purpose for living a meaningful life . . . and having fun in the pursuit of the discovery.

BE YOUR BEST SELF!

Connie Boehm

Practicing self-care establishes a foundation to support your well-being and thriving!

Reflecting on my career, the most important thing that greatly changed over the years is my practice and promotion of self-care. I stumbled through my first year of college with my mental health and lived through suicide ideation. Others were so much better than me at academics, in their social life and in the way that they dressed. I was terribly homesick, but home was very challenging because my parents separated. No one reached out to me to help or recognized how much I was suffering. I ended up moving home and working at a bank. I stayed in bed for days, missed work, and gained 20 pounds. My doctor gave me a strong medication, but there was no mention of ways that I could help myself.

I finally took control of my life after lots of self-reflection and determination. I decided to transfer to a small, private college. I made friends quickly there; the faculty were very caring, and I was so incredibly fortunate to meet a wonderful mentor who encouraged my passion for working in college student wellness.

My mentor introduced me to the concept of wellness. She helped me practice self-compassion, reach out for help, depend on my support system, get moving physically, become involved on campus as a residence assistant and focus on my strengths. From that point, I helped thousands of students develop a sense of inner kindness, confidence to reach out for help academically and emotionally, bounce back after challenges, limit social media use and build healthy in-person connections.

Self-care is self-preservation. Here are five suggestions:

1. Find someone to serve as a mentor.
2. Monitor your well-being and recognize when you are struggling and get help.
3. Keep a gratitude journal that encourages you to focus on the positives.
4. Develop meaningful in-person connections.
5. Limit comparing yourself to others on social media.

What strategies do you use specifically to promote your own self-care? How would these five suggestions work for you?

Connie Boehm spent 40 years providing dynamic, relevant and responsive programming addressing the well-being of college students at comprehensive, Research-1 universities to liberal arts colleges and from Oregon to Ohio.

ADULTHOOD: THE BEAUTIFUL STRUGGLE
Aubrey Whitehead

Experience and self-reflection are necessary components to adulthood.

Your life will be tough, especially when transitioning into adulthood. Who am I? What's important? Why am I here? Spouse? Kids? What will I do for a living? Career? College? Major?

Everyone struggles in some way to answer these questions. Few know. Fewer reach their initial goals. Some will fulfill their childhood plans. Some will start down one path, only to pivot multiple times. Many have no idea where they want to go in life. Any and all of these scenarios are okay. Life is an adventure.

You will have wild successes. They will exceed what you thought possible. These times allow you to examine what led to your achievements. You will bump your head . . . trip . . . stumble . . . fall. Probably several times. You will question yourself and your trajectory. These times allow you to explore the lesson that life is teaching. You will have periods of malaise, boredom, indecision, floundering and uncertainty. You will doubt your motivation and drive. These times allow you to exploit these breaks to plan and do some self-reflection.

Imagine you get everything you want the first time. Where's the fun in that lifestyle? Imagine you score a basket every time you take a shot. Where's the space for development?

Rather than a puzzle to solve or a game to win, adulthood is about the ride. The peaks of triumph. The valleys of tribulation. The doldrums that offer opportunities for introspection and organization. Embrace and learn from them all. Commit to life and all its offerings. Know that all these experiences will challenge you. Mold you. Know that all these events are all necessary to create and refine you.

I wish for you a life that incentivizes and defies you. A life that rewards your efforts. A life that provides hard lessons. A life that allows for self-reflection. A life that challenges your belief system. So you either strengthen your beliefs, refine your understanding of your time here, or completely upend what you think and know. It is in this exploration that you will find an appreciation for life. You are just beginning. Now kick down the door and dive into life. You are ready! Enjoy!

Write down five key words or phrases that describe how you feel today about your life journey. Make a commitment to repeat this at least once a month.

Aubrey Whitehead holds a Ph.D. in educational psychology and is an assistant professor and leadership fellow at the Virginia Military Institute. His research focuses on the effect of close social groups on the motivation and degree persistence of college students.

SAVE YOURSELF BY INVESTING IN YOURSELF
Vaughn M. Roberts

Don't wait for someone else to invest in you!

I owe my financial success to, early in my years, attending various investment seminars on different topics such as stock market investing, real estate investing, company-matched 401(k)s and chatting with others who are financially successful. Sure, the math, science, language arts and history classes that I took helped get me into the profession I desired, but so many professionals are lacking the skills necessary on how to invest in themselves utilizing financial tools available to them. They are out there. Do as I did. Take the personal initiative and seek them out. Your own financial stability is not necessarily based on the type of employment you choose – it is how smartly you invest in yourself.

Starting with your first job, whether it be part time or full time, take a portion of each paycheck (I chose 20%) and stash it away for your future. If you get a raise, add that amount to your investments. Skip that expensive restaurant meal or other nonessential lavish expense every week or two. Trust me, you won't miss it! Over time, you will be amazed – and excited – about all that this does for your financial future.

In addition, talk to others in the job market. Ask them about those things they believe helped them toward their financial goals. Also, ask about those things they "wish they knew and had done before."

In my years through the public school system, I had the usual various topics drilled into me, such as math, science, language arts, history. All those classes were designed to help me become more well rounded, and would assist in getting me into college. They did just that. After nine years of college education and four degrees later, I ventured into the world of full-time employment. Law is my profession. Rest assured that my use of the word "profession" refers not only to those pursuing a career through a college program but also to those who seek a career in the so-called trades, whether it be through a formal technical program or on-the-job training. Regardless of your career path, these basic principles are applicable and critical to your financial future!

For you, my suggested mantra would be "Save yourself by investing in yourself."

What would a reasonable goal be for you today to help with your own saving?

Vaughn M. Roberts, Esq., after public school, obtained a B.S. degree, M.S. degree and ultimately a J.D. degree from the University of Miami. His career path includes serving in the U.S. Army and 32 years in law enforcement.

DO YOU BELIEVE IN YOURSELF OR IN FAIRY TALES?
Tracey Ford

Following your core values and beliefs helps you live a more authentic life.

All my young life, I had bought into the narrative from my family and peers that when I came of age, my Prince Charming would show up in my life, we'd fall in love, have kids, and live happily ever after. The end. But unfortunately, my life didn't turn out like a fairy tale.

I blindly allowed my partner to take control, assuming he had my best interests at heart. The problem was that he didn't. Looking back, the warning signs had been there. I was in a controlling and coercive relationship; however, instead of addressing the problems, I masked them. I started out by using amphetamines recreationally, but I soon became addicted and my life spiraled out of control. It came to a head when hospitalized with drug-induced psychosis.

It was the wake-up call I needed. I found myself at a fork in the road in my life. I believed I had two options: I could either go back into the unhealthy relationship or I could go it alone and focus on having a healthy relationship with myself. I chose the latter.

It didn't take me long to realize that I had been living a lie and had never allowed myself to be my authentic self.

But what did that mean in practice?

- It meant *me* getting honest with *myself.*
- I learned I needed to start expressing *my* true thoughts and emotions, making choices based on what resonates with *me* and not do just what was expected of me by others.
- I had to figure out what *my* core values, beliefs and desires were and live in alignment with them, even if they went against societal conventions.
- I had to start honoring *my* needs and boundaries, celebrating *my* uniqueness and living without masks or pretenses.

I finally got my fairy-tale ending, but it wasn't any Prince Charming that rescued me; it was myself. It was me honoring my needs and boundaries. It was me expressing my true thoughts and emotions, which significantly changed my relationships. It was me clarifying my core values, beliefs and desires and thus guiding my actions and decisions. It was me.

What does "living an authentic life" mean to you, and how closely do you feel you are living in alignment with it?

Tracey Ford lives in the United Kingdom and has worked in the addiction and recovery field for over 30 years. She passionately advocates people finding their true, authentic voice. www.haveawordwithyourself.co.uk.

FINDING STRENGTH IN VULNERABILITY
Dave Closson

Allowing yourself to be vulnerable is the first step toward building true resilience.

As a combat veteran, I was trained to be strong, unyielding and in control – qualities that served me well in combat but that became barriers when transitioning back to civilian life. For years, I believed that showing vulnerability was a sign of weakness, something that could compromise my friendships, my leadership and my effectiveness. But life has a way of teaching you that real strength isn't about being invincible; it's about being authentic, even when it means exposing your fears and uncertainties.

When I finally allowed myself to embrace vulnerability, it didn't just make me a better leader; it opened doors to some of the most meaningful experiences in my life. By letting go of the need to always be the strongest person in the room, a rock for others to lean on, I was able to form deeper connections with others. This shift paved the way for love – leading me to marry my incredible wife, who has been my partner in every sense of the word. Together, we've navigated the joys and challenges of life, including the beautiful journey of becoming parents.

Becoming a father has been one of the most profound experiences of my life. It's taught me that vulnerability isn't just about acknowledging your weaknesses; it's about embracing the fullness of life's experiences. In being open and honest with myself, my wife and my daughter, I aim to show my daughter that true strength comes from understanding and accepting yourself completely.

Recognize vulnerability as a gateway to deeper relationships and personal growth, enhancing both your personal and professional life.

Reflect on a moment when embracing vulnerability led to something positive in your life. Practice sharing your thoughts and feelings with someone you trust, even if it feels challenging.

Dave Closson, a combat veteran and owner of DJC Solutions, LLC, is an author, speaker, podcaster and entrepreneur. His journey from the battlefield to fatherhood illustrates the transformative power of embracing vulnerability.

WORRY
Mitchell Osborn

Worry is a prayer for the very thing you do not want to happen.

Research shows that individuals make an average of 35,000 choices every day. This begins from the moment we open our eyes and choose whether to hit the snooze alarm one or ten times before we actually choose to get out of bed. Then we may choose to get coffee first or the bathroom. When you continually make choices over and over, they become subconscious, and that is what we call a "habit."

One habit many of us have is worrying. We worry about silly things, and we worry about very important things. Either way, it's worry – and the effects of worrying can lead to high anxiety and illnesses.

There is an attentional phenomenon called target fixation that has been observed in individuals. This is when they become so fixated and focused on an object that they inadvertently hit or collide with the very thing they are trying to avoid – like fighter pilots in World War II crashing into their targets or motorcyclist hitting the only telephone pole on a curve as they navigate at a high rate of speed.

The beauty of being human is the gift of "choice." We ultimately have a choice where to place our attention and focus. The habit loop model tells us that when we are "triggered" by an event, we respond with a "behavior" and then receive the "reward" which creates the perpetual cycle. So with something about which we are worrying or wish to avoid, we must bring to our consciousness the habit and then make the choice to replace it with something different and more desirable.

When you find yourself worrying about something, first bring awareness to it. Acknowledge it, and then see if you can find an "opposite" of what you are worrying about and choose to hold that positive outcome as your new focus of your mind. For example, if you are worried about the crazy traffic and getting in a wreck, see yourself as a great driver, a defensive driver and whisper a gratitude for arriving at your destination early and finding a great parking spot right up close to the entrance.

With something small or insignificant that you worry about, flip the script of worry 180 degrees with the steps here and see how that works. Then do the same thing for something larger.

Mitchell Osborn has always been in a role or career where "coach" could describe him. Whether it was working with the body, mind or spirit, he's been there as a type of bridge to help people make their own informed choices and decisions.

FROM FEAR TO LOVE
Bob Rosen

Follow your fears and they will set you free.

Born into a lower middle-class family, I was embarrassed about my upbringing and anxious about financial insecurity. I never felt quite good enough and wondered whether I would ever be successful. So I hid my anxiety and overcompensated by trying to be the best little boy in the world.

I worked throughout my adolescence, received a full college scholarship, got my Ph.D. in clinical psychology by age 24, received a MacArthur Foundation grant by 30 and started my own company. Yet underneath the surface, I suffered from anxiety – and felt a big gap between who I was and who I wanted to be. Acknowledging I was gay only exacerbated my insecurity. My big lesson in this first phase of life was to befriend my imperfect past through the practice of forgiveness.

At age 30, my second phase of life garnered more successes. Professionally, I reached high up into the CEO suite – studying and advising CEOs, writing seven leadership books, building the company and traveling the world. *But* underneath these successes was an anxious guy – obsessed with being special and fearful of decline.

Then came the trouble – medical issues and surgeries and a ten-year opiate addiction from the surgeries. Fortunately, I had my husband, Jay, by my side for 41 years. The big aha at this stage was to temper my attachment to success and the future, stop worrying and strive to live in the present.

At age 60, I started the last third of my life with a dream. I'm a big dreamer, and this dream had me tied up by attachments that were holding me down like heavy baggage, like internal chains that kept me stuck in concrete. That dream helped me begin to see the light. I found myself, slowly but surely, shedding my unhealthy attachments and discovering positive aspirations that freed me. Now in recovery, I am discovering the power of vulnerability and imperfection, the importance of self-compassion and connection with others and being good enough. My deep sense of gratitude helped me to see what was good in my life – my health, partner, career and friends – and how to love freely and well.

I transformed my fears into love – love of myself, of others and in the world – bringing more self-awareness, courage, honesty and resilience.

What would it take to throw out your baggage and live a life of love and freedom?

Bob Rosen is a thought leader on healthy people and organizations. As a psychologist, *New York Times* best-selling author, researcher and business adviser, his work in personal and organizational change is recognized worldwide.

A MATTER OF TIME
Thurston Smith

An extremely valuable asset, if managed well, is time!

From a singular perspective, life is considered the most important thing on earth, as without it, nothing exists. Indeed, second to life itself, time is the most important thing we possess. Time is also among the most complex things we will ever encounter. Ironically, time is the only thing in life that you can have, not have, have too much of, have very little of, take and give away – all at the same time. Like life itself, time is something that should be respected, appreciated and managed with care.

Thinking further along these ideals, whether driving to a job interview or preparing for a midterm exam, time can either work in your favor or against it. It's all about how you manage it. We must learn to protect time. This means carefully managing our who, what, when, where, hows and whys, as well as guarding against the two greatest adversaries of time, complacency and procrastination. Complacency and procrastination are known to rob us of our time and have earned the notorious reputation as "dream busters." If you're not paying close attention, your plans for a new home, advanced degree, new job, car or new gym membership will all be in the rearview mirror (just like that).

Even our subtle, yet casual, movement through the revolving door at a local store requires timing. And even after entering the revolving door, you still need timing to exit, or you'll be going around in circles. This metaphor provides a great example about life: you must always know when and where to move.

If you grow to appreciate time and learn to manage it well, time may become one of your greatest friends. This means learning to devote yourself to the things that are of utmost importance to you: family, health, friends, community, colleagues, home, school and more. This involves setting priorities and maintaining them. Further, be sure to take time for yourself – including being patient with yourself.

FIGURE 4.4
Thurston Smith offers a lecture to "at-risk" youth.

Do an honest assessment of how you manage your time. What might you improve?

Thurston Smith, D.Min., MPA, LAC/S, CCS, is a retired civil servant with the U.S. Department of Veterans Affairs, an Associate Professor at Graceland University and a broadly recognized behavioral health expert.

LIFE ON *YOUR* TERMS
Craig Ullom

Consider these suggestions for ways you can navigate the transition to early adulthood by taking charge of your narrative.

During this transition to early adulthood, the stage is set for **you** to write the next chapter of **your** life. Self-authorship is an opportunity to further define and fully embrace who you are and what you aspire to be. It's time to shift from what others want for you to what you want for yourself.

You are in a space of transition full of opportunities and obstacles – and choices to be made. As you prepare to make those choices and create that next life chapter, here are some things to consider:

- Show up and be present.
- Be open to possibilities of new friendships, new ways of doing things and different perspectives.
- Taking risks is important to move out of your comfort zone. Just be thoughtful in taking them.
- Lean into your intuition. Pause. Breathe. Reflect. Then choose.
- Surround yourself with people who will honor and respect who you are.
- Allow others to challenge you to consider ways of being that you had not considered.
- Listen to perspectives that are different than yours, even if it is uncomfortable.
- Embrace people who unconditionally support and care about you and the choices you make.
- Respect yourself and your fellow travelers.
- Be there for others and allow others to be there for you.
- Invest your time and energy wisely. Once you use this moment, it is no longer available to you.
- There are many resources available to you. It is up to you to ask for them.
- Leverage your privilege to do good in a world that calls for your gifts.
- Make a difference. Be more than a pedestrian. Make an impact.
- Stretch to go beyond what you think you are capable of.
- Enjoy the journey of life – on your terms.

Take a moment to envision your ideal self. Focus on what you want independent of what others want for you. Put that in writing, look at it often and refine it as you continue your life journey. Use that vision as a foundation for making choices as you explore the many opportunities before you.

Craig Ullom has dedicated his career to working with college students as an educator inside and outside of the classroom assisting and supporting them as they navigate life transitions.

TAKING CARE OF YOU
John Welty

It is important to choose some form of exercise or self-care that will help you take care of yourself.

As you address the future, it is important that you choose something that you can do that helps you prepare for each day. It may be meditation, yoga, exercise or something fun. It should be something that you do every day regardless of what you face in a given day. Nothing should get in the way of the activity that you choose. For me, it was running, which turned into jogging as I grew older and is now walking fast on the treadmill as my knees gave way in my later years.

In my earlier years, I would get up and jog three to five miles. This was a special time of the day for me as I could think about what I needed to do that day. It provided physical exercise that was very helpful to me as I went about the day's activity. It also provided a sense of accomplishment.

In my younger years, it was not easy to maintain the discipline of a daily run. Somehow, I felt that I could do without the exercise because I was in good shape and there were more important things to do. However, I soon learned how important this exercise time was for me every morning. If I did not get my run in, I often felt sluggish or not ready for the day.

As I progressed in my career, this daily habit became even more important as I faced increased demands on my time and stress in my work. I believe the 30–45 minutes that I devoted to myself multiplied my effectiveness exponentially.

Thus, it is important to choose what you want to do to take care of you. Decide what you can do that helps you prepare for a day and gives you a sense of accomplishment. Develop the discipline to do it regularly. Nothing should get in the way of doing what you have chosen to do.

If you take care of yourself, you will be much more effective in working with others and maximizing your ability to perform!

Decide what you will do to take care of yourself.

John Welty began his professional career in student affairs work before serving as President of Indiana University of Pennsylvania (7 years) and Fresno State (22 years). He has served as Senior Associate for AASCU Consulting for the past 11 years.

BE PATIENT WITH YOURSELF
Gene G. Lamke

Each life is a unique journey and unfolds in its own due course and time frame, so be patient with yourself.

I hear young adults today quite often express fear that they are falling behind. They feel a need to keep up and "be like everyone else.'" They want success and they want it now. They assume they're a failure because they haven't achieved success compared to others their age. And with the pace of the world becoming increasingly faster, the speed of change may actually heighten their sense of needing to keep up and be on a similar life path. According to Dr. Nigel Barber, an evolutionary psychologist, "We live in an increasingly fast-paced world where communications are instantaneous. Even if the pace of life is speeding up, this does not mean that we must choose to be hurried."

Are you hurrying through life just to keep up with your peers, constantly comparing yourself to your high school and college classmates or young adult friends of similar age? Are they getting ahead of you with their careers or occupations, making more money, getting married or in significant relationships, while you're still figuring out what you want to be and what you want out of life?

Each of us is on our own journey through life, and it requires that we maintain self-confidence and self-esteem as we follow our path, even if it's not the same path and time frame as our peers. This requires patience with oneself. William Langland wrote in is his poem "Piers Plowman" that "patience is a virtue." As a professor who worked with young adults for decades, I witnessed far too many young people stressed out and anxious because they believed they were falling behind.

Young adults benefit from understanding and appreciating that as individuals, we are unique and molded by our circumstances, and in most cases, these circumstances determine how we progress through life. I believe individuals reach their goals by being patient and positive with themselves while continuing to put forth the effort to achieve their dreams and goals.

As has been widely said, "You only fail when you stop trying." It is important to continue to pursue your goals in spite of obstacles in your life.

Are you patient with yourself and persevering in working to achieve your goals? What can you do to improve these traits?

Gene G. Lamke is a Professor Emeritus in Recreation, Parks, Tourism and Hospitality at San Diego State University. He taught for over 50 years in the classroom as well as served as Director of Freshman Success Programs for several years. He continues to work with numerous students and graduates in an ad hoc manner.

BRINGING DESIGN THINKING
TO YOUR WORK AND YOUR LIFE

Alex Williams

If you've ever felt confused or fatigued when solving problems, consider design thinking!

When I was in graduate school, I stumbled upon a methodology that was growing in popularity in education: design thinking. Historically used by engineers and product developers, design thinking deconstructs problem-solving into separate but interdependent steps: (1) discover the problem, (2) define it, (3) develop a potential solution, (4) then iterate and deliver it. This approach separates ideation for problems and solutions, as well as separating the generation and evaluation of those ideas. It is multidimensional: as a methodology, it offers tested and replicable tools to navigate a problem-solving process; as a mindset, it challenges us to approach the world with attitudes, behaviors and beliefs of a problem solver.

In addition to helping me solve problems and be a problem solver, design thinking is also how I approach collaboration, whether at work or in life. Too often, trying to solve a problem feels like trying to shove every tool at our disposal through a narrow door. We've all been there, in the meeting dedicated to brainstorming how to deal with something that devolves into a chaotic spewing of thoughts, opinions, ideas, concerns and so forth. Decades ago, organizational theorists Michael D. Cohen, James G. March and Johan P. Olsen referred to this amalgamation of problems, solutions and decisions as "the garbage can theory." Design thinking provides an antidote to this organizational chaos, intentionally separating "What is the problem?" from "What is the solution?" as well as separating "What should be?" from "What could be?" Whenever I find myself, my team or my students to be stuck, I start to apply design thinking to avoid devolving to the garbage can and instead to feel more satisfied in our collaborations.

I hope you take away two thoughts. First, I hope you will experiment, in part or in whole, ways of learning and applying design thinking. Second, I hope it inspires you to find your own "thinking," to consider how you view, understand and approach problems in the world. I hope this intentional experimentation and metacognition allows you to find more productivity and satisfaction in your life and work. Happy problem-solving!

How do you solve problems? Do you find your approach satisfying or leave you wanting more?

Alex Williams is a career services and experiential learning professional at the University of Louisville. He lives with his wife and two sons in Kentucky.

SETBACKS ARE JUST PLOT TWISTS
Tara Johnson

Your past may have set the stage, but it's how you rise that steals the show.

You don't need a perfect past to create a great future. Starting from age 15, I struggled with my identity and the chaos, violence and instability of my childhood home. I utilized alcohol as a coping mechanism. Later being diagnosed with alcohol use disorder, I discovered I was trying to fit in and live a life that wasn't really mine. I was pretending – hiding my true self – leading to more challenges. Much of my struggle was the fear of facing a past I wasn't proud of. But eventually, I turned my life around. You don't have to come from greatness to achieve it. What matters is how you rise after you've fallen, and every step back is just setting you up for a bigger leap forward.

It took time and a lot of setbacks before I found the courage to turn things around. I had to face my mistakes, stop hiding behind excuses and focus on one thing: building a better future, even if I felt like my past had messed everything up. I have found power in confronting my own mixed-up past; this started with enlisting in the military. Later, this would mean acknowledging where I had played the largest part in my own suffering and making active changes – like making more aligned decisions with who I was, not what others wanted. I have become a better mom, started my own business, obtained professional licenses, run half marathons and continuously reach my hand back out to the person behind me still struggling, always being a lighthouse for those lost.

We all have challenges, especially when transitioning into adulthood. Maybe you feel like your past mistakes define you or that the road ahead is too hard. But you can overcome it. Whether you're finishing high school, entering college or just trying to figure out your next move, the key is not where you've been but where you're going.

So what does this mean for you?

- Your past doesn't define your future. You always have the power to make a fresh start.
- Adversity can be fuel. Use your challenges to push you toward your goals, not hold you back.
- Authenticity is everything. Embrace your real story, the good and the bad.

Think of a setback you've faced recently. What can you learn from that?

Tara Johnson is a mother, avid runner, influencer, veteran of the United States Navy and, most important, actively in recovery using her mistakes to mold a better future for others, determined to leave a legacy of impact and change.

YOU MATTER TOO
Emmy Knowles

Take care of yourself along the way.

I am where I am today because of the community that surrounded me as a teen. I was so grateful for all the love and light poured into me that I thought it was my duty to give it back. I chose social work as my professional path in the eighth grade and vowed my life to lifting up others. The issue is that if you constantly give everyone everything you have, you quickly have nothing left; I discovered that at the very young age of 26. I was already wiped out, and over the next five years, I had to work hard on finding balance between living up to my self-proclaimed purpose and ensuring I was doing what I needed to do to keep living. Life happens outside of work, even if the work feeds our soul.

I hate the phrase "self-care." To me, it's become about expensive things and bubble baths. But self-care is really so much more. It can be taking a walk, saying no, going to bed, taking a lunch break, taking a shower; it can be anything and everything that helps you feel like you. Self-care includes the boundaries you set, the values you embrace and the community you have around you.

It's okay to care for yourself while also serving others. It's okay to be tired and need a break. It's okay to not tie your worth to your productivity. It's okay to feel confused and need to reevaluate. It's okay to make mistakes and learn from them. It's okay to live life on your own timeline and not the one society has made up. It's okay if you don't know what you want your future to look like yet. It's okay to be angry in a job you love. It's okay, my friend. You got this.

As you begin to plan your career or future pathway, it's vital to always have a self-care plan in place. I urge you to create one, to write it in your calendar, and to check in every few months that it's working for you. As you create your plan, check out the seven types of rest, the eight dimensions of wellness, and the social change ecosystem framework. Think about what brings you joy and remember it's okay to say no.

Take a moment to reflect on your self-care. What small steps can you start today to better prioritize your well-being?

Emmy Oakley Knowles (she/her), MSW, is a macro social worker with a deep love for nonprofit work! She is a nature lover, dog mom and wellness educator and passionate about bringing love and light into the work she does.

A CHANGED LIFE WORTH LIVING
Phil McCabe

Listen to your innermost feelings and engage others to provide support.

In our society, it is often assumed that everyone is straight or heterosexual (meaning they are only attracted to people of a different gender). It is also assumed that we all experience attraction in the same way. What if you don't think you are just like everyone else?

My story begins growing up in the '60s. Being gay was rarely actually talked about except with whispers and giggles; jokes and stories mocked effeminate men or butch women. I never read a novel or saw a movie that showed a person just living their life and who happened to be gay.

Throughout my youth, I did not know any openly gay individuals, leading to a sense of isolation, particularly when my peers began to exhibit interest in female companions. To align with societal expectations, I entered into romantic relationships with women – anything to not call attention to my greatest fear: that I might be gay.

The burden of keeping a secret about my inner turmoil was overwhelming. I lived with anxiety and fear. I had thoughts of suicide, believing that if anyone discovered the truth about me, death would be the only solution. I went to my college library looking for some clarity. Unfortunately, there were few resources; the books were listed under abnormal psychology.

I found comfort in drinking alcohol; drinking calmed me, gave me courage and helped me to fantasize about a different life. Alcohol helped me to forget the lie I was living. The plus to all this: under the influence of alcohol, I began to venture out into gay bars. I met people who talked about being lesbian and gay. I met bisexual and trans-identified individuals who, in a safe environment, were able to be themselves. I had a dual existence that I kept separate. It was a juggling act, and I had difficulty keeping all the balls in motion.

I continued my pursuit, and slowly, little pieces of the puzzle started to fall into place. I eventually found a group of people who supported others with coming out. I no longer felt alone.

I knew there were things I needed to change about my life. I slowly began the process of living an authentic life. I am very grateful I found individuals who affirmed each other, raised our consciousness, found our voice and fought oppression of individuals and institutions.

Where can you – or others in your life – find support for addressing important issues?

Philip T. McCabe, CSW, CAS, CDVC, DRCC, has been a health educator at Rutgers School of Public Health since 2000. He also serves as the President of NALGAP: The Association of Lesbian, Gay, Bisexual, Transgender Addiction Professionals and Their Allies.

TRUE GRIT
Nancy Sprenger

Helpful for personal growth is having the courage to try new experiences.

When my son was in first grade, his teacher asked me to come in for a parent-teacher conference. His teacher shared her observations of my son's classroom behaviors. Although he was testing fine, he was not taking risks in her class. In my view, this seemed contrary to being a good student in her class. She explained that he needed to be curious, to ask questions and to share his perspectives on the subject matter. My son had been out of school for a few weeks due to being sick with meningitis. I did not realize he was self-conscious of being behind in class compared to his peers and that he was concerned about being ridiculed by his peers, so he kept quiet in class. I also discovered that he perceived his illness would always define him as being less of a person than his peers.

Thankfully, this new insight helped me teach my son how to reframe a setback as a learning opportunity and thus to be able to develop new skills. In some respect, I had viewed his behavior as simple shyness. I helped him develop a curious mindset, to think about things from different perspectives and to normalize asking questions. His teacher helped me instill in my son a sense of perseverance.

My son has since faced many obstacles in his life; however, he has learned to sit with uncomfortable emotions for some time and then consider different options that move him forward in a positive direction.

In my experience as a college counselor, successful people learn to rebound from frustrations, avoid negative self-talk and have the courage to try new experiences. They have the muscle memory to push past everyday obstacles. These people will find a more enriching journey when they ask questions, face challenges as opportunities rather than knockdowns and use pain as the motivational strength to persevere through any hardship. Mastering the art of stepping outside your comfort zone and taking risks will improve your personal growth – and never giving up is "true grit."

What types of things make you uncomfortable? What can you do to be prepared to take risks in appropriate ways? Who can help with that process?

Nancy Schulte Sprenger is a retired student affairs administrator having served as a mental health clinician at Louisiana State University, George Mason University and Shenandoah University.

MANAGING SELF-CRITICISM
John Watson

It's important to find ways to accommodate imperfections and negative self-judgment.

To my fellow overthinkers who feel like your brain doesn't slow down, I bet you find some of those thoughts are positive and productive and others are self-critical and judgmental. Sometimes our mind is a safe and familiar place to be, and other times it's not! I often feel that those self-critical thoughts might help me reflect and do things differently or even better; and sometimes that happens. Other times it just doesn't work out that way. Sometimes my inner critic gets the best of me and I get stuck in that place of self-criticism, frustration and inner anger. If that goes on too long and unchecked, I start to feel a sense of failure and even shame might creep in. I push those feelings aside and tell myself it is no big deal and just to move on. For an overthinker or a perfectionist, that often doesn't work.

I do find that if and when I share my thoughts, others tell me I am being too hard on myself or that my expectations are too high. I may also hear that I am being unrealistic in my desire to get things right, not even perfect, just right! I bet you have heard that as well.

If and when I hear this same kind of self-critique or negative self-talk experienced by others, it is easy for me to say things like, "Don't be so hard on yourself," "Be kind" and "Show yourself a little grace." In other words, I suggest that they forgive themselves for those little moments of imperfection. When I can do that for myself, the benefits are wonderful! What helps me is to get away from my black-and-white thinking and stop using phrases like "I should have" and "Since I didn't, I failed."

To help yourself, try to use more flexible phrases like "I would like to, but if not, I sure got close and maybe I've learned something" or "I really did my best, but the outcome may be out of my control." I promise, with some practice, this will allow you to be kind to yourself and decrease achievement-related anxiety.

Take a careful look at your own self-talk, and identify ways you can be more forgiving of your imperfections.

John Watson currently is serving as the behavioral health supervisor for an expansion program with Lutheran Family and Children's Services of Missouri. Prior to this, John spent 25 years working in behavioral/mental health and alcohol and other drug abuse prevention in higher education serving as a program director and assistant professor.

FINDING THE LIGHT OF HOPE AND COURAGE INSIDE YOU

Rita Chi-Ying Chung

Finding your own light of hope, courage, strength and resiliency is the road toward a successful quality life.

The multitude of times that I have been told "You're a failure" and "You will NEVER have much success in life," accompanied by laughter and mockery after each failure that became an overwhelming tsunami effect making me feel like retreating and hiding from the world. . . . Yet, there was something deep inside of me, a distant light, that told me, "No. Don't let them define who you are. You are not who they say you are."

As the years went by, the light was fading. I felt the light dimming and going out as I internalized what others thought of me. I still had a chance to prove to myself and others that I am not what they labeled me as. I knew if I did not have the courage now to break out of the vicious cycle, I might as well sign my own death warrant and be a lifelong failure. What did I have to lose? If I failed trying to break free, I would be in the same situation.

You too have a light inside of you. The light of courage, strength and resiliency. Don't let that light burn out! I can proudly announce to the world that I am not that person others thought I would be. I feel proud of myself, I feel comfortable in my own skin and, more important, I believe in myself. I believe you can find the courage to pursue your dreams. Have the courage to go for it!

As you do this, find a safe peaceful space to reflect and find the light of courage. Identify ways that you can stop the negative chatting in your mind and focus on the positive. Reflect on what your gut feeling is telling you about yourself. Identify ways that you can turn your failures into learning moments and reframe them as steps toward courage. Finally, identify ways you can be kind to yourself.

Write down three things that can provide an internal light, and how to keep it burning.

危機

FIGURE 4.5
The Chinese character for Crisis is comprised of the characters "Danger" and "Opportunity." According to Chinese philosophy crisis is not necessarily viewed as negative, rather as an opportunity that can arise from a crisis. It is a matter of having the Courage to do so.

Rita Chi-Ying Chung is a Professor Emerita at George Mason University. She has received multiple national and international awards for her work in social justice and human rights, been an expert witness and has worked throughout the world as an invited speaker and consultant.

ODE TO A CACTUS
Thomas Hall

Self-care relies on trust and perseverance.

Cacti are known to withstand harsh climates, particularly in arid and desert regions where water is scarce. Because cacti thrive in harsh conditions, they embody resilience and unconditional and enduring love. "Ode to a Cactus" describes my awe of people who are grounded as opposed to those who, like tumbleweeds, drift along or, like annuals, bloom for a season and die away. I penned this poem during a period of loss.

Self-care starts with self. Following those who think they have the answers is tempting. Yet, like annuals, their bloom does not last. Trust your inner cactus and persist. Listen to those who listen to you. Embrace your desert and trust you have the power to hold on in difficult times.

Ode to a Cactus
In harsh deserts, you make your home,
Wind, rain, and scorching sun etch their effects on you.
But you stand alone in desolate places,
Enduring, proud, and tall among the annuals.
Tumbleweeds come and go, driven by the wind.
But your roots are firm,
Holding steadfast to solid ground,
Entrenched below the sandy surface.
Fate has transplanted some of your kin to cities,
Ornamental symbols of the free-spirited desert,
But appreciated at a safe distance.
Those who misunderstand your ways,
See your prickly nature,
Not your persistence in harsh climates
Yet, you know the true nature of your being.
Soaring upwards to the sky.
You inspire awe in the hearts of those whose roots are shallow.
You embrace your home in desert places.
Some question the solitude of your ways.
Yet, you are proud of your place in this wasteland.
As the fiery sun sinks into the sand,
A gracious silhouette adorns the skyline,
Tonight, a canopy of stars shines upon you,
And peace fills the heart of those who sojourn with you.

In what ways does this ode resonate for you? What makes up your inner cactus?

Thomas Hall, Ph.D., is a clinical social worker and university researcher.

PRESERVING MENTAL HEALTH
Victoria Rapadas

Achieving your goals shouldn't cost you your mental health.

Born and raised on the island of Guam, I'm a graduate from the Academy of Our Lady of Guam and now a biology student at Saint Mary's College of California. If there is one thing I learned in life this early on at 18 years old, it is that your mental health shouldn't be the price you pay to achieve your goals.

As an ambitious young woman, I thought that I was unstoppable. I took a number of AP and honors courses maintaining a 4.4 to 4.5 GPA throughout high school, on top of student government and captaining two competitive sports teams.

When my list of responsibilities grew and the workload added up, it seemed never ending. My meetings and practices ran late, with games even later. I slept on average at least five to six hours a night, running on coffee and energy drinks to sit upright in class. Whenever I traveled during the school year, I spent my free time on homework – I would finish my assignments on the go, study for tests on the plane and write my college applications while waiting for my next basketball game. This was just the half of it.

Before I knew it, I was burned out.

I tore myself apart by setting unrealistic expectations for myself to succeed. My coaches told me, "You're either all in, or you're all out." If I truly wanted to become great, my heart had to be all in with one thing or another.

My advice to you is to continue to stay grounded as you strive for success. There is so much power in keeping your mental health in check. Take a step back and take it day by day. To my fellow overachievers, remind yourself that you don't only have to rely on yourself for comfort and support and that it's okay to turn to others around you. You don't have to do it alone.

Know that you are capable of so much more than you think. You should be realistic with what you can and can't accomplish, but be comfortable with being uncomfortable.

Thinking about expectations for yourself, which ones appear realistic, and which ones appear unrealistic? What can you do to resolve these to have a healthy and appropriate balance?

Victoria Rapadas (she/her/hers) is an 18-year-old from Asan-Maina, Guam, currently staying in Moraga, California, for school. As a Filipino Chamoru woman who identifies as an Asian American Pacific Islander, she is interested in expanding diversity in the health-care industry and giving back to her community through science and service.

BRINGING WU WEI TO LIFE
Luis Feigenbaum

Incorporating a more natural approach to life helps with higher quality outcomes and a more enjoyable journey.

In a fast-paced world where ambition often drives us to force outcomes, I discovered the profound wisdom of wu wei, or effortless action. The principle of wu wei originates from Taoism, a philosophical and spiritual tradition rooted in ancient Chinese thought. The term itself translates to "nonaction" or "effortless action," and it emphasizes the idea of aligning one's actions with the natural flow of the universe rather than forcing outcomes through sheer will.

Early in my career, I aspired for promotion, but I noticed the more I tried to force opportunities, the more elusive they became. Instead of relentlessly pursuing recognition, I chose to focus on preparing myself . . . for whatever the future might bring. I engaged in continuous learning, sought mentorship and embraced opportunities for growth without the pressure of immediate results. By enhancing my skills and knowledge, I positioned myself as an asset to my team and organization, demonstrating my commitment to my role rather than my desire for advancement.

As time went on, I observed that my efforts were not in vain. Colleagues began to recognize my contributions organically, and I found myself in conversations about leadership opportunities without having to campaign for them. This experience reinforced the idea that by practicing wu wei, I allowed my growth to come to fruition naturally. When the right moment for promotion presented itself, I was ready, not because I forced my way into the spotlight but because I had cultivated the qualities and skills necessary.

Reflecting on this journey, I realized that embracing wu wei not only alleviated the stress of relentless pursuit but also deepened my connection to my work and colleagues. The most fulfilling accomplishments often arise when we align our actions with our values and trust the process, allowing our true potential to shine through effortlessly. I learned that sometimes the best path forward is to simply be prepared and let life unfold at its own pace.

What lessons can you take to improve the quality and direction of your life?

Luis Alejandro Feigenbaum is the Senior Associate Athletics Director for Performance, Health and Wellness, the Program Director for the University of Miami Sports Physical Therapy Residency, and a Clinical Associate Professor in the Department of Physical Therapy at the Miller School of Medicine. He is a two-time graduate of the University of Miami. He also earned his Doctor of Physical Therapy in 2011 from Temple University.

THE VALUE OF GAMES
Cesar R. Torres

Incorporate as many games as possible into your life.

Although games are almost omnipresent in contemporary society, there is a pronounced tendency to consider them as inane or frivolous activities. They are typically recommended, tolerated or prescribed for those who have plenty of leisure time and do not need to engage in what is assumed to be the serious business of life. That includes children and retirees. An exception comprises those who earn a living partaking in games, such as professional athletes or chess players. You most probably have experienced this approach to games while growing up. The more responsibilities you had, the less you were given license to engage at length in games.

An alternative view of games moves them from the periphery of life to its center, turning them into the cornerstone of good living. Following the ideas of philosopher Bernard Suits, this view understands games as artificial problems created and regulated by rules. This artificiality is governed by a "gratuitous logic" that restricts the means allowed to achieve the stipulated goal, making the way to this achievement harder. For example, soccer players are not permitted to use their hands, apart from the goalkeeper and the throw-in, to advance in a match and score. Even more remarkably, they willingly choose to take the more difficult way to constitute the game. After all, handling the ball is more efficient than kicking it.

Besides the utility value that games have for recreation, education, training, socialization or health, among other profitable interests, approaching games as involving efforts to overcome artificial obstacles facilitates perceiving and embodying their inherent value. In inviting to achieve a trivial goal in a more difficult way than needed, games become intrinsically valued activities because they offer to accomplish something difficult for the sake of savoring such difficulty. The process of attempting to solve games' artificially established riddles as well as the commitment to this process is captivating and, at least temporarily, free from the constraints of ordinary life.

Many have argued that this disinterested care is at the core of a life worth living. For sure, games might be infelicitous or exaggerated at certain times and places, but it seems that their current devaluation prevents life from being fully enjoyed. As Suits posits, if all needs were satisfied, humans would devote themselves to games.

Do you have as many games as you would like in your life? How could you explore new and exciting games and incorporate them into your life?

Cesar R. Torres is Professor in the Department of Kinesiology, Physical Education and Sport Studies at State University of New York, Brockport.

DOES MUSIC MOVE OUR CHOICES?

Steve Miller

Music can serve as motivators, reminders and anchors in our lives.

There was a moment in time when any drug or alcohol use seemed unthinkable to me, but a simple suggestion changed my mind, and a single song changed my world. I wouldn't blame a song for my choice, but I understand the powerful influence music has on our lives. When we're young, music helps us navigate emotional turmoil. The song I heard made me fall in love with the band, rock 'n' roll and a lifestyle that became very destructive. I walked through that door without consequence, but by 19 years old, I was stuck in a moment I couldn't escape.

For context, in middle school, the older sister of my girlfriend once said, "You're like the all-American kid, just a cute slice of apple pie." Years later, she amended her statement: "You're the last person I ever thought would come to this. What happened to your life?" This memory, not pretty, is emblazoned in my mind like the song that started it all.

The story would be sad if it ended there, but another song led to a different choice. A priest suggested the words of a song might get someone's attention about their addiction. He was right! A simple song lyric pointed out that sometimes we don't know, and it's okay to ask for help.

Two songs serve as bookends in my life, reminding me that life is filled with choices. The song I was certain was a drug-use anthem turned out to be written to a friend to get their attention and hope they would make other choices; it was a life-affirming message, one I completely misunderstood.

So ask yourself one question when you listen to music: What is this song trying to tell you about your life? If the answer seems detrimental, think again. The muse that inspires all creativity celebrates life with any choice you make.

A song can influence a person to make a decision about their life, albeit inspirational or detrimental.

What song(s) inspire you to live your fullest potential? How can music be helpful for you making positive life choices?

Steve Miller is a person in long-term recovery, loves words and music and helping others navigate life choices.

THE DATA NEVER SPEAK FOR THEMSELVES
Jennifer Griffin-Wiesner

Four simple considerations can help you be a more knowledgeable consumer of information.

At the time of this writing, I am nearing the completion of my dissertation research. My study is focused on *data utilization*: reflecting on, making meaning of and leveraging data to inform decision-making. At 53, I am a doctoral outlier. So why would I invest in graduate school at this stage in my life and career?

I did it largely out of frustration. I kept hearing personally and professionally, especially during the height of the COVID-19 pandemic, the refrain, "The data speak for themselves."

The more I heard people who declared themselves experts, implying that we the people should just take for granted what they had to say, the more deeply I wanted to better understand how all of us can be savvy data consumers in the age of knowledge at our fingertips. Now, after five decades of living, three years of intense review of literature and nine months of interviews, I know that context always matters. The data *never* speak for themselves. In response, I have four lines of questioning, based in experiential learning about which Terry Borton (1970) wrote.

I use these to guide my personal and professional use of data. I offer them here in case they can be of use to you as well.

1. **What?** What data do I have? What do I notice about it? What questions does it raise? What's the source? What do I know about the source? How trustworthy is it? How do I know?
2. **Gut?** How do I feel about it? What reaction am I having? What might that reaction be telling me?
3. **So what?** What additional information do I need? What valid and reliable sources can I use to get it? What are the implications of what I know so far?
4. **Now what?** What actions, if any, will I take because of what I've learned?

How can you use these lines of questioning in your life? What else would you add?

Jennifer Griffin-Wiesner has spent her career bridging research and practice in support of positive youth development.

BEST TIME EVERY TIME
Kirby Boehm

Find the joy in the steps you take.

Life is full of moments that cause each of us to examine our perspectives. Your perspective may shift over time, or the situation may call for you to look at things from another point of view to gain a deeper understanding. Reflecting on my life, I was blessed to realize how one's perspective shapes one's outlook on life at an early age.

During my first year of high school, I entered a program with the mantra "Best time every time." The saying itself referred to giving it your all when running out of the batter's box, putting additional pressure on the defense to make a play. Little did I know the impact this saying would have in my life for years to come.

The same year I entered the program, the head coach was diagnosed with stage 4 colon cancer. Being in his mid-30s, this news came as a shock to everyone, including his wife and four children. This diagnosis may have led some to view the world in a negative light; instead, he attacked each day until he passed away in 2014. He made a conscious effort to remain positive even in the face of adversity. He would often be heard telling people on a gloomy midwestern spring day that he was "grateful for the weather today"; this view was based solely on the fact he was able to wake up and experience the world around him.

Seeing someone handle such devasting news with a positive outlook at such a formative time of my life had a lasting impact on me. The daily monotony of life can cause us to lose sight of how fortunate we are to wake up and have the opportunity to give our best each day.

Certain events may make it difficult to maintain a positive perspective or find joy during those times. However, being cognizant of the perspective from which you choose to see a situation helps shape your attitudes. *Understanding how to shift your perspective may allow you to move through life with more fluidity.* Even on the most difficult journeys, there is a joy to be found in the steps you take along the way.

The next time you face a challenge, take a step back and spin the challenge around to help see the situation from a new perspective. Write down what you find.

Kirby Boehm is a former Division III student athlete and post-graduation pursued a career within higher education. He has worked to provide support as an Athletic Academic Advisor at multiple NCAA institutions and is currently an Assistant Professor of Sport Management.

REAL-TIME RESILIENCE
Jen Schneeman

Reclaim your personal energy and expand your capacity.

Your personal energy is your most valuable, yet variable, currency. Energy capacity is designed to fluctuate, yet we're conditioned to go nonstop. We *know* that each day has differing energy demands; however, it is so easy to exhaust it all with the intention to "restore it later." When self-care is nonexistent or too rigid, we can lose a sense of self and balance. It is exhausting to live in a constant state of go, thereby creating chronic stress, which can lead to burnout.

As a health-conscious go-getter and burning out 4x, here is what I've learned:

1. No bootstrapping can pull you out of burnout.
2. Low-energy states are often shamed; we're rarely taught to honor them.
3. How you transition out of low-energy states is as important (if not more so) than understanding how you got there.
4. It is a common to blast from shutdown to full tilt and then crash harder.
5. The secondary crash can often create a shame cycle, overthinking and disconnection.

I moved states, shifted careers and changed relationships but didn't break the boom-bust cycle until I realized it was my nervous system that needed rewiring for rhythm. Rhythm is life, life is flow, flow is balance and balance is efficient. Finding "balance" stems from a feeling of easeful communication across our nervous system, the communication highway that interprets signals from the environment and sends signals back out to our environment about who we are. The key to ride the highs and the lows of life, without getting stuck in a jolt of stuck survival energy or the deflation of shutting down, is nervous system flexibility. How? *Welcome to the practice of real-time resilience* to reclaim your personal energy – reset in the moment, recharge throughout the day and restore appropriately at the end of each day.

Since stress is simply a demand on our energy, think about how many demands are there on your energy. For some, too much and for others, not enough! We experience life through layers of energy: physical, emotional, mental, intellectual and bliss. When we tend to all the layers of our energy, we care for our whole self – burning bright instead of burning out.

Reflect on what nourishes your layers of energy and what depletes them.

Jen Schneeman, M.B.A., C-IAYT, CDCA, is a soul-driven scientist, cofounder of REAL Human Performance and creator of the Self-Care and Resilience programs.

AFTER LIVING 27,241 DAYS
Nancy Beatty Gleeson

These ten thoughts might be useful for living your life.

1. You'll change direction many times – that's good and you won't stagnate.
2. Don't fear change. It will happen anyway.
3. You will regret some things in life – we all do. Don't dwell on them.
4. You will be hurt by others and by experiences. Don't bury the hurt – accept it.
5. Forgive others. You will need forgiveness too.
6. Search for positive, cheerful people. Be kind and friendly and it will become a habit.
7. Don't hurt yourself. If you think you cannot go on, please get help. Talk to someone about your thoughts. There's no recovery from suicide – not for the person who chooses that route and not for those who are left behind. It is absolutely final.
8. Live your life and practice happiness!
9. Take new experiences when they happen. Try to always learn from them. Travel offers wonderful experiences – new places, people, food, languages and fun! Even your own town, county and state have places you might not have been to.
10. Love someone or something. Begin with the most difficult and learn to love yourself. Only then will you be free to love others deeply and selflessly.

Do an honest self-appraisal for each of these ten thoughts. To what extent are you embracing them? Identify specific areas where you can make improvements.

Nancy Beatty Gleeson grew up in the Washington, D.C. area. She has taught public school music, been a sergeant in the U.S. Air Force Singing Sergeants and taught graphic design at Northern Virginia Community College for 32 years. She has two wonderful children and three terrific grandchildren and finds being three-quarters of a century old extremely entertaining!

A FULFILLING CAREER
Kim Dude

Several key principles are important for making career choices.

"Happy are those who dream dreams and are ready to pay the price to make them come true." This quote by Leon Joseph Suenens has been the mantra of my life. I have always wanted to change the world. I hoped that if I worked hard enough and believed passionately in my dreams, I could make them come true.

I spent my professional career in the drug and alcohol misuse prevention field trying to convince students to make better choices about their health, especially with alcohol. This was not an easy task. The difficulty was in trying to convince other people to believe as strongly as I did regarding the issues.

So what kept me motivated? The health and safety of our students was vitally important to me. But I also loved the challenge, and it was worth the struggle.

If you want to truly make a difference, you are going to have to be willing to work as hard, if not harder, than anyone else. Have the courage to be creative. Excellence is a voluntary commitment, so be willing to make mistakes and stay teachable.

No matter what profession you seek, to make a difference it is vitally important to work in collaboration with others. Helping people feel valued and included is paramount to creating a team. Make work fun and celebrate both small and big wins.

It is also important to understand that change takes time. Being patient while advocating is incredibly challenging. Do not give up. Abraham Lincoln once said, "I will prepare and one day my chance will come."

Two quotes stand out for me. First, Katharine Graham wrote, "To love what you do and know that it makes a difference, how could anything be more wonderful?" Second, Somerset Maugham said, "It's a funny thing about life, if you refuse to accept anything but the best you very often get it." The bottom line is, you only go around once in this life, so pick a career that is fulfilling and uses your talents and passions to change the world.

As you think about your career choices, what talents and passions are currently most important to you?

Kim Dude worked in student affairs for 43 years specializing in alcohol and drug prevention, leadership and wellness. She has always had a passion for changing the world.

YOU CAN WIN THE FIGHT

Gary Levy

Realizing your destiny as a fully functioning person is very difficult to achieve if your life is controlled by anxiety.

My journey has always been challenging.

Along the way, I have often had difficulty getting through that doorway of anxiety. Most times I could, but there were times when it was just too frightening to do so, especially when faced with new social settings. Fear of making a mistake in front of others paralyzed me.

Recently, I had an opportunity to go to a presentation by a famous person whom I greatly admired and wanted to meet. The thought of getting through that doorway to actually get in my car and drive to the event was very scary. Fortunately, I had someone who could mentor me and help me through that door of anxiety: my wife. I went, had a wonderful time, asked questions of the speaker and even exchanged contact information for further conversations. I realized I was not a prisoner of my anxiety. Anxiety can be successfully managed and doesn't have to prevent you from achieving your goals and experiencing joy. It's hard work but worth it.

What can you do to successfully reduce your anxiety to become a stronger, happier person?

1. Be honest with yourself. You are not a terrible, broken or weak person. Talk with a mentor, a friend or significant other, your resident assistant or a teacher or school counselor. You don't have to face this alone.
2. Read books, or articles and workbooks about reducing anxiety.
3. Journal to get your thoughts on paper, especially as you gain new information and insight. It is easier to frame issues and understand them when you can read and think about them clearly, rather than simply perseverating about them in your head.

What situations make you anxious, whether just a little anxious or much stronger? With these, which of the recommendations above would be most helpful for you to not be so anxious and to take better control of it?

Gary Levy is a retired college administrator and armchair astronaut who shares his life with a wonderful spouse, three dogs, three children and six grandchildren. He is still challenged by anxiety but works hard to not let it control him.

BE WILLING TO BE WRONG!
Priya Shukla

The internet encourages the art of always being right
(even when you are not)!

Confirmation bias is the human tendency to seek, interpret and remember information that confirms your preexisting beliefs while dismissing evidence that contradicts them. It's our brain's way of saying, "You're already a genius!" This bias affects every choice we make. In today's world, the internet – a powerful tool for information and communication – has become a breeding ground for this.

The internet reinforces confirmation bias, which impacts us in three ways:

1. *How humans seek information.* Confirmation bias affects how we look at the world around us. My teenage daughter is discovering the world of makeup, and social media content is full of tutorials and products. This selective exposure limits her diversity of information and makes her believe external beauty is more significant than internal beauty!
2. *How humans interpret the information.* Confirmation bias affects how we process what is otherwise neutral information, and it tends to favor our beliefs. When my seven-year-old soccer fan watches videos of wealthy soccer players buying expensive cars, sadly it makes him equate success with possession of expensive things!
3. *How humans remember information.* Our memories are also affected by confirmation bias. We interpret and possibly even change memories and facts in our head based on our beliefs. The polarized news sources on the internet further ingrains confirmation bias.

Why do we do this? In an experiment by psychologists, when presented with evidence counter to participants' beliefs on topics they cared about deeply, brain areas associated with physical pain became more active – as if being wrong *physically hurts.* When opposing facts challenge us, our brain perceives the psychological threat and protects us as if it was an actual physical threat.

What can you do to protect yourself? Diversify your information sources, follow expert blogs with opposing viewpoints! Approach all online information with a critical mindset! Ask, "What evidence supports this claim?" And use search engines for reasons why you might be wrong. The next time you find the internet feeding your suggested reads, just remember, it's a trick to keep your ego nice and warm. But maybe, just maybe, it's time to take control of your digital knowledge and foster open mindedness.

Are you willing to be wrong and learn something new?

Priya Shukla lives in Arlington, Virginia, and practices mindfulness, plotting travels, reading, trying to save the earth and family time.

JUST A PAUSE
Irma Velasquez

Free creativity through quiet stillness.

While attending a life drawing art class, I found myself among experienced artists ready to paint from live models. This setting included a music ensemble of guitar and bass players and a singer. The instructor asked us to express the scene in our unique way. We had an hour to complete the painting.

When the clock started to run, the room became infused with the sounds of the artists preparing their painting instruments to orchestrate their visually creative pieces. The exception was a woman standing calm, focused in front of her easel, unmoved by the passing of time. A few minutes before the hour was over, the quiet woman picked up a brush and furiously covered every inch of her canvas in red paint.

When it was time for her to share what was represented on her canvas, she brought to life a scene on stage before the curtain opened. The curtain, of course, was red.

Creativity often begins when encountering a challenge outside one's comfort zone; this can indeed be a productive struggle. Usually, we rush into an activity before reflecting on our intention or why we would spend energy on such a task. What happens when we stay with the discomfort of silence, stand still and be with the emotions and thoughts inside us? This experience is the creation process at work within us, a productive struggle.

A productive struggle can be experienced as a pause. This space within encourages us to wrestle with new concepts and solve problems without immediate answers. To help with this, you might consider a daily "just exercise": just walking, just eating, just petting your dog.

What are some habitual patterns that could benefit from a pause?

Irma Velasquez is an artist, educator and author of *Fish Dreams: A Mother's Journey From Curing Her Son's Autism to Loving Him as He Is*. She inspires social change through her commitment to higher and special education. She received an honorary Doctorate in Humane Letters from the University of San Francisco for her contributions to social activism and community initiatives.

NOT ALL WHO WANDER ARE LOST: WHAT GOT ME HERE?

Wilson Lam

Find inspiration in your own story.

Life doesn't come with a set of instructions. A lot of times, many things we do are through trial and error, like a science experiment of our own life. It is through this iterative process that our lives unfold. Some of us figure it out a lot sooner; for others, it may take some time.

I am in that latter camp. I spent most of my young adult life figuring out my purpose in life. It wasn't just enough for me to have a job or make a lot of money; rather, I cherish meaning above all else. I developed an interest in fitness right before college, which had led to my curiosity for health and wellness, but I could not point a finger on exactly what that meant for me. What lit a fire in me was the passing of a dear friend in 2022 from pancreatic cancer. It was in that moment that I decided to pursue a career in public health sciences and research in honor of their memory.

In that time, my aspirations had evolved, and I questioned how chronic diseases, such as cancer, affect the mental health of the person living with the diagnosis. These questions led me to the idea that only researching these inquiries would not be enough; I realized I would also need to consider the mental health aspects to understand the psychological underpinnings of the patient. I'm still very far away from achieving my newfound goal and the journey will not be easy, but one day I hope to help alleviate the pain and suffering of those diagnosed with a life-changing disease through my own clinical practice and work as a scientist-practitioner.

Remember that your success may not be a linear path. Failure will be an inevitable part of your journey, so don't let that discourage you. Not knowing where you are now or where you will go, however, is not a failure. In our individualistic culture, we are left to figure things out on our own, but it doesn't have to be this way. Sometimes we need someone to guide us in our reflection; this could be with an apprenticeship, academic advising, career counseling, therapy or other mentor. Don't let obstacles in life stop you, because your potential is yet to be discovered.

What can you do to help find your inspiration? What can help find your aspiration? What will lead you to finding a mentor?

Wilson Lam is currently a data analyst and a graduate student in a public mental health program with aspirations to pursue a PhD.

PREPARE YOURSELF FOR SUCCESS
Alan Herman

It's no joke: The early bird catches the worm.

Spontaneity has its place, but preparation holds the key to life's most important successes. Patrick Mahomes is a superstar quarterback, but think about what he did to achieve his greatness. Mahomes most likely threw thousands and thousands of passes actually and mentally before each game's coin toss and kickoff. Aaron Judge and Shohei Ohtani undoubtedly spent countless hours analyzing and practicing their baseball skills before each umpire said, "Play ball!"

Waiting until the last minute to do anything important is more likely than not to be a recipe for mediocrity or even disaster or failure. Whether one is taking a test in school or completing a job assignment at work, the likelihood of the most successful outcome is usually dependent on thought, knowledge and early action that leaves time for adjustments if necessary. Mahomes might choose to throw short passes in some games as opposed to longer ones. Ohtani when pitching could decide to throw sinkers or sliders rather than fastballs to home-run hitters who feast on 100-mile-per-hour pitches but who struggle when seeing a sinking or slower curving ball.

Unexpected situations often arise in life, and those who opt to wait until the last minute to complete a task often find themselves rushed or in big trouble when hurrying due to their inability to act promptly. These unanticipated forks in the road of life often lead to physical and mental stress. Getting ahead of situations and assignments presents the best path for the most desirable outcome, which often includes appreciation to you by others for a job well done, the possibility for career advancement, inner peace and personal satisfaction.

You will see and become your best self when you prepare early for each assignment and challenge. Waiting until the last minute leaves you little room for error and often results in mediocrity at best.

Think about those times when you did not prepare early or early enough. What can you learn from those situations, and what specific things can you do to improve your ability to be successful?

Alan Herman practiced law for 42 years as a trial attorney and presently works upon request as a mediator and arbitrator. He has experienced the beneficial effects of early preparation and mentored others to do the same.

BREATHE . . . AND BE WHERE YOU ARE
Sue Wasiolek

Although we need to live life to its fullest, we also need to find a pace that works for us, making certain that our focus remains on the here and now.

A fear of missing out (FOMO) has almost always been a part of my existence; it's felt somewhat like a competition *with myself* to try to fit as much as I can into any given day, fearful that I would underestimate or overlook an opportunity that could be life altering. As a result, I have, at times, found myself looking ahead with questions, concerns and anticipation, discounting the joy of being in the moment – of living in the present.

This approach is rather nonsensical, as we have learned a lot through research and practice about what it means to have our total self *be* where we physically are. We know that being mindful can truly be magical, and learning how to be with ourselves, with our thoughts, with our emotions, with our friends, with our classmates, with our teammates, with our family can have enormous benefits to our physical and mental well-being.

As much as all of this seems logical and purposeful, it can be hard to achieve; being and staying present in life takes intentionality and practice. It's more than simply putting our devices to the side, trying to avoid the distraction that these electronics bring into our lives. It is committing, with our total being, to staying focused on the what, the where, the why and the with whom we are, as doing this can help reduce stress, anxiety and regret while improving relationships, happiness, creativity and productivity. We owe it to ourselves and to each other to have our head be where our feet are.

Learning how to meditate/be mindful (sitting, walking, eating), maintaining a journal and expressing gratitude can help us develop this life-enhancing practice of being present.

What can you commit to doing to "breathe" and to "be where you are"? What, specifically, can you do today? What would you like to consider or learn more about?

Sue Wasiolek spent over four decades serving as the dean of students at Duke University where she had the good fortune of working with thousands of brilliant and hardworking students. Although Sue as a child and college student aspired to be a doctor, her rejection from medical school turned out to be the best decision anyone ever made for her, as she found her way to law school and now teaches education law, the First Amendment, civil discourse and meditation.

NAVIGATING YOUR PATH, STEP BY STEP
Judy Palmore

Achieving your goals is much like crossing a moving stream – requiring careful assessment of the landscape, testing each step for stability and deciding which path will carry you forward or set you back.

For decades, I've led diverse communities through an activity that uses crossing a river as a metaphor for achieving goals. This exercise has evolved over time – sometimes it involves stepping on rocks to cross a babbling stream, building a bridge or even navigating past snapping turtles. No matter the challenge, the key is to carefully place your feet, stay focused, add support, minimize challenges and keep your eye on the goal on the other side.

What does this look like in goal setting?

Step 1: Choose a goal – whether it's exercising more, quitting smoking, improving sleep or managing anger. Write it down or sketch it out on a device or a piece of paper. Imagine you are on one side of a rushing water source, and your goal is on the other side.

Step 2a: Now think about those slippery rocks, sneaky snapping turtles and rickety bridges – these are your *challenges*. They represent the obstacles that might hinder your progress. Write down three people, places or situations that could stand in your way as you work toward your goal.

Step 2b: Next, consider the dry and stable rocks or sturdy bridges – this is your *support*. They represent the knowledge, skills, people and resources that will help you achieve your goals. Write down three people, skills or resources that help you work toward your goal.

Step 3a: To reach your goal, you need more support and stability than challenges. List four ways to add the support, knowledge and skills, and resources that will help you achieve your goal.

Step 3b: As you add support, consider how to remove, manage or minimize the challenges you identified in Step 2. List at least one strategy to remove, manage or reduce each challenge.

Great job! Your path is now easier to navigate, and your goal is much closer within reach.

When a goal comes up, use these steps to tackle it with confidence.

Judy Palmore has over 15 years in direct health education and two decades developing adult learning modules in health promotion, communication and leadership and emphasizes experiential learning and sustainable behavior change. She holds a master's degree in counseling psychology.

VOICE OF SELF-COMPASSION
Tom Szigethy

Compassion for self will lead to a life of well-being.

I believe nurturing self-compassion is what provides a meaningful joy-filled life.

Every time I verbalize a desire or a want, I have received the opposite. I wished for wealth and lived paycheck to paycheck. I wanted to be patient and was given a child with cholic (crying all of the time). Through navigating the opposite of my desire, I developed the skill to achieve what I wanted. The process helped me develop self-compassion.

I learned to be frugal and discovered my own creativity to achieve my goals of having abundance. I found I had the capacity to achieve many things on meager resources. My wealth resides in my ability to help others see their own creative beauty. Happiness and sense of accomplishment are not defined by getting what I want.

My son was born a finicky eater and barely slept. He woke easily after hours of working to get him to sleep. I have never known such exhaustion, and once or twice I left him in the crib crying. I eventually learned that life does not show up on my terms – I can fight this reality and be frustrated, or I can choose to accept reality and find serenity. Patience is found in the accepting of reality – change what I can, me. Let all else go.

Responsibilities when handled with grace earn the respect of others, but having too many responsibilities can also breed resentments. I often found that the language I use toward an activity shows me the health of my mindset and I can choose to change my mindset through changing my words. I notice when presented with a task that I mentally say, "I have to" but when I change that language to "I choose to," then my attitude toward the task shifts. Often, people will tell me that they do not have a choice because they do not like the consequence that failure brings. Consequence does not negate choice; it is the motivator of action. Every activity I engage in in life is my choice.

> *What are the tasks that you procrastinate, and what are your inner thoughts that repeat regarding that task? Can you reframe your inner thoughts so that you can see your choice?*

Tom Szigethy, M.A., is the Associate Dean/Director of DuWell at Duke University since 2008. DuWell is the outreach and public health branch of Wellness at Duke. Prior to work at Duke, Tom was the Director of the Department of Alcohol and Other Substance Abuse Prevention at the University of Connecticut. He comes to higher education work after 15 years in the field of social work.

BALANCE AND FLEXIBILITY
Linda Harber

Be intentional with career; learn from everyone. Go with the flow and keep your life balanced.

I wanted to be a librarian. Years ago, we moved to a college town for my husband's Ph.D.; however, the university didn't have a library science degree. So I switched my focus to counseling for postsecondary education. I went with the flow and completed that degree while working – with tuition waiver paying!

Another "go with the flow" moment occurred when we moved for jobs after graduate school. I got a job in the Career Planning Department, working with students and potential employers. Then something opened in the Human Resources (HR) Department and I met the man who would become my mentor – the HR director. I learned so much from him as I moved up the HR ladder; he taught me that life was more important than working, and to work hard but leave work at a reasonable time so you can have a life as well! He taught me to always care about people first.

I remember he would never let any supervisor eliminate jobs right before the winter holidays, and he would always ensure that people received a lot of advance notice so they could end their employment well. We also created an outplacement program when jobs were being abolished to serve laid-off employees.

Maintaining life balance is hard. I remember leaving state conferences early so I could see one of my sons receive a school award. I often rushed home from work for Halloween, baseball games and band concerts. We didn't relocate while our sons were in school so as not to disrupt their school lives.

Going with the flow and moving to another city – to take a chief HR officer position – during midlife was a great decision. I used my HR skills in new ways, met wonderful people and enjoyed the area so much.

How can you best prepare for career risks, going with the flow and maintaining balance?

Linda H. Harber worked in higher education human resources for over 40 years before retiring as Vice President of Human Resources and Faculty and Staff Life at George Mason University.

A BALANCING ACT FOR HEALTH
Oluwagbemiga DadeMatthews

You can embrace a holistic approach to your wellness beginning today.

Integrative health is all about finding balance in our lives by combining conventional and complementary practices for enhanced well-being.

As a medical student, I faced the pressures of academics, relationships and personal growth. My health was often neglected as I tried to find the right balance for my ever-busy schedule.

Fortunately, before I became overwhelmed, I was introduced to the concept of caring for the "whole man – body, mind and spirit." This integrative approach helped me recognize that the mind, body and spirit are interconnected and encouraged me to consider how my daily choices – like what I eat, how I manage stress, and my emotional health – affect my overall wellness. Coupled with good time management practices, I excelled in college. Studies have shown that practices such as mindfulness, exercise and good nutrition can help reduce stress and boost well-being, which is exactly what every person needs: students need this in the fast-paced college environment, those in work settings benefit from this with their productivity, individuals in athletics, dance and the performing arts need this to achieve peak performance, those in the military need this to maintain maximum readiness.

By incorporating integrative health strategies, you can enhance your academic, physical and emotional performance and build resilience. For example, eating a balanced diet packed with nutrients can support your brain function, while staying active helps release endorphins that fight stress. Mindfulness techniques can improve your focus and emotional stability, essential tools for tackling the wide variety of life challenges. These strategies have helped keep me in optimal health and wellness two decades later.

Consider the following action steps beginning today:

1. *Mindfulness Minute*: Devote five minutes daily to practice mindfulness or meditation. Keep a journal of how you feel before and after.
2. *Healthy Eating Challenge*: Add one new nutritious food to your diet weekly and document how it influences your energy and mood.
3. *Movement Goal*: Try to get at least 30 minutes of physical activity three times a week and track your stress levels and overall happiness.

What will you commit yourself to doing to optimize your own health?

Oluwagbemiga DadeMatthews, M.D., Ph.D., is an Assistant Professor, School of Kinesiology, at Louisiana State University. He is a physician and researcher passionate about integrative health and exploring how lifestyle choices impact physical performance. His research focuses on injury prevention and holistic approaches to optimize physical performance and wellness.

FINDING ALLIES IN YOUR BACK YARD
Cathy M. Pinskey

Uncertainty, anxiety and fear can be your very best friends.

I can still remember when I was a teenager in the 1970s, riding in the back seat of my parents' Grand Marquis and listening to my mom ask me, "Cathy, what are your goals?" With my eyes rolling and attitude in my response, I said, "To make $30,000 a year before I am 30." Not exactly what she was looking for in a response. However, I already knew by then I wanted to be an architect when I grew up, but that's about it. I really had no idea about college, internships, licensing, continuing education or even exactly what I would do as an architect. I just knew I needed to make some money and that I liked to draw, which is what I thought architects did.

First step, college applications and visits. This is the point where fear, anxiety and uncertainty almost took over. While I went on some college visits with my parents, I had already decided in my mind I was not going to leave "home" for college. Well, my mom had a very different idea, pronouncing, "I don't care if you go to college across the street. You are not living at home!" With that, I decided to go to University of Buffalo's School of Architecture and Environmental Design, about 1.5 hours from home. It took less than one week at UB to see my mother's wisdom in quite literally pushing me out of the nest.

The opportunity to go to college changed my life in so many ways. For that reason, about 30 years ago I decided to work as an architect for educational institutions as my way of giving back to a place that gave me so much. My goal has been to create environments where learners of all ages and backgrounds can excel and work to solve the most vexing problems of our time.

Do some of the questions you get asked about your future make you feel anxious or uncomfortable? Open your mind and think about "What if" instead of "Why I can't." For me, as an architect, I actually think, "What if one of the buildings I have helped develop supports or even inspires a faculty researcher who then engages a student, and who, together, find a cure for cancer?" What a reward – for all.

What makes you feel anxious or uncomfortable? Now, how can you reframe them to be your allies?

Cathy M. Pinskey, AIA, is an accomplished senior-level architect with 23 years of direct college and university experience working collaboratively to shape the built environment. She incorporates strong leadership with a college/university planning, design and construction background.

Relationships
Bonding

Humans cannot survive in isolation. Relationships are central to life, and they are even more vital for having a thriving life. In the journey of living, a common feature is the wide variety and diversity of relationships in which an individual is involved. This initially includes the relationship, individually and collectively, with one's family of origin, including parents, guardians, siblings and extended family members. It then encompasses relationships with friends and neighbors, classmates in school, playmates with leisure time and others. Yet relationships go far beyond those that naturally come to mind – they include the clerk at the store, the host at the movies or theater, the specialist at the doctor's or dentist's office and the person on the street. Relationships include every human being with whom one comes in contact.

With that broad understanding of relationships, it is also clear that each relationship is not the same. People have relationships with family members, including one's family of upbringing as well as an evolving adult family or a family of choice. Some are based on family background or family relationships – these include those with blood relations, such as grandparents, great-grandparents, aunts, uncles, cousins and beyond. It may be a family relationship not by blood, such as stepparents, godparents, foster or adoptive parents or other family linkage. There are relationships with a spouse or significant other, as well as with children, parents and an extended family. Relationships extend to work, school and community settings, where others are known at various levels and depths.

Some relationships are more long term in nature, and many of these are much more meaningful and intensive when compared with others. Some relationships may be meaningful yet short-lived. Some relationships become intimate and romantic, and some become codified by vows as well as laws. Relationships are diverse in formal structure as well as by constitution and quality.

DOI: 10.4324/9781003541080-5

A central relationship that is often overlooked is a vitally important one. This is a person's relationship with themself. It is one's self-awareness, self-understanding, self-esteem and self-direction. Building on the first three thematic areas in this book – Optimism, Values, and Self-Care – the personal relationship that people have with themselves is vitally important and central to the quality of life. Introspection and reflection are central to this relationship and help constitute the core qualities an individual has and portrays to others.

WHAT IS A RELATIONSHIP?

Thinking about what constitutes a relationship is essential for defining the appropriate qualities linked to that relationship. As noted, some relationships are based on family, some are based on friendship, some are casual in nature and some are much more meaningful. Some may be time limited, based on external factors (such as a work or classroom experience, a travel adventure or a living setting). Some may be framed differently, such as "an adopted family" (not legal adoption per se) and determined by strong bonds.

Furthermore, there is a difference between having a relationship and being in a relationship. Having a relationship can constitute friends and colleagues, work and school settings, neighborly and social settings. Being in a relationship is more long term in nature and typically constitutes something more formal and committed; it would typically be something stated publicly and is often affirmed with a ceremony, jewelry (typically a ring) and other affirmations legal and otherwise.

The nature of the relationship is essential for helping identify more about the qualities essential and appropriate for that interaction. Whether it is a casual relationship (such as when in line at a store, with a store clerk or with a flight attendant) or something more meaningful (like a roommate, study or workout partner, or mentor) or even something deeper (like a soulmate or intimate relationship), different standards and guidelines may be appropriate. The overall focus is that the nature of the relationship will help determine what attitudes and behaviors would be appropriate for being more intentional with the qualities of that relationship.

ENHANCING THE QUALITY OF A RELATIONSHIP

Building quality interactions with others is an opportunity and a responsibility throughout one's life. Whether with a long-term or more proximate, short-lived relationship is the aim of avoiding unhealthy relationships.

Ultimately, it is reasonable to seek quality human interactions so that others are treated with respect and dignity. Beyond "quality human interactions," the aim is having "higher quality human interactions" with others as well as with oneself. With that kind of respect for others and self, the nature and depth of the relationship can be enhanced significantly. Some of these are necessary, if not essential, for an enduring relationship. Some are simply appropriate for a relationship of any type.

At the most basic level, kindness and courtesy are most essential qualities for relationships. These qualities permeate informal and more formal relationships; they are important for relationships to exist and especially for them to thrive. At the same time, having integrity in the relationship is essential for anything meaningful; this means being true to oneself and honoring one's own values and standards.

Communication is a central part of good relationships. That includes stating feelings that are both positive and not so positive. While being kind, feelings that are not as positive can be shared in constructive ways. Communication is helpful for clarifying views and values as well as to review and reflect on assumptions that may be made. Communication includes both verbal and nonverbal approaches, as each complements the other.

Another consideration with healthy relationships is that of respecting differences. Individuals will have varying experiences in their own past, whether distant past or recent lives. These different experiences help influence diversity in points of view, values, approaches, understanding and even the qualities important to a relationship. Essential with these differences is that of respect for one another's differences – and that respect goes in both directions, with you having respect for others' views and differences, and them respecting yours. This means that the relationship involves healthy interactions with one other and that collaboration and respect are found. With relationships, one may not know what is happening in another person's life, whether this is a more casual or more serious relationship.

Related to this is another quality in relationships: how conflict is addressed. Undoubtedly, some level of conflict will exist, whether it involves different values or perspectives, or even in the process of establishing boundaries. Helpful for preventing and managing conflicts, particularly with different values and varying communication styles, is the importance of having boundaries and limits. With this, individuals state any expectations or concerns about what they would like as well as not like in the relationship. Negotiation and clarification of these expectations may occur; what is important is to be clear with oneself, and to make these views clear with others.

With relationships, ideally and essential for longer-term relationships is the opportunity for individual growth and change. While differences in one's past exist and help influence current viewpoints, sometimes things happen in one's life that have a tremendous impact. Related to this is the fact that roles may change in a relationship. A classic example is when a young person adopts a different role with parents or guardians, such as becoming a caregiver. Similarly, relationships exist with mentors and also with being a mentor.

A focus on healthy relationships includes numerous topics and issues. Consider how understanding and skills about a wide variety of topics is helpful for promoting healthy relationships: interpersonal communication, assertiveness, anger management, conflict management and etiquette. Consider also diversity awareness, cultural competence, sexual decision-making, time management, negotiation skills, humor, rituals and traditions, and dependability. Clearly, so many elements constitute healthy relationships.

Ultimately, the aim in relationships is to have healthy relationships. Individuals will encounter new relationships as well as continuing and enhancing existing ones. Through all of this, important is maintaining quality attention to one's relationship with oneself so that relationship is even more thoughtful and grounded for living a full and rich life.

LINKAGE WITH OTHER THEMATIC AREAS

The focus on relationships and having quality relationships is embedded with each of the other six sections of *The Intentional Life*. Whether the focus is on the relationship with others or with oneself, the essential element is that each individual has integrity with how the relationship is and how it unfolds. That is, the aim is that the relationship honors the individual's values and has respect for the qualities of life held near and dear to that individual.

With the thematic areas of Optimism and Values, the key points in those sections of this book are that of being clear with one's own self-view and knowing what is important. And then, to be hopeful and positive that those elements of one's life are helpful and essential. That is, what is important is that individuals believe in themselves and that they are confident that their own beliefs and values are important and to be respected.

The key elements of the Self-Care thematic area are also integrated within relationships, as they incorporate how one views oneself and respects one's own body, mind and spirit. By nourishing oneself with management of stress and time and by elements such as nutrition and diet and exercise, one is demonstrating respect for oneself; that person is taking care of the relationship with themself. Similarly, some of the skills included with self-care, whether it involves mental health, drug and alcohol decisions and financial management, can affect the nature and quality of relationships with others.

Closely related to Relationships is a focus on Community. This is something that works in concert with relationships, as interaction with others is integral to community involvement. Whereas community will be defined in different ways, the undergirding of community activity is interpersonal relationships. This includes many of the qualities identified as important for healthy relationships in this section.

Finally, the linkage to the Nature and Service thematic areas is also found. Nature can be involved to help with nourishing the mind and body and can be done as an individual or group experience. Nature also includes activities such as environmental respect and involvement with causes that help protect these resources. With the Service area, involvement is also that of helping others, again whether alone or in a group. The experience of mentoring can be one of having a relationship with another person or group of people. Similarly, being involved with service activities, such as volunteering or donating time, skill or effort, can help with promoting healthy relationships among those receiving the service as well as with those providing the service.

CONCLUSION

Relationships permeate everyone's life. From birth, to infancy and childhood, to teenage years and young adulthood and then beyond into adulthood and older age, relationships help nourish and sustain one's life. Furthermore, one's relationship with oneself is a vital component, a theme found within this chapter as well as other sections of this book. In this chapter, over six dozen Legacy Letters provide rich insights based on challenges and misgivings, to successes as well as missed opportunities. Attention is provided to some of the qualities that help make a relationship a good one, with it is kindness, caring, outreach, authenticity, perseverance, forgiveness and gratitude. This chapter's contributors cite the importance of culture, whether that is steeped in family background or one's physical surroundings. The linkage with one's values is emphasized, helping the reader to pull things together for themselves. Coupled with the recommendations and reflection strategies, the reader will face numerous opportunities for growth.

Messages What are key points or themes highlighted in the Legacy Letters within the Relationships area?	
Reflections What are your thoughts and feelings about what is shared and recommended regarding Relationships?	
Resources What individuals, groups, organizations or other information would help you better understand and apply recommendations in the Relationships area?	
Commitments What are you willing to commit yourself to doing regarding the Relationships theme, both in the near term and in the more distant future?	

FIGURE 5.1

Legacy Worksheet for Relationships

MOTHER'S STRENGTH:
A JOURNEY OF HOPE, SURVIVAL AND LOVE
Eileen M. Vélez-Vega

Courage and faith help undergird major life challenges.

In an instant, everything changed. At 29, I was five months pregnant with my first daughter, and life couldn't have been more perfect. I was thriving in my career as an engineer, leading major airport projects, and in the blink of an eye, I was hit with devastating news: stage 4 Hodgkin's lymphoma. My world, and of everyone who loved me, was turned upside down.

I couldn't believe it. I was young, healthy and had so much to look forward to. But that diagnosis divided my life into two realities: one filled with chemotherapy and doctors and the other with the hope of a new life. I cried. I questioned everything, but I prayed. I refused to give up.

Despite my body deteriorating, I kept working as much as I could. But at seven months pregnant, I had no choice but to begin chemotherapy. I just needed to get through this for her; we both had to survive. Then, against all odds, on a cold December day, Anna Isabelle was born. Healthy, lots of hair and full of life. Yet I knew the fight wasn't over.

Just when I thought I had overcome the worst, the cancer returned. Anna Isabelle was only one year old and still my reason to keep going. My only chance of survival was an autologous stem cell transplant.

The thought of leaving my baby was unbearable, but I had to act. She deserved a mother just like the one I had. My doctors and nurses became my angels, guiding me through stem cell harvesting, high-dose chemotherapy and isolation. Being separated from Anna Isabelle was the hardest, but my mother was my caregiver, my unwavering support.

After months of grueling treatment, I was alive. My body was weak, but my spirit was rebuilding, just like my cells, slowly but stronger than ever.

Twelve years later, I'm still in remission. I've run half marathons to raise money for cancer research, rebuilt my career and am the proud mother of Anna Isabelle. The scars remain, my badges of courage, and I live a life with more intensity, gratitude and purpose. Life isn't just about surviving but thriving even when all seems impossible.

What helps you – and others – during extremely challenging times?

Eileen M. Vélez-Vega is a two-time cancer survivor, civil engineer and the first woman to become Secretary of the Department of Transportation and Public Works in Puerto Rico. Her inspiring cancer survival journey has fueled her dedication to empowering girls in science, technology, engineering and mathematics, while she continues to improve the island's infrastructure and raise awareness for others facing similar challenges.

LEARNING HOW TO LEARN
Claudia Trevor-Wright and Will Wright

Three steps for learning how to learn are practicing self-compassion, perseverance and reflection.

We have taught each other a lot about how to thrive in a new learning environment as a necessary step in building the life you want. These are the three steps we follow:

1. **Practice self-compassion to give time and space to learn how to learn.**
   Will: As someone who is typically hard on themself, I have always struggled with self-compassion, specifically in sports, where I push myself to be the best I can and always am disappointed when I fail to do so. However, in my academic endeavors, my mother has always taught me that everyone fails sometimes, as we are all human. I have realized that a prerequisite to success in any field is being able to accept failure and moving on from it.

2. **Pair that with perseverance, because we will all fail at some point.**
   Claudia: I avoided academic pathways where I thought I would risk failure. Even though I am proud of my career and love the work I do, I wish I had been more courageous during my undergraduate years. For example, I struggled in precalculus and pursued a major that didn't require calculus. I wish I would have persevered and asked for help instead. I have learned a lot by watching my son play baseball. Baseball players have to fail over and over and keep going. I knew there was a lesson there for both of us about the importance of perseverance.

3. **Pause to reflect on what you learned from your successes and failures.**
   Watching each other succeed and fail and taking opportunities to reflect on those experiences with each other has made each of us better at this step. Sometimes we do this work on our own first by taking quiet time to think. Sometimes we can get right to honest and difficult conversations.

Think of a time when you were in a new learning environment, like a new class or a new job. What were your expectations of yourself? If you didn't meet those expectations, how did you feel? How did you treat yourself?

Claudia Trevor-Wright, J.D., M.A., MCHES, is a health educator and attorney focused on advancing sexual and reproductive health in higher education and community health settings. As a mother, she hopes her children explore things that challenge them and build meaningful lives.

Will Wright is a high school junior who is a two-sport varsity athlete and co-captain of his high school ski team. He hopes to go to a college with a good premed program and later attend medical school.

THE ALOHA SPIRIT LAW: A LEGACY OF ALOHA
Dari Shim Matsuura

The Spirit of Aloha can enhance our lives and our relationships.

My dad was Alvin Shim – attorney, businessman, community leader and influencer, philanthropist, humanitarian, friend and mentor to thousands from all walks of life. The Aloha Spirit Law (HRS Section 5-7.5) is just one part of his legacy – to remind all of us to live with Aloha, to treat each other with respect, dignity and kindness so as to leave others untarnished but rather bigger, better, more valued, more loved having made the connection. That legacy became my brother Pono Shim's legacy and the request by those around him to learn how to live with Aloha. Through the teachings of our kupuna Aunty Pilaki Paki, Pono learned how to practice and live Aloha. Aloha Response started with a handful of friends, colleagues and business leaders interested in learning how to make things better in their jobs, families and lives overall. Aloha Response has now grown to thousands of people throughout the nation who meet online, share their stories and listen and respond with Aloha.

Living in Aloha every day is really hard. It has no monetary or intrinsic value. The only motivation is the desire to be a good person and make the world a better place. What a legacy.

For me, Aloha can be as simple as making enough room for another driver to enter your lane instead of beeping your horn or swearing to yourself meant for the driver in front of you for driving so slow. Maybe it's waving "thank you" to the driver who let you in. As a special education teacher, it's carrying parents through a difficult conversation that you know could dash all the "normal" dreams they have for their child. Doing so with grace, compassion and dignity so as to leave them unbroken yet feeling supported and carried ever so delicately. I hope those after me can say, "She left a legacy of Aloha too."

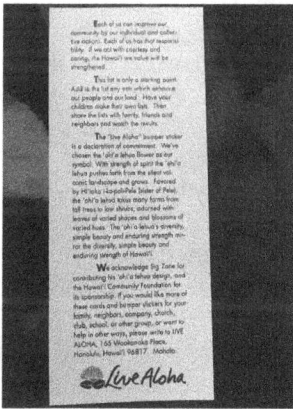

FIGURE 5.2
The Aloha Sprit is real, and even codified into law which is one part of my Dad's legacy.

In what ways does a life of living in Aloha resonate for you? How might you use some of its focus?

Dari Shim Matsuura is one of seven children of Alvin and Marion Shim. She is a special education teacher and hopes that one day, her students and those who know her can say she left her own legacy of Aloha.

RELATIONSHIPS MATTER – MAKE YOURS COUNT
Mark R. Ginsberg

Make a commitment to quality relationships and to caring.

Throughout my career and life, I have learned the importance and value of relationships. They support me, motivate me, inspire me and provide an "emotional glue" that bind together both my challenges and opportunities. I deeply value and appreciate my relationships.

It is often said that we are who we are because of those who have "shaped our being." Of course, that begins with our parents and families. However, it also extends to our friends, mentors and all those who have entered our lives and impacted us personally or professionally, or both.

I have been honored to have many people who have entered my life and had a consequential impact on who I am and what I have become. As a child, my family, teachers, neighbors, spiritual leaders and my peers all played this role. As I grew in age and experience, my professors and academic advisers had an increasingly influential role. In fact, I attribute my career and life success to a few individuals who have had a monumental impact on me.

This begins with my spouse, my best friend and life partner of nearly 50 years. Through all of the challenges each of us have faced, we have always had each other to rely on and to be there during times of calm and times of storm. The strength of this and other relationships has been profoundly important.

The fundamental similarity in the relationships that truly have mattered to me is that their essence is built on a foundation of caring. Caring can mean different things to each of us. For me, consistent with the writings of philosopher Milton Meyerhoff, caring is about helping another to grow. It is this dimension of a meaningful and sustained relationship that has mattered the most – an emphasis on caring and the care that another has had for me.

Yet, caring for another is equally valuable and personally fulfilling. For me, caring for others has been as important as experiencing the care of others.

My suggestions are simple, yet quite complex. Genuinely appreciate those who care for you and helped you to grow. Understand the value and importance of these precious relationships. Concurrently, care for others in the same way others have cared for you. You will be both a beneficiary and the benefactor for others. You will be both inspired and an inspiration.

How can you engage, sustain and make a commitment to relationships as well as caring?

Mark R. Ginsberg is an educator and leader in higher education. Currently, he serves as President of Towson University, after earlier leadership positions at George Mason University and Johns Hopkins University.

LAND HO!

Cathy McCandless

Cherish the people you disagree with; you can learn a great deal from them.

"Three against one," my friends proclaimed gleefully as we started our sailboat voyage. "And there's plenty of time for us to change your mind."

"Bring it!" I countered. "Let the games begin." My friends and I inhabit opposite ends of the political spectrum.

We sailed down the East River past the New York City skyline, and before long, we were out in the Atlantic. Soon, we lost sight of land entirely.

Then came the storm. On the radio, we could hear that boats we couldn't see were sinking all around us. Terrified, we ploughed on, through the wind, through the waves, through the night.

Standing watch together on that dark and stormy night, one of my friends and I got to talking about our hopes and dreams. Apparently, fear had made us philosophical – or maybe it was just that we each had a captive audience. Everyone should have meaningful work, we said, enough to eat, the chance to be happy. Wait, I thought. We're supposed to disagree about this, as we do about so much. Miraculously, we didn't.

The more we talked about our visions of utopia, the more it became clear to me. We wanted exactly the same things to occur in the world; we just had vastly different notions about how to get there. No one could have been more surprised than I was.

In a way, my friends were right. That voyage *did* change my mind (and my life) but not in the way they'd envisioned. It transformed the way I think about the people who disagree with me, however vehemently.

My friends and I are still on opposite ends of the political spectrum, and we're still passionate about our beliefs. However, we can now look back and laugh about how it took being miles from land for us to find common ground.

Think about those with whom you have very different views. On what issues or topics do you actually have common ground?

Cathy McCandless enjoys sailing off City Island, Bronx, New York and has a passion for old wooden boats. "I've had wonderful adventures of many kinds, big and small, during my 75 years," she says. "But it's the extraordinary people I've met along the way that have meant the most to me."

MAKE TIME FOR FAMILY AND FRIENDS
Susie Bruce

Staying connected and helping others benefits your mental health.

Growing up, I can't think of a time that my family missed a wedding, funeral, family reunion or homecoming. It's just what my family did – we were always present. My dad once told me that his favorite holiday growing up was not Christmas but "the Bland County homecoming" because it was a chance to see all his cousins and friends – and I'm sure the bounty of food played a role too.

For as long as I can remember, my dad had his hometown newspaper (only published once a week) mailed to our house. I always felt so famous when our visits "back home" were mentioned in the town news column. As a result, I continue to feel very connected to my dad's tiny hometown (population 343).

Early on in my life, I learned that relationships with family and friends are important. But beyond just "making time" for others, I also learned we should take care of others. My parents often talked about the obligation to help others whenever you can. They taught me that when you're feeling down, helping others can be the best way to distract yourself from your own problems. My parents set an example by always being ready to lend a hand and usually offered help before someone could ask them. Our neighbors all knew they could borrow a tool from my dad anytime; and as a "bonus," he would often give them a few ideas on how to fix whatever was broken as well. Even as my dad's health declined, he would find ways to be helpful to others. When he moved into assisted living, the person in the room next to him could never remember what time meals were served, so my dad would meet her at her door before every meal to walk her to the dining room.

FIGURE 5.3
Make sure you make time for family, friends, and fun!

How do you stay connected with others? Is there someone you've been concerned about but haven't followed up with, and could reach out to in the next two weeks?

Susie Bruce has 30 years' experience in collegiate health promotion, focusing on substance misuse and hazing prevention.

STANDING UP FOR WHAT YOU BELIEVE IN
Eric S. Davidson

Sometimes it takes a lot of courage to do what you believe is best.

The gasps and the chuckles of the wedding guests drew the attention of the old Irish priest as I followed the bridesmaids into the sanctuary. When my best friend had asked if I would stand up as her "maid of honor," I quickly said yes, thinking she was joking. She was serious!

Unfortunately, prior to the wedding, no one had shared my gender with the priest. He struggled greatly with this progressive act. During the rehearsal, he reassigned maid of honor's responsibilities as holding the bridal bouquet and straightening the bridal train to the bride's sister. After the rehearsal, he would not allow me to sign the wedding certificate and license as the bride's witness.

Now, as I approached the wedding altar, I wrestled with complying with the priest or figuratively and literally standing up for my friend as her attendant of honor. As I watched her walk down the aisle, I knew what decision had to be made!

After she took her place, I grasped her bouquet, handed it to her sister and then stepped behind her to straighten the bridal train. Once straightened, I returned to my position and reacquired the bridal bouquet. During the ceremony, I straightened the train five times as well as fulfilling my other duties.

After the ceremony, I avoided the priest. However, at the reception, he caught me seated at the wedding party table. With him standing before us, fear devoured me. However, between the wedding and the reception, a miracle must had occurred! The priest congratulated me on a job well done, telling me I had been "one of the best maids of honors he had ever seen." I thanked him and, as he walked away, gave a sigh of relief and smiled. Had I not stood up for what I had believed in, my friend's wedding may not have been the happy day she had envisioned, and I would not have helped expand the mindsets of the priest and others who held less open points of view.

Think of a situation where you didn't stand up for what you believed in and one where you did so. What conclusions do you draw for each of these situations?

Eric S. Davidson and Anne Lamb continue to be the best of friends. Anne served as Eric's "best man" when Eric married Jill. Both couples relish in telling others the story of their nontraditional attendants.

SUPPORTING EACH OTHER AS WE FIND OUR WAY
Rose Pascarell

*The support of others can make all the difference with keeping
you grounded.*

I've been lucky enough to work with great colleagues and smart students in different roles in higher education. I've spent most of my professional career working at a university I remember feeling exhilarated once I understood that my work could make a positive difference in the world. What's unconventional about my journey is that I quit school as an undergraduate not once or twice but three times.

When I decided to stop quitting, I found I enjoyed being a college student. But the "quit" in me didn't totally go away. Once I graduated with a bachelor's degree, I made my way to Virginia (an area I'd never been to) for graduate school (where I knew no one). I encountered some difficulty, and in two weeks, I was ready to pack my bags and head back to New York. So what kept me going and in school each time? Well, I'd love to say it was my strength and resilience (and no question, I did develop both along the way); instead, it was the kindness, support and connection of others that kept me rooted even when I was ready to bolt.

Kathy Sullivan, my community college professor in New York, encouraged me NOT to quit when I went to her office to tell her I wouldn't be back. I disagreed with a particular assignment she was requiring. Instead of saying goodbye, she listened and asked me to write a paper on the importance of dissent. I did. And I stayed. If not for that interaction, which really triggered my curiosity, I'm pretty sure my higher education career would have ended before it started.

Now, there is no question that other individuals have had a significant impact on my life, but as I realized the significance of one person's support, I began to carve out a life for myself where I might do the same for others whenever possible. Working at a university has provided that opportunity for me.

Who in your life has helped you overcome obstacles, real or perceived? Who have you done the same for? How might you think about yourself as a difference maker for yourself and others?

Rose Pascarell has worked in higher education for over 30 years. A proud graduate of her local public community college, she received her bachelor's and master's degrees from two public institutions. She is currently the Vice President for University Life at Virginia's largest and most diverse public institution.

A MISSPENT LIFE
Lori Hendricks

Value and celebrate engagement outside your core responsibilities.

Back in my undergraduate days, I had an accomplished professor of Russian history. For our midterm, he had a lengthy multiple-choice test – like 500 questions. May have been more; probably was less.

The week after we completed the test, he returned it. He asked for those with 30 or fewer wrong answers to stand. I thought he was going to chastise those who didn't make this cut. Instead, he continued to highlight those with fewer and fewer mistakes. His message, however, caught me off guard.

He went on to say that those with the near-perfect tests had it wrong. In fact, he said those with the perfect midterms were leading misspent lives. We had covered nearly 1,000 years of history in the exam. To understand concepts like liberty and security, one needed to be out of the library and experiencing life. How can you understand conflict or belonging if you aren't interacting with anything but a book?

Sometimes we forget about the learning communities that exist all around us. If you are a college student, whether you are a student athlete, member of the marching band, in Greek Life or member of your student government association, your academic program is elevated when you add cocurricular experiences to it. If you are in another setting, such as working or in the military or traveling or caregiving, your life as a whole is enhanced when you get involved in local activities and culture, volunteering or other things.

In these out-of-classroom or out-of-work experiences, you learn how to be a stronger team member and leader – which on some days may mean patience and kindness and in other moments, accountability and courage. You gain experience performing under pressure. You discover resources available to support you and learn how to overcome adversity. Resilience becomes a skill loaded into your backpack.

Take time to value opportunities that you make space for in your life. Think about their benefits to your physical and mental health. Write down a few bullet points for a future résumé, capturing the skills you are developing.

Lori Hendricks is the Director of Athletics at the University of Massachusetts Dartmouth, former NCAA staffer for the CHAMPS/Life Skills Program and former NCAA Division III student athlete.

THE RIPPLE EFFECT OF INSPIRATION
Roxanne Howe-Murphy

Be curious about what is possible.

In my first professional position, I led the Therapeutic Recreation program at a United Cerebral Palsy Association affiliate. There, I was fortunate to meet a young woman close to my age whose body was seriously affected by this neurological condition but whose intellect and spirit were strong. Her radiant smile and positive energy attracted others to her, even though she was nonverbal, as she was unable to have control over her arms or legs and difficulty in controlling her head movements.

My team became aware that Liza had a story to share. Before technological advances made vocal and written communication more accessible to those dealing with communication issues, Liza relied on using a stick connected to her headband to point to one letter at a time on a language board attached to her wheelchair.

Over several months, staff members took turns sitting with Liza to record her words, which evolved into a moving story. She shared her desire to experience the simple things in life that most people take for granted. But her deeply penetrating message was that most people did not really see who she was as a person, nor did they realize that she wanted to make a difference. Her story was translated into a video titled, *Don't Just Look (There's So Much More to Me)*, which was shown to civic and professional groups across the city.

Since those early days, Liza's message has served as an inspiration for the deep living work, which aims to expand the perspectives and inner capacities for those who are curious about what is possible in their lives. For example, one client chose to be a car salesperson to understand what motivated buyers. She went on to lead an internal coaching program for Harvard Business School's students and staff. Unknown to Liza, her willingness to tell her story created a ripple effect of inspiration.

> *Identify two individuals that are outside of your usual social group to learn more about them as people. Discover what is important to them or inspires them. What did you learn about yourself through this experience?*

Roxanne Howe-Murphy, Ed.D., is a former university professor, founder of a coaching training institute and cofounder of the nonprofit Deep Living Lab. She is coauthor of a therapeutic recreation textbook and author of *Deep Coaching: Using the Enneagram as a Catalyst for Profound Change*, *Deep Living With the Enneagram: Recovering Your True Nature*, and *Underneath Your Personality: Discovering Greater Well-Being Through Deep Living With the Enneagram.*

TAMMY CHANGED MY LIFE
Beth Hotchko

When I turned my rock bottom into a life I never imagined.

My journey of recovery started standing at a bus stop in the skid row area of Los Angeles. I had previously totaled my car in a drunken blackout. That's when I hit my rock bottom. I was a conscientious employee, so I took the bus to work, which was a two-and-a-half-hour journey and three buses each way.

One night, I was waiting at a bus stop for my second of three buses home. A lady came up to me and said, "Hi, where are you going tonight?" I told her I was going home, and then I said the obligatory response, "How about you?" She said she was going to a meeting and I knew exactly what that meant. You see, I had already been arrested twice for DUI and had to attend mandatory meetings. Of course, at that time I didn't have a problem. Yeah, right. Her bus arrived within minutes, and she gave me her phone number and said to call her if I wanted to go to a meeting with her.

I never thought I would be much in my life, but that all changed that night. I called her the next day and have been sober and clean since January 22, 1986, one day at a time. I went to meetings, got a sponsor and worked the steps. Life still had its ups and downs, but I always knew to turn to my sobriety to get through it.

Within nine months, my best friend joined me in recovery. I was so happy we could take this journey together and be there for each other every step of the way. We are still supporting each other to this day.

After being sober for seven years, I met my life mate, my wife. Who knew I would end up getting married, having a child, owning a house and a nice car, getting a great job and have a 401(k)! I credit this trajectory in my life to Tammy, that person I met at a bus stop.

I hope you will be open to new people who come into your life, no matter how brief or how long. They could be your Tammy.

As you think about your friends and acquaintances, who has tried to be "your Tammy"? Who is trying now? And is there someone in your life for whom you could be "their Tammy"?

Beth Hotchko retired from American Airlines as a Corporate Account Executive after 26 years. Beth currently resides in Albuquerque, New Mexico with her wife and likes to travel the world, hike, ski and spend time with her family.

TWO FORCES IN A CONSTRUCTIVIST LIFE
Peter Lake

A constructivist life involves planning and magic.

"Begin each day as if it were on purpose" (Alex Hitchens, from the movie *Hitch*).

When I was four years old, my mom asked me, "What do you want to do in life?" I said, "I am going to Harvard Law School and becoming a lawyer." This was a wild claim for a toddler from a lower middle-class family (no one had ever attended a university like Harvard; my mom graduated college *after* I did, taking night courses in an adult learner "extension" program). These days, when I am in court testifying as an expert witness, even opposing counsel comment on my extensive curriculum vitae and the life I started constructing so many years ago. But I had help.

A constructivist life (one built on purpose) is the result of two forces working together – intent and magnetism. I have learned that my plans and intentions can intertwine with the magic of the universe, which brings, well, *miracles* on my path. Let's turn the page to my college years. There I am, taking mind-bending philosophy courses at Harvard College wondering if I belong and being completely intimidated by my brilliant peers and instructors. My professor, John Rawls, summoned me (yikes!) to his office to "talk about the future." To my surprise, he told me I should become a university professor (!). I could never have dared to imagine being a lawyer and *a teacher*, but my intentions set early in life put me on a path to attract opportunities and mentors than I might have ever imagined that were perfect for me.

I graduated Harvard Law and have become a lifelong law professor. I have learned to plan and aspire but also to let life come to me and open doors I never even knew existed.

My advice: Build your life, and let life build it with you.

> *Keep a lookout for that person who will help you experience life beyond your boldest plans!*

Peter F. Lake is Professor, Stetson University College of Law, Gulfport, Florida.

LISTENING AS YOUR SUPERPOWER
Catherine Malloy

Listening is a core value for relationships.

Put down your devices. Remove your earbuds. Do something extraordinary . . . nothing but listening. A new world awaits. Connect by disconnecting. Open your ears. Pay attention. Listen.

Over my professional career as nurse, educator administrator, mentor and community activist – and throughout my life as daughter, sister, wife, mother and grandmother – and with the gift of longevity, I know the value of listening as a way to communicate. It demonstrates respect of and regard for the other. Listening is a superpower infused with caring, enthusiasm, positivity, optimism and genuine interest in another person. Taking time to genuinely talk to and understand where that person is coming from is an act of caring that embodies optimism. Showing interest by asking questions about what matters to the other person encourages meaningful dialogue. Being authentic, empathic, enthusiastic and having a positive attitude underpin the art of listening. Martin Buber in *I and Thou* posits human life finds its meaningfulness in relationships. Listening is the inspiration for relationships.

I feel confident that my most significant source of inspiration for others is my ability to listen. At least that is what my students, peers and family members tell me all the time. They say, "You listen." Remember, people may not remember what you say, but they will remember how you made them feel.

So can you also hone the art of being an active listener? The short answer is yes! It might require you to think of some ice-breaking questions to ask. You might start with, "Tell me about a time you . . ." I can attest to the fact that it will enhance your life, and you will learn and begin to understand so much about human behavior – including yourself.

How do you begin? First, look at the opening paragraph above for a starting point: *Take out your earbuds.* Start with someone you don't know, such as the cashier at your supermarket or the barista at your local coffee/ smoothie place. Be prepared for an adventure, and enjoy the journey!

How does the art of listening work in your relationships with friends, teachers, fellow students and family members?

Catherine Malloy, BSN, MPH, DrPH, is professor emeritus of Health, Fitness and Recreation Resources at George Mason University. She continues to be actively involved with her coastal community and the League of Women Voters.

STRUGGLES OF THE OLDEST SIBLING
Lijah Rosario

It is important to seek and offer assistance for those struggling with drugs or alcohol.

I remember moments at the kitchen table, staring blankly into space. My backpack on the floor, my homework spilled out like confetti. But my mind wasn't on math or reading comprehension; it was on Mom.

The constant replay of last night's argument echoed in my mind. My younger siblings screaming, Mom crying, the sound of shattering glass. I tried to retreat Mom to her room; she stuffed her ears with pillows to block out the noise.

Fast forward to today, Mom looked different. Her eyes were sunken, her skin pale. She's not smiling. I knew . . . she was coming down. I've seen the evidence on the table from the night before, the way her eyes glazed over.

At school, my classmates talked about their families' bowling nights, board games, movies and popcorn. They described family vacations. I listened but said nothing, and I was aching to join in. But what could I say? "Hey, my mom's addicted to drugs, and for fun I shield my younger siblings from witnessing what I have to witness"? No, I couldn't say that. So I just kept silent; I chose to stay invisible.

One day, my teacher asked to see me after class. She said, "Hey, I've noticed you seem distracted lately. Everything okay?" I lowered my eyes down to my feet while twirling my fingers. "It's . . . my mom." Her expression softened. "Is everything all right?" I stood up straight, sniffled and wiped the tears that were forming from my eyes. "No, but it will be." She replied, "Would you like to speak to someone about it?" And for the first time in months, I felt a glimmer of hope. Maybe, just maybe, I don't have to be strong, and I'm not alone and someone will be able to help me.

I've learned many resources exist. If you or someone you know is struggling with drug or alcohol problems or addiction, please reach out to local treatment centers or support groups, as well as the National Substance Abuse and Mental Health Services Administration Hotline: 1-800-662-HELP (4357).

FIGURE 5.4
Heading to an interview with the state, exuding an air of professionalism and pride.

Think of others in your life whom you believe have a problem with drugs or alcohol. Identify where you can seek advice about the best ways to help them.

Lijah Rosario is a photographer, writer and the eldest sibling with an old soul. His journey on earth is to lend an ear and try to provide words of wisdom.

LEAN INTO YOUR FRUSTRATION TO FIND YOUR PATH
Stevan Veldkamp

Frustrations and challenges can serve as a window into productive opportunities.

Work frustrations can often feel like insurmountable obstacles to productivity, fulfillment and happiness. However, it is, in fact, important to pay attention to those perplexing feelings as they can be powerful catalyst for change.

When we confront challenges that vex us – the ones that get under our skin – we have an opportunity to transform these feelings into purposeful action. This transformation begins with acknowledging our perennial frustrations that reoccur and delving deeper into their root causes.

By understanding what truly bothers us, we can turn turbulent emotional energy into a blueprint for positive change and, surprisingly, a career.

My own experience, in a high burnout field of working with college students, has frequently exposed me to disillusionment. I found myself grappling with the feeling that my efforts didn't contribute to any real change, particularly within the realm of fraternity and sorority life. Instead of retreating from these frustrations, I chose to immerse myself in understanding them. This decision not only led to personal growth but also paved the way to leading a research center aimed at addressing these complex issues.

The key to navigating frustration is to view it not as a dead end but as a guiding force that can help illuminate a path forward. For instance, my initial conflict regarding the inherent values of fraternities and sororities compelled me to seek solutions that went beyond polarized views. I began a mission to explore how practices could be adjusted to better support groups toward safer and meaningful experience.

As I engaged in this inquiry, I discovered a wealth of perspectives on governance, funding and volunteer involvement. This newfound knowledge allowed me to not only advance my career but to also find a well of motivation.

Ultimately, our frustrations can serve as a compass, guiding us toward significant change. By investing our heart and energy into the issues that concern us, we not only elevate our own purpose but also create opportunities for others. Embrace your challenges; they could be the very spark that ignites a transformative journey and unlocks sustained satisfaction.

Identify three things that frustrate you. For each of these, how can your shift your perspective to create opportunities for moving forward in positive directions.

Stevan Veldkamp, Ed.D., is executive director of the Timothy J. Piazza Center for Fraternity and Sorority Research at Penn State. His career spans 30 years of mentoring leaders and researching best practice for student learning and safety.

BOUNDARIES, LIMITS AND GROWTH
Steve Piscitelli

Establishing clear boundaries and limits helps with healthier relationships, including with yourself.

Whenever you see Igor in the gym, he rants about political issues. You keep walking on the treadmill, hoping he will stop so you can concentrate on your exercise. Igor continues to ramble. Rather than verbalize your boundary, you fume to yourself.

Personal **boundaries** tell others what is acceptable and unacceptable when they interact with you. These boundaries establish a metaphorical property line: "Please do not cross." But you need to communicate your boundaries. If you assume people will know what or what not to do or say, you could be setting them and yourself up for failure. In the gym, you want to focus on your physical well-being. But did you tell Igor? Did you state your boundary?

Personal **limits** let people know what you will or will not do in a given situation. Without established limits, you may give more (physically, emotionally and professionally) than you want to give. Resentment, exhaustion or hurt feelings can be the result. But you do it to yourself.

Now consider Tami. She volunteers at the local animal shelter for four hours weekly. Due to a lack of volunteers, the supervisor has asked Tami to work an extra weekly shift for the last two months. Rather than refuse, Tami skips pickleball matches with her friends. She is beginning to resent her volunteer work, but she has done this to herself.

Remember, *boundaries* are for *others*, and *limits* are for *you*. Based on additional information or changing circumstances, they can be adjusted along the way. Tami could do extra work for a week or two to help at the shelter. How will the supervisor know if Tami doesn't communicate her limits?

Your goals, intentions and purpose help you grow. However, continually violating or miscommunicating your boundaries and limits might set you up for disappointment or worse. As you work on your boundaries and limits, ask yourself whether they are sensible, fair and respectful. Also important is that you communicate each of these to make sure they are known.

Take a moment today and review one of your goals. What is one boundary that you need to establish as you move forward? What is one limit?

After nearly four decades of classroom teaching and national speaking engagements, Steve Piscitelli devotes his time to writing and community-based activities.

THE CHOICES I MAKE MAKE ME
Mitchell Moore

Stop – THINK – Act.

It is 4:00 a.m. as we hurriedly made our way to the dock. After selecting our place aboard the deep-sea fishing boat, we settled in for a three-hour ride before dropping a line into the water. What would we catch, I wondered – snapper, ling, a shark? A storm that was threatening to cancel our trip was now upon us. Returning to the dock, disappointed and a cash refund in hand, I happened by a tattoo shop. Without much thought I went inside, pointed to the wall and said, "I'd like that one in blue." After a quick exchange of cash from my hand and ink into my bicep, I left with a brand-new tattoo not stopping to think that this decision, like all choices I make, lasts a lifetime.

Because each choice we make makes us.

So I offer this suggestion: Stop – THINK – Act. Had I stopped to think about the tattoo, my 20-year-old self would choose to get it. But my 30-year-old self would have asked me to move it up so the "1" that is below the end of my shirt sleeve wouldn't be a distraction in the classroom.

My 40-year-old self would like to have considered the colors fading over time, and my 50-year-old self is glad I didn't get a creature performing lewd acts under a mushroom.

Today, my 60-year-old self looks into the rearview window of life and thinks, "I am what I am today because of the choices I made yesterday. I will become what I will be tomorrow based on the choices I make today." Good or bad, right or wrong, each decision I make makes me.

I offer this suggestion: When someone shouts "Go," you might think, "Whoa." Stop and think before you act. And ask yourself whether this decision will advance you toward who you are choosing to be.

Think about a time in your past when you did not stop and think before you acted. How you feel about that today? How can you ensure that your decisions help advance what you truly seek?

Mitchell Moore has chosen to become a valuable member of the helping profession as a licensed chemical dependency counselor and internationally certified prevention specialist. He is also a husband, grandfather and beekeeper and daily enjoys his one and only tattoo.

SELF-ADVOCACY
David Gitlin

To achieve goals, one must know oneself, one's needs and how to get what one wants.

Mental health issues were a challenge throughout my childhood and adolescent years. By my sophomore year of high school, I was frustrated and misunderstood – anxiety taking tests, grades going down, self-esteem issues and emotional pain. Throughout high school and college, I sought mental health treatment. With a therapist, prior to attending college, I practiced role-playing different scenarios and formulating appropriate responses. Cognitive behavioral therapy was helpful, and I was able to assert needs confidently and also improved my communication skills and relationships.

In college, I put forth the effort to and was able to utilize Disability Support Services so I could meet my academic goals (this was personally challenging for me to request an accommodation, but I did). Communicating my needs helped overcome challenges and meet goals. Challenges faced in an academic setting were test anxiety and perfectionism. I needed to speak up for myself and be responsible to communicate with professors for accommodation requests to take tests with extended time in a quiet environment. I should not have to feel embarrassed about myself but be empowered to stand up for myself and know my worth and that I can achieve with the appropriate accommodations. I knew the material but needed more time.

Navigating social situations in the workplace was problematic, and early in my career, I was "let go" from multiple jobs. I learned to stand up for myself and advocate for myself. Staying employed while managing mental health issues was difficult.

A lack of self-advocacy skills can lead to frustration and misunderstandings. Self-advocacy skills will allow you to communicate needs, feel understood and be included in society. Accept and be proud of who you are and what you can accomplish. People are receptive to help when you reach out and are willing to put in the effort. Employment is not always stable, and revenue dries up at times; saving for the future with retirement planning, spending money wisely, eating healthy and exercising all contribute to a quality life.

Think of situations in your life where you can practice advocating for your rights and needs, connect with others and learn to ask for help.

David Gitlin is an only child, born in New York to supportive parents. He earned a master's in Rehabilitation Counseling and is a Certified Rehabilitation Counselor who provided vocational services to people with disabilities. His interests include music, reading, photography and stand-up comedy.

LATITUDE FOR THE ATTITUDE OF GRATITUDE
R. Brit Katz

Including politeness and an attitude of gratitude with others is often overlooked, yet vitally important.

What ever happened to a thank-you note? As a proud baby boomer, I was carefully tutored to hand-scribe my appreciation for every gift received. From my earliest cognitive days, I printed those brief but sincere expressions of affection for the tangible gestures extended to me. As I aged, my cursive letters became my common practice in politesse. As age inexorably changed many of my behaviors, my penchant for providing "thanks" – verbally, visually (e-cards), written – did not mellow. And it seemed that most persons of my acquaintance acknowledged personal and professional presents in a similar way.

My preoccupation with politeness carried into my four decades of leadership, teaching and service in higher education student affairs. Carrying a leather valise with me into meetings and engagements, I obsessively noted every positive contribution made by colleagues, students, families, donors and friends. At the end of a day, a week or a month, my fingers grasped pen and stationery to script a letter of recognition. If the other person's efforts were significantly beyond expectations, then a small personal gift of esteem could escort the card or letter. I felt guilty if I did not set aside time and effort to remember others through my penmanship.

So I worry about the media-reported "coarsening of the U.S.A." Have Americans become less interested in demonstrating an attitude of gratitude in our families, in our work, in our lives? Social media images leave me insensate with the videos and posts of uncivil, profane, pugilistic and generally antisocial transgressions. In carefully posed reactions, I've added workshops and presentations on the impact of positive reinforcement of all things good!

As a supervisor and leader of nascent and seasoned professionals, I love cultivating a latitude for the attitude of gratitude in our lives. Write a note. Pay a visit. Send a gift. Celebrate an achievement. Condole with a sweet memory. Take the lonely to lunch. Smile. Love. Embrace. Smile again.

I'm still working full time, as passionately as ever about commending upbeat, gracious demonstrations of our humanity. My youth's yellow hair and white teeth gradually morphed into white hair and yellow teeth. But my latitude for an attitude of gratitude is evergreen.

It's important for me to thank you for reading this! Then I pray you'll grow the latitude too!

In what ways can you incorporate acts of gratitude in the lives of others?

R. Brit Katz, Ph.D., serves as Vice President and Dean for Student Life, Southwestern University. He specializes in hiring happy, grateful student office assistants to spread the gospel of goodness and gracious gift giving.

THE SPEAKING TRADITION
Craig Esherick

Building community health starts with a smile or simply saying hello.

When my son was a high school senior, he was being recruited to play basketball by a number of Division III schools. On a recruiting trip to a university in the South, my wife and son met with a representative of the admissions office. In that meeting, the woman explained about a long-standing tradition that was an important part of the culture of the school. It's called the "speaking tradition" – it holds that you say hello to the people you see as you walk around the campus. When my wife returned home from that visit, she was excited about the school and was eager to tell me about this quaint but powerful "tradition." I'm not sure my son was equally excited. He attended a different school in the South and had a great college experience.

Fast forward to today. The COVID-19 pandemic put us and the communities we live in through a terribly disruptive ordeal that worked to distance us from those around us. The social psychologist and author Jonathan Haidt has published a new book to much acclaim, decrying the influence that cell phones, earbuds, the internet and social media has on young people today. The influence of the pandemic and many of the issues discussed by Haidt have made me think about the value of the speaking tradition.

What if every teacher, employer, coach, pastor, school principal or community organizer instituted a speaking tradition? During COVID-19, my wife and I would walk around our neighborhood and say hello to perfect strangers walking past us. Some folks were taken by surprise that a stranger was saying hello. But more often, we would receive back a friendly hello and a slight smile.

We wonder why we live in such polarized times. Maybe all we need is our own speaking tradition. Smile at your neighbor. Say thank you when someone holds the door for you. Building community *starts* with speaking to people, even perfect strangers.

What behavior or tradition can you embrace for yourself, and perhaps for a group of which you are a member, to help build community?

Craig Esherick is a longtime faculty member of sport management at George Mason University; he is the program coordinator and internship coordinator for this nationally respected program. Craig is a former Georgetown University basketball player and coach. He also was an assistant basketball coach and scout for the 1988 U.S. Men's Olympic Basketball team.

KNOW THYSELF:
RECLAIMING THE MOST IMPORTANT KNOWLEDGE

David I. Anderson

Turning inward to enhance self-knowledge increases authenticity and the opportunity for growth.

Humans possess an extraordinary gift: the ability to learn and transform. Although I resist the notion of human exceptionalism, our capacity to accumulate and share knowledge – and to change – is truly unparalleled. We have housed our learning in vast repositories of understanding: libraries, institutions and cultural traditions, each a testament to our collective intelligence.

Yet, for all our wisdom, we have developed a paradoxical approach to knowledge. The scientific method, our most celebrated tool for understanding, encourages a detached, third-person perspective that often neglects the most crucial subject of all: ourselves. We have forgotten the ancient Greek imperative to "know thyself," instead prioritizing external knowledge over internal exploration.

Our educational institutions epitomize this disconnect. Colleges and universities champion critical thinking and reasoning but rarely turn these skills inward. We learn to analyze the world but not our place within it. Science's pursuit of objectivity has inadvertently marginalized personal experience, treating our inner world as somehow less valid than our external observations.

This approach is fundamentally backward. True understanding begins with self-knowledge. Our biases, experiences and inner narratives shape how we perceive the world, yet we invest little time in understanding these basic filters. We need to harness our unparalleled learning capacity to interrogate our own thoughts, behaviors and sensations.

The most profound learning often involves unlearning – dismantling patterns that no longer serve us, challenging our assumptions and developing a more nuanced, compassionate understanding of ourselves and our world. Ultimately, by turning our remarkable capacity for learning inward, we can gain deeper insights into the problems we confront daily, become more authentic and create meaningful change within ourselves and in the world around us.

What are some things you can do – alone and with others – to increase your knowledge of yourself?

David I. Anderson is the Director of the Marian Wright Edelman Institute for the Study of Children, Youth and Families at San Francisco State University.

LIFE EXPERIENCES
Dwayne Delaney

Strive to be unselfish through the walks of life.

The most important roles within my childhood were dealing with the murder of my father and watching my grandmother, mother and sister grieve with tears running from their eyes and screams of shock and loss. While looking at my grandfather, angered and filled with disbelief, he never once shed a tear and provided the officer with a statement of vengeance and promise. While I was being questioned by the sheriff department, I witnessed my father being carried out of the home by medical professionals and deputies. The officer said that my father was fatally shot in the head.

Torn with so many emotions with vengeance in my heart, I became the man of my home and swore to be the shepherd of my family. I remember sheltering my sister from the ordeal and helping family members clean the home and my mother cleaning the bloodstained floor while witnessing dried flesh of the brain.

I was left not knowing whom to trust, being sleep deprived and with thoughts of retaliation while listening to C-murder on repeat. Refusing to assist with funeral preparation, I decided to attend school to help minimize the thoughts of my father's death. I knew the responsibility and well-being of my family fell into my hands on that day.

All this provided a lesson of value to be thankful for grace and appreciation to those that provide substance to personal development because life has no guarantee. So be selfless and not selfish. I dealt with my trauma by staying active in sports, all with the protection of my guardian angels being my coaches and family. My coaches provided structure, discipline and accountability by creating a vision of playing collegiately, thus changing the dynamic of my surroundings. Even though being mentally unstable at times, they stayed by my side without having to meet with therapists or counselors. Football and after-school activities became my protective factors, unleashing my rage one snap and one whistle at a time. It provided a release and peace necessary to change the cultural normalizations of my life to refrain from becoming a victim of my environment.

To make a change, you must be willing to help your neighbor to allow your family and community to bloom in positive ways.

Look at your relationships with family and friends. Are you being as selfless as you can? What might you be willing to modify?

Dwayne Delaney is a country boy from rural Virginia who enjoys the thrills of the outdoors, friendship, beagling, hunting and comradery. He is a regional prevention coordinator and provides in-home services to children or adults.

THERE ARE NO REGRETS
WHEN DOING THE RIGHT THING
Jerry Weiland

Learn from everything you do to lead you down the right path.

Growing up, I remember watching all sorts of television shows but fondly recall watching Officers Reed and Malloy on *Adam-12*, Ponch and Jon on *CHiPs* and Sully and Bosco on *Third Watch*. Although I never really thought of working in law enforcement, it seems like this kind of work was on my mind.

After leaving high school, I worked some maintenance and landscaping jobs. I also had a part-time security job at some concerts. There, I began working more closely with law enforcement and seeing the good that could be accomplished when dealing with various people and situations.

For example, working at a Jimmy Buffet concert, I remember a Tinley Park, Illinois police officer wearing funny margarita glasses. While performing his job, directing traffic and maintaining order, he wore those silly glasses. He was able to make a connection with everyone in a positive manner yet remain professional. The funny thing is, I don't remember his name.

After moving to Florida and working in security for Walt Disney World, I learned about speaking and dealing with people from around the world. Their mannerisms, clothing styles, vocabulary and more taught me a lot but mostly helped hone my skills speaking with people.

At the ripe age of 31, I entered the law enforcement academy and became a deputy sheriff. After almost a quarter century in this job, I have faced many life and death situations and have saved some lives along the way. I've also had to tell family members that their loved ones had died.

In looking back at the people I've met, their stories and lessons in life I learned, I can say that I have no regrets in anything I've done. I hold these experiences dearly and am proud of my accomplishments and how I have been able to make positive impacts in people's lives.

To me, doing the right thing sometimes comes with a price. However, the payoff in life more than makes up for it. While life is full of bumps and lumps, make sure to keep your eyes and ears open, learn from everything you do, each job you work and each person you meet. Those stories and the lessons will always lead you down the right path in life to be successful.

My hope is that years down the road, someone will remember a story, maybe not my name, but something I've done. Remember, no matter the jobs you do or the levels you achieve in life, wear a silly pair of glasses every once in a while.

What can you do to make sure you keep your eyes and ears open?

Jerry Weiland serves as a deputy sheriff in Osceola County, Florida.

GRACE EXTENDERS
Georgina Manahan

Looking to build communication bridges will enrich our relationships.

I'm concerned we've become a society that looks to be or feel offended. All too often, a sticky point comes up with a friend or acquaintance – or even a random stranger – and we want to revel in having been offended or in having been wronged. We will wear that cloche for a very long time, showing it off to anyone who will look and listen, ruminating on it and spinning it until, like yeast bread dough, it doubles in size.

We've become intolerant to others' opinions, different from ours, which further widens the divide in interpersonal interaction. I remember extended family dinners years ago where current event subjects were discussed passionately without repercussions. I remember a time you could offer advice or an observation to someone without them reeling in offense.

My sage advice, in the words of Bob Newhart, "Just stop it!" To get our society back on track, we need to be a people that looks to extend grace. In personal disagreements, grace extenders are open to seeing another's perspective and are open to admitting wrong. They don't allow offense to take hold in them, and they are quick to look within and offer an explanation and, yes, an apology if warranted. Grace extenders can agree to disagree and remain civil. They look to bridge the conversation gap, finding common ground if it's there and accepting that there may not be that common ground.

In many different religious faiths, we are called to love one another and extend grace to one another and, yes, to forgive one another. Let's be a people of grace extenders and let the healing between us begin.

Think of a recent situation where disagreements occurred. How would an approach of extending grace have affected the process and the outcome?

Georgina Manahan is a wife, mom, business owner and Christian counselor. Her practice, Grace & Hope in Loss, LLC, is located in State College, Pennsylvania. She has a B.A. in Psychology from Boston University and an M.A. in Human Development and Counseling from Liberty University.

YOU CAN'T DO IT . . .
Vicki Highstreet

Don't let them take away your dreams.

I was told by a high school counselor that I was not college material, but I wanted to be a teacher. Being an aspiring first-generation college student, I didn't have good resources at my disposal to help me navigate the process . . . or at least I wasn't aware of any. My parents never gave me a reason to believe that they would help me finance my education, so I worked three jobs to cover expenses of tuition, fees, books and other expenses. Thankfully, I was able to live at home. Based on these jobs, there were not enough hours in my day to include studying, so that happened when I should have been sleeping! Living at home didn't help me navigate all my fears; my parents couldn't relate and between work, classes and studying. With all this, I didn't allow time for what I needed most for my health and well-being.

I remember being so lost on campus but soon realized the importance of developing relationships. Relationships to help me study, relationships to encourage some sort of social life and relationships for sharing my hopes, dreams and concerns. This was the beginning of me looking after my emotional, social and mental well-being. I wasn't sure I'd return to school after my first year, but I persisted. It was me overcoming some of my fears of reaching out to faculty members when I needed help that was instrument for encouraging me to continue with my education. Graduating in four years and acquiring my first teaching job was an "I can do this" moment.

> What will you do to take the initiative to seek out resources to help you navigate your entrance into a new experience, such as college or a new job?

Vicki Highstreet's passion was realized through her professional association involvement working with college students and young professionals to help them see their potential, resulting in her spending 50 years in education. Her ability to facilitate workshops and individual sessions on trust and engagement brings everything full circle from the first "you can't do it" moment.

ACTING FOR REAL LIFE
James Lange

Consider nontraditional approaches to improve social interactions.

I want you to take an acting class, preferably one that includes rudimentary *improvisation* skills. But I suppose before you react to my persuasion goal, I should admit that I am not an actor or an expert in the realm of performing arts. But I once took a college acting class, so hear me out.

I took that class because the course description said it would introduce basic acting practices that may help with general presentation skills along the way. But it ended up being more transformative than I expected.

Shakespeare's line "All the world's a stage" was not necessarily intended to describe our social existence as merely a performance on a grand scale. Yet in some ways, it is. Building up the skills of an actor can truly change your real-life interactions, especially within the realm of humor and fun interactions.

It's my belief that humor is a critical skill for a happy, successful life. But there are many types of humor, some of which I'm good at, others befuddle me. For instance, I am horrible at remembering jokes, and the class didn't help that. It's the *improvisation* lessons I believe are the more transformative skill you should develop. Social interactions (almost always) benefit from a few skills: listening, empathy, validation, contribution and play (when appropriate). Learning some of the basics of improv will help for carrying out better interactions.

First, improv demands that you *listen* to your partner(s) and *understand* where they are going with the story (i.e., *empathy*). At your turn, you take a positive orientation and build on the story. The concept of "yes . . . and" reflects that improv is best if the reality created by the first person can be built on. Indeed, through that building process, a whole new direction may emerge that is better than anything you alone could have constructed. Often, this results in humor because of the surprising and often absurd twists that emerge.

Now imagine that you take these skills to various social interactions. From the weird elevator small talk to work meetings, to dinner with friends, if you approach these interactions with the skills of an improv actor, you may more successfully be spontaneous, impactful and downright funny. So I say again, take an acting class.

Whatever your setting, look up what classes, workshops or other opportunities exist and try one. Then see if it improves your social interaction skills.

James Lange has a doctorate in social psychology and is on the faculty at San Diego State University. His research studies mostly focus on how people interact with one another in ways that may either enhance or detract from better behavioral health choices.

THE JOURNEY TO HOLISTIC WELLNESS
Shawnte Elbert

True fulfillment comes from nurturing every dimension of your wellness.

In the early days of my career, I was constantly trying to figure out what I needed to do now to reach my next goal, juggling responsibilities and chasing every opportunity. I was determined to prove to myself and everyone around me that I could excel. But in my relentless pursuit of success and helping everyone along the way, I began to "feel" the impact of my decisions and lost sight of what truly mattered. My physical health started to suffer, my resilience waned and the spark of joy that had once fueled my passion began to dim.

Then one day, everything came to a halt. I was faced with anxiety attacks and burnout – a deep, overwhelming exhaustion that left me questioning everything I had worked so hard for. In that quiet, vulnerable moment, I realized that I had been so focused on the outward signs of success that I had forgotten to care for the very essence of who I was. It was a painful awakening, but it was also the beginning of a profound transformation that was truly needed.

As I embarked on the journey of healing, I had to fully embrace what I had taught others for decades: the power of wholeness through holistic wellness. I was reminded that true success isn't just about professional achievements; it's about finding harmony across all aspects of life – physical, occupational, emotional, financial and spiritual. I began to practice grounding, learned tapping from my twin sister, nurtured my relationships and reprioritized self-care and comfort in ways I had never done before. Slowly but surely, I started to feel whole again.

For young adults, especially those navigating the challenges of growing up, it's vital to understand that your wellness is the foundation of everything you will build in life. Thriving isn't about doing it all; it's about doing what matters most to you in a way that honors every part of your being. Embrace the journey of holistic wellness, and let it guide you to a life of true fulfillment and joy.

Create a simple wellness routine that includes activities that nourish each part of you. Commit to it for the next 30 days and observe how it transforms your energy, focus and overall sense of well-being.

Shawnte Elbert, Ed.D., MCHES, CWHC, is a public health leader, faculty member and wellness coach dedicated to guiding individuals toward holistic wellness and intentional living. She is the founder of Elbert Innovative Solutions and co-CEO of Sister W.E.L.L.S., PLLC.

FRIENDSHIP BY DESIGN
Jessica Abramson

Sometimes making friends requires intention, vulnerability and explicit invitations.

In college, there was a classmate in a few of my classes whom I really wanted to befriend. I could tell from her comments during class discussions that she was thoughtful and kind, and I just had a feeling we might really get along. Those few classes were our only overlap, and I assumed she had a whole, full life on campus outside of what I saw.

I made a few subtle attempts to befriend her but nothing overt enough that I risked feeling let down. It wasn't enough; we never really got to know each other. We had lunch together a few weeks before graduation. We talked about how we felt about graduating, and she told me she was more than ready to leave; she had never really found her people at our school. I was completely surprised. I'd assumed that she wasn't looking for more friends; it was part of why I hadn't ever really invited her to hang out. I felt like I'd let myself down, not taking that chance. I don't know if we would have become good friends, but whatever knowing each other would have been, we missed out on it.

Making friends, especially close friends, gets more complicated during adulthood. I've had people tell me they feel more comfortable asking someone on a date than inviting a potential friend to spend time together socially. In friendship, I think it can feel like more is on the line. Asking someone if they want to hang out is something I still find scary today, but I think an often-untold truth about life is that sometimes close relationships require immense vulnerability. Sending a text or direct message can be a good option if an in-person invitation feels too awkward or vulnerable!

You are worthy and wonderful even if someone you want to be friends with doesn't feel the same way. So take the risk. Friendship is far too precious for it not to be worth it.

> Think of one person in your life whom you'd like to befriend. What feels like the right next step in getting to know them? Reach out and make the invite!

Jess Abramson is a Clinical Psychology PhD student living in Maryland. She loves to write, analyze data and accidentally stay up far too late talking with one of her favorite people.

TO TELL THE TRUTH
Jerry Rehm

Feel confident to share the same and true you in various settings.

We are used to presenting ourselves in different ways to different people, such as parents, friends, teachers, teammates, relationship partners, supervisors, colleagues and store clerks. Humans are even good at keeping these different curated personas separate. Many of these personas withhold or add information because of cultural norms, levels of trust, or desired privacy. We add details to the stories we tell to make them more dramatic or funnier or to serve some other purpose. We may be driven by our desire to appear more confident, wiser or happier than we feel. Also, we might withhold information that would show us as depressed, sad or not conforming to our parents' or friends' social values. In the beginning, these personas aren't necessarily vastly inaccurate, and we continue to mostly reveal who we are. We might tell ourselves that these embellishments of truth are not lies and don't hurt anyone.

The trouble is that the more we blur our real self to others, the more work it takes to keep the fabrications straight. Because we become good at keeping these personas separate, it is easy to stray further and further from the truth with significantly fabricated details. Some of us keep up vastly different personas and may do so in different ways in different settings, thus substantially blurring our real self to others. We can even put ourselves in danger of separating from our own self and our personal history. In the extreme, we start reducing our participation in free-flowing interactions to avoid accidentally revealing misrepresentations. This does great harm to relationships that depend on trust. We become inauthentic and must exert a great deal of effort to keep up the multiple facades. In the end, we must face the destructive nature of this behavior and the high price we may pay for its utilization: It's a slippery slope worth avoiding.

Why even start down this path? Maintain your sense of self and reject adding embellishments. Seek out people who like the way you really are and those who still like the way you really are as you change and grow over time.

Reflect on your interactions with various people in your life, and assess how consistent you are with your own authentic self.

Jerry Rehm is retired from a career in business management, which culminated in 24 years at the United States Holocaust Memorial Museum. He is a happy man living in Arlington, Virginia.

CROTALUS ADAMANTEUS
Jon Dodrill

First impressions can be limiting and misleading.

One sunny but unseasonably cool October morning, I was starting an environmental stewardship effort to partially restore longleaf pine on a four-acre lot in southwestern Georgia. Scanning the ground, I saw an adult eastern diamondback rattlesnake (*Crotalus adamanteus*), the largest venomous snake in North America. It lay motionless in the sun, stretched arrow straight to a length of 5.5 feet, excluding its silent 12–13 segment rattle.

I remained motionless for ten minutes, closely observing the lifeless rattler. It looked bloated; its girth as thick around as my bicep for half of its body length. It must have been slowly swelling in the sun for at least two days. It was a beautifully marked snake and I felt sad. My conclusion: The rattlesnake was clearly dead; cause of death based on its large adult size could only have been human induced. Eastern diamondbacks, their numbers in decline, have long been persecuted by man commercially for their skins, venom extraction, meat, snake oil, to collect bounties, for rattlesnake roundup spectacles, for mere sport and target practice. Suburban sprawl gnaws away at wildlands, destroying diamondback rattlesnake and longleaf pine habitat.

I took the snake's body home and showed my son and grandson, maybe find out more about eastern diamondback rattlesnakes and share that information. As I bent down to grasp the tail, the rattle suddenly became erect and twitched once. I immediately backed off and walked way; when I returned, the day had warmed up, and the snake was gone.

As I reflect on this, one thing I wished I possessed more of when younger was situational awareness – being less distracted, not paying attention, being more aware of what was going on around me. We didn't have the distraction of smartphone-checking every few minutes, but I still believed I wasn't paying full attention to my surroundings. Sometimes gut feelings, first impressions and internal bias snap judgments don't tell the full story when you are dealing with sentient creatures, including humans.

This story was a personal lesson on the hazards of jumping to conclusions about people and their behavior and taking action or saying things based on false first impressions. It's also a lesson on respecting nature and appreciating the role of animals in the ecosystem of which people are a part.

What can you do to fire up the embers of your curiosity, ask questions, dig deeper, do more research to answer your questions and enhance your legacy of learning?

Jon Dodrill's career involved federal or state government–related work with both marine fisheries and terrestrial land management/resource management activities. Currently, he volunteers with assisting unsheltered individuals, promoting affordable housing and working to reduce gun violence.

A LETTER TO MY GRANDCHILDREN
Larry Moneta

Consider what makes you unique and the obligations associated with your history and ancestry.

Some of you have reached the age of "young adult," and others of you will soon get there. Your parents are wonderful role models and your individual strengths, insights and emerging life purposes serve as a reflection of your immediate environments, your own personalities and your extended families. Your other grandparents have each contributed extraordinary history and culture, and genetically you reflect distinctive elements derived from your extended families. You are each truly unique, crafted from within and without and poised to be remarkable adults.

My parents and their ancestors before them represent aspects of your lives that I hope you'll remember. My mother and father – your great-grandparents – were Holocaust survivors who lived through unspeakable horrors and yet found the resolve to overcome debilitating trauma and thrive. They survived because they resisted the urge to succumb. They survived because they refused to concede defeat. They survived by becoming clever, crafty and creative. Their strength of character has been passed down to you both in narrative and genealogy. Part of you comes from part of them.

In the years ahead, as you evolve into the next generation of adults, you'll face considerable challenges and opportunities. What you will do is less important than who you will be. As you further mature, your individual and personal values will become clearer, and aligning your behaviors with your values will ensure a joyous and fulfilling life ahead. All I ask of you is that you know your family history, that you honor each of them by being the best person you can be, that you learn from difficulties and failures, that you practice *tikkun olam* (repair the world) and that you speak out and act out in the face of injustices.

I share these thoughts with every young adult.

Ask your parents for details about their families. Ask your grandparents the same. Record the oral histories of your living family members. If they're willing, capture their DNAs.

Larry Moneta, Ed.D., is a grandfather to five including one soon to begin college. He spent more than 50 years working in higher education focused on support and service to college students. He is a child of Holocaust survivors.

IT MAY SEEM INSIGNIFICANT
Leslie Dill

Every interaction is an opportunity.

I wish someone would have told me sooner that within every interaction you have with another human, there is sometimes a not-so-obvious opportunity. Have you ever attended a meeting, event or class and met someone whom you would love to engage with on a deeper level? This has happened to me many times in my roles as both a student and a professional.

I have learned a few tips and tricks along the way that will support your engagement and relationship building efforts.

- Let me buy you a cup of coffee!
  - Or tea . . . This is a budget-friendly way to get someone out of the office or classroom and into a relaxed setting to engage with you. Find a local, quiet spot and treat the person to a cup! For some reason, people always remember this gesture.
- Be interested, not interesting.
  - People often think that others will remember you because you have done XYZ thing. In my experience, people are more likely to remember you if you are sincerely interested in what *they* are saying. Pay attention. Remember names. Bring up something specific they said during your last encounter. This will make *you* memorable.
- Treat everyone as if . . .
  - Several times in my life, I have met someone, and that person later became my colleague or supervisor. You never know when this will happen. It may be during your next class, meeting or conference. Always treat everyone you meet as if they will be on the search committee for your dream job. You never know!

I challenge you, the next time you are engaging with someone for the first time, to implement one of the above strategies. Then pay it forward by sharing these simple tips with others. It makes the world more beautiful when we encourage and support the success of others.

> *Think of someone in your life with whom you'd like to have a stronger relationship. Identify at least one strategy you will commit to doing with this person.*

Leslie Dill is a progressive southerner who has spent the past 20 years in various public health settings across North Carolina. She spent 12 years working with students at a local university and 3 years with historically marginalized populations. Leslie currently works for a consulting group providing evaluation and technical support to tribal groups.

MENTORING
Susan Marshall

The most important step in figuring out what you want to do in life may be to cultivate a mentor.

A mentor is someone who is doing something that you would like to do and who takes an interest in you. Finding a mentor requires building a network of relationships in your community. A mentor can be a teacher at school but is just as likely to be someone in the workforce whom you admire. It could be someone in your neighborhood or sport/recreation group, in your faith setting, in a support group or elsewhere in other settings where you find yourself. In fact, you may have more than one mentor.

A mentor can provide early guidance on whether you are heading in the right direction by anticipating obstacles and identifying alternatives that you may not have considered. A mentor can also facilitate access to opportunities you might be unaware of. And a mentor can provide support through your decision-making and action processes.

As a child growing up in a military family that moved every year or two, finding a mentor proved difficult. By the time I started high school, we had moved ten times and I had attended six different schools. Each move required us to start over making new friends and building new relationships.

It wasn't until I started my first job that I fully appreciated the importance of mentors. I was an associate at a Wall Street law firm. Much to my surprise, it had a very nurturing environment. Senior lawyers were willing, even eager, to mentor me. Their success depended on how much quality work they could turn out quickly, and that in turn depended on having well-trained associates working for them. I was stunned at how easily doors opened for me. I learned that I needed to be proactive in cultivating the relationships; I constantly checked in with lawyers I wanted to work with and never left for the evening before they did. I was elected to the partnership with their support and, through their teachings, became an authority on securities law and structured debt financings – things I had never even heard of before starting work.

Some action items for your consideration center on being proactive in cultivating mentors:

1. Volunteer for assignments.
2. Be available for less-than-stimulating tasks.
3. Be open to new ideas.

> *Who could serve as a mentor for you? What can you do to help establish this relationship?*

Susan Marshall is a retired partner from a corporate law firm.

LESSONS LEARNED FROM RUNNING A BUSINESS
Dave Pavlin

Some insights from our personal and professional lives can help with your life journey.

After working for other companies, my brother, wife and I started a medical equipment business. After 20 years, we sold the business after reaching several professional and personal goals. Getting away from our day-to-day responsibilities has given us a front-row seat in building relationships, managing resources and understanding human nature better.

Personal Takeaways:

- One regret is not spending more time with those who mattered. Spend as much time as possible with the ones you love and who make you feel good.
- Forget those relationships that don't bring value; they won't matter. Surround yourself with people who reinforce the good things in life. They provide insights and challenges that contribute to a better way of life.
- Do not try to please others. It is draining and damaging. Live your life the way you want. Follow your instincts. Believe in yourself early and often.
- Success comes in many. Follow your path knowing that certain key values like "mean what you say," moral character and financial health are common elements. The difference between a nurse and a doctor is the level of education attained. They both have similar passions for caring for others.

Professional Takeaways:

- The marketplace will reward or punish you, whether you work for someone or manage company employees.
- Place value on others; it improves their lives, plus you will benefit directly.
- Prepare early with education and experiences outside your comfort zone, and know a higher power exists. The earlier you prepare for life's challenges, the better your chances for success.
- We want to be proud of ourselves through stable families, good health and cherished friendships, all requiring diligent work and detailed gratification.
- An impressive résumé doesn't always translate to successful work experience. Don't be fooled by salesmanship.
- We want to trust those we interact with. We expect honest and reliable outcomes. Trusting people is admirable, but verify actions and results.

As you review these personal and professional insights, which ones do you agree with fully? Which ones do you disagree with? Which ones best apply to your life?

Dave and his wife, Ruscell, have extensive backgrounds in medical and real estate business start-ups. They are active in their community through philanthropy and volunteering. They reside in Springfield, Missouri.

THE POWER OF RELATIONSHIPS
Laura Simpson

Relationships are your greatest asset personally and professionally.

In my career journey, I've come to realize the profound impact of relationships. From the very start, building and nurturing connections has been crucial not only for career advancement but also for personal growth and happiness.

With my career, I was eager to make a mark. However, it soon became clear that success wasn't just about individual effort; it was about collaboration and mutual support. The company where I worked thrives on teamwork and provided the perfect environment to witness the magic of relationships firsthand. I found that reaching out to colleagues for help and guidance often led to innovative solutions and creative breakthroughs. These interactions allowed me to learn from the wealth of experience around me.

One of the most significant aspects of relationships is the support system they create. There were moments when challenges seemed insurmountable. During these times, the friendships I had fostered became a lifeline. Whether it was a tough project deadline or a personal hurdle, having a network of supportive colleagues made all the difference. The encouragement and advice from these relationships provided the strength to push through and succeed.

Moreover, relationships at work were not just about work. The camaraderie extended beyond office walls, leading to unforgettable experiences and lifelong friendships. From team-building activities to casual get-togethers, these moments of fun and connection added immense joy to my life. They reminded me that work could be enjoyable and that the people were as important as the tasks at hand.

FIGURE 5.5
Mickey Mouse always brings a smile to everyone's face and it reminded me daily that I had to bring smiles to my team, my colleagues and partners every day!

Relationships are invaluable; they provide support, open doors to new opportunities and enrich your life with joy and friendship. Invest time in building and nurturing these connections. Meet with people personally, get to know them, listen to what they have to share and, most important, continue to nurture your relationships over time.

Think about how support, collaboration and friendships can be pivotal for achieving you goals and finding joy in both your professional and personal life.

Laura Simpson has over 30 years of marketing experience, with almost 20 years at Disney Parks Synergy, where she held the position of synergy director.

PRIORITIZE FRIENDSHIPS
Angelo Gadaleto

Friendships are central to a fulfilling life.

Who did you think of when you read the title that had the word "friendship"? Can you identify five or more people you consider friends? Friendships come in varying degrees of intensity. We might have a continuum of friends, from close friends to acquaintances. Our frequency of interaction and history of shared experiences often determine how close we are. It's a rare and fortunate person who can identify multiple people they consider close friends. Our closest friends are those we trust to be there for us without being judgmental when needed. It is essential to know you have someone in your corner when you need emotional support.

When we are younger, there is often more opportunity to develop close friendships. I think of my friends from grade school and high school. We had spent much time together, both unstructured and structured, like being on the same sports team, sharing other activities or just hanging out. In college, we lived in close proximity and often shared similar life joys and challenges.

Unfortunately, as we progress through adulthood, it can become easy to neglect developing or maintaining close relationships outside one's immediate family. It's important to recognize this potential neglect and take proactive steps to address it. Often, you might not recognize the lack of close friends in your life until you are in a situation where you want to turn to such a close friend for support or sharing.

Developing and maintaining close friendships is easier when we make a regular effort to do so. Consider making the first move when you identify someone with whom you would like to develop a closer relationship. Plan shared activities like going to lunch or dinner, attending a sports event or activity, or any opportunity to spend time together. Reach out and stay in touch with close friends you have drifted away from and reinvest in the friendship. These shared activities not only build and strengthen bonds but bring a sense of excitement and joy, motivating us to invest further in our friendships.

If you prioritize your friendships, you will not only be happier but also experience a greater sense of comfort in life.

What steps can you take to strengthen various friendships of yours?

Angelo Gadaleto is a retired Emeritus Professor of Counselor Education who, earlier in his career, served as the director of a university counseling and learning skills center. He coordinated with his friend Dr. David Anderson in developing and administrating the College Alcohol Survey. He is the author of the popular online program *Proven Methods to Better Grades*.

BE KIND
Marguerite Phillips

Being kind to others is an important trait.

Young adults who are graduating can often be narcissists. Everything revolved around them for the last couple of years. They have received awards in sports, scholastics and the arts. Their pictures have appeared on Facebook, Instagram and in yearbooks. Now they are graduating, going to college, in the military or in the workforce. What message can I give them that will help them throughout their life whether they become executives, teachers, artists, farmers, army captains or rock stars?

I implore them to be kind. Aesop said, "No act of kindness, no matter how small, is ever wasted. It's not." Dr. Seuss wrote, "Unless someone like you cares a whole awful lot, nothing will get better."

What is a person's worth if they are not kind and compassionate? With a simple smile or making direct eye contact, you are telling a friend, stranger, illiterate person, ill person or elderly person that "I see you! You are not invisible! You matter! You are not alone!"

Young adults can practice kindness daily. Start by saying hello, opening doors and saying thank you. It will propel you to more simple acts of kindness. Hand a homeless person a bottle of water. Share a pizza with a roommate. Feed a stray cat or dog. Pick up trash when you are taking a walk. Call an old person, like your grandparents, and say, "I love you." Give them five minutes of your life story; it will lift their spirits and yours too.

Do not flaunt your kindness; just quietly give without expecting a trophy or hundreds of YouTube likes. To expect a reward for kindness negates your gift. It is not about quid pro quo. Do not expect anything in return other than knowing a simple act of kindness makes you a better person.

What can you do to extend your reach of kindness? How can you make this more central in your life?

Marguerite Phillips is a grandmother of five young adults, all finding their way in life. Her kind husband and she have been married 58 years. She is a writer, artist and a good Samaritan.

CARING
Tom Goodale

Caring is central to life.

A well-known adage tells us "life is what happens while we're making other plans." Some high school seniors have plans; some work out, some don't. Most seniors face the question, "Within the realm of possibility, what's next?" Being realistic and practical, the answer is, beyond high school, how do I prepare to make a living? With certificates and degrees, apprenticeships and trade schools, community colleges, four-year colleges and universities, *whatever* is within the realm of possibility. We need jobs, then occupations, even careers. But our "work" may be different; it's infused with moral and ethical value.

We have to figure that out while being bombarded by every sort of media clamoring for attention. So we face the question, "To what should we pay attention?" In essence, we need to determine what matters to us and what we truly care about. Here, we confront the philosopher's (David Hume) "is-ought" question: "How do we get from what is to what ought to be, from description to prescription?"

Surely no one is satisfied with what is; there is always room for improvement. Although tempting, "should" cannot replace "ought," a word in which moral and ethical imperatives are embedded. What kind of persons ought we be? In what kind of world ought we live? How can we make this our home?

A more recent philosopher (Milton Mayeroff) addressed Hume's question this way: "The extent to which persons can be said to be at home in the world, they are at home not through describing or explaining, but through caring, and being cared for." Is that not a world we dream about? Do we not hope to have occupations and careers that build that home? Because at the confluence of our work and our dreams, the current is the strongest, carrying us the furthest.

Find great mentors, head for the confluence, cultivate everyone within your reach because in the final analysis, our greatest resource is each other.

Identify at least five specific ways you can demonstrate caring in your life.

Tom Goodale is Professor Emeritus, George Mason University.

PAY ATTENTION
Daniel A. Nathan

Key to a higher quality life and success is paying attention.

By vocation, I am a professor. It means that I teach, mentor, think, research and write. And sometimes I profess, like right now. One of the primary reasons I went into this business is because of the opportunities it provides to learn all manner of things from all manner of sources—scholarship, colleagues and students. Sometimes we learn valuable lessons from unexpected sources. For that to happen, though, we usually have to do something that is challenging, which I can sum up in two words: *pay attention.*

I cannot stress this enough. Good things happen when you pay attention. When you pay attention to directions you are given, you get where you are going. When you pay attention to people's words, reactions and body language, you become a better communicator and more empathic.

When you pay attention to the world around you, you get in fewer accidents and make fewer mistakes. You also see some amazing, unexpected sights. To do so, you need to keep your eyes (and ears) open and be in the moment. You need to minimize distractions, which is hard, I know. Is there a worse distraction than a smartphone?

For reasons I don't recall, a few years ago I read a book about poker (which I don't play). The author, Maria Konnikova, a Russian American woman with a Ph.D. in psychology, was in the process of becoming a professional poker player. She sought the advice of Erik Seidel, a world champion poker player.

She writes, "When I inevitably ask him the question he gets asked most frequently—what his single piece of advice would be to aspiring poker players—his answer is two words long: pay attention. Two simple words that we simply ignore more often than not. Presence is far more difficult than the path of least resistance."

In effect, paying attention is a way of living in the now, of focusing on things that matter, of keeping your head on a swivel, of being present and mindful. It is not easy. But it's often remarkably rewarding.

Think about the numerous things you do every day, and identify ways you can increase the extent to which you are paying attention.

Daniel A. Nathan is Professor of American Studies at Skidmore College. He is the author of the award-winning *Saying It's So: A Cultural History of the Black Sox Scandal* (2003) and the recipient of a Fulbright Fellowship.

VALUING QUALITY RELATIONSHIPS

Bridget Guernsey Riordan and Collette Riordan

The nature and quality of the wide variety of your relationships can be enhanced with some straightforward approaches.

Your relationships and how you navigate them will impact your personal and professional decisions throughout your life. Having the tools to handle the complexities of relationships will help you grow, develop and learn how to be successful in a variety of situations. The relationships include family, friends, teammates, club members, coworkers, romantic partners, social media, the internet and yourself.

Research shows that learning can be enhanced by experiencing it with others. Therefore, it is important to ensure that your relationships are positive and continually support you as you experience various stages of life. Even in situations where you fail, you want to learn and have others help you make meaning of your successes and disappointments.

Many relationships are those you do not choose (e.g., family, professors, teammates, coworkers). However, you choose how to behave and react to them. Some relationships, such as friends and romantic partners, are often based on something special. Other relationships occur based on timing and locations (e.g., roommates, teammates or club members). As your preferences change, your choices in relationships likely will change too.

Caring and respecting yourself is one of the best ways to prepare yourself for healthy relationships. Being mindful of maintaining a sound body, mind, spirit and identity will prepare you for dealing with diverse individuals encountered.

In valuing yourself and your relationships, keep the following in mind:

1. Seek out the value in each person and strive to maintain mutually beneficial relationships.
2. Understand that each person is an individual with imperfections.
3. Offer grace in relationships when needed, while never allowing another to hurt or harm you.
4. Share joy, compassion and understanding with others.
5. Love yourself; find those who provide unconditional love and support.
6. Value and nurture relationships where you can be your authentic self.

For each of these categories, assess how you are doing with the recommendations cited. Where can you improve, and what goals would be reasonable?

Bridget Guernsey Riordan, Ph.D., has spent her career in higher education where she has served as Dean of Students and assisted students with identity, wellness and personal and leadership development. Colleen Riordan, M.A., has worked in environments that include service, wellness, engineering and finance.

THE ATTITUDE OF GRATITUDE
Katrina Wieberg

Live your life with gratitude.

My husband and I have always lived a pretty simple life motto – *Everything happens for a reason.* Our three children have heard this motto more times than not and often respond to situations with this very same saying. As I'm writing this, I'm preparing to celebrate my 45th birthday, and I will be thanking God for allowing me to live another day – a life with gratitude. Because of my faith, my thanks go to God. If that's not your belief, just be thankful to your higher power or just be thankful.

Centuries ago, Plato said, "A grateful mind is a great mind which eventually attracts to itself great things." I believe it is important to wake up each day and be thankful for another day. And at the end of each day, being thankful for another day. Live life with gratitude!

Be a glass half-full kind of person. A look on the bright side of a kind of person. Don't get caught up in all the rhetoric of this world. See the good in things. The attitude of gratitude!

Gratitude takes effort. Do something as simple as baking. One of my favorite things about baking is that it allows me to take my mind off things that might be weighing heavily on me. Bake with love!

Another one of my favorite things is exercising. I don't necessarily love the physical efforts during the workout, but I think about all the benefits – both physically and mentally – you gain just from giving a little bit of effort; and they really don't cost you a dime. No pain, no gain!

Live your life with gratitude, especially around the holidays, on birthdays and for special occasions. Life is precious! Not everyone in our lives will live with us eternally. I often find myself, after a special event, being so thankful that I was able to spend another day with my people. Family is everything!

Prepare a list of people, groups or situations in your life for which you can be grateful now. Reflect on this and see how it grows over time.

Katrina Wieberg is the Director of Finance & Operations at a nonprofit agency. When not at work, you will most likely find her with her husband of 22 years spending time outdoors with their children and family dogs.

EMBRACE YOUR ROOTS
Gioia Caiola Forman

Your unique heritage should be understood, respected and nourished.

As a first-generation Italian American woman, I was the first to graduate from high school, the first to go to college, the first to hold a professional job, the first to attend graduate school and the first to move away from family and relatives to teach in another state.

First, embrace your unique heritage. Be proud of your family's background and the culture that shaped you. Share traditions, language and customs with others, introducing them to the richness of your roots. Learn and cherish family recipes passed down through generations, and share them with your friends.

Understand that not all family members may embrace new ideas and customs as readily as you. Strive to excel academically and professionally, demonstrating your capabilities and contributions to the community. Embrace the opportunities available to you and make the most of your education and career.

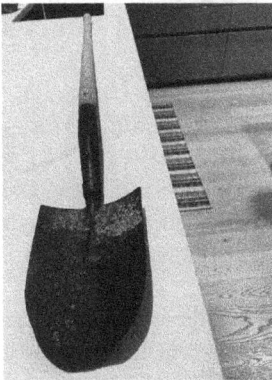

FIGURE 5.6
In 1917 my paternal grandfather immigrated from Italy with this shovel and a package of tomato seeds hidden in his pocket. I used this shovel as I became an Extension Master Gardener.

Most important, master your family's language proficiently. Reading, writing and speaking it well will not only connect you deeply to your heritage but also make you an interesting and valuable asset in any setting. It will open doors to new opportunities and allow you to communicate effectively with all members of your community.

Living in two worlds can be challenging, but it is also an incredible privilege. By embracing both your heritage and your new surroundings, you will develop a unique and multifaceted perspective that will serve you well throughout your life.

Success is not defined by conforming to one culture or another. It lies in finding a harmonious balance between the two, respecting and honoring both your past and your future. With determination, resilience and a deep appreciation for your roots, you have the potential to achieve great things. Embrace the challenges and opportunities that come your way, and never lose sight of your unique identity.

What do you know about your family heritage? How can you learn more about it?

Gioia Caiola Forman taught for a few years before spending most of her professional life as a principal. After 30-plus years in education, she went back to college to get a certification in horticulture and became a Master Gardener.

RETHINKING OUR THINKING
Amr Abdalla

Our relationships with others can be improved if we reshaped our approaches in more peace-oriented ways.

Each of us has been engaged in conflicts. Some of these are at the personal level with our family or loved ones. Some are in work settings, some are in classrooms and learning environments and others in community settings. We find conflicts when we are purchasing what we thought was a high-quality item. And some of us are, or will be, in leadership positions in our organizations, work settings and government. Conflict is often a part of our daily lives. In these various conflict settings, we often get into an either/or, good/bad, better/lesser situation. We pit one against the other and perhaps with unrealistic expectations.

How often have we engaged in such process? How much violence have we committed because we insisted that we, and only we, are the good ones? How much damage to our friendships and relationships have we inflicted on ourselves and others because we could not see that they too woke up in the morning thinking they were the good ones? And how much peace could we gain by embracing a different approach – a more understanding and peace-oriented one not only for us but also for the other?

Students come to me years after attending my workshops and sessions on peace and conflict to tell me that a reshaping of their thinking, with a new mindset, had changed their lives! They learned to make a genuine space for listening to the other and try hard to learn how they, too, wake up in the morning thinking they are the good ones! They brought more peace into their lives!

I am sure that everyone has, and likely is, engaged in conflicts at their personal, family, workplace or community level. Please try the following steps:

1. Choose one of these conflicts and reflect on the motto "No one wakes up in the morning thinking they are the bad person."
2. This time, apply the motto not only to yourself but also to the other.
3. Try hard to understand how they, too, woke up in the morning thinking they are the good ones.
4. Do it genuinely and try hard to see the situation from their side being the good ones.
5. Ask yourself, "Should I do things differently now?"

The rest is yours. Enjoy the journey!

How can you apply this different perspective to your own life? What situations are you in now where you can try this out?

Amr Abdalla is a professor emeritus at the United Nations – mandated University for Peace. He is an Egyptian American.

BE SKEPTICAL
Susan Bradford

If it's important to you, question everything you are being told.

As a teenager, somebody is always telling you what is right, what is best for you. What most teenagers don't realize is that that sort of thing, while coming from well-meaning people, doesn't always wind up being what is actually right for you. That doesn't mean you should throw out everything you are being told. But it does mean that when it is an important decision, you should do the work to make up your own mind.

Think about what people are telling you. Does it make sense? Is it coming from a place of possible bias on their part? Delve into books and scientific journals to explore the topic further. Don't rely solely on the internet or local news, as these sources often have their own agendas. Scientific journals can be *hard* to read! But you really don't need to understand it all; just go to the last section and read the Discussion section for what you actually need to know.

Emotions are important to include too. If something seems like it will make you happier, that's also a data point. Once you have all the data gathered, take time to reflect on it. Make pro and con lists – rarely is something all good or all bad. Both sides provide important information.

You will sometimes be tempted to oversimplify things to force it to come to the conclusions you prefer. Don't do that. You always get the final choice no matter what the data says, so don't lie to yourself. At the end of the day, you make what you think is the best choice and try it out! No matter what happens, that becomes an important data piece to carry forward into the next decision. Then, over time, decision by decision, you become wiser.

You will not always make great choices (nobody does), but by learning how to think for yourself and challenge assumptions that may have been baked into you before you were even able to talk, you will guide your life on the best path for you. And that "for you" really is important. It is your path, and it doesn't have to look like anyone else's.

What process do you use to make important decisions? What sources do you find to be useful and why? What sources have you found that are not helpful to you at all? How do you learn from past decisions to make better ones in the future?

Susan Bradford grew up in foster care and had a disastrous first marriage that launched her into adulthood. After a lot of self-reflection and a series of deliberate choices, she now has a loving (mostly found, not born) family supporting her in St. Louis.

FRIENDSHIP: WE DID IT
Danielle Lafrenière-Ciell

Developing and maintaining a friendship requires key features.

Friendship is one of the most precious interpersonal relationships we can develop in our lifetime. It is distinguished by its depth, sincerity and impact on our emotional well-being. In a society where human interaction is often superficial, authentic friendship offers a refuge, a space where we can be ourselves without judgment.

One of the essential characteristics of friendship is trust. This trust is built over time, through shared experiences and moments of vulnerability. A true friend is one who accepts us as we are, with our faults and our qualities. This unconditional acceptance creates a strong bond, allowing everyone to express themselves freely. Open communication is also crucial. Friends share their thoughts, concerns and dreams, which strengthens their connection.

However, friendship is not without its challenges. Misunderstandings, conflicts and differences of opinion can arise. How these obstacles are managed often determines the durability of the relationship. A healthy friendship relies on the ability to resolve conflicts constructively, to listen actively and to show empathy. These interpersonal skills are essential to maintaining a balanced and fulfilling relationship.

To what extent do the friendships in your life have these features? What else helps make them strong friendships?

Danielle Lafrenière-Ciell was born up north in Quebec, land where the sun sets very late and the snow starts very early, where the forest blends with majestic lakes and where the other becomes our survival.

LIFE'S JOURNEY
Kevin McNamee

The journey of life, coupled with adversity, can reap great rewards.

It was 1976 and my senior year at St. Bonaventure University, situated in the Allegheny Mountains of southwestern New York State. St. Bonaventure is a university founded and anchored in the principles of the Franciscan order. The Order of Friars Minor (OFM) was founded in 1209 by the Italian saint Francis of Assisi.

I had enrolled in a senior seminar that was taught by an emeritus former president of the university. Fr. Brian Lhota, OFM, was a gentle giant of a man in both size and reputation. His optimism and wisdom left a massive mark on my past, present and future. The seminar was titled, "The Teachings of Thomas Merton."

It was in this classroom that I learned that life comes with the gift of adversity. The most optimistic person is buoyed by their ability to handle what life throws at them. As a devastated 11-year-old boy who had lost his father to a war, I grew to learn at the age of 21 that I had the privilege of carrying my father's wonderful legacy of selflessness and courage to defend others' freedom – a father who fought valiantly to live as long as possible to be a husband and a father. Passing that story to my children and grandchildren has been an important privilege and gift.

The profound effect of Thomas Merton's teachings led me to the experiential laboratory of a college coaching career. It was here that the highs and lows of learning collided. Teaching young men and women to turn inevitable competitive lows into highs was everything. From here, I could only hope the seed to a full life was planted.

As Thomas Merton said in *The Seven Storey Mountain*, "Souls are like athletes, that need opponents worthy of them, if they are to be tried and extended and pushed to the full use of their powers, and rewarded according to their capacity."

The Franciscans talk about the good journey, and these are only two examples of what goes into that journey. Their mantra is, *Pax et bonum*; the simple phrase means, "Peace and goodness." Embrace the journey.

> *What and who are core influencers of your life journey? How do you learn from life's highs and lows?*

Kevin McNamee worked on the backstreets of NCAA college athletics/higher education for over four decades. Husband to a saint, father to three beautiful daughters and "Gipi" to eight gorgeous grandsquirts.

ACCEPTING THE CHALLENGE
Lee Kooler

Challenges can be truly rewarding.

As a psychology professor, students who would present me with challenges would spend time in my office, and to my surprise, these special students would give me my most rewarding experiences.

As I walked into my classroom of 100, I was struck by the appearance of a student on life support – Christamae Zimple. She was on oxygen and had a feeding tube and was reclined in a specialized wheelchair. She presented me with a multitude of challenges. My inexperienced response would have been, "Oh no, this is going to drain my energy and make it hard to teach the other students." However, I knew I had the patience and compassion to help her succeed; plus, she would give me much more than she received.

I nominated her for "Disability Student of the Year." At the ceremony, she was joined by her mother and sister. As I looked at the three wheelchairs with life supporting devices, I thought how fortunate I was to have met such an incredible student. She earned an A+ and became my best teaching assistant!

Teachers know the signs of a student who is going to require extra help and patience. They interrupt class, stay late to ask questions and visit our offices spending an exorbitant amount of time seeking help. Multiple emails daily ask for directions and exceptions to the workload. Although I may think, "Here I go again with another needy student," I often found that these students brought me an opportunity to have the exact experience I was hoping for when I aspired to be a professor. I valued being a mentor to nontraditional students.

I encourage you to accept the challenge of someone who requires more from you than you want to give. Also, I encourage you to approach them with the gratitude that they will stretch you to serve them. Know you will be rewarded with the satisfaction of doing so. These may be your coworkers, students, patients, clients, neighbors or relatives. They are going to come into your life and help you find the blessing that awaits.

Identify who in your life may require extra attention or assistance. How do you feel about aiding them?

Lee Kooler was a professor of psychology for over 40 years at a community college. Each semester, she taught 340 students. She loved teaching these students and helping them realize their dreams!

SMALL ACTS, BIG IMPACT
Jean Chin

Small sincere acts are powerful and will uplift, enrich and positively impact others.

How did you do it? How did you create a culture where people felt valued, respected and nurtured? I've been asked these questions many times and since retiring, I have had ample opportunity to reflect. I led an organization that grew to over 300 staff. With so many, I needed to make small, everyday actions count. Grand gestures like those movie moments that take your breath away aren't scalable or practical. Small acts are simple, inexpensive and repeatable and leave long-lasting impressions.

I learned names: Using someone's name conveys value and respect. I met every new staff member during their orientation. Five minutes was enough time to learn their names, their role and what I could do to help them succeed.

I actively listened: Active listening requires focus, a willingness and ability to understand and practice, practice, practice. To avoid distraction, I stepped away from my computer. I learned to listen without interrupting and without planning my next question. I learned to listen with the right body language, leaning in, eye contact and an open posture. Active listening takes patience, but the payoff in understanding the other person's perspective, context and reasoning is worth the investment.

I sent handwritten notes: I sent birthday cards to every staff member annually. The notes were brief, no more than four sentences, but they were personalized and included words of appreciation for their contributions to the organization. Text messages and emails are expedient, but nothing is more meaningful than a handwritten note.

These actions require intention and a sincere effort to understand, recognize and appreciate someone. As a result, people feel valued, respected and empowered. You don't need a staff of 300 to start. Try one small act on one person. The return on investment will be astonishing. No one states this better than Maya Angelou: "I've learned that people will forget what you said, people will forget what you did, but people will never forget how you made them feel."

What small acts can you engage in, starting today, that can have a positive impact on others? Once you do some of these, reflect on how it feels.

Jean Chin is a physician educator who teaches medical students the power of active listening and learning and using patient's preferred names. She continues to handwrite notes of appreciation in her many roles as board member, educator, health-care provider, clinic supervisor and mentor.

MAKING YOUR HOBBY YOUR JOB
Kirsten Agla

Making your hobby your job means turning a fun activity into work, which has its pros and cons.

Let's say your favorite hobby is playing video games. You get home, sit down after a long day of school or work and start playing. "I wish I could do this all day every day!" you think to yourself as you smash the buttons on the controller. You even go so far as to play all weekend. Then your wish becomes a reality as you are offered a position as a game tester in which you play video games 40 hours a week!

You love your new job at first. You brag to your friends and family about this amazing way to make a living by doing something that you love. But as the months drag on, you notice that you are enjoying the job less and less. The company chooses which games to play and sets quotas. After a long day of work, you get home and don't know what to do with yourself. The idea of playing video games to decompress after having just spend eight hours playing video games makes you recoil. Your wrists hurt. The activity that you used to look forward to has become work, and now you need to do something else to relax after a long day. You take up hiking. "I wish I could do this all day every day!" The cycle continues.

So, is making your hobby your job a genius move or a misguided mistake? The answer is really for you to decide.

Is your hobby a potentially lucrative career? Will putting financial pressure on your hobby make it less enjoyable?

Kirsten Agla turned her hobby of learning languages into a job, regretted it, then changed her career path to work as an academic adviser at a college. She now enjoys her hobby again.

TOMORROW CAN WAIT

Susie Reece

When you don't want to see tomorrow, simply breathe through today.

They say at 10,000 hours, a person becomes a "master" in a subject. I estimate I've spent 33,800 hours over the past ten years of my life trying to understand suicide. People have called me a "suicide prevention expert" for some time now. I guess, according to the saying and time I've invested, one could say it's true. However, I know better.

You see, suicide is my experience. It is one I have lived through in several ways, but the one that matters most right now is that I lived through wanting to die. I can't count the number of hours I've spent wishing I weren't alive. I wonder what they would add up to if I could count them. I know suicide isn't something I can master. But despite those hours, I am still here.

During those dark times, I could never have imagined my life being what it is today. I didn't believe I deserved any of what I have now. I felt like life had been wasted on me and that I had nothing to offer anyone, this world or myself. I was hopeless, but I continued when I didn't want to. I made it through, even when I was doing everything I could think of to destroy myself.

Today, life isn't perfect by any means. I will always struggle within my mind to keep going, but I know now that means I have a chance to see things I could never dream for myself.

If you are reading this and you've felt the soul-numbing urge to leave this world, know you are not alone. You can make it through. There is no telling what tomorrow might hold for you, but in this moment, tomorrow doesn't matter. Only today does. And all you need to do today is breathe. Just breathe past your brain, that sinking feeling and anything else that might make you feel like you shouldn't be here.

Take a deep breath through your nose. Hold it and count to five. Release it through your mouth. Do it again and again.

Breathe through today. Tomorrow can wait.

Think about a dark time that you or a friend have experienced. Identify now places, people or resources that you could have called on for assistance.

Susie Reynolds Reece has been a recognized leader and suicide prevention strategist for nearly a decade. Reece's lived experience ensures she continually centers the needs of those most affected by suicide. You can connect or learn more about her at susiereece.org.

AVOIDING THE HUMPTY DUMPTY DILEMMA
Shane Varcoe

Understanding the context is critical for any decision-making.

Humpty Dumpty sat on a wall.
Humpty Dumpty had a great fall.
All the king's horses and all the king's men
couldn't put Humpty together again.

It still surprises me how many Gen Now punters know this old nursery rhyme – even finish it for me in various speaking contexts. Although most would not consciously understand what I'm about to say, I think this age-old rhyme resonates even louder today than any other time in its history. It's an inventory on so much of what has become "Western culture."

Let's interrogate the tune. First, this current Gen Now is the most potential-optioned generation in human history. Greatest potential for knowledge, good health, longevity, productivity and so forth, yet it would appear simultaneously the most vulnerable.

This begs the following questions:

1) How did Humpty Dumpty today get so fragile?
2) What's a fragile individual doing in a precarious place?
3) Did Humpty fall, or was he pushed? What caused that?
4) Why can't governments (all the king's resources) fix this problem?
5) And to where do "kings" go to find solutions?

Decision-making is always the key to any success or failure in life, but in what context you make those choices is key.

Context is everything! What you do, how you do it, when and with whom are all important, sure. But they are not as important as why? If you don't have a sustainable why or a sound "because" for your choices, you are fodder for the system. You are easy to manipulate, coerce, seduce and con. I don't know anyone who knowingly wants to be in that space, but that's the key; if you don't know you don't know, then you're easily chewed up and spit out. If you don't have a solid framework for rational, sound, wise and well-considered decision-making, then you'll simply default to the M.U.S.T. (mood, urge, taste and symptom) does. These anchorless psychosocial *bullies* will almost always bring you and/or those around you undone.

How can you better understand the context for your decisions, large and small?

Shane Varcoe has worked with children, youth and young adults for over 40 years in varied settings. As a youth and child care worker and a credentialed minister, he has journeyed through the many vicissitudes of life.

HOW TO NEGOTIATE A SALARY AND A LIFE
Shirley C. Golub

It is important to know your worth as you pursue professional compensation and your life overall.

As a former recruiter-turned-therapist, I know that salary negotiations can challenge your confidence and sense of self-worth. I have negotiated hundreds of salaries over the course of my career and want to share what I have learned over the years.

First, always negotiate your salary, especially if you are a female. As a recruiter, I always expected to negotiate with candidates. Yet, I discovered that men almost always negotiated, while women rarely did. I believe there are a confluence of reasons for this, including societal messages to women. It can be an uncomfortable experience, but it is a skill that you can and should learn and continue to improve on.

Second, take the time to learn the mechanics of negotiating salaries, including doing research on your industry and knowing the market. There are many credible resources online for this.

Third – and this is the hard part – know your worth. This search does not happen on Google; rather, it happens within. A salary is just a number, but it does not represent you as a person.

What qualities, skills, values and experiences do you bring to the table, not just to this potential job but in life? There is no need to detail these in the actual negotiation, but this knowledge will empower you. Be honest with yourself but also be kind. If you are unsure of where to start, you may want to reach out to a former teacher or mentor. This exercise may take a few hours or a lifetime, but it is important.

Finally, regardless of the number you land on, do not conflate your job with your life. Your job can be an important and meaningful part of your life, but do not let it be your entire life. Make genuine connections with others. Do the things that bring you joy. Make time for what matters to you. The more enriching your life is *outside* of work, the more value you will bring *to* your work.

What can you do, including people to talk with, about gaining clarity about your worth in your work setting?

Shirley C. Golub is a licensed professional counselor and career coach with a private practice in northern Virginia. Prior to working in mental health, she was a recruiter and human resources generalist in various industries for over 16 years.

LIFE IS WORTHWHILE, MAKE THE MOST OF IT
Robert K. Barney

Our lives benefit from quality relationships with others.

Read the title again. Truer words were never spoken! As far as we know for certain, one comes down the pathway of human life only once. If one desires to live that life with the least degree of discomfort, the greatest amount of personal pride and satisfaction, the finest levels of physical and emotional health, then consider following a pathway of balance between family, community, professional and worldly involvement.

As I write this short reflection, I am one month short of my 93rd birthday. I just may reach 100, as my mother did before passing away peacefully three months short of her 104th birthday in 2011. I was a Great Depression baby, a World War II teenager, a military enlistee during the Korean War, a college student with a growing family in the 1950s/'60s, a professor of physical education/kinesiology at four universities in the United States and Canada, and a professor emeritus at Western University in Canada for the past 25 years. My mother, an accomplished concert pianist performer/teacher in Boston, and my father, a military officer of high rank whose career spanned from the heroics of horse and saber to the catastrophic consequences of nuclear weaponry, were folks worthy of emulation.

From my superb parents, I was given a deep spirit of responsibility to others through service. I confess to being an eternal optimist, wedded to a "glass half-full" mentality and demeanor. To some, I'm sure, I am an embellishment of the term "Pollyanna." Nevertheless, that "responsibility root" translated to an important consideration underscoring my life among human beings – the power of human relationships.

None can escape the fact that our lives are embedded in engagement with others. For me personally, the effort has long existed to make personal relationships a core priority in the pursuit of a happy lifelong pathway. I strive to seek the friendship, collegiality and company of those that share my "optimism toward life." In that respect, I find much sense in carefully contemplating and applying the challenge laid before me by the 20th century's most distinguished scientist, Albert Einstein: "Stay away from negative people. They have a problem for every solution."

Reflect on your current relationships. What can you adjust with them to make them most appropriate and helpful for your current life journey?

Robert K. Barney is Professor Emeritus at Western University. As an undergraduate, he was an intercollegiate athlete – football, baseball and swimming. Specializing in Olympic research, he has published 300 scholarly items.

PERSPECTIVE
Eric Anderson

Breathe, just breathe.

My story comes from a solo trip through Thailand. What better place to get lost! The trip started by my losing my wallet in the airport I was leaving. I realized it after trying to buy a sandwich while standing in front of my next gate. "Now boarding for Tokyo." It was a 15-hour flight. I was off to a great start.

Fast forward. I had spent two weeks wandering Thailand. I spent a week on the beach in Phuket and a couple of days at an elephant sanctuary. I ate things I didn't know what they were. Next thing I know, I was sitting in a packed Chiang Mai food market around midnight, eating alone when a female, about my age, asked if she could join me. Normally, I keep to myself, but not having spoken English in weeks, I smiled and she smiled back. She had an eastern European accent but knew English quite well. She knew slang and probably was more formal than I. A spy perhaps? We visited for hours. We talked about our families. What we did for work. She finally got around to asking what an American was doing alone in northern Thailand. I was escaping my divorce the year before. I felt like I was starting over. While feeling sorry for myself, it was her turn. Little did I know that my sorrow would quickly turn into a large piece of humble pie. She was from Russia, escaping the war in Ukraine. *Sigh*

All too often, we spend our time looking to fit in or looking down on someone. Some people are just looking for their next place to sleep.

I check in on her from time to time. She's currently in Hanoi, Vietnam until that visa expires. Then who knows? There's a saying when things aren't going right, go left. I say breathe, just breathe.

Life will be scary, but it will also be fun. Smile. It can be overwhelming at times. Laugh. You'll get lost. Ask for help. Your train will break down. Be patient. You'll spend more than necessary. It's okay. But you'll walk away having learned a thing or two, perhaps about someone else and about yourself. See as much of the world as you can. Step outside your comfort zone. Say yes, but take care of yourself. Talk to people with a different point a view. Even though we may speak a different language, we have so much in common.

Someone once said, "The best time to plant a tree was yesterday. The next best time is today."

What perspectives can you incorporate in your own life today?

Eric Anderson is a travel and sports enthusiast. He is always willing to help, and you won't find him without a smile on his face.

SENSE OF BELONGING
Ricardo O. Sánchez

Expressions of kindness provide a welcome foundation for so many people.

Compassionate messages rooted in a deep sense of humanity have the power to change lives. As an immigrant from Peru to the United States arriving as an unaccompanied minor, I experienced firsthand the shift from having a large family, many friends and a caring community to having none. The greatest challenge wasn't the lack of social connections – I knew that would come with adjusting to a new culture. Instead, the hardest part of the immigrant experience was the lack of a sense of belonging and the feeling of being out of place or even unwanted in this new society.

I have seen nonimmigrants as well as people from all walks of life experience similar feelings of loneliness and a lack of a place to call home. During my own year of feeling like an outsider – empty and without a sense of belonging – I encountered a stranger on the street. He sensed my vulnerability, my struggle to fit in and my desire to be accepted. With eyes full of compassion, he looked at me and said firmly, "Ricardo, I want you to know that you are welcome in this country. Your presence matters here. You are a valued member of our community, teaching us about courage and reminding us that dreams and hopes have no borders." I was stunned. I never expected to hear such a heartfelt message of welcome from an American. His words were like music to my ears – powerful words that lifted my spirits and, in many ways, changed my life.

We all have the power to heal and unite. No matter your background, you can touch someone's life or be the recipient of a blessing from a total stranger. As you go through life, take any chance you have to reach out to a stranger, a neighbor or someone from afar. Share something heartfelt that makes them feel at home, that makes them feel wanted. Small acts of kindness can be the spark that lights someone else's path, giving them strength to move forward. You never know, you may change someone's life or even your own in the process.

Think about some specific ways you can extend your hand of welcome to others over the next week and beyond. How does that feel?

Ricardo O. Sánchez, Ph.D., is codirector of Eagle Condor Center, a private practice group in Virginia. He has worked with immigrant families on topics related to family reunification, unaccompanied minors and domestic conflicts. He provides consulting and training on immigrant integration and inclusion, cultural competence and promoting social inclusion and equity.

PARENTS' STORIES
Jennifer Murphy

Do not let your parents slip away without discerning their stories.

When we lose our parents, especially the last parent, we typically lose the thread of generational reach. Our parents' young lives – as children, as newlyweds, as 20- and 30-somethings – are gone. And yet, those are often the events that formed those people who helped nourish us to be the individuals we are.

Of course, we all know the basics of the contours of our parents' lives. But everyone has a past that is rich in stories – some are simple such as adventurers of a childhood hike – some more complicated such as teenage friendship intrigues. Some stories are eventful such as travel stories; others are just funny as in how Santa's real persona was revealed. You will find there is infinite power in learning the rich elements of your parents' lives.

Beyond your parents' lives, imagine how much detail they can give about events that occurred before your memory and how much color they can add to events that you remember, yet only from a child's perspective.

Here are several things you can do so you can learn more about their backgrounds and what shaped them.

1. Think about stories your parent has talked about or gaps in your knowledge of them. For a special holiday or a birthday, give those questions to each parent in little strips along with a notebook. Ask the parent to answer the questions in the notebook and suggest the notebook be given back to you the following year.
2. Show your parents how to record onto their phones and how they can save the recording. Then, when you think of a question, send a text and request that they record their response.
3. Find some pictures of your parents as children. Ask them for the stories behind the pictures.

While this is focusing on your parents, you might consider doing the same with grandparents, other relatives and even special people in your life.

Ask and be persistent!

Identify at least one new way you can learn more about your parents.

Jennifer Murphy spent her career in university research administration, serving as Assistant Vice President for Research for several years before retirement. She enjoys being a mother, grandmother and now great-grandmother and further enjoys volunteering with the Amadeus Concert Series, local garden club, and her Episcopal church.

TIME IS REAL
Kevin Wang

Take the time to focus on what is important in life.

My legal name is Yingwei Wang, and I am from mainland China. Kevin is the nickname that I picked for myself from the famous movie *Home Alone* because I was naughty and always home alone when my parents went to work.

I thought a childhood like that would make me a strong and independent person. However, I found that I am demanding and I am longing for love, especially love from my father.

One thing I regret is that I did not spend enough time in understanding him or even knowing about him. Believe it or not, I don't even know what he did for a living, and he passed away five years ago.

We always think we will have plenty of time to be with our family, but this is not accurate. Yes, we should focus on what we want to achieve in our career as well as in our lives overall, but it should not become the excuse that we do not spend much time with our family. Put down the smartphone and all kinds of smart devices that you use to kill time, Be a real smart person to treasure the ones you love and the ones who love you. We don't kill time, but time kills us. Oh yes, it kills all of our beloved family eventually.

> Think about what is most important in your life today. Now do an honest appraisal of the quantity and quality of time you spend focusing on that.

Kevin Wang was born and raised in mainland China, who luckily received a lot of support and guidance from family and friends to study in college and universities in China, the United States, and Australia and is now working as a data analyst at National Australia Bank in Melbourne, Australia.

CHOOSE YOUR TRIBE
Rikki Barton

You have the choice to be intentional about the people who are in your life.

"Show me your friends and I'll show you your future." Ever heard that? I used to roll my eyes when my parents would say that to me. Granted, I had some pretty great friends growing up. We were do-gooders – volunteering, going on mission trips and being active in community activities. My teenage friends and I made choices that put us on a path toward becoming responsible adults, and we supported one another in the development of strong belief systems and values.

However, after graduating from college, I moved 1,800 miles away to challenge myself to start a brand-new life. It was a fun adventure, but the initial friends I made in this new setting lived their lives differently from how I did and how I wanted to. Although I tried to tag along in their fun, it was incongruent with who I am as a person. After three to four months of trying to fit in with this group of friends, I realized that they weren't my tribe. I didn't want to cultivate those friendships because they weren't beneficial for me and who I wanted to become. If I stayed in those friendships, my life would look very different today. I made the conscious choice to end those friendships because it was more important to me to live in congruence with my beliefs than it was to feel accepted or have that social life. I'm thrilled to say that after some time, I cultivated a wonderful tribe of new friends who aligned with my future.

So how much does who you surround yourself with influence and affect who you become? The answer, I believe, is very much. We have the right, and dare I say the responsibility, to intentionally choose the people we want to be surrounded by. Choose your friends wisely. If there are people who frequently put you in situations of discomfort, danger or risk, it's time to move on from those relationships. If you feel used, undervalued or misunderstood, seek to find people who treasure your thoughts, perspectives and time. Decide who you want to be, and get yourself a tribe that fuels that future you.

Thinking about what kind of person you want to be, who in your life affirms that? Who draws the good out of you? What relationships can you cultivate to aid in your development, success and overall well-being?

Rikki Barton has a passion for travel, including public speaking/training all over the nation as well as adventure trips to do things like the Everest Base Camp trek, summit Mt. Kilimanjaro and visit just about any country to play outside.

AUTHENTIC SELF
Sara Hussain

Embrace your true self by finding your voice and maintaining your core characteristics despite external forces.

As a Sudanese Muslim girl, I grew up accustomed to certain cultural norms and values. When I came to America, I was very excited. However, the cultural shock was gut wrenching, as I quickly learned how unkind some people were due to how different I was.

I often endured a lot of criticism. While changing every bit of myself, I lost track of who I truly was. The girl who once read Quran for a hobby, competed in piano playing and enjoyed grocery shopping with her mother slowly began to fade. The older I became, the more lost I was. I rapidly learned how the color of my skin, my religion, the texture of my hair and the certain confidence in my voice were all a problem, and soon the word "racism" surfaced. I never really knew much about racism until I came to America, where I was boxed in just for being a certain color, where I was looked down on by certain people and denied jobs due to my hair being "unprofessional."

My passion for my job and the goals I wanted to achieve in the world would become tainted by the judgment of those who hated me, felt as though I was inferior to them and had the upper hand. Through it all, I always wondered where the kindness of people hid. I made a vow to remain myself and balance the two cultures by remembering the moments when friends were kind, helped me learn English and reminded me how charming my Arabic/African accent was. I highlighted those mentors who encouraged me to embrace myself, never missed an opportunity to tell me how beautiful my hair was, how passionate and intelligent I am and inspired me to dream big.

I began to love my sharp edges, how gentle my heart was, the beauty in the sound of words that I spoke, the passion and assertiveness in my tone and in all my work.

Although it is difficult to assimilate to another culture, do your best to remain who you are, value your core characteristics and your own cultural values and find a way to balance these without losing who you are. In a world that doesn't like different, choose to stand out and be your own person.

Reflect on your self today. Were you kind? Did you make someone feel welcomed and help them embrace a part of them?

Sara Hussain is a daughter, a sister and a friend who prides herself in helping those around her embrace their resiliency and difference. She is a therapist helping others adjust to a new world while remaining themselves.

HAPPINESS IN A RELATIONSHIP
Lon Tosi

It is important to establish a lifelong happiness game plan in a relationship.

My wife and I have weathered many storms, like losing our first child. We have survived lost jobs, losing friends and our entire families. My wife survived bouts with a deadly autoimmune disorder and cancer. However, we have thrived – together! But how?

Happiness in a relationship can be a precious gift. Achieving it should be a goal. It can be empowering. It needs to be nurtured.

The following captures our happiness secret:

FIGURE 5.7
Prior to the start of an Orlando area wedding ceremony, Lon Tosi, at 76-years old, keeps an active and positive mind, and a strong exercised body.

Speak often about anything and everything.
Seek praise, understanding and support from each other.
Share both significant and insignificant daily things with each other.
Listen, strengthen, support and praise.
Smile, laugh, strut and dance, even if you can't dance.
Show strength, courage, weakness and need in equal measures.
Bolster each other, and praise all accomplishments.
Do not display selfishness but rather selflessness.
Be fiercely loyal. Be a best friend.
Act like you are still dating.
Listen to the little sounds that you each make, and smile at them.
Work hard. Play even harder.
Sing, even if you can't do it well.
Chase each other, and breathlessly giggle about it.
Touch, hold hands, bump, pat and hug.
Pay attention to each other. Share looks, wink and make funny faces.

Believe in "I am."
With little efforts each day, happiness will occur in spite of all obstacles.
Act happy, and happiness will act like it has found you.

What can you do to build and improve the happiness in your relationships?

Lon Tosi is a sales professional with over 50 years of experience. He currently is a professional wedding officiant, with nearly 3,000 weddings conducted.

EMBRACE YOUR COMMUNITY
Isabelle Louhisdon

Take intentional steps toward self-discovery by leaning into the support of your community.

As I approach my 40s, I reflect on a journey that has taken me from uncertainty to clarity, and I want to share a piece of wisdom that has guided me: Turn to your community for help.

Growing up, I wasn't sure what I wanted to do after high school. I didn't have clear guidance, and I struggled to find my path. What I now realize is that sometimes the answers we seek lie not within ourselves but in the people around us. During the years I spent as a special education teacher, I witnessed firsthand the power of community. The teachers, parents and students I worked with taught me more than any textbook ever could; they taught me about resilience, vulnerability and the importance of hard work.

After the pandemic, like many, I found myself questioning everything – my career, my faith and my purpose. I felt stuck, as if I were living a life I hadn't planned. This led me to a deeper exploration of who I really am and what matters most to me. Through this journey, I came to understand that being intentional and proactive in my choices has been the key to finding purpose and happiness. Life is not about perfection but about growth and change. The lessons we learn during each season are the stepping stones to understanding our true selves. When we have setbacks, we have to ask ourselves, "What lesson can I take away from this experience?"

I urge young people today to take time to connect with their community – family, teachers, mentors, religious leaders and neighbors. These people can help provide clarity when you feel lost. Don't be afraid to ask questions, seek guidance and embrace the wisdom around you. It's through these relationships that you will find the courage to carve out a path that resonates with your true purpose.

Reach out to someone you trust – a teacher, mentor or family member – and have a conversation about your goals, struggles and dreams.

Isabelle Louhisdon is a Black Haitian American woman in her 40s and believes that connecting with community and finding one's life purpose leads to true fulfillment.

SEEING THINGS FROM ANOTHER'S POINT OF VIEW
Steve Schmidt

Having greater empathy with individuals and groups will provide rich rewards.

Empathy, or in simple terms, "putting ourselves in someone else's shoes," is important in our interpersonal relationships. However, it can be a powerful guide in our careers as well. I have found it to be a valuable attribute in policy and program development, organizational management and communications.

Many of us are faced with challenges of solving problems or bettering a current situation that requires working with populations and organizations with diverse perspectives. Many times, those individuals or groups with whom we work have conflicting goals. Understanding why these differences exist is an important part of the research, development and implementation of policies and programs. Often, our challenges require balancing these diverse perspectives and reducing as many barriers to success as possible. Asking ourselves the question, "How will this be viewed?" or "Why would there be opposition?" and *sincerely* seeking to answer these types of questions can often help us to enlist skeptical, even adversarial, players. This can also help us be prepared for how to respond to or alleviate concerns.

Empathy is also important internally in our work settings; it helps with understanding the priorities and processes of our organizational leaders, other departments and our coworkers. This is especially helpful with our supervisors and those we supervise, who can be critical about how we interact, prepare and carry out tasks. In addition, empathy helps us to see those around us as individuals coming from diverse backgrounds, with varying perspectives and at times experiencing challenges we may not fully understand.

Last, when communicating with external and broader audiences, my preparation would include seeking out the issues of concern, knowing the circumstances that may be at the top of their minds and being sure to direct my communications in a way that respects their current situations.

I believe that this empathetic approach has not only contributed to a satisfying career but also many lifelong friendships and the respect of others.

As you actually incorporate greater empathy in various settings and situations in your life, what do you notice regarding your interactions?

Steve Schmidt has held leadership positions in government and nonprofit organizations focused on alcohol issues, policy and regulation for over 40 years. He continues to mentor and consult with persons and organizations that are focused on improving policy and programs to improve communities.

AUTHENTIC RELATIONSHIPS
THAT STRENGTHEN YOU
Alex Voorhees

Build relationships that nourish you, inspire others and walk alongside you.

Now a decade into my post-college life, I'm reminded just how difficult it can be to build meaningful relationships that last. The few high school and college friends I keep in touch with are rare connections, while the most significant friendships in my life now have been built in the last ten years, many in the last three. Building a community that means something to you is not accidental – it takes work and is built with intention.

Sustaining friendships requires recognizing three key roles in your life: those who pour into you, those you pour into and those who walk beside you.

Think about who is pouring into you. These could be mentors, guides or friends who are further along and challenge you. These are the people who push you to grow and can offer something that you don't have yet. This allows you to grow and cultivate healthy friendships all around you.

Reflect on who you are pouring into. Giving is a fundamental part of building relationships. There are people around you who are not as far along and can benefit from your wisdom. I'm not sure why it's important, but I've found that I become personally encouraged in those relationships where I am lending my time and attention to others.

Finally, who are the people by your side? These are your peers, the ones who are doing life with you. You celebrate wins together, grieve losses and laugh through the mundane moments. These may be colleagues at work or school. They may be those with whom you are serving in the military or volunteering in the community. These may be others on a local athletic team or even dealing with some family or community issues.

As you consider how to apply these perspectives, think about who fills these roles in your life today, and whom you might need to reconnect with. Consider ways you can organize your schedule to accommodate these relationships regularly. Taking steps to build a lasting community around you can be so rewarding. Life is so much richer when shared with others!

Make plans to reach out to someone in each of these roles – express gratitude, offer encouragement or simply spend time together.

Alex Voorhees holds a degree in finance and is a certified financial planner. He and his wife and two children are actively involved in their church. Alex serves on the board of a nonprofit organization that raises scholarships while educating students on financial markets.

DON'T BE AFRAID TO TALK: CONVERSATIONS MATTER!

Elaine Pasqua

Humans are social creatures. Effective communication and connections are the essence of human interaction and success.

As a professional speaker for three decades, I was recently asked by a podcast interviewer, "What is the number one thing you owe your years of entrepreneurial success to?" Without hesitating, I replied, "Talking to people."

Humans are social creatures, yet we've been slowly disconnecting from one another, largely due to the increased use of technology and social media.

The hallmark of effective communication is the ability to ask questions and, more important, to listen. Questions permitted me to learn about my client's challenges and needs. This allowed me to grow, help solve my client's problems and sustain my business. Gaining a greater understanding of their issues resulted in my ability to remain relevant.

Fearless networking led me to unimaginable opportunities. I was never afraid to call people to introduce and promote my services. Relationships matter! Through these relationships, I garnered introductions to those who opened doors for me. Don't be afraid to ask for help or for contacts. You have a 50-50 chance of hearing yes. If you don't ask, you have zero chance.

How can you connect with others with confidence? First, put your phone down and talk to people around you. Many are buried in their phones, causing them to miss out on opportunities around them. You never know who is sitting next to you. People have lost the ability to establish eye contact, along with the skills or confidence for a casual conversation.

Small talk is a great start! We all share things in common no matter who we are. We can talk about the weather, news, music, sports, . . . many possibilities.

Many are reluctant to adopt this strategy for fear of rejection. Rejection is part of life. We must learn to accept it with grace, dust ourselves off and pick ourselves up again. With every rejection, my resolve grew stronger to rise above it and move on to the next opportunity.

Don't be afraid to start a conversation. You never know where it will lead!

Make a commitment to initiate at least one new conversation every day. See how that feels, and then commit to growing your confidence with more new ones.

Elaine Pasqua, CSP, is a professional speaker who has presented to more than 1 million people nationwide. Her ability to talk to people and network fearlessly has led her to work with 32 teams across the National Football League, the National Basketball Association and Major League Baseball, 700 universities, countless businesses and associations and the military.

A LITTLE CHAOS GOES A LONG WAY
Dan Dustin

A small action can have a monumental impact.

Chaos theory teaches us that little actions can lead to big differences down the road. You just can't predict them. Popularized as the "butterfly effect" (a butterfly flapping its wings in South America can influence weather patterns in the United States), chaos theory reminds us that we often have to proceed on faith when wondering whether we are making a difference in life. The theory reassures us that a kind word here, a positive gesture there can make all the difference in the world.

I once had a student at San Diego State University who was mourning the passing of his mother. His name was Eric, and I suggested that a good remedy for what was ailing him would be to hike the John Muir Trail along the backbone of California's High Sierra. That small suggestion was my contribution to Eric's life.

Twenty-five years later, Eric tracked me down to ask if I would like to read a book he had just published based on a story he had discovered along the John Muir Trail. I was happy to do so. Soon thereafter, his book, *The Last Season*, was nominated for a Pulitzer Prize in nonfiction. The book was an inquiry into the disappearance of a backcountry wilderness ranger named Randy Morgenson. Today, Eric Blehm is a *New York Times* best-selling author.

Would Eric have reached such heights, both literally and figuratively, had he not followed my advice? And what if I hadn't offered that advice? I don't know the answer to either of these questions. What I do know is that Eric acknowledged my contribution to his life in the back of his book, and he made an effort to reach me a quarter of a century later to tell me in person about the impact of my few words of advice.

Has anyone ever said or done anything to you that had a monumental effect on your life years later? Have you taken the time to thank them? You should. Otherwise, they may never know.

Think of at least one person who has had a positive impact on your life as a result of something they said or did at an opportune time, and make plans to thank them for it.

Dan Dustin is Professor Emeritus of Outdoor Recreation Studies at the University of Utah.

MY YOUNGER SELF WOULD HAVE THANKED ME
Len Annetta

As a young man, I thought I had it all figured out – until I didn't.

The world is *yours*! When I was younger, a late-night show would always have a top-ten list that was often ridden with comedy. What follows is the top-ten list my younger self would have thanked me for had I known then what I know now – void of any comic relief.

1. Follow your passion and not the money. It will take sacrifice and persistence.
2. Remember where you came from and who helped you get there. Be humble, or you will stumble.
3. It is often not *what* you know but *who* you know. Expand your network and stay connected.
4. You *will* fail. Babe Ruth hit 700-plus home runs and struck out over 2,100 times. It won't be easy, but it will be worth it. Take calculated risks. Adversity doesn't build character; it reveals it. Embrace disappointment. It will make the success infinitely more gratifying.
5. Save for retirement. Even a small amount when you are young will grow into something you can use when you are old.
6. Have faith. We have free will, but not everything is going to follow your plan on your timeline.
7. You can only control your attitude and effort. Have *pride* (personal responsibility is a daily effort).
8. Begin with the end in mind. Reverse engineer your life. Where do you want to be? Plan in chunks and set SMART (specific, measurable, attainable, relevant and time-based) goals. Keep learning. The separation is in the preparation.
9. Pay it forward. Help the next person succeed and do better than you.
10. Family first. Friends and colleagues come and go, but your family is your rock.

I was a first-generation college student whose parents were not formally educated but highly valued education. This list consists of items they tried to teach me, but I had to learn the hard way on my own because I didn't always listen to them.

Make a commitment to further your exploration of this by readings books, watching videos of people you deem successful and commit to a healthy mind, body and soul.

Len Annetta is Dean of the Zucker Family School of Education and Zucker Professor of Entrepreneurial Education Leadership at the Citadel College.

AN ATTITUDE OF GRATITUDE
Chris Cole

Gratitude is when what you have becomes more than enough.

I have a daily discipline of writing a list of at least five things for which I am grateful to begin my day each morning. No matter what is happening, there is always, always, always much to be grateful for. This practice has changed my life.

Gratitude is a powerful force that can shape the way you experience the world. It's not just about saying "thank you" when something good happens; it's about developing an attitude that sees the beauty in everyday life, even during tough times. When you practice gratitude, you begin to notice and appreciate the little things, like a sunny day, a kind word from a friend or the smell of fresh coffee in the morning. These moments, though small, add up to create a sense of happiness and fulfillment.

Gratitude also has a way of shifting your focus from what you lack to what you have. In a world that often tells you to want more and be more, gratitude reminds you that you are enough and that your life is full of blessings. This shift in perspective can reduce feelings of envy, stress and dissatisfaction, replacing them with contentment and peace.

Moreover, gratitude strengthens your relationships. When you express appreciation for the people in your life, it deepens your connections and fosters a sense of mutual respect and understanding. It's a way of showing others that you value them and that their presence in your life matters.

Gratitude is like a muscle – the more you use it, the stronger it becomes. By cultivating gratitude daily, you'll find that your life becomes richer, your challenges more manageable and your heart more open to the joy and love that surrounds you.

What are some specific things you can do to cultivate gratitude as part of your daily living?

Chris Cole is CEO of APNH: A Place to Nourish your Health, a health center providing services to those who face stigma or challenges in receiving culturally competent care. Previously, Chris was Director of AIDS/LifeCycle and National Director of the AIDS Rides. Chris is in the process of becoming an ordained minister in the United Church of Christ.

TO ERR IS HUMAN, TO FORGIVE IS . . . HEALING
Keri Schwab

Forgiveness and boundaries are two overlapping concepts that can help protect – even foster – relationships with others.

I recently dined with a friend who said our former colleague was temporarily living with her. I was shocked. This colleague had undermined, backstabbed and lied when we all worked together. She caused pain and embarrassment, damaged relationships and fractured teams. My friend simply said, "I had to do a lot of forgiving, and now we have a great friendship."

Forgiveness must be a careful, intentional process. The person who wronged us was usually wronged in their life, with injuries and pain they can't or don't know how to nurture or discard, and may be incapable of forgiveness.

To forgive is to offer compassion to the pain living inside the one who hurt you. This is not easy, but if you imagine a small, frightened child inside them, the idea of nurturing instead of chastising them becomes an easier way.

We should not forgive and forget, though. Forgiveness is not to forget the actions taken or what precipitated them. We might let the same scenario happen again if we forget. Forgiveness is to simply show empathy and compassion for the pain in the other.

As young adults, you will learn by navigating many new relationships – friends, professors, coworkers and supervisors. Forgiveness and boundaries are important life skills. You will have conflicts, misunderstandings and perceived wrongs done to you. How you handle the fallout will determine how you move forward. Forgiveness can help with the emotional weight of relationship conflict. It's not always necessary to tell the other person; you can simply hold forgiveness in your heart and mind – maybe not even for the act but for the ethos and suffering that led to it. Then, by setting boundaries, you prevent yourself from being wronged in the same way again.

Forgiveness is not tolerating bad behavior but rather a choice of how to react and live through situations, how to move forward with compassion to self and others. Learning to forgive and set boundaries can lead to emotional resilience that does not let your past rule you but instead allows for more meaningful connections in important relationships.

In what relationship are you resisting forgiveness? How does this resistance serve you? What could forgiveness and boundaries look like for a calm and equitable relationship?

Keri Schwab is a professor at California Polytechnic State University, San Luis Obispo.

WHAT'S YOUR FORD TRUCK?

Jason Anderson

While life's experiences certainly shape our opinions, it can be hard to move away from what we are taught first.

In the span of the 35 years that I have possessed a driver's license, every pickup truck I've owned (and I've owned a few) has been a Ford. Is that a product of my having conducted thorough research at the time of each purchase? Did I pore over consumer satisfaction data – based on reliability, features, comfort and capability? Or did I thoughtfully investigate the projected resale value of all makes and models before coincidentally landing on the same brand?

Nope. I drive a Ford because my dad drove a Ford. The first of his I'm old enough to remember was a '71 short bed. He bought it to haul firewood, and I thought it looked bulletproof. In my teenage years, he had a '79 with an engine so big that when you stepped on the accelerator, gas poured through the carburetor like you were flushing a toilet. On the day I acquired my driver's license, it was in that truck that I took my first unaccompanied drive. I *felt* bulletproof.

So I still drive Fords. No matter what positive (and sometimes negative) experiences they give me, I've yet to really open my mind to other opinions, let alone objective data. To be fair, objective data *might* steer me in the same direction I'm on with vehicle selections.

This self-awareness I've recently discovered has helped me to humbly recognize that there are things I hold as "truths" that are simply opinions that I am reluctant to let go of. And it's my awareness that others in my life have their own "Ford trucks" that allows me to give them a little bit more grace when I struggle to understand why they believe what they do. We all have our "Ford trucks." The distinction between facts and opinions is an important one. Sometimes we hold an opinion very dearly, yet are able to recognize that it is an opinion. The challenge for each of us is to be able to distinguish these two for ourselves and others.

How will you apply this in your own self-awareness and your relationship with others?

Jason Anderson is an army veteran, husband and father of two grown boys and resides in northern Minnesota. After a 25-year career in probation/parole, he currently supports organizations across the country as a professional development trainer. His passions include all things outdoors and his faith, and he dabbles in community theater.

RESILIENCE AND KINDNESS
Juan-Carlos Aviles

Support and inspire others.

The world seemed full of contradictions in the 1980s as I grew up in a Spanish-speaking home in small-town Colorado. At eight years old, I decided I wanted to learn how to roller-skate. As I fearlessly careened out to the middle of the ring, I fell, ironically as the music "Another One Bites the Dust" played. To my surprise, a pair of strong arms came up from behind, lifted me up, smiled and said, "You are okay." It was the skating ring monitor. I did not know why then, but I still remember it was an unforgettable moment.

My strict immigrant mother who worked as a house cleaner most of her life was built tough and had no time for softness or sympathy. She taught me what she knew: the importance of hard work, putting your family first and keeping a good sense of humor. My childhood consisted of bike rides, sunset curfews, high school track, wrestling, cross-country and student council. During a few summers, my mother had me join family in the onion fields to teach me a lesson about hard work. In her words, you either "work hard to get an education for a better life or work like a mule and get paid nothing." Message received. In addition to graduating high school, I earned a bachelor's degree in philosophy and a master's degree in public communication.

Throughout the years, I learned that we all have stories of resilience in the face of hardship or challenges. I also learned that people help others along their life journey. Angels open doors. My mother taught me never to give up and the value of education. My grandmother wrapped me in unconditional love. The skating rink monitor demonstrated an act of kindness and encouragement. Teachers, bosses, friends and strangers over the years opened doors. It was my responsibility to make the most of every opportunity.

I once read about a person walking to the Golden Gate Bridge; if no one smiled at them, they planned to take their own life. We never know what others are dealing with. Regardless of circumstances, be positive and give hope whenever possible, even if it's as simple as saying hello to someone passing on the sidewalk. Reach out, offer support and be kind to others. It can make a difference, save a life or create a lifetime memory.

Where does your resilience come from? How can you provide it to others?

Juan-Carlos Aviles was born in Texas, raised in Colorado and came of age in Los Angeles. He enjoys a low-key married life in Washington, D.C., works in the federal government, loves to garden, enjoys photography and continues to smile, says hi to strangers and offers acts of kindness and encouragement.

AN UNEXPECTED TRANSITION
Monica Canfield-Lenfest

Be open to the possibility of change.

Halfway through my senior year of high school, my father came out to me as transgender and started transitioning to live as a woman. As I was on the verge of becoming an adult woman, my father became a woman too. It came as a total surprise to me at the time and taught me a few core lessons that have continued to influence my life.

First, *be open to the possibility of things changing unexpectedly.* When my Dad became a woman, I learned that even things that feel unchanging can transform. This person who had been my father for 17 years, who had lived as a man for more than 50 years, did not feel like a man. If my dad could become a woman, what else might change?

It has been said that change is the only constant, but as humans, we long for predictable stability. We only have so much control over the conditions of our lives and the people around us. This brings me to the next lesson.

Stay curious about other people's experiences. At first, I couldn't understand why my dad would want to transition genders. I told my dad I loved her no matter what but wondered how this might change our relationship. When I took a step back and got curious about my parent as a whole person, my view shifted. What changed most was my empathy for her journey and a growing appreciation of her commitment to live authentically.

This leads to my final lesson: *be true to yourself* even if you have to make big changes. If my parent could have the courage to truly become herself in midlife despite the risks and challenges, what capacity might I have to become the person I am meant to be?

My experience in my late teens taught me valuable lessons that I come back to when things change suddenly. I may not know what's coming next, but I can be open to the possibility of each transition. Hopefully these lessons will serve you as well, particularly in moments when your life transforms unexpectedly and when it's hard to make sense of other people's choices.

What changes would you be willing to make to live authentically?

Monica Canfield-Lenfest is a dynamic communicator, convener and facilitator who sees personal transformation as a key ingredient to building a more just and compassionate world. She has authored a resource guide for people with transgender parents, coordinated a Compassionate Leadership Summit with the Dalai Lama and taught the principles of Architecting Curiosity.

Community
Connections

What is Community? What is community health? What makes for a vibrant and effective community? What helps sustain a community today and tomorrow? In brief, community is often seen as a group of people with some shared interests or background. Community involves multiple people, expanding on the Relationship thematic area of the previous section of this book. A community incorporates multiple relationships all at once.

When thinking about communities and their health, this can be viewed in many different ways. One way has to do with the nature of the community – is it physical or virtual? Is it an ad hoc group or something more permanent, perhaps with bylaws and operating procedures? Is it based on some shared interest, similar or same background or something else in common? Is it relatively new in formation, is it more established or is it floundering?

Communities may be of different sizes as well as be based on other dimensions, such as longevity of its existence or shorter term or longer term in planned duration. They may be based on a specific set of values or with a foundation in a religious faith or political belief.

Ultimately, the aim with a section on Community is having a positive experience with the community and on having a community that is nourishing and supporting its members. It is also about having the community itself get nourished so that it, as a community, continues to grow and mature in the desired ways sought by its members and leaders.

WHAT IS A COMMUNITY?

Consider various communities. One that immediately comes to mind is that based on one's living arrangement – in a residential community, with a neighborhood. Some of these are called "planned communities," when a plot of land is developed in an arranged manner, with the homes often built by a single builder and with similar styles. This type of living situation may be a residential area where homes are built in a less systematic manner. Another community may be with an apartment building or complex, and those living there, in similar circumstances, may have a community.

DOI: 10.4324/9781003541080-6

A community can be short term in nature (such as a traveling group or conference) or much longer term in scope (such as a membership organization or extended family group).

For those in college, there may be a residence hall or residential area with a set of buildings and labeled a community. Similarly, with the military and the residential setting of barracks or other living areas. And the settings of these – a college campus as well as a military base – may attempt to foster a community. Moving beyond that, consider those living together on a submarine – with such close spaces and similar experiences, a community may develop.

Some living areas have a community feeling or at least aspire to one. This may be found in a retirement community, with housing, activities, social services, recreation, and more housed under one organizational framework and even one larger physical structure or interconnecting structures.

Communities may take another form as well. There are communities that develop with the shared interest of sports and recreation, found with clubs and teams as well as ad hoc groups (such as a pickup basketball game on certain afternoons). Communities exist in the workplace, perhaps based on job function or role. Communities may emerge with study groups for school or discussion groups within the faith community setting. There may be communities of shared interests or activities, such as reading groups, walking groups or other skill-building groups. Consider the self-help groups, such as Alcoholics Anonymous (AA) or Narcotics Anonymous (NA); a community of those dealing with drug or alcohol issues find common support with those meetings as well as with the 12 Steps. Other support groups may also have community as their basis – consider those for gambling, overeating or other issues.

A community may develop within a larger community. For a college campus, for example, within the larger campus community may exist the communities in residence halls or among those majoring in a certain topic. There may be communities of students who are adult learners, veterans or commuters. Communities exist based on race and ethnicity as well as sexual orientation. And beyond the college campus, many of these communities (e.g., veterans, LGBTQ+, people in recovery) have a presence and serve important functions.

One important factor regarding communities is that individuals are likely members of multiple communities. With this, their community involvement in various groups may meet different needs of theirs. For example, a person may consider their residential setting as one community, their involvement with a faith setting another community, their athletic or recreation group effort as another community and their racial/ethnic background as another community. Beyond that, they may be a person in recovery (and participate with an AA or NA meeting), be involved in an online forum regarding a hobby, identify as LGBTQIA+, have work colleagues and enjoy a weekend outing with like-minded enthusiasts. These different group affiliations may have more or less importance for individuals, and may have higher or lower priority for different personal and professional needs, and may change over time. An awareness of one's community involvement and the roles they play in one's life is important for heightened engagement and productivity.

WHAT IS A HEALTHY COMMUNITY?

In an overall sense, community health emphasizes the enhancement of the quality of group interactions so that the group's aims and purposes are more likely to be achieved. A healthy community addresses the functioning of the group so it is more effective and efficient, more engaging and a quality experience for those involved. Community health is valuable as an aspiration for formal groups as well as less formal groups that seek to be well-functioning and effective.

Communities can flourish if they are built on sound foundations; typically, these are based on the factors of shared interest or background that help constitute the community to start with. If the community is not healthy, the consequences can be multiple: dysfunction, lack of productivity, loss of membership and dissolution.

When communities are first formed (such as with a new group in a workplace, or a new residential setting, or a new classroom setting), they typically undergo a process of establishing their foundations. These communities are in development or in the process of becoming a community. They may have been formed because of a need (such as a local issue) or because individuals signed up for it (such as for a class or a training event). The community in process may be initiated because of a leader, whether charismatic or otherwise identified. As the community begins to get established, various issues will emerge, including differences of opinion or varying perspectives. There may also be further clarification of the overall operating foundations for the group, which may be exemplified with operating standards (e.g., bylaws) or guiding principles (e.g., an articulation of processes important to the group). Sometimes groups develop these standards in advance, and sometimes they are done when faced with a crisis (e.g., with the emergence of a health pandemic or a natural disaster). Those overall foundations can be helpful in staying on track with what was envisioned and developed during "calmer" times with less urgent needs.

Numerous elements are important for a community's health. Some of these include communication, decision-making, organization, activities and functions. Helpful with communities are leaders, whether self-identified, elected, appointed or otherwise specified. There may be rotating leadership (e.g., for a specific period or based on an identified milestone). Leadership may be shared, such as may be the case with coleaders, or a young member paired with a more seasoned member. Leaders have an important role with setting the tone for a healthy and productive community.

With the identification of a healthy community, a first step is that of identifying clearly what "community" means for that group. That is, what is important for the group at a particular point in time? What is it that is valued – is it a certain outcome, a focus on a specific initiative, or a certain process or set of processes? With this, specific components are viewed as important for a functioning and vibrant community. Many of the key elements for a well-functioning community parallel those found with healthy relationships. One is basic human respect; individuals in the group respect one another for their different backgrounds and experiences as well as different points of view. Another is dignity and kindness, including how one treats others. Communication is central to a healthy community so that individuals are up to date on current needs, issues and strategies. Related to that is engagement, whereby individuals feel their points of view are respected.

Communities also incorporate safety so that vulnerabilities within the community and with individuals are minimized. Conflict is minimized, with a focus on being constructive and positive. Healthy communities engage in advance planning and one that is highly participatory and engaging of key constituencies. This also involves anticipating issues and concerns and identifying strengths and assets of community members and other resources for addressing these. A healthy community stays positive and continues to monitor its own health to maintain and enhance its viability and value to its members and its surroundings.

Implicit with community health is that members feel welcome and valued. Since individuals may belong to multiple communities, each of these community memberships is important to retain the involvement of its members. From the perspective of a college campus, students gain much experience and exposure through getting involved on the campus, whether through their academic or nonacademic activities; this can be enhanced by participation in social, recreational and cultural activities. In other settings and walks throughout life, engagement as a valued participant is an important ingredient in community membership. Although individuals may have different points of view, the important feature of a healthy community is that individuals feel comfortable with speaking up and speaking out and that these views are listened to and respected by others in the group.

Related to that perspective is the issue of teamwork and collaboration. Communities involve different individuals in different ways. This incorporates engaging different people and drawing on their strengths and unique talents, as well as identifying specific and helpful roles in which they can serve the larger whole of the group. With this, individuals' different talents, perspectives and experiences are used in helpful ways. While various points of view are respected, different individuals may have different roles and different responsibilities, helping the community as a whole move forward in an orderly and effective manner.

Also involved with communities is the way in which it comes together in a crisis or emergency situation. Sometimes intact groups have to shift roles and responsibilities with such a situation (imagine a weather-related emergency affecting a few or many). Sometimes a community may have some immediate and localized situation, such as a medical situation or death involving one of its members. This is a time that community members may draw on some of the core foundations for the group and its membership, and how they demonstrate quality outcomes based on shared responsibilities.

LINKAGE WITH OTHER THEMATIC AREAS

The linkage of community with the other six thematic areas is similar to that found with relationships. Founded in optimism, the focus of a community is based on shared values and needs and a commonality of some factors important to individuals in that group. The Optimism theme is one of hope and positivity and one that permeates communities. Communities, when healthy, have a shared purpose, and that purpose is for a positive and desired outcome. Without a sense of optimism, the communities that exist may be more destructive or nonfunctional in nature. Similarly, the issue of Values is important, as there is some sharing of foundations that are similar among the community members. Whether it is the value of healthy aging, or managing health or safety issues, or a social or civic cause, or some societal distress or discrimination, the shared value tends to be the glue that binds things together for group members.

Self-Care is important for the community group. That is, a community cannot "just be established" and then "let things work out." That is a type of wayward approach and lacks the foundations for a healthy community. The self-care elements, whether those be with time management, stress management, interpersonal relationships or drug or alcohol misuse, can all be part of a functional community – by managing and helping shape individual and group decisions around these various dimensions. Similarly, the themes within the Relationships area – whether human respect or conflict resolution, or listening and promoting growth – are all important for a community's health and development.

The attention to Nature is linked to community, as communities are surrounded by the natural world, whether urban, rural or suburban. Many communities, particularly those of a physical nature or defined by physical boundaries, incorporate environmental factors as part of their mission as well as activities. Some communities help shape the environment so that it works in harmony with the overall aura desired by the group members. With Service, community groups are often organized based on a service orientation, and group members may bond as a community when they are doing their service activities (e.g., mentoring, volunteering) together.

CONCLUSION

With the wide range of communities in one's life, this chapter and its Legacy Letters help provide some perspectives about promoting greater health and functioning with these group relationships. From attention to the networks one has, as well as the physical spaces, from leadership and connections, to thinking about change and possibilities, as well as the importance of a constructive spirit, the contributors provide rich insights. With over 50 contributions in this chapter, the reflection portion of each Legacy Letter provides the reader with some ideas about how to nourish and sustain communities in their own lives. With the acknowledgment that each individual is a member of multiple communities simultaneously, the important message is that communities are as impactful, in positive ways, as they are allowed and encouraged to be.

Messages What are key points or themes highlighted in the Legacy Letters within the Community area?	
Reflections What are your thoughts and feelings about what is shared and recommended regarding Community?	
Resources What individuals, groups, organizations or other information would help you better understand and apply recommendations in the Community area?	
Commitments What are you willing to commit yourself to doing regarding the Community theme, both in the near term and in the more distant future?	

FIGURE 6.1
Legacy Worksheet for Community

FIND COMMUNITY
Gerardo M. González

Being part of a community can help people gain inner strength to withstand prejudice and the damage it can cause.

My family and I came to the United States as refugees from Cuba following the Castro revolution when I was 11 years old. At first, it was very difficult for my parents to find work, and we had to move from Miami to Pittsburgh to West New York, New Jersey and back to Miami within three years. As our immigrant family moved from city to city, I felt like an outsider. I didn't belong. I longed for local communities of other immigrants or people who spoke my language to serve as safe and trusted groups with whom I could discuss common problems and ideas for making my way.

FIGURE 6.2
I am with my sister Maritza walking home from school by ourselves in our first snowstorm. I am carrying an English/Spanish dictionary covered by plastic to protect it from the weather.

In New York, I discovered other Spanish-speaking kids. Suddenly I had a peer group, people who understood my language and my culture. That young community brought me out of my shell. I began to develop confidence and inner strength. When I was able to band together with kids like me, I felt good about myself for the first time; now I spoke all the time. I gained in confidence. On top of being "different," my newfound friends were also adolescents, struggling with painful rites of passage. In our little group of Spanish speakers, we supported one another through our identity crises and the prejudice we encountered.

Years later when I left Miami to attend college, I again stuck out amid the predominantly white student population. Not only did the campus lack diversity, but there were no special services for Hispanic and Latino students. Our small group of Cuban and other Hispanic students became our own tight-knit social and support group. And in the long term, when it came time to advocate for a new Institute for Hispanic and Latino Cultures, we were successful because we were able to speak with one voice.

Whatever your path in life, find a community that makes you feel you belong. Reach out and get involved. You can find strength in numbers.

Think about a time when you felt isolated; how did you regain inner strength?

Gerardo González, Ph.D., is Professor and Dean Emeritus of Education at Indiana University. Recognized as a leading founder of the peer education movement in America, his memoir is titled *A Cuban Refugee's Journey to the American Dream: The Power of Education.*

WATCH WHERE YOU CHOSE TO PARK
Sandy Potter

One act of kindness can last a lifetime!

I'll never forget a time I was running late to class and looking for a parking place when I whipped directly into an open parallel parking spot. After I whipped in, I noticed a car on the street that was actually trying to back up into the spot. I thought, "I guess I'll just have to pull out and find another spot." I didn't look at the person who was waiting to back into that spot, but the person looked at me.

It took me another five minutes to find a spot and I ran to class getting there five minutes late. As I arrived, the teacher said, "It's okay. I know why you're late." After class, she asked me to stay back and then told me that she really appreciated me pulling out of the spot so that she could park there. My heart stopped. What if I had just parked and ran to class! Instead I made a friend for life. I ended up having Dr. Williams for four more classes in my undergraduate program, and we are still friends to this day.

After that moment, I realized I needed to become more aware of others and act with intentional kindness. This became a strong part of my focus in life and in my career. At work, my leadership style is to be intentionally kind, honest, respectful and funny! But I'm naturally a funny person.

Of course I work hard, think fast and read everything, but I think I have excelled as a leader by being a real person, being nice and having fun intentionally! Oh, and never cutting someone out of a parking place!

Go joyfully!

Where in your life can you incorporate more kindness?

Sandy Potter, LCSW, has been a social worker for her entire career. She is currently the Vice President of Medicaid Care Management, and Population Health Training at AmeriHealth Caritas.

THE SPIRIT OF ALOHA
Dari Shim Matsuura

The Spirit of Aloha helps with a balanced and peaceful life.

Alo (in the presence of) ha (divine breath). The values of Aloha are not unique to Hawai'i. When the Aloha Spirit became law in 1986, I remember thinking "Okay, now Dad's gone too far, but people will entertain the idea of conducting business and relationships with ALOHA, not because it's now a law, but because when Alvin talks, people listen." The Aloha Spirit Law was an esoteric idea whose time had not yet come. But Dad knew "the world will turn to Hawai'i as they search for world peace because Hawai'i has the key . . . and that key is ALOHA."

My dad would write poetry, sending me some in birthday cards. Here is one of them.

Spirit of Aloha *by Alvin Shim*

In the land of trade winds, the sun, the sand and sea
With clouds floating by, in skies of blue
Where children and elders laugh, and sing and dance
There's a spirit, of Aloha

When I accept you, the way you are
And you accept me, the way I am
And we accept others, the way they are
There's a spirit, of Aloha

When we stop pushing others down, to make ourselves tall,
When we are motivated by kindness and sharing for all to win and succeed,
There's a spirit, of Aloha

When we help others anonymously,
And are sensitive and aware to assist unconditionally without being asked
There's a spirit, of Aloha

When you have wondrous feelings of serenity and your smiles show your
*   inner souls,*
And experience feelings of beautiful bliss
And share your lives with patient peace
There is a spirit, of Aloha.

Take a section of the "Spirit of Aloha" and identify ways it can apply to your life. If you were to create your own aphorism or poem, how would it read?

Dari Shim Matsuura is a special education teacher and hopes that her students and those who know her can say she left her own legacy of Aloha.

YOU'RE SO LUCKY
Mark Weber

Take the risk, do the work and seek positive impact.

Luck has a significant role in life if you are prepared to take risks and do the work. As luck would have it, in the tenth grade I read the book *Hidden Persuaders*, a 1950s examination of how thoughts and feelings are manipulated by business, media and politicians. I was mesmerized.

As an undergraduate, I wondered if the tools used to manipulate could inform choices about health and wellness. With the support of consumer behavior faculty and campus health services staff, we developed an HIV/AIDS education program at Virginia Tech in the mid-1980s. The work and my academic studies led to my first job – a staff assistant for a project preventing HIV/AIDS in adolescents. The work and connections made soon led to my next job at the U.S. Department of Health and Human Services (HHS). I took the first of many risks at HHS and wrote a speech for a top official on HIV/AIDS and federal immigration policy.

During my 32-plus years at HHS, no two days were alike. I often compare the projects I worked on to Mr. Toad's Wild Ride. Any and all success I was part of is a tribute to the people who went on these wild rides with me and the trust we placed in one another. Common purpose and trust make the difference. Trust is the foundation of real teamwork.

As a finale in 2020, I was given a once-in-a-lifetime opportunity to develop and lead the HHS COVID-19 public education media campaign. Evaluations of the campaign showed that for the year starting in April 2021, an estimated 55.9 million doses of COVID-19 vaccines would not have been administered absent the campaign. For every $1 spent, the campaign and corresponding vaccination costs resulted in benefits of almost $90.

People tell me I am lucky that I was able to "retire" at age 57. Yes, luck had something to do with it. So did taking risks and doing the work. And let me be clear – please do not confuse the technical term "retirement" with my demise. I'm not done yet!

Where in your life can you take a risk, do the work and make a positive impact?

Mark Weber enjoys riding slow trains to nowhere and just getting stuff done.

COURAGE, CONNECTION AND CREATIVITY
Amy Yamashiro

Imagine a world where everyone lifts one another up, where we all take a moment to connect and create – courage, connection and creativity help us to speak out, build friendships and work together.

Lessons learned on the schoolyard formed my moral compass. Speak out for what's right, build friendships and work together to create community. I use these values to navigate through life.

Courage. Stand up for what's right, even when it's tough. While in elementary school, I saw Kim who had an autoimmune disease sitting alone on the swings. A group of kids began to tease her mercilessly. I didn't know her well but couldn't just stand by and watch. I took a deep breath and walked over, my heart racing. I faced the bullies, repeating their taunts back at them, asking, "How does that feel?" As their laughter faded and they turned away, I saw her eyes light up with gratitude. That day, I gained courage to stand up for myself and others.

Connection. Reach out and include everyone. In middle school, I felt like a fish out of water, the only one from my old school in a sea of unfamiliar faces. During a break, Evelyn, a friendly girl, invited me to join her group, but another girl sneered, "Who do you think you are?" My heart sank, and I felt like I was sinking in quicksand. But that incident lit a fire in me. I silently vowed I would never treat anyone that way. From then on, it was my mission to welcome the new, shy or excluded students. I found joy in helping others feel included and integrated.

Creativity. Be a problem solver and see things in new ways. After school while working on a class project, my group faced a challenge: how to present our ideas in a fun and engaging way. I suggested creating a skit to bring our project to life with costumes and laughter. The excitement was electric as we worked together. That experience taught me that creativity is not only about thinking outside the box but also in finding joy in teamwork.

These values – courage, connection and creativity – steer me toward success at school, college, the workplace and in the community. When we support one another, we make the world a brighter place.

Find the qualities that speak to you and live into them! Your words and actions can inspire others, creating ripples that make the world a better place.

What qualities speak to you most loudly? How can you live into them even more?

Amy D. Yamashiro, Ed.D., serves as a budget analyst in the Technology Directorate, Federal Student Aid, U.S. Department of Education. She has taught elementary, secondary, university, graduate teacher education students and holds a pre-K–12 teaching license in English and TESOL.

"NO ONE WAKES UP IN THE MORNING THINKING THEY ARE THE BAD ONE!"

Amr Abdalla

Reframing conflict situations can result in healthier outcomes.

Ever since I was a child and a teenager, I was notorious among my friends and peers for being the peacemaker in the group – the one who dislikes violence. It seems that such inclination has guided me toward a full career in the field of peace and conflict studies, after a few years of law practice as a public prosecutor in Egypt. My prosecutor work set me in the middle of contentious dealings with conflicts – everyone in a conflict used all possible means to prove they were right and their opponent wrong. Sadly, this tendency often proliferates into higher levels of antagonism when we dedicate time, efforts and resources to prove that the other is not only wrong but also bad, dangerous, demonic or unhuman.

Through my study and work in the field of peace and conflict, I came to realize that such tendencies do serve a crucial purpose for us humans when we are in conflict, because our default as humans, it seems, is to pursue our needs peacefully. However, when confronted with threats or obstructions to fulfilling our needs (be it material or nonmaterial) or to our identity, beliefs or values, we have to take action to reduce such threats or obstructions. This is when we may resort to force, which we would never call "violence." Instead, we call it self-defense, protection or preemptive strike! Of course, the recipient of such actions call them "violence," and they too would engage in a similar process.

FIGURE 6.3

Celebrating 20 years of teaching at the University for Peace with Class of 2024. Twenty years of service with honor, growth, and joy!

I formulated this awareness into the motto, "No one wakes up in the morning thinking they are the bad one." Since then, it has become one of the key premises with which I start my classes and workshops. Having weaved my professional and personal experiences, struggles, disappointments, successes and rejoicings with my teaching, practice and research in the field of peace and conflict studies, this motto has become the guiding light and inspiration for my students worldwide!

Thinking of a situation in your recent past when you have been in conflict with another person or group, how might you approach this differently now?

Amr Abdalla is a professor emeritus at the United Nations–mandated University for Peace. He is an Egyptian American.

BE THE CHANGEMAKER
Angie Asa-Lovstad

Embrace your role as a changemaker by challenging the status quo, envisioning possibilities and taking action to improve your community.

Too often, we notice things in our community that could be better but fail to act. The change formula (from Richard Beckhard and Reuben T. Harris) {D x V x F > R} explains why. If there is no Dissatisfaction (D) with the current state, no Vision (V) of what could be and no clear First Steps (F), Resistance (R) to change will prevail.

Imagine a community where mental health is prioritized, and young adults start peer support groups, advocate for mental health resources and create safe spaces for open conversations. Picture a neighborhood where physical health is promoted through community sports, fitness programs and healthy eating initiatives. Envision an environment where sustainability is a collective effort, with cleanup drives, recycling programs and community gardens flourishing.

Think about the power of social connectivity in building stronger, more inclusive communities. Events, volunteer opportunities and support networks can bring people together, fostering a sense of belonging and mutual support. Consider the impact of accessible health-care services, ensuring everyone in the community has the care they need.

You can be the changemaker by questioning the status quo, painting a vision of what is possible and rallying people to take action. Challenge yourself and those around you to not accept things as they are.

As an example, I once worked with young people to reimagine their community. They identified blocks to their vision and started conversations to overcome them. One group transformed an underutilized tennis court into Skate Central by securing funding through a grant and local fundraising. Twenty years later, the city continues to make improvements to Central Park and Skate Central, and those young people pursued careers inspired by their involvement in the change.

If you don't like something, envision what is possible, find allies and make a plan. By minimizing resistance to change, you can achieve great things.

FIGURE 6.4
Life's full of twists and turns, and sometimes the path isn't clear. Trust that you're right where you're supposed to be, soak up the lessons, and you might score a hole-in-one!

What change will you inspire in your community?

Angie Asa-Lovstad is a master connector, coach, and facilitator with ASA Facilitation who helps people discover their potential and embrace change.

WHAT I LEARNED IN BASIC TRAINING
Nancy Beatty Gleeson

Admiration of basic human qualities often comes from unexpected situations.

I know now how snobbish and intolerant I was at 23 when I enlisted in the air force. With a four-year college degree, marriage and a year of teaching behind me, eight weeks of basic training would make me a sergeant. The other women in the flight, or training group, would only be airmen. In my narrow-minded view, I was sure they were uneducated and inferior.

My first experience was a sergeant yelling in my ear to line up and put my nose in another person's neck. How dare he? It all went seriously downhill from there. We arrived at Lackland Air Force Base at 2:00 a.m. to sleep in un-air-conditioned World War II barracks – all part of breaking us down to build us up into airmen.

Dragging ourselves out of bed at 5:00 a.m., our training instructor yelled at us to make our beds and line up outside. That first day we marched to breakfast and then marched to get uniforms and shoes. We marched to lunch, classes, exercise, marching practice, how to salute, when to salute and how to salute an officer while marching. Next we cleaned the barracks, washed and ironed uniforms, showered and fell into bed. That was 24-7 for eight weeks.

One woman, who was 19 years old with five children, enlisted to have free medical care, lower-cost food and other privileges for life. She was one of the smart women in the flight. One night, she showed her courage while we were ironing. Everyone was talking when one woman suddenly, silently, put down her iron and stepped back. A tarantula, about six inches wide, was crawling down the wall. We were all terrified except for one person. Yup, the one with the five kids said, "Oh for ___ sake!" took off her slipper, whapped the spider and went back to ironing. We were in total admiration of our fellow airman. My last feelings of superiority disappeared that night.

Some experiences you don't forget. I hope she went to Officer Training School because she would have become a general! That night was a turning point, changing my outlook and opening my mind. That memory is still vivid 51 years later.

What human qualities do you admire in others and that you can adopt for yourself?

Nancy Beatty Gleeson grew up in the Washington, D.C. area. She has taught public school music, been a sergeant in the U.S. Air Force Singing Sergeants and taught graphic design at Northern Virginia Community College for 32 years. She has two wonderful children and three terrific grandchildren and finds being three-quarters of a century old extremely entertaining!

HUMOR, HUMILITY AND HUMANITY – KEY INGREDIENTS TO LEADERSHIP

Christopher M. Jones

Leadership is defined by how you show up to work every day, not by your position on the org chart.

Throughout my career, I have had the fortune, good and bad, of experiencing many types of leaders. Some were leaders in name only due to their position in the organization. Others were leaders through their actions – sometimes this coincided with a position of responsibility.

I vividly remember the traits of those who were leaders in name only – barking orders to subordinates, regularly devaluing staff and demoralizing the organization. These "leaders" trafficked in inflated egos, condescension and callousness.

Those who were true leaders – regardless of where they sat on the organizational chart – demonstrated something different, something people wanted to be a part of. What I remember most is their humor, humility and humanity – the hallmarks of how I try to show up to work.

Humor – Jobs are hard. Spending 40, and often more, hours a week navigating personalities, politics and difficult decisions can weigh heavily on your spirit. For me, injecting humor into the workday has been an essential element to finding balance, joy and a common bond with others.

Humility – No task is ever "above my paygrade." Regardless of my position, I view myself as just another member of the team. I am always willing to take on whatever task is needed to get the job done, whether big or small. This is a cornerstone of servant leadership, and this approach has enabled me to build trust with and respect from staff, peers, and leaders above me.

Humanity – Life happens. The people you work for, work with and those you lead bring all aspects of their life and their lived experiences to the workplace, whether they know it or not. You do as well! Showing up as your authentic self, knowing and owning your strengths and your limitations and understanding and embracing the humanity of others is perhaps the most challenging part of leadership. But once you can tap into this leadership ingredient, your potential knows no bounds.

Think about your interactions with others and ask how you showed up today, including the use of humor and how you embraced your humanity and the humanity of others.

Christopher M. Jones currently serves as the Director of the Center for Substance Abuse Prevention at the Substance Abuse and Mental Health Services Administration. Dr. Jones has served in a variety of leadership positions at the Centers for Disease Control and Prevention, U.S. Food and Drug Administration and the U.S. Department of Health and Human Services.

DEVELOP A PASSION FOR SOCIAL ADVOCACY!
Gary Kreps

Stand up strong for fairness and equity in society.

As a health and risk communication educator, researcher and author, my efforts to help champion human rights as a health advocate by addressing health inequities have been tremendously meaningful for me. My advocacy projects focus on promoting health equity by combating serious health disparities. This work involves conducting engaged research projects that identify, examine and respond to significant impediments that many at-risk and vulnerable populations face when trying to achieve personal well-being and a high quality of life. I've found that many of these at-risk groups could benefit from efforts to support their health information needs and represent them within complex and bureaucratic modern health-care systems

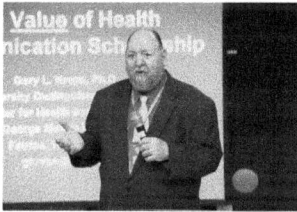

FIGURE 6.5

Here I am presenting a keynote speech about The Value of Health Communication Inquiry at the University of Peking in Beijing, China.

My health advocacy projects are a form of translational research to guide development, implementation and institutionalization of evidence-based programs, policies, practices and technologies for identifying and preventing serious impending health risks, detecting significant health problems when they are most treatable, and providing health-care consumers and providers with the best diagnostic and treatment information to guide their health promotion efforts.

My work as an advocate has involved addressing debilitating health problems such as cancers, serious infectious diseases (including pandemics), adverse environmental crises and difficult mental health issues like dementia, depression and suicidality that are most dangerous for poor, elderly, migrant and minority communities. To address these thorny health risks, I have worked collaboratively with individuals who are directly involved in confronting these problems – patients and both formal and informal caregivers. I become their health advocate by providing them with evidence-based insights into the causes and potential solutions to their health problems, working directly with them to codesign new strategies for responding to their health problems and then evaluating the effectiveness of responsive programs, practices, media and campaigns to help promote health equity.

Think about how you can serve as an advocate for groups of people in society who are in need, such as helping them access relevant information and support.

Gary Kreps is a Distinguished University Professor and Director of the Center for Health and Risk Communication at George Mason University.

CONNECTING THROUGH ALOHA
Sadae

Family and culture are vitally important to adapting in a multicultural environment.

I live in a multicultural place. The Asian, Hawaiian, local and other cultures merged with my life experiences and has taught me many things. The Asian way of "don't bring shame to your family" was ingrained at an early age. It meant having good character, values and having your elders be proud of you, which included those who had passed on – my ancestors – as they worked hard and sacrificed for the next generation to succeed.

The Hawaiian, local and other cultures taught me the importance of connecting to people through Aloha (not the contemporary translated version of love or a greeting but a deeper meaning in living one's life; a practice of connection to others versus trying to correct them; listening to beyond what is being said, what are their intentions).

The practice of Aloha wasn't always with me. Western practices of communication conflicted with my Asian heritage. Through my work, I learned how to balance East, West and Hawaiian cultural values. It impacted me and my work with others where I could connect with them as we shared the same values of compassion, empathy and positivity.

My legacy for the next generation?

- In a world where things are moving at a fast pace, take the time to slow things down and be patient with yourself and others.
- Be open to what different cultures can teach you about who you are and how to deeply connect with others.
- Practice empathy.
- Be grateful. Listen beyond the words. Listen to their stories on who they are so you can connect.
- Look forward, not backward. Acknowledge the past, but steer forward.

Keep those connections with family (however you define it) and its traditions; it can keep you grounded. It's okay to be vulnerable at times; it's what makes us human. Don't be afraid to ask for help. It is not a sign of weakness. You are resilient! I see you.

So who are you? What is your story? Is there someone, a place, a thing, an activity and so forth where you feel that connection? Find it and steer it forward.

Sadae has lived in Hawai'i all her life. She is well traveled and works collaboratively with federal, state and local agencies, along with many cultural groups who are mindful of the practice of Aloha to better connect to the community.

ECOLOGY AS A HUMAN RIGHT
Philippe Michelot

It is important to build a society where human and environmental health are prioritized.

From the outset, it is crucial to acknowledge that ecology does not belong to any political party or religion; rather, it is a fundamental human right that touches on our shared responsibility to safeguard the planet and its resources. Without ecological food practices, we risk jeopardizing the future of humanity.

The Shakespearean quote "'Tis the time's plague when madmen lead the blind" resonates deeply in our contemporary society, where decisions and behaviors often driven by short-term interests can lead to devastating long-term consequences. This reflection finds parallels in Plato's allegory of the cave, where individuals are captives of their limited perception of reality, as well as in Theodore Kaczynski's critiques in "The Ship of Fools," highlighting the dangers of excessive dependence on technology and manipulation.

In the agricultural realm, this metaphor applies to modern practices that often prioritize convenience and immediate yield at the expense of sustainability and environmental health. The intensive use of pesticides, consumption of out-of-season products and excessive plastic packaging are examples where society seems blinded by illusions of progress and food security.

I stress an inspiring alternative to these destructive paradigms. I maintain a complete absence of pesticides and phytosanitary treatments and manage orchards left grassed to promote biodiversity and regulate soil warming.

I believe individual choices and responsible agricultural practices can not only provide sustainable solutions to food and environmental challenges but also inspire a collective transformation toward a healthier and more balanced future. I invite all to break free from contemporary illusions and embrace a more conscious and respectful vision of our food and planet.

At the heart of this transformation lies the recognition that ecology is a fundamental human right. We must safeguard biodiversity – be it ladybugs, butterflies, dragonflies, bees, the songs of birds and cicadas, fish in the sea or animals in the forests – as they are essential for the well-being of our planet and future generations.

What concrete actions can you take that contribute to promoting and prioritizing human and environmental health?

Philippe Michelot lives near Saint-Rémy-de-Provence, France, where he has managed his estate and farm Mas des Figues for over 25 years using permaculture. He is actively involved in tourism and agriculture within the Alpilles Regional Natural Park.

I'M NOT A ROCK OR AN ISLAND
Steve Miller

Grounding yourself in community settings is critical for a healthy life.

For most of us, when we were children, our imaginations and innocence helped us make friends and play with carefree abandon. During that time in our lives, we belonged to a unique and exclusive community: childhood, a place where only children can belong. Sure, older siblings, parents or other family members may have joined in our play. However, when I reflect on that period of my life, it's clear there was a magic present, one that now seems out of reach as an adult. It's as though I can see it and want to touch it, but it exists in a time and space beyond my grasp, like it's behind a fogged window with sounds muffled in the distance.

What this tells me is that childhood was an important time in life. This also tells me it is essential for me to keep alive the parts of it that I still feel connected to. Community is a wonderful thing – it keeps us connected and grounded and assures us that we're not alone. These were things we didn't have to consider when we were young; they came automatically. Now that I'm older, I recognize how crucial connectedness is.

I know this all too well as a person in substance use recovery. Addiction thrives in isolation, and being part of a community is the best-known antidote. Whether through self-help groups such as Alcoholics Anonymous or Narcotics Anonymous or through other community-oriented settings where we live or work, exercise or enjoy life, practice our faith or other activities, community is essential.

For all of us, while life changes – people come in and out of our lives, we change jobs, move away from friends and family – we need some anchors. Finding a place we call home among people we feel close to, share common interests with and who challenge us with their differences is what community is all about.

What communities are you connected to? If you are feeling alone and not connected, what is one thing you can do today to invite yourself into community?

Steve Miller belongs to communities of art, faith, recovery and storytelling and believes in blooming where we're planted.

SELF-IDENTITY
Tim Gerhardson

Increase your cultural hybridity today.

I met my mother when I was 30 years old. With her nose, eyes and immediately recognizable mannerisms, I finally saw my reflection in someone else. But I always knew I was adopted. Prior to meeting my biological mother, Sharon, my mother, Audrey, had raised me in rural Minnesota. I had bonded to an identity from northern Minnesota with Scandinavian roots. Thor was my hero, lefse a staple food. I had an important internal narrative about my Scandinavian membership.

It wasn't until my grandmother died that Sharon told me I was not only Norwegian but mostly Irish with some Cree Indian from Manitoba. How interesting. A chance to change my self-identity! It didn't take me long to jump ethnic ships and adapt corresponding Gaelic traditions and Celtic beliefs, seek new heroes and taste newly ethnic cuisine. What I learned from my self-discovery is that we all seek our internal story and personal narrative – maybe true or not. What's important is that we believe in ourselves.

This earlier lesson in self-identity helped me in my career to understand better the idea of cultural relativism and how to manage cultural differences and cross-cultural communication more effectively. Establishing a cultural identity is achieved through meaningful relationships with people of the host country. An awareness of where one is on the strong-weak cultural identity continuum is critical to traversing successfully from a strong cultural identity toward a weak cultural identity or vice versa.

One's cultural self-identity is a work in progress. Some people have a strong cultural identity – I am a Zimbabwean from Chinoyi, speak Shona, celebrate only Zimbabwean holidays, believe in Shona religious figures and eat only sadza. Some have a weak cultural identity – I am a citizen of the world, a global nomad with no ties to any place or ethnicity and believe in all religions.

After 30 years of international work and 100 countries visited, my cultural self-identity traversed from very strong Scandi to weaker and weaker with each passport stamp; now I am a mere curious flaneur. The best souvenir I received from travel is the understanding that even though the people I met were different in many ways, we were the same across the globe: we all want to live with dignity, enjoy human rights and freedoms and have an opportunity to make life better for our children and others.

How would you describe your cultural self-identity? What could you do to enhance it?

Tim Gerhardson retired from the U.S. Foreign Service with 27 years' expertise in public diplomacy. He is a returned Peace Corps volunteer, international student, father and student archer.

BELIEVING
Phil McCabe

The strength of recovery helps with reconnection and purpose.

Looking back, I made previous promises to myself, and each time, I made excuses that maybe I wasn't that bad. It started with booze, then pot, then I added pills and eventually, it was anything I could get my hands on. Yes, anything, and this was before I could drink legally. I inhaled industrial cleaner, spray paint and any chemical in an aerosol can, which was a cheap and dangerous way to catch a buzz, just to change how I felt.

I was living a bad after-school special often shown to scare teens. I had no fear. Booze and pills were my best friends; they took me out of myself, and they made every situation more bearable. I can't say I felt much emotional pain; I worked myself into believing I didn't want to feel anything. I know it wasn't all bad; family and friends cared about me, but the problem was that I didn't always care about myself. I loved the highs and hated the lows. Sometimes even the alcohol, pills and pot didn't do what I needed. I lived week to week, making money and using it to buy more drugs. I did my best to hide everything from those who cared about me. I was in a death cycle, and the worst was having no fear of dying.

On April 10, 1985, I finally surrendered and admitted I needed help. And help was available. I met a group of people who chose to remain anonymous. We shared a common bond that only someone who had been there could genuinely understand. It didn't matter that we came from many different walks of life. Some had lost all; some lost less. They experienced jail or other institutions, and some just decided they didn't want things to worsen. They tried the best they could to hold themselves together and often failed. They reminded each other that it didn't matter if they came from Yale, jail, Park Avenue or a park bench. We ended up in a similar place, physically, mentally, emotionally and spiritually bankrupt. I had had enough.

Recovery allowed me to reconnect, and I transformed into the man I originally wanted to be. I wanted to stop thinking only of myself and think about my place in the universe. Recovery is not easy, but it is possible. The important thing is finding your path and believing.

Identify ways you can learn more about the important role of recovery for people you know, including yourself.

Philip T. McCabe, CSW, CAS, CDVC, DRCC, has over 40 years' experience as a community educator. He has been a health educator at Rutgers School of Public Health since 2000. As an openly queer professional, he proudly identifies as a social justice warrior.

NOTHING ABOUT US WITHOUT US
Nathan Monell

Engaging perspectives of those being served can make help achieve impact.

Many adults who grew up in foster care call themselves "alumni" of foster care. And one of their rallying calls is "Nothing about us without us," signifying a belief shared by consumers of any public system. The individuals for whom a service is provided should be involved in the design, delivery and evaluation of those services. Their perspectives are different from the provider community, the funding source, the politicians and any other stakeholder.

For-profit entities invest millions in customer research before they launch a product. The human services our public entities provide are much more essential to the well-being of those who consume those services, but public systems of support rarely take the same care as companies and manufacturers.

When working with young adults at Foster Care Alumni of America, I learned even greater lessons about the power of the consumer voice. One Wednesday before Thanksgiving, we brought about 20 alumni to Capitol Hill to host a Thanksgiving dinner – white tablecloths, a massive turkey and all the fixings. In the shadow of the Capitol, in the same space where the January 6 insurrection later happened, the alumni had dinner sharing their often heartbreaking foster care experience as dozens of boom mics and cameras carried their messages to the world listening in. A staffer from the congressional committee that oversaw federal foster care funding and policy came out of the Capitol to witness the event. The stories had captured his heart.

FIGURE 6.6

Adult alumni of foster care traveled to celebrate Thanksgiving dinner on the Capitol grounds. Eating there was their free speech expression to lobby legislators (the federal funders of foster care) that changes needed to be made for kids still in care. Photo Credit: Gediyon Kifle.

Simultaneously, one of the alumni met with Representative John Lewis, his congressman, to talk about the challenges he faced in foster care. Lewis's office called us as they drafted potential legislation. The questions they repeatedly asked were, "If we wrote the legislation this way, the congressman wants to know if that would solve the problem Kevin described." You see, policymakers decide with their heads and their hearts. Telling human stories moves the empathic heart to want to act. Marrying the narrative with facts gives the head permission to embrace the solution.

How can you blend narrative with facts to help advance a policy or initiative?

Nathan Monell worked with Foster Care Alumni of America whose leadership elevated his understanding of the human condition. It also prepared him to be a better father to his two adopted children.

GIVING BACK
Cynthia Conigliaro

Volunteering not only benefits others, but it also benefits you.

Our lives are busy. Most of us have limited time. The idea of volunteering can sometimes seem daunting, like an impossible task. However, volunteering doesn't have to take up too much time. I have found so many benefits from giving back.

I volunteered in soup kitchens throughout high school, serving food to the homeless. I listened to their stories or simply sat with them as they had a warm meal. I also volunteered as a hospital assistant in high school. It was an eye-opening experience to walk into waiting rooms with coloring books for the children of parents who were having surgery. The simple act of bringing coloring books and crayons to the children put a smile on their face. I loved my role as "big sister" in high school as well, working with a young girl who was looking for some guidance. We would spend a few hours a month and we would do everything from just talking over ice cream, walking in the park or preparing for an upcoming history exam.

Studies show that the more you volunteer, the more benefits you'll experience. It has been found to reduce stress, decrease depression and provide a feeling of purpose. Volunteering doesn't have to involve a long-term commitment. Even giving in simple ways can help those in need and improve your overall health and happiness.

One thing I really love about volunteering is connecting with others. I have found that going through a challenge is a powerful way to support others as it allows you to empathize with what they are going through. It also is incredibly rewarding to you personally.

I have found that volunteering helps to create a sense of accomplishment. When my children volunteered for the Special Olympics, it gave them a sense of pride and helped boost their self-confidence; it took them out of their natural comfort zone and environment and stretched them to do new things. It did the same for me and it continues to do that.

Without a doubt, volunteering has helped me to feel better about myself. It is an amazing thing to think that in helping others, I am helping myself.

What type of volunteer opportunities can you identify that would be of interest to you?

Cynthia Conigliaro is an independent health and wellness coach and social worker. She works for a wellness training firm delivering trainings in resilience and stress management to people all over the country.

WHAT MATTERS MOST
James Hartman

It really matters that we do the best we can, that we show up, that we appreciate the life and gifts we are given and that we help one another as much as we can.

My latest friend is 102. Her name is Babs, and she has lived above my wife and me for the last 34 years. She lives in a corner unit in a condo complex with a spectacular view of the Pacific Ocean. Pat and I love knowing and celebrating life with Babs.

Our view is ideal for living life to the fullest. In that quest, we can hear the waves beating against the shore. We can smell the saltwater below where we live. We see the pelicans flying by. To live within yards of this great ocean is a blessing, and we enjoy the blessing together.

I write stories and often share them with Pat and Babs to get their input. My latest writing venture is about five old men who meet weekly. I titled it the Organ Recital Group since they spend a lot of time talking about their organs that no longer function. It is a great socialization activity for these older men to gather and try to comfort one another. It's at a tavern. It is special.

So are Pat and Babs. They tell me to change this and that, and I listen and rewrite. Sometimes I change what I wrote and sometimes I do not. An important aspect of this is that I value their feedback. I love them actually even when I may not agree with them. We are aging in place. More important, we are supporting good practice among seniors in the area of nutrition and sleep, exercise and stress reduction and the final biggie, less alcohol. That one may be the toughest.

The lesson for young people is clear. Appreciate those of us who are older and have many experiences to share. Preserve a sense of community by participating in community building and enhancing vitality. Love each other and appreciate the days we have on earth. This gift we are all given of life is an incredible opportunity to thrive and to live life fully.

Identify specific ways you can demonstrate community such as join a service club, get involved with local community matters, practice your faith, volunteer to help others and inspire others to get involved and help each other.

James Hartman has a lengthy record of serving others through his work in higher education at Ohio University; Radford University; California State University, Dominguez Hills; K–12 education at Chadwick School and his work with the Salvation Army College for Officer Training in Los Angeles.

BE AN AMBASSADOR FOR RECONCILIATION
Colber Prosper

Active and constructive engagement in groups and communities can help both their health and your own health.

I have taught in K–12 and in higher education and currently own a consulting firm. I've worked in over ten counties, and I'm passionate about education, spirituality, social justice and people.

When I was a junior in college, I played Romeo Montague in William Shakespeare's play *Romeo and Juliet*. According to the play, Romeo's second love interest was Juliet Capulet. The major problem for Romeo and Juliet was that their houses (the Montague and Capulet families) despised each other. Prince Escalus, ruler of Verona, wanted the houses to reconcile, but (spoiler alert) reconciliation didn't happen until the deaths of Juliet and Romeo.

This play and the community of Verona troubled me. I'm a senior consultant and I've worked with more than 1,000 communities and organizations in multiple countries. Through this work, I have found that reconciliation within communities is hard to come by. But the benefits of having a strong, engaged and well-connected community are exhaustive. Having positive relationships with the people around you increases mental and physical health outcomes. But when an incident or crisis takes place and separates people, community health outcomes decrease.

What does this mean? I implore you to be an active participant in your communities. Join clubs and associations or volunteer for a cause you're passionate about. Second, be the person to encourage reconciliation between individuals and groups of people. Reconciliation reminds us of our humanness: our capacities to make mistakes and, importantly, to forgive, learn, support and change. It also reminds us that we love, fall out of love and develop vulnerabilities to love more and much deeper.

I think that's what the human experience is about. As we embrace such struggles, we increase our abilities to relate to one another and empathize. I think we deserve these virtues from one another.

Romeo and Juliet is often described as a tragedy between lovers. Maybe it is actually a cautionary tale of delayed reconciliation.

In what ways can you be more active, particularly with reconciliation efforts, with the various communities of which you are a part?

Colber Prosper, M.S., is the CEO of Prosper & Partners International Consulting Firm, LLC. He has authored the book *No Entry: Examining the Powers That Undermine Our Full Potential*. Colber is an expert in education, organizational development, community public health and prevention, all centered on building community and creating inclusive spaces.

DEFEATING THE BYSTANDER EFFECT
Rebeca Segraves

One intervention can restore humanity.

I was working as a physical therapist in the hospital when I evaluated a 13-year-old patient after an abdominal surgery. It was common in my field to help people recover during their hospital admission when their surgery affected their ability to get out of bed, walk and negotiate stairs. When several of my colleagues, including a lactation consultant I worked with, chose not to treat this patient, I found myself in the middle of the bystander effect. The 13-year-old patient we were asked to see had undergone a cesarean section the day before.

Social psychologists Darley and Bibb Latané (1968) developed the bystander effect theory to describe how people are less likely to help someone in need when others are present. Within health care, many of my colleagues were aware that the United States has the worst maternal outcomes of all high-income nations, particularly among Black women. The chance for this young Black patient to receive physical therapy in another hospital after cesarean section was slim to none despite being an adolescent who was recovering after an open abdominal surgery.

The first manuscript I wrote a few months later for a major research journal was added to the repository of the Johns Hopkins Center for Humanitarian Health within days of our publication. The topic: physical therapy in the hospital after cesarean section, the most common surgery performed in the United States. What I discovered through that one intervention later became the foundation for the only program in the world with the mission of providing access to rehabilitation in the hospital after birth, regardless of age or race. It was the strategy we used to defeat the bystander effect and restore humanity in women's health. The strategy we teach is this: Ignore the crowd when the crowd is not serving the person in need.

Reflect on a time when you stood apart from the crowd to help someone in need. Reflect on the outcome, how this person responded to you and how it made you feel.

Rebeca Segraves is a Doctor of Physical Therapy and clinical director of Enhanced Recovery After Delivery. Her international network is dedicated to improving maternal and infant health sooner through women's health education.

A FRIEND'S LEGACY – FOR LIFE

James Wilkinson

These words provide inspiration throughout a lifetime.

In the fall of 1990, I was called up to the Gulf War as part of the U.S. Marine Corps Reserves. I was an undergrad student at the University of Maryland managing a pizza place. Jim Paradiso, the owner of the pizza place, took me out to spend an evening with me before I shipped out. Jim treated all his staff like family and trained us for life well beyond pizza and college. For me, he was a father figure at a time when my relationship with my own father was strained, and he was there when I needed it most.

At the end of our evening of bar hopping, he presented to me a copy of Marcus Aurelius's *Meditations*, which he inscribed for me in his inimitable, unmistakably curly cursive. That book traveled with me to the Gulf and saw me safely home and has stayed within easy reach no matter where my home has been over the intervening years and decades. The book itself isn't thick, but it is difficult, having been translated from the Latin. But when I reach for it, it's not to muse on the sage stoicism of the philosopher emperor.

Instead, I return to Jim's timeless inscription which offers me the same nine lines of ancient wisdom each time, yet newly received with each reading:

Before you speak, Listen.
Before you write, Think.
Before you spend, Earn.
Before you invest, Investigate.
Before you criticize, Wait.
Before you pray, Forgive.
Before you quit, Try.
Before you retire, Save.
Before you die, Give.

Jim was taken from us in 2005 at age 46 in a horrific automobile accident. I touch his legacy with my hands every time I open *Meditations*.

Jim's legacy letter still speaks to me through the years and from beyond the grave, as I hope it will speak to you, dear reader.

In what ways do Jim's words speak to you?

James Wilkinson, M.A., CAE, has served for over 20 years as the chief executive at several nonprofit organizations and on the boards of several others. He is a contributing author to the upcoming anthology *Leadership DNA* and lives in suburban Maryland.

THE LEADER WITHIN
Peter J. Joyce

Everyone has the opportunity to be a leader, once discovered and embraced.

When I accepted a special assignment as the Senior Advisor on Youth at the U.S. embassy in Nairobi, Kenya, I devoted much of my time to listening – learning firsthand about the dreams and challenges of young people and exploring ways to reimagine youth as leaders. In these conversations, I often shared a story about a small African village where a young boy accidentally fell into a dried-up, 50-foot well. As word spread, people rushed from their businesses, schools, churches, hospitals and homes, each bringing a short rope, determined to save the boy. Yet, as they arrived, it became clear that no single rope or person could reach him. Then someone called out, "Tie the ropes together!" United, they linked their ropes and, working together, lifted the boy to safety.

This story illustrates a new understanding of leadership. Leadership was once seen as the province of a select few – those with grand visions and many followers. Today, however, leadership is a role that calls to each of us. A leader may not hold the entire solution but can bring together others with diverse perspectives and ideas, creating something far more powerful. A leader may offer an idea or strategy, which may serve as a catalyst or springboard for others to build on. A true leader draws people toward a shared purpose, helping them find and implement solutions collectively.

Consider your projects at school, work or in the community. Perhaps you're working on a group assignment where people seem divided, and progress feels stalled. Maybe you're organizing a fundraiser or tackling an issue at work that seems unsolvable. Here, you can step into a facilitative leadership role – bringing people together, gathering ideas, finding common ground, and inspiring action. Discover the leader within you, and embrace this role today.

In what kind of leadership role can you serve? What opportunities exist for you, today and tomorrow?

Peter J. Joyce holds a doctorate from Harvard University and works under Reimagining Education and Work, LLC on global projects focused on youth.

HOPE IN ACTION AND ACTION IN HOPE
Peter Moll

I sat there, at a community meeting in the heart of the land of the giants, Amboseli Ecosystem. With Mt. Kilimanjaro in the background, the meeting progressed and elders and leaders were being introduced. They wondered who this young-looking guy was and why he was here in their world.

But then, community members with whom we have worked and whose lives we changed, started to stand up one by one to testify to our work. You could tell the change in the community, because they could see the hope in the stories being shared and more – not just empty hope but hope in action.

The local leaders and elders could not understand how this young man could have done all that, but they were moved by those stories, and guess what they got? HOPE!

They never understood how our worlds could be one. But when they saw what we did in the worlds of others, they resonated, understood and something within them was stirred, the conversation was shifted and everyone started to speak of challenges they had – including solutions with hope they could move from dream to reality.

The last speaker was a woman not dressed in traditional attire. She started telling us about her women's group that cooks at events and for children at school. But for these children, their school is under a tree. I could tell this lady had been bitten by the hope bug by the stories shared by others.

FIGURE 6.7
During the launch of one of the classrooms, I am welcomed with a community traditional greeting, welcoming me back to the community, it's a sign of love and respect.

What I learned is that as young people, many times we are doubted by many. We are often compared to the young people that the people doubting us know in their world. So we must build our small community of those who not only believe in us but have seen us perform in the area of life and purpose and let those people inspire action in hope.

Do not tire of standing in rooms or worlds that do not recognize what you have to offer. Do your little thing, build your community and they will help open up rooms and worlds. They will see you as an action-in-hope changemaker!

Identify a setting or cause that would benefit from your hope and your action.

Peter Fredrick Moll is a 32-year-old Kenyan who is the founder of Stand Up Shout Out, now based in over 20 countries and 60 cities, as well as CEO of World Leaders of Today.

EVERYONE "WINS"
Ned Parke

Active involvement of stakeholders helps promote higher quality outcomes and rewarding processes.

In both my business career and personal life, the most rewarding endeavors are situations when all stakeholders feel good with the outcome. Seeking and creating situations where everyone "wins" likely achieves the best results and outcome.

An example from my business life was a situation when I assumed responsibility for another production department. Prior to assuming responsibility for this new department, a quality assurance project to install an automated detection system was planned. Initially, the project had not involved any operators and the planned equipment layout was not operator friendly. I immediately included operators on the design project team. After operator involvement, the layout was modified and corrected. Once the detection system was installed, operators embraced the new system that, in their words, "made their job easier." In addition, the project was recognized as the company's most successful quality assurance project. By creating a situation where all stakeholders were involved in the design and implementation, everyone "won" and felt good with the outcome.

> Think of a situation or project with which you are now involved. What can you do or say to help promote the involvement of all stakeholders?

Ned Parke enjoyed a career in various supply chain management positions, primarily with Procter & Gamble and Abbott Laboratories. He and his wife raised three sons and a daughter and currently enjoy eight grandchildren. He is a loyal Ohio State fan, plays tennis, enjoys the outdoors and is always working on a DIY project.

CONNECTING WITH OTHERS MAKES ALL THE DIFFERENCE
Tim Burkhalter

A life well lived is to be done with and for others.

In a society that often celebrates self-gratification and individual achievement over altruism and community success, it may seem a worthless exercise to first consider the value of the group or others as the greater virtue. I offer this not to minimize personal pursuits but to challenge the popular narrative that in some cultures and societies prioritizes the focus on "I," "me" and "mine."

As a borderline introvert-extrovert, independent thinker and one who appreciates solitude in a world that feels full of "noise" and distractions, it took me a long time to understand and adopt this paradigm. That said, when I am truly being honest, I realize I experience greater fulfillment and completeness when I am doing life with and for others.

I encourage you to consider the following succinct "truths" I have found:

- Serving others increases empathy.
- Forgiving others enhances compassion.
- Saying "thank you" and sincerely meaning it facilitates gratitude.
- Learning about other cultures and life experiences broadens your worldview.

Let's take it a step further. When opening yourself up to the teachings and stories of mentors and elders, you discern more about shared wisdom and life lessons. When celebrating accomplishments and milestones of others, you learn pathways, have examples to emulate and are presented role models to follow. When mourning the loss and death of a family member, friend or colleague, you better understand the impact one's life can have on others, and you are reminded that life is finite.

Following such examples, I would argue, increases your interrelatedness and humanity. When I made the connection between being an educator to transforming lives and impacting communities, I understood my vocation and professional purpose. When I connected my role as a life partner, father and son to breaking generational curses that plagued my family, I became a legacy bearer and catalyst.

I encourage you to consider these prompts and contemplate your own interconnectedness to others (and their impact on you). As you do so, think about other examples that you can identify that resonate for your own life.

What greater purpose(s) are you preparing for that connects you with others?

Tim Burkhalter, Ph.D., is an educator, student affairs professional and well-being advocate. He finds purpose and joy in quality time with his family, random acts of kindness, nature, personal fitness, sports and the arts.

YOUR NETWORK, YOUR WORTH

Sharon Alexander

Take bold steps to build meaningful connections while exploring diverse paths to success – your future self will thank you.

Like many, I was raised believing in a traditional pathway to career success: get a college degree and pursue a career directly aligned with that education. My first job perfectly matched my degree field. But here's what's fascinating – my career journey took unexpected turns, leading to two subsequent positions that diverged significantly from my academic background. What made these transitions possible was the authentic relationships I had cultivated over years of genuine interactions and a commitment to continuous learning. These opportunities emerged because people knew my professional capabilities and my curiosity, adaptability and eagerness to grow. This experience taught me that whereas formal education provides a foundation, it's a willingness to learn continuously and build meaningful connections that truly shapes career trajectory.

The beauty of building social capital lies in its compound interest – every authentic connection has the potential to lead to countless others. The key is to approach relationship building with curiosity and generosity rather than calculation. Whether through internships, volunteering, informational interviews or community involvement, each interaction is an opportunity to learn, grow and contribute.

Here's the truth that took me years to understand: There is no single "right" path to success. Some of the most fulfilled and successful people I know never completed college, while others found their calling through apprenticeships, entrepreneurship or unconventional careers. What they all share is a rich network of relationships built on trust, mutual support and shared values. Their willingness to embrace new learning opportunities and step beyond comfort zones has been just as crucial as formal credentials.

Numerous strategies exist to help achieve a more positive future. One is to identify three potential mentors in fields of interest and reach out to one with a specific, thoughtful question about their journey. Another is to create a "connection journal" to track meaningful interactions and follow-up actions. Third, before pursuing any major educational or career commitment, arrange three "shadow days" with professionals to gain real-world insights. Fourth, practice the art of genuine curiosity; in every conversation, ask at least one question that goes beyond surface-level small talk.

Make a plan to enhance your own personal and professional growth.

Sharon Alexander, B.A., M.H.Sc., has dedicated her career to youth development, evolving from a child development specialist to a dynamic nonprofit leader who has guided countless young people.

NOW HERE THIS

Lara Herscovitch

Recentering helps you be your best, healthiest (and happiest) self.

I wrote this poem (and song) to remind myself to recenter in the current moment. When my brain is ruminating about yesterday or worrying about tomorrow, some things I turn to include going for a walk, listening or dancing to a favorite song, catching up with a trusted friend, doing a closed-eyes 15-minute meditation, playing guitar, baking, singing, writing . . .

Now. Here. This.
Now.

Can I borrow you for a minute?
   Maybe two or three
Bring the beautiful broken pieces
   from you and me
Now. Here. This.
Now.

Can we forget about the world for
   a minute? Maybe two or three
What used to be trades in for
   infinity
Here. This. Now.
Here.

We can glitter, we can shine
Swallow tails on the telephone line
Waiting for the call – to arrive
It's This. Now. Here.
This.

Lakeside icy edges thin
Bored of the shore but what if we
   fall in

Oh what then, oh what then
What Now. Here. This.
Now

Some savored sadness till it won
We were climbing trees to catch a
   little more sun
Waiting for the future to come
Right Here. This. Now.
Here.

We can glitter, we can shine
Swallow tails on the telephone line
Waiting for the call – came just in
   time
It's This. Now. Here.
This.

Sure as the blackbird delivers
   spring
We will try and fail, try again
Little did we know that everything
   is
Now. Right Here. This.
Right here right now.

The poem was released in 2020 as a part of my album *Highway Philosophers*. (c)(p)Lara Herscovitch 2020 (BMI). Used with permission.

> *What do you like to do to recover and recenter?*

Lara Herscovitch is a singer-songwriter, policy social worker, accidental author and former State Troubadour of Connecticut (yes, that's a thing).

BE THE AUTHENTIC YOU!
Paora Te Hurihanganui

Today's actions draw from your past and shape your future.

Legacy is not a destination; it's a path and it's your birthright if you choose it to be. When we reflect on our purpose, each of us is bound by the threads of those who came before us, those who are present now and those generations that are yet to come. Life is not just about you but an opportunity for the authentic you to thrive and flourish.

As I see it, whakapapa, our genealogy, provides a powerful framework to approach life. Embracing where we come from – our people, our places, our stories – sets a compass for a life of purpose, values and community.

Growing up in Rotorua, New Zealand, and deeply rooted in our tribal teachings, I learned early that legacy isn't only about personal achievements but also about contributing to collective imperatives. A strong sense of purpose and intent has carried me through countless roles – in the arts, education, sport, healing practices, Māori performing arts and as a leader.

For young people today especially, there's so much external noise about what matters that we overthink and underfeel in these contemporary times. So lean into your whakapapa and let it shape your path. Traditional sites of significance, like the forest (*ngahere*) or the ocean (*moana*), are where I find strength and reflection. Those places hold DNA memories and lessons that ground us in our life's purpose, giving us the courage to face challenges with optimism and resilience.

In your journey, nurture your spirit with connection – to land, to people, to the values that define you. This is your legacy, unfolding one choice at a time. The actions you take will echo into the future, shaping others' lives.

"You are the sum total of all there was, all there is and everything that is going to be."

Here are several action steps for you to consider:

- Spend time in a place of significance to your family or community and reflect on its meaning.
- Decide on three enduring values you want to live by and revisit these when making big decisions and let it inform your future potentiality.
- Seek mentors who can guide you with wisdom from lived experience – let them challenge and inspire you.
- Hang out with people you admire and would like to replicate their x factor.

What action steps are you willing to do adopt to be your authentic self?

Paora Te Hurihanganui is a father and the CEO of Te Arawa Whānau Ora, with a Ph.D. in Public Health. He is passionate about ancestral knowledge revitalization, traditional healing and the transformative power of whakapapa.

LEARN FROM YOUR VILLAGE
Luther McKinney Jr.

Continue to observe and learn to develop a better self.

It is imperative that we take the time to learn from all of the opportunities in our "village." There are numerous activities and individuals within our communities that are available for us to learn valuable lessons and develop into productive individuals. Every second of our lives is an opportunity to gather valuable information that helps develop our goals, visions and degrees of wisdom.

I am a product of the 1950s and 1960s. Thankfully, I had parents, family members and extended family members who shared their experiences and encouraged my siblings and me to further our learning through gaining education and exercising an open mind. Not only have my five siblings and I obtained degrees from higher education institutions, but we learned to gain exposure from every situation around us.

After leaving the Marine Corps in 1975, I entered the University of Maryland Eastern Shore and obtained a bachelor of science degree in business administration. From 1979 until 1995, I gained practical business experience and decided to obtain a master of science degree in computer science, which I completed in 1997. Then, in 2008, I received a Ph.D. in organizational leadership. In addition, I have been a mentor to young people and "Certified Peer Support Specialist" for over 20 years.

I believe we must take the time to become aware of our surroundings. Becoming aware affords us the opportunities that enable us to develop holistically. I believe it is important and helpful to observe the clouds in the sky, the birds overhead and the flowers. Strive to gain knowledge from each aspect of our lives. Do your very best to utilize each opportunity you have to become the very best that you can be. When you experience new aspects of life and meet new people, you are then able to begin developing the better you.

Identify some specific opportunities that surround you about which you can take greater advantage for your own personal and professional growth.

After leaving the U.S. Marine Corps in 1975, Luther McKinney Jr. entered the University of Maryland Eastern Shore and obtained a bachelor of science degree in business administration, followed by an M.S. in computer science and a Ph.D. in organizational research. He was director of institutional research for several institutions of higher education and has been an advocate for K–16 students for over ten years.

LESSONS LEARNED ABOUT SAFETY
Bill Modzeleski

Communities have been struggling to find ways to make schools, colleges and universities safer.

The following are a few lessons learned over the past several decades.

1. Partnerships are essential. Schools face a myriad of educational, emotional and social problems. There is no way they can effectively address every problem. Numerous federal/state agencies as well as not-for-profit organizations can provide help in a wide range of services including health, mental health, alcohol and drug cessation, violence prevention and threat assessment behavior.
2. Involvement of youth/young adults is essential. Repeatedly, we find that even though youth/young adults know best what is going on in their communities/schools, their opinions are often ignored. Success with things such as the reduction of alcohol and drug misuse and abuse can't happen until this group is included.
3. Priorities must be established to match the needs. Schools today are confronted with a wide range of issues that they must face. These issues range from alcohol/drug use to the onslaught of illicit pills, and from harassment/bullying to terrorism. Learning to deal with all these different incidents demands the use of a comprehensive management strategy that pushes funding to strategies that are supported by research.
4. Lack of funding is not an excuse to do nothing! Programs can be redesigned, alternative funding can be found for activities such as training and programs that haven't proven effective can be modified and made more effective.
5. Arm yourself with facts, not fiction. Too often, decisions regarding controversial issues such as arming teachers and viewing alcohol and marijuana as not being harmful have the tendency to be more harmful than helpful. Gather facts from reliable and valid sources.

What can you do to help ensure that your setting – whether a college, school, workplace – are as safe as possible? How can you get local leadership to have safety as a top priority?

Over the past 40 years, William Modzeleski has played a key role in the manner in which elementary schools, high schools and institutes of higher education address behavioral and social issues facing their student body. His efforts have led to the development of programs that forge new alliances and aim at improving data collection surrounding those topics with government agencies such as the Centers for Disease Control and Prevention, the Federal Bureau of Investigation and the United States Secret Service.

MAKE IT COUNT
Jordan Foster

Aligning your career and your identity together is central to a meaningful life.

For better or worse, no one lives forever. As a result, we have to fit a lot into a small amount of time. Recently, I read Octavia Butler's 1980 science fiction novel *Wild Seed* in which she explores several themes. The most interesting to me was the power struggle between the two main characters, Doro and Anyanwu. Both are immortal beings, and although they have different approaches to life, they are similar in their longing for community and fellowship. They seemingly developed strong identities of themselves, but after building and losing wealth and influence several times over, they realized that they were both actually motivated by creating and maintaining lasting community.

While reading the book, I considered my own journey, motivations and values. As an undergrad, I was very selfish, caring only about myself and my future success. I hardly spoke to my family and friends, taking their presence for granted. I also was not concerned with travel or most other leisure activities.

After struggling in law school, I seemingly faced my own mortality. Having placed my sense of worth in titles and prestige, I did not know who I was without these external factors. This led to a long internal rebuilding where I did the difficult work of discovering who I was and what I actually valued. By the time I had a strong sense of self, I was 31 years old and had to figure out how to create the life I really wanted after building one not aligned with my values.

My advice is to recognize your mortality and the brevity of human life. You don't have the luxury of endless time, so build your career and your identity at the same time. As you strive academically and professionally, take time to build your community and identity, and find someone or something to trust (start with yourself). Move as if you've been given a life with which you can do whatever you want, but you only one and when it is gone, it is gone. Make your life count.

What are you doing now or making preparations to do to make your life count?

Jordan Foster serves as an attorney for a national nonprofit organization.

CASTING CALL
Joseph J. Cicala

Beyond talent and skill lies a necessary intangible.

During our college years, my closest friends in our student theater group had a code that included these elements:

- If you audition for a show and you are offered a part, accept it graciously – even if it's not the one you wanted – and give it your all, supporting and applauding everyone.
- If you are not cast (and even if you are), play a role offstage: advertising, ticket sales, stage crew, club leadership . . . maybe all of the above.
- On closing night: no cast party until the set has been struck and the stage is ready for its next use.

I've thought about this a lot through the years since we last said "break a leg" (the actor's substitute for "good luck") to one another. On my best days, I've aspired to similar standards in both personal and professional settings and encouraged my partners to do the same. I look for the others-oriented qualities that inspire such standards in teams I seek to join and in teammates we bring aboard. As an educator, I've been proud to see their impacts ripple forward in the lives of my students and in their own good works.

Make no mistake, talent and skill are necessary but, I think, insufficient. After all, one can be sharpened and the other learned. But the intangible, the commitment to shared purpose for the common good: that must be present – and then actively fostered – if individuals are to truly join as cast and crew.

When we come together as a team, we set the stage for our best possible performance. When we share the spotlight, it shines more brightly for everyone.

I don't think it's a coincidence that the people mentioned at the outset remain among my closest friends. Seek and find castmates like them, dear reader. Bring to life a code like ours . . . and break a leg.

Identify the key people whose lives have touched yours and whose own lives you been privileged to touch.

An award-winning professional, Joseph J. Cicala, Ph.D., has served and studied across the sectors of American higher education. He is most proud of the contributions his students make to our world.

BUILDING AND LEADING TEAMS
Brett A. Wright

The ability to develop and lead teams is a skill set that is critical to success in contemporary society.

Teams are ubiquitous in today's world. Teams are found in corporate offices, small businesses, athletic organizations, educational institutions, community organizations, the military, religious institutions and families. Most work today is conducted by teams; rarely does a person work alone. After 40 years in higher education, I continue to scratch my head regarding why educators still test and evaluate students largely on individual performance.

My first associations with the concept of teams came through athletics, playing on myriad teams from youth to varsity. Although I remember the joy of playing and the friendships made, I was too immersed in the activity to notice all that was going on around me.

In the military, I learned something that has had a positive effect on my life and my leadership in developing teams – that is, to intently observe the human dynamics that occur when someone is leading a team. If you make this a habit, there is lifelong education occurring around you that will translate into better leadership on your part and more success among your teams. Ironically, you may find that you can learn more from bad leaders than you can from good ones. Good leaders and team builders conduct themselves in such ways that are frequently subtle, often unnoticeable. A person must look hard to see the nuances of speech, body language, reactions to others and so forth. However, poor leaders and people with poor team-building skills are more obvious, allowing you to learn valuable lessons in what "not to do."

When I entered academia, I had to adapt and learn the craft of academic leadership. One lesson I learned while observing department heads and deans who were my bosses was that successful leadership was not just about how intelligent a person was. I have known professors who were absolutely brilliant in their scientific fields but absolutely awful when elevated to a formal leadership position. They had IQ in large volumes but had desperate deficiencies in EQ. This EQ can be enhanced through casual observation and analysis of behavior. Plus, it gives you something positive to do while waiting in airport boarding areas watching the crowds.

Recall the image of a person from your past who led a team and list three things they did that motivated you. Now recall three things that hindered you.

Brett A. Wright is dean emeritus of the College of Behavioral, Social and Health Sciences and professor of parks, recreation and tourism at Clemson University. He served for eight years as director of a four-university consortium (all tiger-mascot schools), dedicated to saving the world's declining populations of wild tigers.

THE UNHOUSED
Brad Miller

Look for your unhoused neighbors and engage.

My recognition of the plight of the homeless did not start early enough. Despite living in my eighth decade, I have substantively supported my unhoused neighbors for less than ten years. Upon reflection, it is disappointing; I could have done so much more. I certainly encountered the homeless condition throughout my professional career. Hands were extended, reaching for sustenance. I saw people huddled in doorways, sleeping on benches, just existing in their tents. I realize that, by my early thirties, I had bought into many assumptions regarding the homeless.

Certainly, there were opportunities where I participated in food and clothing drives, made my annual donations to the Salvation Army and various charities, volunteered at soup kitchens, and even occasionally filled an extended hand with a nominal dollar amount.

Looking back, there were ample opportunities to do more. I could have sought understanding of the needs of the unhoused, to meet and talk with those living on the street, and to understand how they met their situations. I could have learned earlier about the value of a hand up versus a handout. Another one of my regrets was not involving and educating my children earlier regarding the obligation to support their unhoused neighbors.

Almost too late in my career, I was introduced to wonderful people engaged in providing support at our local homeless shelter and currently serve on their board of trustees. Over several years, I met, talked with and helped many of my unhoused neighbors. I encountered a vast amount of factual information about the homeless, busting myths and assumptions within our society as well as myself. I have learned much, through hands-on experiences, while giving me an appreciation for just how much there is to be done.

Further, I have been active in a program to expand awareness of the unhoused. This has included leading conversations to share education to fellow service-minded citizens, while calling for action and engagement in their communities. Much is underway in various communities that can be shared as models, for improving and preventing the homeless condition. This is the message that I carry forward.

You can act now by reaching out to your community's homelessness resource network. Volunteer, become informed and engage to make a difference.

What are you willing to commit yourself to doing to engage more with this issue?

Brad Miller is a retired Insurance professional, married with three children, California native and active Rotarian.

LIVE LIFE . . . GIVE HOPE
Tammy Lee

Ripples in our lives give us the purpose to leave a legacy.

Tuesday, October 26, 2021, the day my life changed forever. My oldest son, Dylan, was with some friends in the early morning and went into cardiac arrest. They helped him out of their car and left him two miles from the Celebration Hospital. When the police arrived, he barely had a pulse. The hospital called at 9:30 a.m. to let me know he was in the intensive care unit. When I arrived, he seized every minute for over 36 hours before they put him in a coma to stop it.

On Thursday morning, the doctors informed us that Dylan had no brain activity and that we needed to decide on his care. We asked if he could be a donor because it was not on his driver's license. We signed the papers on Friday afternoon to stop lifesaving care to comfort care, and the diligence process began.

On Saturday morning, three matches were found, and our "go" time would be 2:30 a.m. Sunday. They came in to take measurements of his organs, and we were able to listen to his heartbeat one last time. One by one, family and friends came to say goodbye.

At 2:15 a.m., everyone lined the halls as we gave him the honor walk he deserved to the operating room. We all gathered around his bed and prayed that he would give life to these three people and that we loved him very much. They took him off the machine, and we watched him take his last breath. We left the hospital that morning very numb but hopeful that the transplants would be a success.

Later that morning, we received the call that all three were a success. We cried with joy and pain at the same time. Our boy was a HERO. Three months later on Dylan's birthday, I received a letter from his left kidney recipient thanking us for such a special gift and that he was very sorry for my loss. This letter gave me the strength to keep moving forward.

I attended my first Donate Life event on Mother's Day weekend that year and met other bereaved mothers. The love and support that I received from these special ladies that day has become my strength to keep Dylan's legacy alive. MomStrong they call us.

What can you do to help promote the gift of life to others, whether through organ donation or other effort?

Tammy Lee is a donor mom whose motto is "Live life . . . Give hope." She and her husband, Ken, own and operate Celebration Sanitation, serving Celebration, Florida, and providing broad community awareness locally and beyond.

THE POWER OF COMMUNITY: BEING YOU, BEING ENOUGH

Alex Williams

If you're ever unsure or confused about some part of you, one step can be to find a community of those with similar feelings or experiences.

"Can't sit properly in a chair? Congratulations: You're bisexual!" When I read this post on Reddit's r/bisexual page several years ago, I nervously chuckled to myself. "Well, that checks another box for me." Other signs included using finger guns (check), regularly dropping puns (check), and enjoying lemon bars (half check). While this was perhaps the author's intent, whimsical posts like this helped me discover that there was a community out there for me and, in turn, helped me feel comfortable and not alone in my identity.

From rare medical conditions to common life occurrences, communities can help us make sense of ourselves, our identities and our experiences. Before I discovered my community, I felt shame, rejection, hopelessness. My relationships, both platonic and romantic, felt pulled between heterosexual and homosexual norms, creating an identity crisis: Am I 50% gay, 50% straight? Am I "gay enough" for a gay bar? Am I "straight enough" for a hetero relationship? Although I didn't realize it at the time, a lot of the self-doubt implied in these questions was caused by a sense of aloneness: that others don't struggle with these questions, and therefore something is wrong with me.

Scrolling past the r/bisexual page one day, I clicked on it out of curiosity and initially approached with caution. Some posts felt academic, like reading a journal article whose data specifically reference bisexuality; other times it was more casual, like posts about celebrities who were out bisexuals. At first, I only read, observing from a safe distance and containing my thoughts. But the more I engaged this community – sharing articles, posting comments, texting memes – the more I started thinking about it as *my* community. Each of my interactions, in sometimes significant but more often incremental ways, affirmed for me my stubborn uncertainties and budding certainties.

And what about those questions of self-doubt? Even though I don't believe they'll ever be fully gone, it is because of my community that I appreciate that I am 100% me and that my identity is justified through me alone. This, for me, is the power of community.

In what aspects of your life do you feel alone? Is there a community – in person or online – that may be appropriate and helpful for you?

Alex Williams is a career services and experiential learning professional at the University of Louisville. He lives with his wife and two sons in Louisville, Kentucky.

COMMUNITY NOW
Craig Ullom

Building community involves key elements that support a meaningful and rewarding experience.

A haiku is an unrhymed Japanese poetic form that consists of seventeen syllables arranged in three lines containing five, seven, and five syllables, respectively. A haiku expresses much and suggests more in the fewest possible words. As you read these haiku, reflect on how being part of a community has impacted you.

> Cocreating paths,
> Convening lives that matter.
> Community roots.

> Companions emerge,
> Collegiality forms.
> Community lives.

> Connection begins,
> Collaboration ensues.
> Community thrives.

> Combining our gifts,
> Communicating our thoughts.
> Community grows.

> Cooperation
> Coalesces human change.
> Community Now.

Think about a community you are a part of. What might you do to enhance the community experience for you and for others? How might you create a community that would do good in our world?

Craig Ullom has dedicated his career to working with college students as an educator inside and outside of the classroom assisting and supporting them as they navigate life transitions.

LESSONS LEARNED THROUGH LIVING

Ray Quirolgico

Three suggestions can help enhance a meaningful life.

Through the different jobs and volunteer and leadership positions I have worked, I have found opportunities to reflect on lessons that my mentors, teachers, advisers and friends have shared with me.

My first lesson is, **Learn something new every day.** I believe that feeling good about my value and worth in the world is evidenced when I feel my lived experiences have taught me something that day. Sometimes this is just a reflection I commit myself to in an evening meditation (in my thoughts or in a journal). Seizing any opportunity to recognize that my mind and heart are still growing reminds me that there is joy to be had in life.

That brings me to my second lesson: **Notice as much as you can.** This means being aware of as much as possible in the past and present to fuel the imagination for the future. Sometimes I am reminded that there is laughter in my workplace, or beautiful colors in the surrounding landscapes, or amazing engineering in the places I move through. Sometimes I just notice that my physical body has changed and noticing that might change how I am feeling in my emotional form. And so on.

In addition to paying attention to as much as I can and hoping to end each day with more knowledge than when I started that day, I am joyful that my life has clarified a sense of personal purpose, which is my third lesson: **Make other people better than you.** Someone once told me that nobody pursues a career in education (as I have done) expecting to become rich and famous or to get glories of titles and accolades of honors. But every once in a while, rare though the moments may be, someone has communicated to me how I have affected them, and usually that memory is a form of appreciation for having touched their life in a way that changed them for the better.

If I have lived an intentional life, then I am happy to have had it peppered with those moments of gratitude: my personal internal thanks for learning from my experiences and the external thanks from others that I have contributed to their own experiences.

In what ways, specifically, can you apply any or all of these lessons in your life?

Ray Quirolgico, Ed.D., is a native New Yorker who has worked in higher education administration for over 30 years. He continues to fill his life with joy from theater, books, dinosaurs and Lego.

TRAVEL, LIFE'S ELIXIR
Bill Norris

Travel, near and far, can teach you many things.

Some of the best advice you will ever get is to find and pursue a passion. Having grown up on a very small farm outside of a very small town, my passion became travel to discover the world beyond my childhood. Starting with a very limited budget, early trips were limited to visiting family, school friends, close beaches and occasional bus trips to New York. In those days, any hotel was limited by my very meager finances. As finances permitted, travel expanded to eventually include Antarctica and 70 countries in Europe, South America, Asia, Australia and Africa.

The three distinct phases to any trip include planning, execution and remembering. Each phase has its own rewards and frustrations.

The planning phase is often as much or even more enjoyable than the trip itself. This includes researching different possibilities for things to do, transportation, lodging and special food a region is known for. The challenge is trying to decide what to see in the limited amount of time you have.

Actually, doing the trip can be the least favorite part of the process because you deal with the difficulties travel can bring. Finally seeing those sights you wanted to see is amazing, but worrying about missing a connection, trying to locate your hotel and finding a restroom in an unknown city will be stressful.

Your memories will last forever. Our minds can do a great job of filtering out unpleasant aspects of a trip. Memories of that 13-hour flight to Japan are replaced by memories of okonomiyaki savory pancakes of Hiroshima. Memories of the restroom facilities on the Inca Trail are superseded by memories of entering Machu Picchu through the Sun Gate at sunrise.

My favorite vacation spots are private game reserves in South Africa, the Grand Canal from my balcony in Venice and hiking remote sections of the Inca Trail and the Great Wall. The strangest place I visited is Pyongyang, North Korea, where I visited the embalmed remains of the country's first two rulers.

Travel shows you how similar people are around the world and how lucky we are to live in the United States. No matter how much you travel, there are always future trips to plan for and do.

What kinds of travel have you done – or plan to do – to help expand your own horizons? What lessons has your travel taught you?

Bill Norris attended Virginia Tech and finished with an MBA with a concentration in finance. The majority of his career was spent with Oracle Corporation where he retired as a technical director.

NOTICE THE SPACES YOU ENTER
Emil Chuck

The spaces you occupy can have intended and unintended outcomes.

When I interviewed students as Director of Admissions at a dental school, one question I posed was how they would redecorate my office reception space. I had a cup containing colored pencils and pens (for the essay) and some coasters from around the world.

The answers made by these very smart students revealed creativity and a desire to make the spaces more welcoming. Many drew from their own favorite spaces to relax and study. Suggestions included a coffee bar, comfortable or humorous decorative pillows, and some video games. I was able to imagine how they would design their own reception spaces that welcomed new dental patients, anxious and nervous about seeing someone to address their pain.

When given a "white room" challenge, everyone finds a way to personalize their spaces. Photos and posters recall happy moments, aspirational heroes or placid peacefulness. Colors and materials for furniture items further ground oneself with affirming emotions that can help someone rest (in the bedroom) or encourage togetherness (in a dining or living room). Heirlooms may be kept in a cabinet so everyone can see their pride in their culture or history. In reality, you will

FIGURE 6.8
Standing on the outdoor guest terrace of the Cleveland Museum of Natural History.

find some people who want to completely remake you while others are willing to help you manage your perceived flaws into strengths.

The interviewed candidates would later ask me if there was a "right answer." A few years later, the school was moved to a brand-new building with an open-air atrium with a four-story-high ceiling, a coffee bar and some food vending machines nearby. Modern metal chairs matched the white, utilitarian design of the atrium with dark granite floors and some trees to offer more feng shui. My aged student lounge was replaced with an austere, intimidating hospital-like reception space in a larger, noisy atrium.

When it comes to the spaces you cherish, think about what those you would welcome will learn about you from what you put on the walls, the tables, and the furniture. Notice those things that make others happy or comfortable when you enter their safe spaces. Your room decor says a lot more about you than you know.

How can you decorate your home and work spaces to reflect you and your priorities?

Emil Chuck, Ph.D., has advised aspiring health professionals as Director of Advising Services for the Health Professional Student Association and publishes articles on the Student Doctor Network.

HAVE AN EVENTFUL DAY!
Seungwon "Shawn" Lee

Plan one special event per day in your life.

The well-respected Joe Goldblatt, known as the father of modern event management education, defined a special event as "a unique moment in time celebrated with ceremony and ritual to satisfy specific needs."

Decades ago, I crossed the Pacific Ocean from South Korea to learn how to plan special events. Some compare the speed of life to age, suggesting life moves at 10 mph in your teens, 20 mph in your 20s and 60 mph in your 60s. Even though I want to reject this formula, there are moments when I feel its truth – as if a year has flown by without any memorable memories or accomplishments.

Reflecting on my teens and 20s, I often woke up with exciting ideas for the day about playing, feeling that one day wasn't enough to explore them all. My days were eventful and filled with creativity and fun. However, in my 30s, 40s and now 50s, my time has often been prestructured around work schedules, leading to fewer unique moments or times of particular excitement.

A special event doesn't have to be grand or expensive. What makes a day special are the small, meaningful celebrations. It could be sending a heartfelt message to someone you've been thinking about, picking up a cookie for a friend and including a kind note or rewarding yourself with your favorite drink for a day honoring your self-view of "I was fantastic." In event management, planning is only part of the process – execution is what brings it to life.

By celebrating small moments, you can create eventful days for yourself and others. Start your greetings with, "Have an eventful day!" and may it truly be so.

> Plan one event each day and track its delivery. With this, also consider inviting others to join in planning or enjoying events together.

Seungwon "Shawn" Lee, Ph.D., is an associate professor of event management and technology at George Mason University in Fairfax, Virginia. He came to the United States in 1999 to study business event management (conventions and conferences), leaving behind his computer programming position in South Korea.

WHAT'S THE MEANING OF LIFE? YES

Joe Norskov

Embrace uncertainty, focus on today and find meaning in curiosity, community and service.

When someone asks, "What are you going to do with your life?" does it fill you with excitement or dread? These questions, often posed with good intentions, can feel overwhelming and unhelpful. They filled me with dread when I was younger.

A more practical question is, *What will I do today?* Life is not about figuring out everything all at once. Each day is the rest of your life, and it's the only space in which you can act. You can't leap to the absolute or change the entirety of your future in one move. As the Zen saying attributed to Layman Pang goes, "Chop wood, carry water." There will always be tasks in life that feel mundane but are essential.

When I was younger, I thought adults had answers. Most people I know, even in middle age, laugh when asked if they've figured life out. Now I've realized most of us are still figuring it out as we go – and that's okay. Over time, I found solace in this: You don't figure it out; you live it. There's freedom in not knowing.

Society often values what's marketable and purchasable – things like wealth or status. But your bank account won't call you on your birthday. The things that truly matter are relationships, curiosity and service. Call a friend you haven't spoken to in a while, pick up a book on a topic that intrigues you or volunteer for a cause that matters to you. These small actions can lead to big shifts in your perspectives about life.

Invest in your community. Share without expecting anything in return. If you focus on being useful and curious, many of life's answers will emerge. Obviously, you must only share what you have to give. Give what you can, but remember to take care of yourself too. You can't pour from an empty cup.

Questions themselves are the answer. Every request for help and every moment of curiosity are opportunities. By embracing the paradox of seeking and uncertainty, you'll discover that meaning lies not in finding answers but in asking better questions. So don't worry about having all the answers or any of them. Instead, stay curious, keep asking and trust that the journey itself will reveal what matters most. Sometimes the journey and the questions are the answers.

Identify what is needed or nourishing for the meaningful areas of your life (e.g., your family, yourself, your career, your home). Pick one thing, and do that today.

Joe Norskov lives in Knoxville, Tennessee and likes questions.

THE POWER OF YOUTH INFLUENCERS
Carlton Hall

The most important lesson I learned was from my grandchildren.

When I visit my grandchildren's home, every detail is carefully childproofed. Gates block stairways, cabinets have locks and sharp edges are padded. This isn't just caution; it's love in action, ensuring the safety of those most vulnerable. This same principle applies to the prevention of addiction and substance misuse. To truly make a difference, we must identify the most at-risk populations and create environments that protect and empower them.

The National Child Traumatic Stress Network reports that nine in ten people addicted to nicotine, alcohol or drugs started using before age 18. Those who begin before 15 are nearly seven times more likely to develop a substance use problem than those who wait until 21 or older. As young adults, you have a profound role to play in this. Think of prevention of drug and alcohol misuse not as a distant policy but rather as a shared responsibility to build a safer, healthier community. Your actions, words and leadership can help protect those who may not yet see the risks around them. By becoming influencers for prevention, you can create social "childproofing" that helps shield your peers and younger generations from harm.

FIGURE 6.9
Prevention is about prioritizing the most vulnerable populations and identifying where they are most vulnerable.

Youth influencers possess a unique power to engage equitably: the ability to connect authentically. Your voice resonates deeply with peers, making you and your peers natural leaders in shaping attitudes and behaviors of others. When you advocate for healthy choices, challenge stigma or create safe spaces for honest conversations, you are setting up protective gates at the top of life's stairways. You're making "invisible" vulnerabilities obvious and avoidable.

Prevention is much more than saying no to risks; it's about saying yes to opportunities. When you inspire someone to make positive choices, you're planting seeds of resilience that grow into strong, supportive communities. You're not just a bystander; you're an architect of change.

Think of the impact you can have: a friend choosing counseling over coping through substances, a peer choosing to speak up about pressures rather than staying silent, or as a role model of thoughtful living. These ripples create waves that transform lives.

What specific actions are you willing to take to be an influencer in positive ways?

Carlton Hall is the President and CEO of Carlton Hall Consulting LLC, a firm specializing in customized solutions to drive measurable change for communities, organizations and individuals.

BUILDING EFFORTS WITH PRIDE
Todd Rose

It can take a lot of effort to build quality with organizations and individuals, but it's worth it.

I have taken college students on several service trips. One year, we went to a rural part of Illinois. Floods had devastated this area and towns needed to be rebuilt. One student team was assigned a neighborhood where structures were uninhabitable, needed to be taken down and the land cleared. The second team went to an area where the land had been cleared and structures were being rebuilt.

The team working on destruction needed little training to get started. If a structure was standing, they took hammers and mallets to it to knock it down. Their lone safety guidance was to wear hard hats and watch for falling material. The work was easy. Relatively little skill was needed. You could imagine how many dilapidated buildings they were able to take down – and how much fun was had in the process.

The team assigned to work on the construction of a new facility had a different experience. Drawings and daily objectives were shared each morning. New tasks were assigned. The tools used were as varied as the jobs, and different skill levels were called on. The last day, the team was finally able to see the roof going onto the lone house they worked on all week.

The last evening, we launched into a group discussion to understand how the students were reflecting on their week. A variety of comments were shared about the value of the work, the need for community to come together and economic disparity in communities.

One student who had been part of the team tearing down structures noted that it appeared that it took far more time to accomplish the work of construction and building, and that other team's progress appeared to be slower. However, those students actually involved in this process seemed to be more satisfied with their work that week and inevitably had something to show for it. It took more coordinated effort and time to "build" than to "destroy" organizations and communities – even friendships. The builders, though, had something tangible of which to be proud.

Reflect on your current relationships as well as groups or organizations of which you are a member. What are you doing to help build these?

Todd Rose, Ph.D., has worked with college and university campuses for most of his career. He currently provides leadership for a language and academic program supporting international students at George Mason University.

GET INVOLVED: IT WILL CHANGE YOUR LIFE
Ralph S. Blackman

Getting involved in positive ways can help make your community a better place.

I got involved in my first political campaign when I was in high school. Back in the days of retail politics when a politician's popularity was measured by buttons and yard signs, political campaigns ran on the energy of young people who acted in the name of a particular politician, common cause or shared values. In my case, it was Eugene McCarthy in 1968 and we were going to change the world! McCarthy's stance against the war in Vietnam drew young people from around the nation to his cause, and his run for the White House put pressure on Lyndon Johnson to withdraw from the race for the presidential nomination. Even though perhaps we didn't change the world, we found community around a common cause.

Political action became my way of reaching new people and taking action to accomplish something positive. I was only in high school, barely old enough to drive. I passed out buttons, I put flyers on doorknobs and signs in yards. But I also met others who shared my views and who I remember to this day.

That small step led me to statewide politics and a job in a governor's office and from there to the speaker of the state house of representatives. From there, I went to work for a national political party, and from there, I went on to work for two presidents. In each different role, I became part of a bigger community; I stood for something with others, and I felt like I was doing my part to make my community a better place.

No matter how small your initial effort may be, taking positive action for a common cause will make you part of a larger community. Don't stand on the sidelines. Being part of something will change your life.

Identify at least one issue about which you feel passionate. Now identify specific ways in which you can get more involved.

Ralph S. Blackman spent nearly 30 years in politics serving the governor of Illinois, the Speaker of the Illinois House of Representatives, working for the Republican National Committee and Presidents Ronald Reagan and George H. W. Bush. Blackman also served as President and CEO of Responsibility. org. Blackman has a bachelor of arts degree in political science from Western Illinois University and a master of arts degree in public administration from the University of Illinois, Springfield.

CREATE YOUR OWN LOCKER ROOM
Craig Esherick

Being a team player in various places is vital for positive results.

When I read articles about former athletes, they talk about what they will miss most about their lives as competitors. Invariably, it is some version of the locker room or being part of a team. As someone who was involved in college basketball for more than 25 years as a player and a coach, I understand this sentiment. As a member of a team, you form special bonds that last a lifetime. There's just something about the locker room that is difficult to replicate in life after sports. The locker room isn't just a physical space; it's also a mindset where dedication, perseverance, sacrifice and grit turn a group of disparate people into a team.

However, once you stop playing team sports (or even if you have never played team sports), it doesn't mean you can't be part of a team and create your own locker room. Life is full of *teams* that make up a community. A family is a team. Small and large companies are teams. A classroom is a team. And each of these is a type of locker room. Church, synagogue and mosque are teams. If you work for a local government agency, you're a member of a team. All of these teams have goals, and when they function well, it is a sign that most team members are working together to "win."

Each team member has a talent and a role that their teammates rely on to reach the collective goal. Sacrificing is just as important in a teammate on the basketball court as a teammate in a company or in a family. As a former coach of mine used to say, "We can't have any tourists on this team." Everyone has to pull their weight. The team member AND the coach can create team chemistry and foster a productive team atmosphere. In a family, the parents are NOT the only members of the team that must share the responsibility of a healthy family. Become part of a team, embrace your role and take responsibility for creating your own locker room, wherever you find it.

FIGURE 6.10
Craig Esherick's thoughts about team building and the 'locker room' were shaped by his 30 years at Georgetown University. Photo Credit: Georgetown University Athletic Department.

Think about groups or settings where you are a member of the team. What can you do to enhance your roles and responsibilities as a team player?

Craig Esherick is a longtime faculty member of sport management at George Mason University. Esherick is a former Georgetown University basketball player and coach. Craig also was an assistant basketball coach and scout for the 1988 U.S. Men's Olympic Basketball team.

FINANCIAL WORDS OF WISDOM
Bob Tucker

Having sound financial footing is based on four key elements.

Breathing is an involuntary but necessary process for living. Sometimes it is easy. Sometimes we struggle, especially when going up a steep hill! Sometimes it just comes out in an enjoyable laugh.

Another necessity for living is dealing with money. Here are some words of wisdom from my personal and professional life that I have found most useful.

- **Earning** – this has to start with a good work ethic and a focus on always being a learner to improve our vocation. Working diligently and gaining the 10,000 hours necessary to be proficient at a skill or profession will produce a solid start to a career. Work may begin as more physical or at an entry level. Eventually, however, earnings will come more from knowledge and experience than from the toil or sweat.
- **Spending** – spend first on what is needed, then spend wisely on what is wanted. To help determine the difference, make a short list of what is needed to get to work and care for yourself and a family (shelter, food, transportation, etc.). Do not spend future earnings (i.e., what is anticipated or promised but not yet in hand) on things that lose value (e.g., cars, toys). Learn to be your own bank. Being wise and frugal today ensures the ability to spend more on wants and experiences later.
- **Saving** – having money for emergencies (accumulating 20%–30% of your annual income) is vital. Also essential is to save 10% annually for future plans and retirement. Invest wisely in assets that grow over time (stocks, real estate, your own business). Invest in your future self wisely by starting early – with your first paycheck.
- **Giving** – start by giving time, and then give money; either blesses others and is a great way to pay it forward. Almost everyone in the world is likely living on less than the average American. It is our responsibility to care for our family and others, whether in word or deed. Consider this and learn to enjoy being a generous giver.

While financial health can be much more detailed, these four themes serve as lifelong anchors for peace of mind and an enhanced quality of life.

Do an assessment of your own financial well-being. How do you measure up with each of these today?

Bob Tucker is a business owner, team leader, wealth manager and learner for 37 years.

FRIENDS AT WORK
Patrice Levinson

Having a best friend – or friends – is important for staying on track.

According to a recent Gallup study, having a best friend at work is one of the most important factors in job satisfaction and performance. Throughout my career, I have taken this advice seriously. I foster my work friendships and nurture them in multiple ways. In the hospital units and primary care practices where I have worked as a nurse or nurse practitioner, we start our workday with a "team huddle." The staff meets for a few minutes to say our good mornings and review pertinent information for the day. Then we head to our offices and patient care posts.

We meet up at lunchtime and go for a two-mile walk. Every day. Rain, shine, snow or summer heat. We encourage each other to take this time for exercise even on days where we might not be prioritizing our own health and well-being. It's hard to say no when your work best friend asks, "Are you ready to walk?"

Our walks take us across our beautiful campuses and through the surrounding neighborhoods, where we can enjoy fresh air, sunshine, flowers and trees. We have helped each other through life stressors, family and medical challenges and personal and family milestones and celebrations. This daily time with our work best friends is restorative and important.

Making a best friend in your post-college or work setting enhances your overall well-being. College students who make a best friend the first week after arriving on campus graduate on time and their college years are more successful and more fun with a best friend at their side.

FIGURE 6.11
Although these work friends walk at lunchtime most days, on this beautiful spring day, they are promoting the university's annual Health and Fitness Expo. Photo Credit: GMU Office of University Branding.

People in the military feel more valued and supported. People working at home, as caregivers or entrepreneurs, will find energy, focus and a sense of purpose with the encouragement of their best friends.

What are some ways you could make that best friend in college, work or other setting – both in person and when working remotely?

Patrice Levinson is a nurse practitioner at the Student Health Services at George Mason University. She enjoys working with college students, who are open and interested in learning positive health-care practices.

MY SHORTSTOPS
Diane Fedorchak

Asking for assistance can help you as well as aid those helping.

Even if I were the greatest softball catcher of all time – which I'm not – I would still need a shortstop to catch my blazing throwdowns to second base. When I start to believe I don't need help, that I can handle everything on my own and that asking for assistance is a sign of weakness, I think about those shortstops who caught my throws. It's a reminder: A team makes me stronger and better.

Recognizing the need for help – and then asking for it – can feel deeply vulnerable. What will people think? Will they see me as incapable, weak or lazy? Will they roll their eyes, judge me or dismiss me?

Here's what I've learned. The answer to those fears embedded in those questions is "maybe" – but far more often, "no." In my experience, every time I've asked for help, whether for something small or in moments of great need, people have shown up. They weren't just willing to help – they were eager, even grateful, for the chance to step up.

During some of my toughest times, when I didn't know where to turn, I've looked to the sky and simply said, "Help me." What's amazed me is how often the universe responds in ways I never could have predicted.

I share this lesson with the students I'm privileged to work with – emerging adults facing substance misuse and bravely reaching out for support. Pushing through the vulnerability, fear and uncertainty that comes with asking for help is not a sign of weakness. It's a profound act of strength.

What many discover through this process is something unexpected and powerful: by asking for help, they also give others the opportunity to heal and grow. Helping becomes a gift – a reciprocal exchange that reminds us how deeply connected we all are.

Life was never meant to be navigated alone.

Think about some times when you needed help but didn't ask for it. How might things have been different if you had handled things differently?

Diane Fedorchak has over 20 years of experience working in alcohol and drug misuse prevention, intervention and recovery at UMass Amherst. As a person in long-term recovery, she is honored to support others through their healing journey as they discover the transformative power of fellowship and connection.

THE POWER OF ONE
James F. Murphy

Take time to recognize the gifts of each person.

During the early years of my academic career, I was trying to forge a path that including trying to publish articles in professional journals and author textbooks – all while teaching four classes and directing the campus intramural program. I found myself needing to become more immersed in the teaching of my classes, as there were students who needed assistance and guidance.

In a leadership class I was assigned to teach, I broke up the students into small groups to team up and plan and execute an event. In one of the groups, a student was not very engaged in the planning process and had difficulty expressing himself to group members and was being marginalized by the others. After their event, I met with all the groups to evaluate the process and outcome. In meeting with the team where the student felt ill at ease in the group, the other members voiced their criticism of him and believed he was a burden and an obstacle for the group to achieve success. During the evaluation process, I came to understand how this young man who was intimidated by members of the group needed understanding and support as well as recognition of his unique gifts which were less obvious than other, more outgoing individuals.

That shy, less self-assured student went on to have a long, successful career at Oracle. Some 40 years later, he reached out to me via email to thank me for recognizing his less obvious leadership traits and helping him to gain confidence and allowing him to see himself as a valued team member working with others. This enabled him to realize he had unique gifts that could help team members in the workplace and be cognizant of other coworkers who might need a boost and helping hand.

Leadership skills of individuals may not be as obvious in everyone with whom you engage. It is important to take time to reach out to individuals with whom you interact. It's amazing to see how people can blossom with support and encouragement.

Identify some individuals in your life who may benefit from some outreach and encouragement. Then make a plan to reach out.

James F. Murphy, Ph.D., is a professor emeritus, Parks, Recreation, and Leisure Studies, San Francisco State University. He is the author and coauthor of nine textbooks, including *Recreation and Leisure Service for the Disadvantaged*; *Recreation and Leisure Service: A Humanistic Perspective*; and *A Career with Meaning: Recreation, Parks, Sport Management, Hospitality, and Tourism.*

THE PLACES YOU'LL GO, THE PEOPLE YOU'LL MEET
Mary Wilfert

Lessons learned can help guide one's professional journey.

Upon finishing my master's degree in community health education, I struggled initially to find a job in my profession. So having to make rent, I got an office assistant job at a large law firm and learned about office culture. I kept my eyes and ears open for health educator jobs, and a few months into my law firm experience, I found an opening at the local health department. It was an exciting (though not very lucrative) find, and it started me along my professional path, highlighted by middle school puberty education, parent forums on head lice control, community drug prevention awareness and high school sex education guest lectures (favorite video, *Hope Is Not a Method*).

Early on, I was offered many opportunities for professional growth, and my first lesson was, **connect/collaborate with and learn from other professionals** across local, state and national forums.

FIGURE 6.12
Professionals from various disciplines (college health, psychological services, administration, athletics) collaborating to teach student-athletes bystander intervention!

This was also the start of the AIDS epidemic, and **relying on courageous professionals** was critical to advancing my professional knowledge and understanding of intersectionality.

Through outreach and professional collaboration with other community organizations, I entered another phase of my career with local social services. A request for a guest lecture led to securing a position in higher education. Lesson: **Offer your services to others in the community.**

When a family move prompted another job search, I found a position at the NCAA (college athletics governing body – talk about getting out of your comfort zone!). Through this position, I was able to work with a variety of professionals across the nation, advancing prevention efforts in this unique population. Another lesson: **Recognize your transferable skills, and collaborate!**

So, collaborate, continue professional development, respond to others' needs, and recognize your value – and you'll make great friends!

For each recommendation, identify ways you can do them today and enhance them.

Mary Wilfert studied health education and community health education. She enjoys reconnecting with the fabulous folks she's met along her professional journey.

SOCIAL PURPOSE
Martin Ford

The desire to accomplish goals that are larger than yourself and of benefit to others is the motivational fuel that has enabled humankind to soar above all other species.

In Western societies, we are socialized to believe that people are naturally motivated by self-interest, and almost everything else is a facade. And yet, evidence from biologists, psychologists and neuroscientists overwhelmingly demonstrates that social purpose is an equally powerful motivational force, one that enables humans to thrive in families, communities and groups organized around shared goals and objectives.

Social purpose includes four types of motives: **belongingness** (focused on interpersonal relationships and group involvement), **social responsibility** (focused on obligations and commitments to others), **equity** (focused on fairness and justice) and **resource provision** (focused on caring and giving). It is now clear that social purpose is literally a life-sustaining force, as those who prioritize these concerns experience greater well-being and better health outcomes. Moreover, caring for and about others appears to be part of a larger, self-enhancing pattern of seeking to engage life in ways that are rich in meaning and emotional vitality.

Adding social purpose to self-interest is like adding color to a black-and-white photograph. To experience that transformation, practice engaging with others by first focusing on THEIR thoughts, feeling and concerns. Listen, learn and consider ways to be encouraging and supportive. You will soon find that when you focus on more than "What's in it for me?" or "Why should I care?" your thinking will become more flexible and inspired, and others will start to see you in a more approving and appreciative light. That in turn will enhance their motivation to listen, learn and support you as well.

And that is the beauty of social purpose: in the long run, the most reliable way to improve your own life – and to be seen as an effective leader – is to find ways to improve the lives of others.

What opportunities can you find that would enable you to help improve others' lives in small ways, modest ways and in large ways?

Martin Ford is the cocreator (with Peyton Smith) of the thriving with social purpose theory of motivation and optimal functioning, as detailed in *Motivating Self and Others: Thriving With Social Purpose, Life Meaning, and the Pursuit of Core Personal Goals* (Cambridge University Press, 2020).

Nature
Nurturing Yourself

Each person is surrounded by the natural world. More than that, each person needs the world to survive. Consider it – the air needed to breathe, the water required to live, the food grown from the earth to sustain human and animal life, the oceans and rivers that nourish fish and aquatic life. All too often, nature is taken for granted; yet it surrounds all human beings, whether in a country setting or urban environment.

Beyond the essential parts of nature, the natural world is also important for the human heart and soul. Whether it is the sun on one's face or the distant stars in the sky that piques curiosity and wonder, the natural world can revitalize individuals. It may be the shade and the trees of the forest, or the sound of the babbling brook or ocean waves; it may be the sand between one's toes or even the rustling leaves. And it may be the texture of the pine needles or the beauty of the color of the changing leaves. Nature surrounds everyone, and nature has its beauty.

At the same time, nature deserves respect. For the natural world to provide all that it does, whether for one's body, mind, soul or more, it needs to be protected. Certainly, humankind can harness so much of what nature offers, whether through crops, nourishment or even energy. However, nature must not be taken for granted or overused to depletion or abused.

WHY ATTENTION TO THE NATURAL WORLD?

The purpose of having an entire section on nature and the natural world is to help increase an overall understanding of the role of nature in one's life and for sustaining a quality life. Further, its presence is designed to help increase an understanding of the important role each person plays within the larger context of the natural world. Thus, attention is important for understanding the sights, sounds and smells that surround people in different settings and ways of each person can increase an appreciation of the nature surrounding them. It also includes gaining greater understanding of the interconnectedness of the natural world and respect for all that nature brings,

DOI: 10.4324/9781003541080-7

including being environmentally engaged with behaviors such as recycling and sustainability.

From a broad perspective, it is important to think about natural capital. Nature is essentially a finite resource, although some parts of it are renewable. For minerals in the earth, limits exist. For crops grown regularly, these can be sustained, albeit with quality earth and nourished grounds. Things like the wind and the sun can be harnessed for energy; however, damage and harm can result from natural or human causes.

A core question with an understanding of the natural world is how humans are leaving the earth for others who follow on the planet. How are people collectively sustaining each other in their daily lives and with daily habits and behavior. Central to the natural world discussion is an examination of the larger systems, including naturally occurring and politically or organizationally generated systems, that affect these issues in both harmful and helpful ways. Attention to systemic change can be an important and vital component of the natural world and demonstrating respect for it.

Implicit with this understanding is the role of individuals in helping to shape nature in positive and constructive ways. This can be termed "environmental justice," as such an approach can acknowledge the respect necessary to sustain and nourish the natural world. This view also acknowledges that individuals have their own spheres of influence, whereby they can take action to help promote quality outcomes with positive outcomes. From the broad policy and social justice perspective, many organizations, governments and individuals can take action to promote sustainability.

An important first step for positive change is educating ourselves and others about opportunities. As education is a multilayered process, it is helpful to learn more about positive and harmful things that can be done and promoting the positive and reducing or eliminating the harmful. It is helpful to connect with the community, both local and more broadly. Through connecting with organizations and through promoting partnerships and collaboration, much can be done to promote sustainability. Further, through connection with experts who remain up to date with the latest science, greater understanding and application is feasible.

NATURE'S APPLICATIONS TO INDIVIDUALS

Individuals have many opportunities to become involved with nature and to promote greater respect for nature. Whether it is through conservation or renewal, through observation or engagement, or through awareness or advocacy, numerous approaches exist for personal involvement.

First, it is important to have a basic respect for the natural world. With that foundation, so much else can follow. Related to that respect is one of awareness and understanding. That involves learning ways that individual actions, or inactions, can affect the surrounding natural world. Consider the age-old saying found when hiking: "Leave only footprints; take only memories." That can apply to so many places beyond a trail in the woods; noticing the litter on roadways, playgrounds and so many settings can give one pause about the source of those items.

From an individual perspective, the attention to reusability and recycling is commonplace. This includes reusing things or limiting one-time-use products. It attends to the local standards and procedures for recycling various items. It can translate to the products one chooses to purchase. Individuals may also consider, based on specific local standards, using their yard as well as food waste in a composting bin or setting. Extending beyond one's individual lifestyle, people can identify ways to recycle in their school, work or community setting and advocate for more convenient and appropriate ways of promoting this sustainability.

Individuals can also create positive spaces with property they own or inhabit; if that's not found based on one's living situation, individuals can strive to promote similar outcomes with the leaders and influencers in their setting. For example, consider identifying ways to beautify the local setting, including the use of natural plants and flowers. This might include a small habitat that is consistent with the natural setting and one that promotes the use of natural pest control rather than using artificial pesticides.

Extending beyond individual activity, it is helpful to consider ways of supporting conservation efforts. This may be with service projects and other hands-on opportunities, such as waterway or roadway cleanups as well as tree plantings. Individuals may also reach out to a local conservation organization or nature center, or an organization that supports such initiatives to identify ways they can be better educated and even volunteer to serve.

A final consideration with individual applications vis-à-vis the natural world is to identify and engage in ways that nature can be helpful in sustaining one's own mental and physical health. This could be a run through the woods or along the ocean. It could be sitting quietly on a hillside and appreciating the natural beauty. It could be standing on a rooftop and becoming absorbed by the clouds by day and the stars at night. It could be sitting with a book and listening to the babbling brook or the rustling of the winds. It could be reflecting on ways in which the surrounding environment is nourishing and inspiring.

The important things are to start with yourself and to learn as much as possible to build on the respect – and hopefully a growing respect – for the natural world. It's important to not be intimidated by lack of knowledge, experience, or engagement. These can each grow over time and as needed. Even though greater attention to and incorporation of nature can feel overwhelming, a larger and more sustainable future can be the ultimate result.

LINKAGE WITH OTHER THEMATIC AREAS

Each of the other thematic areas in this book can be linked to this section on nature. Consider, for example, how optimism can and must be embedded with efforts surrounding the natural world. From an individual perspective, one must believe that their efforts do in fact make a difference. And if they are not clear with that, they can learn more about what specific initiatives by them, individually or as part of a group, are meaningful and helpful. A vision for a more healthful and inspiring future is embedded with the optimism theme.

Similarly, having a value placed on the importance of the natural world is important. Imagine what the near and distant future would be like if people didn't care about the quality of the water or air, or the nourishment embedded in the foods they're eating. What would it be like if rubbish was tolerated widely as well as the decimation of forests and streams and grasslands? Consider the value of nature within one's own life, including but not limited to whether it promotes awe and wonder. If respect for and care of the natural world were not valued or encouraged, where would creativity and perseverance and an engagement in the future be? Clearly, having a value for nature, both individually and collectively, is central to this area. The Self-Care thematic area is indeed a large part of this focus, as involvement with the natural world is important for stress reduction, for mental health, for physical health and for spiritual wellness. Similarly, active engagement with nature, as a core part of one's life, can reduce the desire for drugs or alcohol misuse, as well as promote greater self-esteem and overall quality of life.

The thematic areas of Relationships and Community also link to nature, as the shared experiences with oneself or other relationships, as well as with a group or work setting can help nurture quality interactions. Surrounding individuals and groups with nourishing natural beauty provides an environment that is helpful and grounding. Similarly, the involvement with the Service area is present, as many individuals and groups involve themselves with volunteering to help promote positive surroundings. They may also want to identify ways they can be part of giving back and promoting quality external and environmental settings.

CONCLUSION

In this chapter, the importance of nature is highlighted. That focus is not meant to be solely passive, with attention to how nature can help heal and sustain, and nourish and motivate individuals. While those are important features, attention is also provided to the important advocacy and engagement role with the natural world surrounding everyone. With the over 25 contributions included in this section, readers will be encouraged to be more "green" in their lives as well as finding how a tree can be an integral part of life. The contributors offer perspectives about nature's power as well as the inspiration found with nature's beauty and abundance. Even viewing nature and the outdoors as a quality playground can be helpful for readers. The inspirations and reflection pieces add further value about how the readers can engage with and help shape the natural world around them.

Messages What are key points or themes highlighted in the Legacy Letters within the Nature area?	
Reflections What are your thoughts and feelings about what is shared and recommended regarding Nature?	
Resources What individuals, groups, organizations or other information would help you better understand and apply recommendations in the Nature area?	
Commitments What are you willing to commit yourself to doing regarding the Nature theme, both in the near term and in the more distant future?	

FIGURE 7.1
Legacy Worksheet for Nature

NATURALLY: KNOWN . . . AND BEYOND
Ray Quirolgico

The joy and power of nature actually emanates from what is undefined and not fully understood.

As a child, I always enjoyed nature documentaries probably starting with my fascination with dinosaurs, whales and dolphins, and astronomy and so on. As an adult, my enjoyment of these science nonfiction stories has deepened to include appreciation for their cinematography, narration and even music scoring. Most important, I continue to value the ceaseless **sense of wonder and the value for learning** that these documentary journeys offer.

To paraphrase a lesson that the renowned astronomer and educator Carl Sagan offered decades ago, when someone asked him how someone could be a person of faith and a person of science at the same time, science (as explained in these documentaries) requires human convictions that parallel faith: the search for meaning, truth and understanding, motivated by **the yearning to understand and the belief that there is more to discover in the unknown and the unproven.**

In my younger years, nature seemed like a set of solvable puzzles and science was the playground that would (eventually) figure them out. Now I appreciate nature not for its answers but more for its questions. I feel a real humility when I think about mysteries that might not get proven or disproven in my lifetime: Is there extraterrestrial life? Do other animals have language and culture? How does life originate? How did everything begin and how might it all end? And so on. In my personal life, I try to notice things that might still spark that feeling of awe and curiosity: **feeling resolute that there is so much more beyond me and accepting the limits of my own humanity.**

FIGURE 7.2

Long-exposure of the morning sun rising over winter landscape, gazing out the window of a moving train.

As much as I strive to do, and to achieve, and to make a difference with my life, and as much as the next nature documentary might teach me something concrete, there is so much more to love about nature (and science) that comes from the undiscovered and undiscoverable, from the undefined and from the not-yet understood. To exist in a cosmos of possibilities and limitless ideas feels comforting, perhaps as the universe has always intended.

How does the natural world inspire you with awe and wonder? What do you commit yourself to that is unknown or unproven?

Ray Quirolgico, Ed.D., has worked in higher education administration for over 30 years. He fills his life with joy from theater, books, dinosaurs and Lego.

GROWING PLAYGROUNDS
Scott Kretchmar

It's time to grow playgrounds!

Gather your rake of curiosity, your shovel of creativity and your watering can of serendipity and head to the garden of play. No time to waste.

Perhaps you have heard the aphorism, "All work and no play makes Jack and Jill dull people." Surely, you don't want to become one of those – that is, a dull person, someone who is unhappy, who has been worn down (or worn out) by the requirements of work.

That is a danger because you are heading into a lifetime filled with work. You will have to make a living. Hopefully, that work will be interesting and, to a certain degree, enjoyable. However, whether it promises good days or not, having a job is a requirement. And requirements can become onerous, heavy and have that life-robbing "dulling" effect.

Fortunately, a well-tested antidote is available. It is called play. Play keeps us fresh. It renews us. It gives us something to look forward to. In contrast to the rational duty to make a living, it provides a kind of irrational alternative. The only thing it is designed to make is joy.

All play takes place on playgrounds, and potential playgrounds exist everywhere. But many of them are underdeveloped and need to be fertilized. Others have not yet broken ground. They need to be watered. It should be easy to see why that fertilizing and watering is necessary.

They require attention because the lake will always be an underdeveloped playground until someone learns how to swim, or fish, or canoe. Novels will always be weak playgrounds at best until one cultivates a taste for good literature. Mountains will not become healthy playgrounds, and nobody will fall in love with mountaineering until one develops requisite degrees of fitness and skill, learns some mountain lore and rubs shoulders with the slopes. That's where you come in.

It is your responsibility and privilege to cultivate playgrounds that will adorn your life. It is up to you to develop the skills, attitudes, knowledge and tastes that grow your current playgrounds and, over the years, help you foster new ones. Good luck! And play on!

Where are your playgrounds today? What can you do to grow your playgrounds of tomorrow?

Scott Kretchmar is Professor Emeritus of Exercise and Sport Science at Penn State University. He specializes in sport philosophy and ethics, is a Fellow in the National Academy of Kinesiology and has received its highest honor, the Heatherington Award.

SAVORING NATURE
Hollie M. Chessman

Be present and curious within the natural world.

By the time I was ten years old, I could identify about a dozen different trees just by looking at their bark. Looking at the leaves was cheating because it would be a dead giveaway on what type of tree it was. The challenge was to figure it out without looking at the leaves. And so it went every time my father would take my sister, brother and me on a hike in our over 25 acres of woods.

These hikes were the foundation of my childhood, and I have often thought about how being in and among nature just feels different – more centering, heart-opening, and mindful. I am still able to identify a lot of trees without looking at their leaves, but more than that, I have remained forever present, curious and drawn to nature.

When was the last time you spent several days within the confines of a city or an urban environment? What do you remember experiencing? The noise from the cars and ambulances; the persistent honking or car alarms; the smell of car exhaust or from a fast-food restaurant venting their grease and burgers. You may have felt energized, but you also may have felt exhausted, overstimulated or overwhelmed.

There is a reason green space is so important to urban planning and colleges and universities. Not only does it look nice, but it also provides a sanctuary for humans, birds, squirrels, chipmunks, flowers, trees, frogs and fish (if there is water, of course). It provides a place to listen to the birds. A place to feel the grass between our toes or fingers. An olfactory experience when the flowers are blooming or the grass is being cut. Shade from the hot sun under the trees. A landmark to gather in community with others.

Next time you are out in nature, a park, the beach, the campus quad or hiking or biking a trail, pay attention. Be present. Notice the sights, sounds, smells and feeling of being in nature. What do you notice? How do you feel?

Do you know what type of tree you are seeing? Can you identify the song of the bird you hear? Do you know what type of flower is growing beside the trail? If not, dear reader, find out!

Hollie M. Chessman has worked in and around higher education for over 20 years. She loves to spend time in the woods, on the Oregon Coast, New Orleans and lying in the grass on a blanket listening for birds.

SUNRISE: OUR DAILY DO-OVER
Eileen Crawford

Through life's ups and downs, we are given a reset button daily, if only we open our eyes early enough to take it.

My first introduction to the power of the sunrise didn't involve the actual sun at all. It involved my mother. As a child, I carried my troubles locked inside. But when night cast its dark quiet over my bedroom, they were stirred and unpacked, and tears would flow. Mom magically heard me every time. Into my bedroom she crept, and I would pour out my drama of the moment. She would listen, hug me and say, "That was all today. But today is over. Tomorrow is a new day, and every new day brings new possibilities for great things to happen. Close your eyes, and when you wake, the new day will be here, and you will feel so much better." And damn, she was always right.

Mom's magic worked for a while, but as I grew, so too did some of my troubles. Some days, I awoke still as sad or worried as the night before, and on others, I never slept at all. In my realization that dawn was coming, a strange thing happened. I discovered that I loved seeing it arrive. So much more happens than I had ever realized. Birds wake up and start calling out to each other. They scurry for food and shake up the trees and backyard dogs. On days when I am lucky enough to be by the ocean, I make it a point to wake not just for sunrise but for the 20 minutes or so before. The sky fills with colors – blues, purples, reds, yielding to pink, orange and yellow – clouds taking turns to shield and then reveal what is behind them. And in all this, I always come back to that feeling of being a tiny part of something so much bigger and grander than myself. It is a moment of glory and awe, announcing that indeed, anything is possible.

When you find yourself feeling down, overwhelmed or discouraged, make it a point to wake at least a half hour before dawn for one week. Find a peaceful spot in nature to take in the sunrise and feel its healing energy. Nature beats antidepressants with surprising frequency. Try it!

Eileen Crawford is a mother, grandmother and Licensed Mental Health Counselor in private practice in Ponte Vedra, Florida. Her research area of interest is resilience, and she writes, speaks and teaches on building strength-based resilience individually and in families.

THE POWER OF NATURE
Dave Closson

Nature has the power to clear your mind, calm your soul and energize your spirit.

I was fortunate to grow up immersed in the outdoors. My dad worked in conservation law enforcement, so I spent my childhood traveling the state, learning to appreciate everything nature offers. From driving a giant boat on Lake Michigan to hunting deer, turkey and waterfowl, and fishing using bank poles and nets, the outdoors became my playground.

As I got older, my love for nature only deepened. After earning a degree in environmental biology, I achieved my dream of working in the Rocky Mountains of Colorado with the Division of Wildlife. During that time, I spent my weekdays backpacking to high-altitude mountain lakes above 10,000 feet, measuring fish populations to monitor ecosystem health. I cooked over open campfires, marveled at star-filled skies and found profound peace in the stillness of the mountains.

Even now, when life feels overwhelming, I turn to nature. Whether I'm hiking in the woods or simply stepping onto my back porch to feel the sun on my face, nature helps me recharge. Although I now live in a busy suburb far from the remote mountain lakes of my past, I've learned that even small moments outdoors can provide clarity and calm. Observing the squirrels and birds, breathing in fresh air and noticing the movement of leaves in the breeze reminds me of the beauty that surrounds us daily, no matter where we are.

Here are some things you can do to help bring nature into your life. First, consider taking a few moments each day to step outside, even if only onto your porch or balcony or on a walk, and observe the natural world around you. Second, take notice of the nature around you during your daily routine – as you drive to work, school or anywhere; observe the clouds, the sky, the trees and the birds. Third, reflect on how spending time in nature clears your mind and rejuvenates your spirit, and make it a regular part of your self-care routine.

Take an inventory of the ways in which you currently observe and appreciate the natural world around you. With that assessment, what specific changes might you consider?

Dave Closson, a combat veteran and owner of DJC Solutions, LLC, is an author, speaker, podcaster and entrepreneur.

IF YOU CAN'T BEAT THEM, DON'T JOIN THEM
Warren Doyle

Musings of a traveler on the way to becoming.

I have come to the conclusion that I have seen too many acts of human kindness and generosity and feelings of authentic freedom. These have occurred in the miles (i.e., 38,000) I have walked on the Appalachian Trail, along with the miles I have danced on the contradance floor. These miles keep me from ever feeling beaten down by the hate, anger, violence and greed of a dehumanizing world which is propagated by the media. I will neither buy into nor believe in their narrative that the world is a dangerous place for an individual and that a person needs an institution to save or protect us from ourselves. My feelings on this are as deep, thick and gently soft as the moss I have slept on and the pine needles that I have trod on.

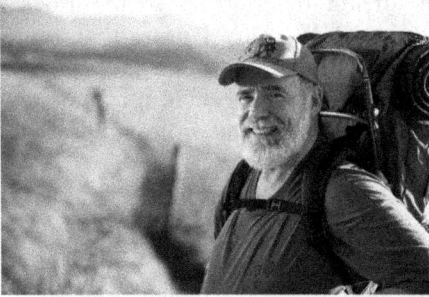

FIGURE 7.3
Atop Max Patch Bald on the NC/TN border illustrated by Maurice Herzog's quote "Only at the summit can we straighten our bodies that always lean uphill."

I know I can't overcome societal institutions' mistrust of the individual, and its desire to control us for our own good, but *even though I can't beat them, I don't have to join them*. And that creates an adventure filled with constant observation fueled by a never-ending curiosity of the wonder of it all.

How about you?

- Will you be a member of the herd feeding in a crowded, muddy corral or an independent outlier eating remnants of winter hay high on the side of a pasture being content with your place?
- Do you want to remove yourself from an environment that is causing you self-doubt or confusion about your future and go on a pilgrimage of self-discovery through challenge in an environment (i.e., nature/Appalachian Trail) that knows neither prejudice nor discrimination?
- Do you want to set forth on a difficult quest for a tabula rasa?

The choice is yours and yours alone.

What potential action steps would you consider in the near and more distant future?

Warren Doyle, Ph.D., has successfully flowed between the two worlds of the practical and of the ideal without becoming trapped in either of them.

GROW, COOK AND EAT, GARDEN TO KITCHEN
Philippe Michelot

It is important to build a society where human and environmental health are prioritized.

The concept of "Grow, Cook and Eat" and associated movements like "farm to table" and "garden to kitchen" represent an integrated and sustainable approach to food. These provide opportunities for each of us, regardless of where we live or our rural, suburban or urban settings. These shorten the distance between producer and consumer; by minimizing intermediaries, they ensure fresher and often higher quality products. This also involves increased support for local farmers and a reduction in the ecological footprint.

GROW includes selecting organic seeds, managing soil ecologically and promoting biodiversity. Sustainable agricultural practices, such as crop rotation, composting and using natural pesticides, are preferred to preserve soil health and ecosystems. COOK emphasizes healthy cooking methods that preserve nutrients. Recipes prioritize fresh, local and seasonal ingredients, thereby ensuring better flavor and nutritional quality. EAT promotes fresh, local and seasonal foods, resulting in health benefits of nutritional quality, reduced exposure to chemicals and improved well-being.

From my experience as a farmer for over a quarter century, I know about the health impact on several fronts. First, there's the nutritional factor: organic products are often richer in nutrients, including vitamins, minerals and antioxidants. Eating seasonal fruits and vegetables ensures a varied and balanced diet throughout the year. Second, there's mental well-being. Gardening and cooking with seasonal produce can have beneficial effects on mental health, reducing stress and fostering a sense of satisfaction and accomplishment. Third is the disease-prevention focus. A diet rich in fresh, organic and seasonal products can help prevent many chronic diseases, such as cardiovascular diseases, type 2 diabetes and certain cancers.

Also, consider the importance of seasonal fruits and vegetables. These are at their peak flavor and texture, enhancing culinary experience and taste satisfaction. They are generally richer in nutrients because they are harvested at maturity. Consuming seasonal products reduces dependence on energy-intensive production systems (such as heated greenhouses) and long-distance imports, thus decreasing the carbon footprint.

These concepts are within reach for each of us. Even though it's a lot of work, our health is certainly worth it!

How can you incorporate the principles of Grow, Cook and Eat in your lifestyle?

Philippe Michelot lives near Saint-Rémy-de-Provence, France, where he has managed his estate and farm Mas des Figues using permaculture.

GO GREEN!
Tokeitha Wilson

Numerous strategies exist for being more environmentally committed.

Reduce, reuse and recycle today! For many people, "green" means nature and suggests lush grass, overgrown trees and majestic forests. Other common associations are money, luck, health and the negative emotion known as envy. I find green to be refreshing and exotic.

We all have heard the phrase "Go green." "Going green" typically applies to the actions you take to lessen your impact on the planet. But how many of us actually respect our environment and make a conscious decision to go green. Going green can be defined as "environmentally friendly decisions" as well as to "reduce, reuse and recycle." By choosing to go green, we are helping to make the world a better place. It's about creating places and spaces to simplify life. After all, our overall wellness is closely tied to our environment.

Every day, we get to choose how we want to live our lives. In our natural environment, we should never take for granted the freedom to access clean air, food and water. In our social environment, we have the liberty to stop bullying, harassment and racism. We have the power to build harmony in our place of residence, anywhere in the world. We can preserve resources, making the planet safe and sustainable for generations to come.

You can go green by recycling, composting or conserving energy or water. Perhaps you are in a transition in life – you can choose to remove some toxins by surrounding yourself with people and things that you find positive and inspiring. If you are exploring a new hobby, consider developing a green thumb as a gardener. Make an ecofriendly choice: more green time, less screen time. Detox! Personally, I love exploring flower beds. As the saying goes, "Stop and smell the roses"; I like to stop and observe the flowers, colors, textures and scents of flower beds.

To do your part with going green, think about your environment.

- Are you recycling whenever possible, and buying recycled products?
- Do you limit the power and water you use?
- How often do you take public transportation?
- What was your last outdoor activity?
- When have you visited a public park to learn, play or walk?
- Do you organize your living space and add things that make you happy?

Review ways you can increase your commitment for going green in the near future.

Tokeitha Wilson is a public health executive who has influenced corporate and government infrastructure. She is a lover of sports and comedy, a mother to a musical genius and an aunt to three fur babies.

BUILDING BONDS
Jeanne Martino-McAllister

Cross-pollinate your friends.

When I turned 60, I went to Italy with a relatively disconnected group of friends. Not one of us knew every one of us. To explain, my "60 Circle" of friends came from Virginia, Pennsylvania and Bermuda and were in my life at various stages but did not always know each other. Ages ranged from 34 to 74. Some called the grouping risky; we just called it amazing.

On our first full day in Italy, we hiked the Path of the Gods, high above Positano. It was spontaneous and beautiful, magnificent and challenging. The shared experience, breathtaking views, light conversation and gentle encouragement created bonds that carried us through a fantastic and memorable trip.

Interestingly enough, the blending of friends with curvy connections to one or more of someone else in the group was repeated twice since the Italy trip – both times on intentional, self-guided hiking trips to Ireland and Switzerland.

Witnessing the beauty of the landscape and the building of new relationships with "relatively disconnected" people in my life was invigorating. We knew there would be challenges to overcome and solutions and compromising. The feeling of creating this people space that spanned ages and continents was immensely satisfying.

Bringing strangers together can be a risk, but it can also be socially and emotionally rewarding when done thoughtfully and intentionally. Can you think of people from your school, classes,

FIGURE 7.4
Taking turns, leading and following, opening the pathway for new conversations.

church, neighborhood, workplace or community who may benefit from coming together? Invite a cross section of people in your life to go on a walk or hike. It does not have to be in another country! Ponder commonalities – activities, clubs, music, places, things. Encourage connections, watch how they pair up, change up and chat with each other. You do the same. Never leave anyone behind or alone. Be a connector of people in your life.

In what ways can you cross-pollinate your friends?

Jeanne Martino-McAllister, Ph.D., is Professor Emerita, Department of Health Sciences, James Madison University.

HARDSCAPE

Jim Williamson

Finding a new way in an unfamiliar space can be so rewarding.

I was born and raised in New Jersey, ten miles outside of New York City. My natural world was hardscape. It was the buildings of NYC, the parking lots of the Giants Stadium, and the streets of suburbia. Nature was not in my world.

I went to Gettysburg College and got a job as a salesperson for a big company. They asked if I was willing to relocate, which I was. They said, "Great, you are moving to West Virginia." I had to get a map to find out where that was.

I moved there at the beginning of spring. I knew no one and since I was a salesperson, I had no office to go to. I worked all day and drove the state wondering where all the people were. It was lonely, depressing and sad. Then a client asked me if I was interested in going rafting with her and her friends that weekend in the New River Gorge. I immediately said yes, and it changed my life.

The rafting was so amazing and beautiful that I started spending all my weekends in the gorge – hiking the mountainous terrain, watching the people raft and going by myself when I could. The New and Gauley Rivers in West Virginia are world-class rapids, I found out, and decided it would BE my social life.

I interviewed for a rafting guide job at North American River Runners that fall and got a job on the weekends as a guide. I trained for three months with 15 men and women all around my age. We became close friends quickly and spent every weekend that year rafting, hiking and enjoying the beautiful natural landscape of West Virginia. When I got a new job back in New York, I was sad to leave the greenspaces of West Virginia, but it was back to the hardscape for me.

So, say yes. Say yes to new ideas and opportunities. It just may change your life.

> *Think about what's around you – places, people, events and more. What is something new to which you can say yes?*

Jim Williamson lives in New Jersey still with his wife, dog and occasionally his grown sons. An Ironman triathlete, Jim is also the chief revenue officer for AFCO Direct.

A SERENDIPITOUS JOURNEY
John Heidke

Be an intentional steward of your ecosystem and contribute to its preservation.

I grew up in a small town in Wisconsin and was schooled in the work of Aldo Leopold, the great author and conservationist, as well as tromping around the land with my father and friends. It was idyllic!

Fast forward to today where I have the honor of living in the Greater Yellowstone Ecosystem – often referred to as the "American Serengeti." My small ranch is 25 miles north of Yellowstone National Park with all its critters, geysers, waters and wonders. *Stick with me. I have a point, and it involves you!*

In my time here in Montana, I have seen the devastating results of climate change, calamitous natural events such as wildfires and 1,000-year floods, unbridled growth, mining, and other conscious and unconscious human acts often of a shortsighted and destructive nature. I have also seen the heroic act of teenagers taking on the state because it was not meeting their constitutional right to "a clean environment." And they won!

I have mindfully made a commitment to be a steward of "my" ecosystem. And it has become my moral contribution to the future of my grandkids. I see my community in a broad way, not unlike the vistas outside my window – the mountains, rivers, large and small critters, the soil, rock and plants. But as Leopold opined, "The relationships between people and land are intertwined; care for people cannot be separated from care for the land. Thus, a land ethic is a moral code of conduct that stems from these interconnected caring relationships."

Now it is time for you, with intention, to determine your commitment. Metaphorically, this is like planting a tree that can grow to hold a swing that three generations hence can play on. Consider how you can hardwire ethical stewardship into your life. Spend five minutes every day focusing on your ecosystem. Make it a high personal priority. I promise it will bring you immense joy and satisfaction, as it has me.

FIGURE 7.5
Looking southward from Carter's Bridge near Livingston, MT up Paradise Valley toward Yellowstone National Park – 1000-year flood of June, 2022.

What are you willing to commit yourself to doing to improve your environment?

John Heidke, after careers in higher education and consulting for organizations worldwide, actively contributes his time and talent serving and volunteering.

EARTHING
Gina Firth

Connect with earth's natural healing energy by grounding yourself daily.

The earth beneath our feet holds wisdom older than anything chronicled by humans. It also holds tremendous healing energy and grounding. In a world of constant digital noise and chaos, nature offers a profound sanctuary of connection, perspective and renewal.

Grounding to the earth, often called "earthing," offers profound physical and psychological benefits. By directly connecting with the natural ground – through walking barefoot, sitting on the grass or making direct skin contact with soil, stone or a tree –humans can experience significant healing and restoration.

The earth's surface carries a subtle electrical charge that, when in direct contact with our bodies, helps neutralize free radicals and reduce inflammation. Research suggests this connection can lower stress hormones, improve sleep quality and enhance overall immune function. The earth's natural electromagnetic fields seem to recalibrate our body's internal rhythms, counteracting disruptions caused by modern environments.

Psychologically, grounding provides an immediate sense of calm and presence. By feeling the literal ground beneath us, we interrupt mental spirals of anxiety and reconnect with the fundamental stability of our physical existence. This roots us in the present moment, reducing mental chatter and promoting a sense of peace and interconnectedness with the natural world.

Regular grounding practices can help reset our nervous system, decrease cortisol levels and promote a deeper sense of personal equilibrium and well-being. The forest doesn't judge your career trajectory; the ocean doesn't care about your social media status. They simply exist, resilient and interconnected, teaching us about adaptability, patience and the beauty of diverse growth. Spending time in nature isn't a luxury - it's a fundamental way of recalibrating our inner compass, balance and reconnections.

FIGURE 7.6
Discover how direct physical contact with the earth can provide physical and psychological benefits.

Spend 30 minutes this week in a natural setting – a local park, a hiking trail or even a small garden – and spend at least 10 minutes barefoot. Observe without judgment and feel your connection to something larger than yourself.

Gina Firth is the assistant vice president for wellness at the University of Tampa and the proud mother of four amazing daughters.

THE ARTFUL LIFE
Neena Jhaveri

Live and walk with art.

The roots of my journey began in India, where I grew up . . . with the richness of colors, sounds and people . . . that my sensory faculties were infused and overwhelmed at the same time. As a little child, I took retreat in my imagination and then, when a little older, in the natural world around me. Soon, I learned that you can imagine anything – an internal landscape that only *you* know.

A new fascination began by the sounds of birds, nature and colors, whenever, wherever, anywhere I went. As this world of imagination became active, an inspiration came to me – that I could create art. As a young child, I said to my family, "One day, I will become an artist and go to America to live there."

The journey from that point on was being active with school – dance training at an early age, drawing and painting in my free time all through school until I graduated from high school. I attended two colleges simultaneously – one for my bachelor of arts degree where I majored in economics with a minor in psychology, the other was going to a fine arts college for drawing and painting. That was my dad's advice, which at that time I did not like. Needless to say, having both areas of academic studies have helped with running an art-based, woman-based small company where I make art, create one-of-a-kind ceramics and design accessories and linens for home. I have a few other women who help me in that vision.

The imagination to create was a candle that was always burning in the deepest part of my heart, as it brought joy to me as a child. That feeling of joy has taken a meandering path with vision, learning from my surroundings and other people – observing and soaking in their experience and wisdom. All of this continues to compel me to create joy that I can bring to others.

You give the gifts you become by receiving on your journey. Feeling life and nature deeply has the ability to create rich depth – an artful life!

Life is a painting on a blank canvas, creating from a ball of clay. Possibilities are endless when you just follow your joy, keep the imagination alive and strive to be your authentic self.

All rest will follow.

In what ways can you engage nature more deeply in your own life?

Neena Jhaveri is an accomplished artist, ceramicist and designer based in the Shenandoah Valley of Virginia. She has always had a strong appreciation for nature's beauty and is a master at bringing nature's miracles to life in all her creations.

GETTING OUTSIDE IN NATURE
Jon Dodrill

Sometimes a side project with a noble goal can make a difference.

I enjoy trees. One of the southern yellow pines, the longleaf pine (*Pinus palustris*) is my favorite. A continuous 92-million-acre longleaf pine–dominated open-canopy forest once stretched across the southeastern coastal plain from southern Virginia to eastern Texas. Now less than 5 percent of this fragmented ecosystem with its high biodiversity remains with only about 1 percent in an original old-growth-forest condition. The longleaf pine ecosystem is the third most endangered ecosystem in the United States.

My personal side project, unrelated to my job as a marine fisheries biologist, was to plant, over time, grass-stage longleaf pine as well as lost native ground cover to partially restore a disturbed four-acre vacant property in rural Grady County, southwestern Georgia. The property during the previous 75 years had an environmental history of turpentining, logging, sod farming, pasture grass and other invasive plant species encroachment, plus land clearing for someone's house that was never built. Only six second-growth longleaf pines remained.

In my brief 19 year stewardship of the four-acre property, I personally was not able to return this patch of disturbed land to the pre-Columbian condition nearly five centuries ago. That was when Hernando de Soto, one of the world's richest men, still bent on more wealth, crossed the nearby Ochlocknee River in late March 1540 a few miles south of the lot, leading the first Europeans headed into the interior of the southeast.

I'll be happy if my legacy for this project is a few dozen pines planted as slow-growing foot-high grass-stage specimens continue to survive. And then, after another 20 years, they are 35–40 feet tall and producing pine cones. Plus, that fire-tolerant wire grass plugs placed in the understory ground cover remain and have expanded.

I sold my restoration project property after 19 years, taking a monetary loss. It was difficult letting go; there could be someone's mansion there with all the trees cut down for a spacious lawn view. In the end, as some Native American once said, "No one owns the land."

I am still dealing with letting go of doing something I enjoyed as a side project and a chance to get outside in nature, as altered as it initially was.

What might you do to help protect some part of nature or some other worthwhile investment in the future?

Jon Dodrill's career involved federal- or state government–related work with marine fisheries–related and terrestrial land management/resource management activities. He now volunteers with assisting unsheltered individuals, promoting affordable housing and working to reduce gun violence.

ADVENTURE IS OUT THERE!
Rikki Barton

Nature has many benefits, large and small. Go find them.

I have always had an appreciation for the beauty of nature, and my adult life has given me a whole new level of respect for it. I've been able to capitalize on opportunities that take me all over the world to explore different parts of nature. For me, there's just nothing like a mountain to take my breath away (both literally and philosophically)!

I've become a long-haul hiker, having accomplished several 20-plus-mile/day hikes as well as several multiday hikes across incredible terrain, like the Himalayas and the African plains. No matter the place or people I am with, I come away from nature more inspired and changed by its influence.

What if you could shift your mental state by spending a few hours in nature on a weekend? It doesn't have to be hiking like I do. It could be sitting in a cozy cabin with endless amounts of tea and books to read from the comfort of a rocking chair. It could be a beach bungalow with a paddleboard. Try it all! Head out into nature and see what it speaks to you.

For me, a consistent message I receive after being in nature is how grand the world is and how my small, albeit important, role in it is. Each of us plays a part in this world we live in, and there's nothing quite like nature to help us zoom out to see the bigger picture and how all of that plays together.

Adventure doesn't have to be something requiring courage or death defying. Adventure could look like going into nature to find out more about yourself in the context of the world we live in. Adventure is out there.

FIGURE 7.7
Ama Dablam is an important stop on the way to Everest Base Camp. The name means "mothers necklace" as the long ridges on each side are like the arms of a mother protecting her child. Photo Credit: Pramod Regmi (trek guide).

What plans can you make to take advantage of the gifts that nature has to offer?

Rikki Barton has a passion for travel, including public speaking/training all over the nation as well as adventure trips to do things like the Everest Base Camp trek, summit Mount Kilimanjaro and visit just about any country!

PRICELESS GIFT OF THE OUTDOORS
Brenda Wiggins

Staying connected with the outdoors and nature has tremendous power in many ways.

As a child, my mom, dad and sister along with many aunts, uncles and cousins all camped out together for a week each summer at a beautiful location between Sequoia and Yosemite National Parks. Nine cousins would slide down small waterfalls, ride horses with ten adults and always make it a point to hike up to the fire lookout. We would drink water collected from a natural spring while my uncle whittled each of us a tiny waterwheel from twigs that would spin in the creek and my cousin charmed chipmunks to eat peanuts out of his hand. Everyone sat around the campfire singing familiar songs accompanied by a harmonica and talked about the flowers, insects and trees we could identify nearby.

Those teachable moments helped me decide on a professional career in recreation. I was drawn by the magic of nature while camping, listening to park rangers' campfire talks and eating s'mores while interacting with one another and sitting under the stars.

The socialization, cognitive and behavioral opportunities as well as economic benefits of nature instilled in me by my family have resulted in a lifelong love for the environment and my belief in the need for preserving it. Many professionals from an assortment of professional fields of study recognize how essential nature is to reduce stress and offer each of us well-being and an enhanced quality of life. When a child goes to their pediatrician for a wellness check, the doctor will often write a prescription "to go outside and play." Where better to improve physical skills, like balance, when scaling a rock or the development of skills necessary to identify a bird's call? Few other things in life are like nature – with the same power to inspire, heal, connect and nurture us no matter what our age, ability or disability.

When I think about the gift of nature and what I experience, it is hikes with others where I use my senses to smell fresh air, listen for the wind in the trees and touch a babbling brook. Not only does it bring back my childhood memories, but it also keeps me connected with so much of what is important today.

> *What do you experience in nature? How can you realize the necessary balance of nature in your life?*

Brenda Wiggins, Ph.D., is an Associate Professor in the Recreation Management Program at George Mason University.

THE AWE AND WONDER OF NATURE
Jim Moore

Nature surrounds all of us and provides rich opportunities for personal nourishment.

Do you find yourself stressed all the time? Are you overwhelmed by issues at work, with family, volunteer commitments, expectations of others and/or self-expectations – all of the "shoulds" in your life? Do these issues weigh you down or lead you to feeling immobilized?

Many people find that an effective antidote to the stressors in life is to schedule "time-out" breaks in nature. Examples include time at the lake/ocean, in the mountains, in the desert, in a park or a large garden, in the vastness of the plains, relaxing in the sun or having fun in the snow.

While time spent in each of these settings is itself important, the renewal of your spirit is greatly enhanced by *how* you spend your time in each of those settings. Perhaps you've heard of the saying, "Take time to smell the roses" – not just look at them but get close to experience the fragrance and color of those flowers.

In nature settings, seek wonder and awe to deepen the experience, which in turn will further nurture your soul. Focusing on the moment – what you are doing in that setting, while letting go of the stressors back home – will sharpen your senses and enhance your appreciation of the beauty of the world around us.

Consider camping in a desert or spending an evening in a "dark community" marveling at what you can see in the night sky, away from city lights. In an old-growth forest, ponder what a 1,500-year-old tree has seen during its life. Notice how the birds and critters in the forest are not worried about what did or might happen. They live for today, focused on food, shelter and parenting.

Nature can also evoke awe in urban settings. The power of this life force enables a flower (or a weed) to grow in a crack in a concrete sidewalk. A canopy of trees provides shelter for animals and cooling for people.

Strive to find awe and wonder in nature and in the world around you. Doing so will enhance your life.

Make a commitment to spend some time discovering the natural world around you, and write down some observations and feelings.

Jim Moore has worked in a machine shop, been a busboy in several restaurants, served as a night watchman, and held multiple positions in the administration of higher education, including Vice President for Student Affairs/Dean of Students at three universities.

OUR PART OF THE CLIMATE ISSUE
Laura S. Privalle

Each individual has an opportunity and an obligation to help our world's climate.

I give my pledge as an American – this is the first part of the conservation pledge – *to save and faithfully defend from waste, the natural resources of my country, its soils and minerals, its forests, water and wildlife.* This pledge was originally crafted in 1946, and I learned it at Nature Camp where we said it every day, from the time I was 11 until my junior year in high school.

The impressions this made on me have been deep and long lasting. My family started recycling newspapers, glass and aluminum back in the 1960s. We organized newspaper drives and litter pickup activities, which I continue to do even now. It also influenced my career choice.

FIGURE 7.8
Laura Privalle, Head, Product Safety, examines a genetically engineered insect-resistant cotton plant in a regulatory field trial being conducted as part of the product's safety assessment.

Now recycling is commonplace, compostable disposable dishware is available, electric cars are much more common and awareness of climate change has increased. However, it takes everyone to really make a difference.

Points to consider may include:

1. Do you eat produce out of season that had to be flown in from far away (large carbon footprint)?
2. To conserve water, consider using a dishwasher.
3. Combine your errands to conserve your fuel.
4. Support clean energy (nuclear, wind, solar, hydro).
5. Recycle, reuse, compost.
6. Discuss the issues with your friends – for their reactions and suggestions!

Review your habits and find a way that you can make a difference. Be mindful of your personal impact on the environment – your carbon footprint.

What are you doing to address these issues individually and as a community member?

Laura Privalle received her Ph.D. in biochemistry from and spent her career in the agricultural biotechnology sector with Syngenta and BASF.

BE YOUR OWN NORTH STAR
Laura Hettinger

Tune in to nature and remain centered.

For millennia, wise men extolled the virtue of nature. Hippocrates promoted the necessity of "airs, waters, and places" for physical and mental well-being. Ralph Waldo Emerson wrote, "There I feel that nothing can befall me in life – no disgrace, no calamity (leaving me my eyes), which nature cannot repair."

However, many of us are required to commute long distances and spend most of our waking hours indoors. Many of us are hunched over a desk, staring at computer screens for hours on end. Exacerbating the situation, we are also surrounded by concrete, metal and glass – essentially devoid of earthly sensations. These converging forces led environmental writer Richard Louv to coin the term "nature deficit disorder" – a form of suffering that comes from a sense of being disconnected from nature and its powers. So it's no surprise that we are drained, feeling confused and uncentered – lost and out of touch with ourselves!

Hundreds of studies have shown that being immersed in nature benefits our physical and mental health, helping us to feel "centered" – a feeling of peace and calmness. Understandably, after a day's work, we find ourselves so tired that even going for a walk is just too daunting or we don't have the time for such a "luxury." On the weekends, catching up on household chores can limit any time for "ourselves."

My advertising career required me to work very long hours, and combined with a long commute, I had little time for myself. I was chasing the bigger accounts, the promotion. The stress had a way of catching up to me. I was amazed at how taking a walk in a park nearby would calm my spirit. Or how a day trip hiking in the National Park centered me. I would tune in to all my senses. Seeing the setting sun cast a golden light on the tree trunks was breathtaking. I loved listening to the birds chirping and feeling the cool breeze on my cheeks. It would put me in a meditative state – feeling centered, I could once again face the world.

No matter what, muster up the energy and get out in nature any chance you get. I promise you, the reward will pay you back tenfold and your North Star will always guide you.

Make specific plans to get out in nature, near and far.

Laura M. Hettinger is a retired advertising executive who pivoted from her long career and raised two children. She recently moved to rural Virginia on three acres with a view of the Shenandoah Mountains, never missing a chance to be in nature, and is a Master Gardener.

HAVING A TREE FRIEND
Changwoo Ahn

Having a tree friend will nurture and teach you valuable lessons in life.

We all need friends. Friends that nurture and sustain us. Friends that are there for us, and we are there for them. I offer the following as a different, yet important, kind of friend. You won't be disappointed.

Plant a tree. If you cannot do that, adopt one and tend to it. You can also pick a tree near you wherever you are and visit it at least once a month, ideally more often. Watch the tree change over the seasons and the years. When you visit the tree, spend time with it by watching, taking pictures of, sitting with, and trying to listen and talk to the tree. It will grow on you, and you will feel like you are having a friend you have never had, who will always be there for you like a book. Learn the tree's scientific name, and its characteristics. Name the tree in your way if you wish and call it by the name every time you see it. Carefully observe how the tree responds and adapts to environmental changes around it. In time, you will have established an emotional relationship with the tree, which may lead you to (re)think our inevitable association with nature and even being part of it.

FIGURE 7.9
My beautiful oak tree friend who is always there through the seasons and the years for my musings on people and nature.

The tree may not need you, but you need the tree: it will solace, comfort, and love you as long as you let it. Establishing a deeper connection with nature through keen observation and tending can start with a simple act like having a tree friend. Having a tree friend will enrich your life and provide you with many life lessons, including how to love and live, which you will appreciate more and more as you go through your life.

And if you move away, carry with you the special memories of and feelings about that tree. Come back and visit it. And find (or plant) a new tree for yourself. It's all part of the circle of life.

Have you leaned on and/or hugged a tree long enough? You can start sitting right next to one calmly for five to ten minutes every day.

Changwoo Ahn, Ph.D. is a Professor of Environmental Science and Policy at George Mason University.

THE CURE FOR ISOLATION

Kurt Larson

Spending time on the trails can be a perfect antidote for our physical and mental health.

Twenty-five years ago, my exercise routine consisted of a daily three-mile run through a local cemetery. I liked the cemetery route because it was quiet, the grounds and its majestic trees were beautifully maintained, and no one ever bothered me in that setting. Not interacting with others in nature was glorious, or so I thought.

A friend persuaded me to join a club to train for a marathon. It soon became clear to me that there was something extraordinary about exercising with others in nature. Conversation came easy. We ran through the seasons and shared our observations about the beauty of nature around us. We shared the pain of the miles of pavement we pounded each week. We shared the smells of our environment, including ourselves. As the weeks passed and the long runs got even longer, we had time to get to know each other better. We shared laughter and some tears too. The relationships I formed during that time of training felt truer, deeper and more real than any I have ever known.

Although I did not know it at the time, my future wife, Sally, was among the many friends I met in that training group. As the years pass, it has become clear to Sally and me that we are at our best together on the trails. Life's challenging issues and pivotal decisions get their proper consideration during long, slow conversations on runs, walks and bike rides. As our marriage evolved, the trails remained our training ground and our refuge from the world. Out there, we still rehearse our various roles, attempting to find the right balance to any given crisis, while untethered to a cell phone and without all the distractions of life outside the confines of four walls.

If you tend to withdraw from the world and many of the people in it, I encourage you to venture out on nature trails and discover what they have to offer you. Trail users are generally a friendly bunch. I think they are softened by the environment around them. The eye contact is better. The friendly greetings are more common. And the trail vibe is very relaxed. You may discover, as I did, that time on the trails interacting with others can have a profound impact on your physical and mental health.

Identify some opportunities for getting out on the trails near you – where, with whom and when.

Kurt Larson lives in Springfield, Missouri, and remains convinced that the best strategy for juggling his roles as husband, father, grandfather, lawyer and professor is exercising outside with friends.

THE FUN, JOYS AND BENEFITS OF TRAVELING INTERNATIONALLY

Joel Meier

International travel broadens perspectives in immeasurable ways.

There's nothing quite like taking a trip, especially an international adventure. Whether you're going somewhere for the first time or returning to a familiar place, getting out of our "comfort zone" is transformational. It helps us appreciate what we have, strengthens relationships and aids creativity.

I'm fortunate to have set foot on all of the world's seven continents. That puts me in an elite group that constitutes less than 1 percent of the world's total population. My travels have been by various means – airplane, car, motorcycle, kayak and boat.

I've learned so much during my travels. It helps us learn about others as well as ourselves, and we do this all while making lifelong-lasting friendships and memories. Many benefits include personal growth, gaining a deeper understanding of different cultures, facilitating problem-solving skills, gaining rejuvenation from a change in scenery, increasing physical activity, reducing stress and deepening satisfaction with life in general.

A lot of folks are hesitant to travel internationally due to the language barrier and fear generated by the media about crime. Sure, there are isolated incidents of crime, just like there is in any place. International travel is not a problem if you use common sense about where and when you travel.

History, culture, food and adventure travel are fantastic wherever you go, but most of all it's the kindness, friendship and camaraderie of the people. You will find that people everywhere are accommodating, helpful, and accepting with open arms, and they go out of their way in every way to welcome visitors to their interesting and beautiful countries.

Wherever you travel, cell service is available almost everywhere, and there are few difficulties in exchanging money, finding available fuel or locating comfortable and clean lodging. Simply research the requirements and recommendations for entering any country, and away you go.

So hop on a plane, board a boat, rev up your motorcycle or launch your kayak, and you'll be on your way to an exciting adventure. Have fun, enjoy the world and create beautiful memories.

Think about some travel plans you can make within the not-too-distant future.

Joel Meier is Professor Emeritus and former Associate Dean of the University of Montana's College of Forestry and Conservation. He also is Professor Emeritus and former Chair of the Department of Recreation, Parks and Tourism Studies at Indiana University.

ASPEN CATHEDRAL
Paul J. Kachoris

We must safely guard our Earth, or we are all lost!

Their spires reach for the sky.
White Grecian columns embrace us
as we enter:
their hallowed sanctuary.

All is still – a hush;
except for the soft rustling of their leaves:
a choir of fluttering butterfly wings
chanting for our entrance.

Ferns are our carpet
as we step onto their welcoming softness.
Our necks craning,
looking upwards
into their shimmering, canopied dome.
We are compelled instantly – in a sudden gasp
to catch our breath in awe.

Numinous sunlight
plays through their
filigreed fingers
allowing packets of filtered light
to fall down upon us,
touching us ever so lightly, and
blessing us to their presence.

We walk reverently, silently,
through this memorial garden
populated by so many
spiritual beings,
who for eons, standing tall,
have been holding silent vigil
on this highest mountain peak.

Reminding us
of the grandeur of "The Infinite"
and "Its" constant invitation
to join in and share,
through the eyes of our heart,
all Creation with "Itself."

"Aspen Cathedral" is my poem of homage to the cosmic connection between our Mother Earth and the Heavens above. The aspen trees high up in the Rocky Mountains are the conduits that translate the Life-enchanting energies from the vast Cosmos, nurturing and giving us Life eternally here on Earth. We are the entrusted guardians of our living organic planet. We must safely guard our Earth, or we are all lost! This poem provides inspiration about numerous ways you can take action. Consider, as a start, the following: Plant trees; Cultivate gardens; Use wind and solar power; Fight for worldwide climate change; Eliminate plastic; Revere Mother Nature; and Worship Life.

What can you commit to doing to help protect our natural world?

Paul J. Kachoris, M.D., is a child, adolescent, adult psychiatrist in active clinical practice for 60 years. He has received First Prize, Religious Category, Poets & Patrons 50th Annual, Chicagoland Poetry Contest, 2006, for "Aspen Cathedral" and has a book of poetry, *Unmasked: Poetry of Self Expression.*

THE GIFT OF THE PRESENT
Larry Beck

One of the most critical components of an intentional life is awareness of what's going on around us in the present moment.

We seem to be distracted. It has only been recently, in our human history, that we have not paid close attention to the world around us. In the past, this has been essential to our survival, knowing where to hunt and gather successfully. But now our attention is often diverted away from the world around us. This is most evident in our often total absorption with our smartphones.

A vast literature shows that too much screen time, especially as it relates to social media, can lead to depression and anxiety. Constant distraction can also compromise friendships. Thich Nhat Hanh wrote, "The most precious gift we can offer anyone is our attention." Similarly, Simone Weil wrote, "Attention is the rarest and purest form of generosity." Therefore, our full attention reveals our concern and respect for others and they will appreciate our generosity as better friends and acquaintances.

But there is even more to gain from intentional attentiveness that comes, in this instance away from others, from time spent in nature. When outdoors, our capacity to recognize natural beauty is linked to our attention to the present moment. We can be captivated by clouds in the sky, a colorful wildflower or the cacophony of ocean surf. This time outdoors boosts our immune systems and our moods. We find ourselves in awe of the majesty that surrounds us.

By practicing the gift of the present, then, we can achieve healthier lives, enhance social relationships and become more attuned to the beauty and wonder of the world we are a part of.

With all these benefits in mind, I encourage you to look at your smartphone less, especially when engaging with another person. The next time you are in conversation with someone, give them your full attention, then do it again and again. Furthermore, commit to spending more time in nature, at least once a week, and focus on one new thing to devote your full attention to for at least five minutes.

What, specifically, will you commit yourself to doing to provide more attention to the people and beauty surrounding you?

Larry Beck is an emeritus professor at San Diego State University.

THE INTERCONNECTION OF NATURE AND SELF-LOVE
Peter Moll

The greatest act of self-love is taking care of nature.

I happened to cross paths with a longtime friend who had known me before I started my nongovernmental organization on conservation and leadership, and he said, "You really love elephants and trees, dude. That's so inspiring"

I said, "Hmm, it's really more about loving yourself more than it is about loving elephants. I mean, do not get me wrong, there is nothing more exhilarating than being out in nature, by a campfire with friends and colleagues with the stars glistening, and hearing the lion's roar and the elephants grumble, and your heart is full." He just stared at me and said, while chuckling, "Dude, you see? You really love it!"

I added, "And, of course, elephants are the gardeners of our savannah as they eat 300 kilograms a day and excrete 100 kilograms rich in fertilizer and seeds." We both smiled, and of course I could see his point of view. But I needed him to understand what it meant that it is more about loving oneself. "I hear you, but let me break it down for you. You have dreams right?" He replied, "Yes."

I said, "Those dreams matter to you a lot, yes?" He said, "Yes, they do. It's my purpose and ambitions." I replied, "And to achieve that dream or those dreams, you need time, yes?" He said, "Of course."

I stated, "So if your dreams need time, it means your dreams need tomorrow, and it needs tomorrow to have food security, clean water, clean air and a stable climate. Which then means our tomorrow needs a thriving nature, and hence your dreams need nature. So loving yourself is allowing yourself to live a life of your dreams, and taking care of nature is the ultimate act of self-love, as you are securing your future for your dreams for you."

He paused for a moment and replied, "Makes total sense. I never looked at it like that."

The greatest act of self-love in our generation is to take care of nature in small or big ways. Directly or indirectly play your role, for your dreams, for you.

Identify some specific ways that you can take care of the natural world around you.

Peter Fredrick Mol is a 32-year-old Kenyan who is passionate about positioning the African youth in a structured and meaningful way to play their role. He is the founder of Stand Up Shout Out, now based in over 20 countries and 60 cities, as well as CEO of World Leaders of Today. He is the youngest on the board of directors of Kenya Wildlife Service (KWS) in the history of the service.

GET OUT, SEE THE WORLD AND PROTECT OUR PLANET

Jay Fisette

My bohemian year abroad was most formative and foundational.

At 25, I cycled from England to Greece, then settled in Paris while continuing to explore Europe. I had anxiety of not being productive, as college buds were getting corporate jobs and starting families. In retrospect, it was the most formative and foundational year of my life. I read, kept diaries on travels and life's challenges and opened my mind to the world. Total cost: $8,000.

I learned I was lucky to be born in the United States, yet we are not perfect. Fascinating cultures abound across the globe. History provides important context and lessons. Perspective coming with age also comes from travel and worldly curiosity. Diversity, including biodiversity, is a treasure.

My travels cemented my awareness and respect for nature. I've always admired the stories of Native Americans who lived off the land and used only what they needed. As they wisely warn, "We do not inherit the Earth from our ancestors; we borrow it from our children."

The man-made alteration of our one planet's ecosystem is on track to upend civilization as we know it. Earth is resilient, yet the unlocking of fossil fuels and creation of plastics, chemicals and nuclear power since the Industrial Revolution have put our planet's future in jeopardy.

Climate change is the existential threat of our times. The concentration of carbon dioxide in Earth's atmosphere recently hit a level not seen for over 3 million years. Then, the globe was 3.6–5.4 degrees Fahrenheit warmer, sea levels were 30–60 feet higher and *Homo sapiens* didn't exist. To those who dismiss that a couple of degree change in the earth's temperature can be problematic, harken Thomas Friedman's words, "If your body temperature goes from 98.6 to 100.6, you don't feel so good. And if it goes from 100.6 to 102.6, you go to the hospital. So does Mother Nature."

I have tried to infuse sustainability into all parts of my life. Reduce, reuse, recycle. This efficiency helps shrink my personal carbon footprint. I bike, walk and use transit, and I keep using the same dozen plastic sandwich bags!

So, see the world and protect the planet. Those with more have a greater responsibility. It starts by modeling behavior at home by incorporating sustainable practices and products into your life.

What commitments can you make to live your responsibilities as a world citizen?

Jay Fisette was born in New York City, landed in Arlington, Virginia and became Virginia's first openly gay elected official – serving 20 years on the Arlington County Board. Jay and husband, Bob, have been together for 41 years.

GROUND YOURSELF WITH NATURE
Cindy Andrews

Find purpose in lifelong learning about the world around you.

Want to love your life no matter what you do for a living? Get outside! There is calmness and simultaneous excitement being under the trees, next to a river or hiking through a meadow. There is *purpose*. Learn to be quiet outside and you might find you can think more clearly, cope with your "regular" life more easily and feel passionate about something new. Start exploring with sunrises and sunsets, listen to and watch birds, find diverse insects, learn about amazing fungi. Learn how bivalves, like oysters and mussels, clean gallons of water every day. Spot the delicate spring ephemerals that grow nearby. Stumble on a pond of tiny baby tree frogs or a migrating warbler rarely seen.

Nature will ground you. Nature will amaze you. You will find a place in the wider world and an appreciation for what happens around us every day, sometimes loudly and vibrantly and other times silently and unseen. You will find yourself becoming a nature warrior as you learn what we humans are doing to our planet. And our planet needs more warriors. Find a nature club or become a master naturalist to connect with people who feel similarly about the environment.

FIGURE 7.10
Who can't look at the stained glass-like wings of a dragonfly and not be amazed by nature? This Selys' Sundragon (Helocordulia selysii) rests from a day devoted to feeding and mating.

We were once toddlers playing in the dirt, fascinated by the things we found outside. Time to reconnect with your inner toddler and stay entranced and at peace with the natural world around you.

One thing you can do is to take a walk in a local park; however, do not make distance the goal. Practice seeing the flora and fauna around you. Download some of the free nature ID apps such as Seek or iNaturalist. Using your cell phone with these apps, name the things you find. Start a life list of sightings of those things. Reflect on what you learned that day and how it relates to your place in the world. Was it interesting learning about something new? Did you feel the peace that comes with a walk in the woods?

Commit to connecting with nature, as described here, within the next week. Reflect on that experience, and determine what you want to modify for another connection.

Cindy Haddon Andrews is a certified master naturalist. She believes passionately in native plants and conservation efforts to protect our planet.

GET OUT(SIDE)
John H. Blacksten

The natural world holds so many benefits for each of us if we take advantage of them.

Something my parents did that was incredibly beneficial for me – and that I have impressed on my own kids – is to get outside early and often. Expose them to nature, explore with them different environments and let them witness the "circle of life" firsthand.

Go to parks, the shore, camping, hiking, biking, canoeing. Or explore the outdoors in a local green space or your own backyard. John Muir, a renowned naturalist and advocate for national parks, said, "In every walk with nature, one receives far more than [they] seek." Being immersed in the natural world broadens one's perspective, fosters a sense of wonder and inspires curiosity. Hopefully, each of us learns to appreciate the interconnectedness of all living things and the delicate balance of ecosystems.

It's amazing to see how being in nature can have a profoundly positive impact on our kids' – as well as our own – physical and mental health. Studies have shown that exposure to natural environments can reduce stress levels, improve mood and enhance cognitive function. Getting kids outside encourages physical activity – away from phones and other devices.

But beyond all the practical benefits, the most important thing that nature can give each of us is a sense of purpose and identity. As Muir noted, "Everybody needs beauty as well as bread, places to play in and pray in, where nature may heal and give strength to body and soul." Experiencing the beauty, wonder and vastness of the natural world leads many young people to become more environmentally conscious and motivated to make a positive impact on the world. Remember, there is no Planet B.

So get outside as often as possible. It will pay dividends. As Gifford Pinchot, the first chief of the U.S. Forest Service, said, "The earth gives us everything we need. We only have to learn to use it." By learning and teaching others to appreciate and care for the natural world, we're passing on a gift that will last a lifetime.

After an outdoor adventure, draw, paint a picture or write a poem about what you saw, heard and felt. If others shared that adventure, discuss each person's creation – with similarities and differences.

John H. Blacksten lives in McLean, Virginia, with his wife, Deborah, and adult children. A public relations and communications professional, he has traveled to 50 states, enjoying the unique natural beauty in each.

ROOTED IN NATURE
C. Oliver Tacto

Engagement with nature is vital to our nourishment and our future.

Reflecting on my life, one constant has always brought me peace, understanding and purpose: my relationship with nature. From my childhood to my work, nature has been my steady companion. Its beauty, stillness and cycles of change have taught me invaluable lessons about myself, my purpose and the world.

Growing up, I was always captivated by the beauty of sunsets over the Pacific Ocean. There was something magical when the sky seemed to be painted in hues of pink and orange – a reminder that beauty exists even in the quiet moments. As a young person, especially in times when I struggled to understand my identity as a gay Filipino American male, nature was my escape and sanctuary. On those sunsets, I found a deep sense of comfort, an understanding that no matter how lost or uncertain I felt, there was something greater than myself that was constant and always found its way back.

These quiet reflections became even more significant as I navigated my life's path. I came to understand that nature wasn't just something to admire from a distance; it should be embedded in our everyday lives, workspace and learning environment. The presence of nature can soothe the mind and heal the soul. It reminds us of our connection to something far more significant than ourselves, something eternal.

FIGURE 7.11
This row of palm trees pressed against the sunset sky shows the perfect silhouettes of palm trees – representing my home and hometown.

So, whenever you find yourself at a crossroads or in a moment of doubt, step outside. Close your eyes, breathe deeply and let nature speak to you. Whether it's the soft rustling of the leaves, the warmth of the sun on your skin or the quiet stillness of a calm evening, nature has a way of putting things into perspective. It has a way of reminding us of who we are and what we are capable of.

Lead with purpose, embrace nature and inspire positive change for people, places and planet.

C. Oliver Tacto, DSW, is the Dean of Student Wellness at Maryville University, leading initiatives on holistic well-being, purpose and community engagement.

Service

Giving Back

Unselfishness. Volunteering. Donations. Mentoring. Sharing. These, and more, are what the thematic area of Service is all about. Service is a way of giving to others. Service involves sharing the gifts held by an individual, whether those gifts are knowledge, skills, expertise, time, companionship or comfort. Service also includes gifts that are financial or materialistic in nature. Service gifts also include things like personal support, such as is found with endorsements and networking.

Service is giving back; it can also be seen as paying forward. Service is a matter of sharing some of ourselves with others. So much attention is generally given to individuals and their own personal and professional development. In fact, the thrust of *The Intentional Life* is anchored in ways that individuals, both alone and with others, can have a life that is more fulfilling, rewarding and successful in the eyes of the individual. That is, individuals have hopes, dreams, desires and ambitions; by incorporating many of the insights found throughout this book, the belief is that individuals will be more likely to achieve their own goals. Service, however, appears to have a different thrust, as it is focused outward to the benefit of others. While that is indeed the focus of service, the result is that, in fact, the person providing the service is also the beneficiary of these efforts. That is, engagement in service is helpful for the growth and development of individuals.

UNDERSTANDING SERVICE ACTIVITIES AND EFFORTS

The theme of service is about providing something helpful for and to others. The focus is on "the other," whether that be an individual or a group and whether that be a setting or a cause. Service may be provided through volunteer or paid work in an organized way, and it may encompass an attitude of helping others and giving. It may be orchestrated with a requirement, such as is found with an academic setting; it may also be incorporated as a standard for a club or organization, perhaps found with a charity event or cause, or even a fundraiser on a regular or one-time basis.

    DOI: 10.4324/9781003541080-8

Consider a wide variety of examples of how service is embedded throughout the culture. Service includes volunteering time and energy, and it involves the pro bono activities with which one becomes involved. Service is embedded in institutions of higher education, with "service" being one of the three standard expectations of college and university faculty members; this may involve providing workshops or lectures to community groups or workplace settings, and also includes participation as a member of a local or national governing board. Service is found with mentoring of or leading others, such as is found with many youth organizations. Service may be seen with tutoring or training, and with personal, mental and spiritual development. Service can be seen with spending time with hospice organizations or volunteer time for errands and home chores. involvement with the faith community or service organizations and time providing guidance to others.

Whether a requirement or expectation exists for engagement with service activities, the focus is universally on helping improve the life experience of others. While this is clear from the perspective of an individual who benefits (e.g., mentoring, coaching, training), this can also be seen with group benefits (e.g., a worksite or housing setting that had physical improvements or even a training provided) as well as with general improvements (e.g., cleanup of a trail, roadway or waterway, artwork on public walls or buildings, development of a memorial garden).

Service can also be found with fundraising or related activities. Some of these are long term and ongoing, such as found with established nonprofit organizations. These may be incorporated within the ongoing activities of a group, such as an annual fundraiser for a specific cause or an effort to gather resources (such as food for a food bank, clothing, household items, glasses or hearing aids). They can also be found when a tragedy occurs, whether that be a personal individual or family event (such as family losing the chief breadwinner or a medical emergency facing an individual); it can also be found with weather-related situations, such as a tornado, hurricane or flood, resulting in devastation of buildings and settings.

Overall, opportunities for service abound in communities and other settings, at the local, national and international levels. It is when people actually become engaged and take action so that their surroundings, locally or even the larger world, are made better. Furthermore, a service orientation is found throughout the culture, found at the individual, group, organizational and systemic levels. Whether codified through policies and priorities or through tradition and history, service plays a large role with the lives of so many, whether the recipient or the donor.

SERVICE BENEFITS FOR THE INDIVIDUAL

As noted, service activities are also helpful to the individual providing that effort. Much of the theoretical underpinning for inclusion of Service as one of the seven thematic areas of this book is based on the fact that much is gained by those who give. For example, the helper therapy principle, initially provided by Frank Riessman over 60 years ago, served as the foundation for many altruistic and empathy-oriented approaches. Riessman's focus was on the individual who is helping also receiving benefits. These benefits may emerge from self-reflection and personal growth. They could also be embedded within Abraham Maslow's highest level of self-actualization in his hierarchy of needs. The involvement with service activities can help with overall individual self-esteem as well as overall well-being.

How can individual benefits be further enhanced? One of the best ways of enhancing one's own benefit is by engaging in reflection. With this, individuals review what was done, what was learned and what feelings were generated. Reflection also, importantly, incorporates how to best apply those learnings to one's daily lives. This is typically done with a commitment to reflection, so it is more than casual thinking about the service activities. One way is that an individual writes down thoughts and feelings on a regular basis (perhaps on completion of a specific project). Another approach is with discussion, where individuals share their different experiences and perspectives to see varied viewpoints and interpretations; this helps with strengthening the views of individuals and the larger context within which the experiences exist. Again, an important component of the reflection effort is the application of the insights toward future service activities as well as with life in general.

Service activities can also be viewed as "service learning." That occurs when the connections between the service activity or event are linked with one's life and larger learning outcomes. For example, service activities are often embedded as a classroom assignment in a school or college setting. The benefits for the individual are enhanced when learning objectives are developed around which the service activities are based. Then, during and following the service activity itself, attention to the objectives and the applications of the service activities can be reviewed and discussed. When coupled with reflection, students can see the linkage to identified – and typically desired – learning objectives and use that knowledge with the development of their own life applications.

Also embedded with service efforts is the theme of "servant leadership." This extends the role of an organization's leader beyond the traditional activities of personnel, financial and structural management. The focus of the leader is outward and on the development, satisfaction and engagement of employees and those served by the organization. The emphasis is on providing an environment, through formal and informal structures, where individuals and groups are valued and encouraged. Although a somewhat different twist on the general role of service, the relevance of servant leadership is that it focuses even more clearly on "the other" rather than on the self.

LINKAGE WITH OTHER THEMATIC AREAS

How does the theme of service link with the other six thematic areas? First, Optimism is embedded in service: a person engaged in service activities will believe and generally experience that those activities will make a difference in others' lives. Particularly if the motivation to engage in service is internally based, the perceived value for the recipient is viewed in a positive manner. With Values, service plays an important role because an individual has placed importance on getting involved with providing service. Whether through the donation of time or skill, or the participation in unselfish giving of one's self, the importance of this effort is present.

Self-care is found embedded with service, as one's skills and one's belief in oneself are likely enhanced. Through participation in volunteer activities, one may become more skilled at, for example, building homes such as is found with Habitat for Humanity efforts. Or an individual's own self-esteem and feelings of self-worth may be improved. The reflection activities associated with service can further enhance one's own attitudes and one's own mental health with the belief they are doing something worthwhile that requires their own involvement.

The thematic areas of Relationships and Community are also embedded with service activities. When an individual is working with others, and with reflection and discussion during and following the service activities, greater and stronger and deeper relationships are built. With group efforts and teamwork, the community feeling is further enhanced.

Finally, Nature is often found with service activities, as so many service activities involve working with nature and being in natural settings, as well as doing things to help preserve and protect the natural world. With efforts of cleanup as well as site enhancement (e.g., signage and structures), the beauty of one's surroundings for oneself and for many others is paramount.

CONCLUSION

This chapter on service has a focus on other people. While the audience for these 40 Legacy Letters is the young adult, the emphasis is on the importance of giving back to others. The contents of this chapter emphasize not only how and why such activity is important but also ways in which the person providing the service will benefit, often in innumerable ways. The ways that service involvement and service learning provide nourishment to others is clear. At the same time, attention to what can be learned from travel, from volunteering, from mentoring and from incorporating personal values by engaging with others is highlighted. The inspiration and reflections shared by the authors and ways the reader is encouraged to think about and apply some of these insights provide for a rich and meaningful engagement with life.

Messages What are key points or themes highlighted in the Legacy Letters within the Service area?	
Reflections What are your thoughts and feelings about what is shared and recommended regarding Service?	
Resources What individuals, groups, organizations or other information would help you better understand and apply recommendations in the Service area?	
Commitments What are you willing to commit yourself to doing regarding the Service theme, both in the near term and in the more distant future?	

FIGURE 8.1
Legacy Worksheet for Service

LIFE MEANING: THE GIFT THAT KEEPS ON GIVING
Martin Ford

You can change people's lives by actively seeking to cultivate meaningful and inspirational experiences in others.

When opportunities arise to help or support others, the focus is typically on practical, short-term concerns: What do people need from you right now or in the near future? And yet, what if some of your efforts to assist others could have a more *enduring* impact on their well-being, like a gift that maintains its value to the recipient for years to come?

This kind of impact is hard to engineer, but when it happens, the results can be profoundly gratifying for both the helper and the recipient. That is because deeply meaningful experiences heal and inspire people. **Life meaning** is a distinctive feeling that arises when a person believes that their life makes sense, has purpose and is worthwhile. Humans evolved the capacity to experience deep feelings of life meaning because such feelings help motivate us to care for others and to remain resilient when we experience adversity or profound suffering.

The potency of life meaning as a renewable source of positive energy raises the question, how can such feelings be fostered and sustained? Life meaning scholars emphasize the following themes:

1. Persistently reinforce an **action orientation** that focuses attention on progressing toward a positive goal (rather than ruminating about current circumstances).
2. Encourage people to choose actions that feel personally **authentic and worthy,** even if that is not the easiest path forward.
3. Help others see their decisions and actions in terms of broader principles, whether they be of a **philosophical, ethical or spiritual** nature.
4. Try to create **uplifting experiences** that can change a person's point of view and inspire hope for a better future. In doing so, steer people away from transitory sources of life meaning such as fame, fortune and material possessions.

Life meaning is a fundamental source of motivational strength and vitality. Identify several events in your life that have been deeply meaningful in a memorable and impactful way.

Martin Ford is the co-creator (with Peyton Smith) of the thriving with social purpose theory of life meaning, as detailed in *Motivating Self and Others: Thriving With Social Purpose, Life Meaning, and the Pursuit of Core Personal Goals* (Cambridge University Press, 2020).

YOU CAN DO IT!
Antonia C. Novello, MD (with Jill S. Tietjen)

When preparation meets opportunity, the result is success.

It is possible to start with a normal background and through education and hard work achieve your dreams and still be close and loving with your friends and family. I'm from a midsize town in Puerto Rico. Our family – my mother, stepfather and brother – wasn't rich, but we weren't poor either. My mother was a teacher and school principal. I had a good education but not at a mainland university. Education was crucial. You don't have to be golden to be number one; you just have to have the desire to be beyond what you are today. And it is okay if it takes you longer to graduate from college than other students.

Decide what legacy you want to leave. I kept getting additional education. Thus, I was prepared, and preparation successfully met opportunity which equaled success. Do the job that nobody else wants to do and do it well. Underpromise and overdeliver. Pick your battles carefully. Surprise wins the war.

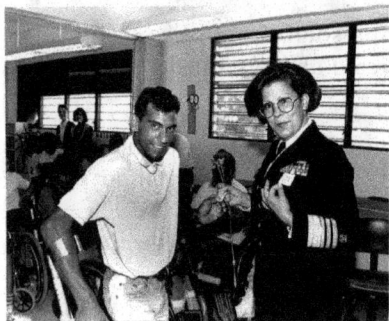

FIGURE 8.2
Dr. Antonia Novello speaks with a patient at the Society of Education and Rehabilitation of Puerto Rico.

I was born in Fajardo, Puerto Rico, with a disease (congenital megacolon) that caused me to be hospitalized for two weeks every summer until I was 18. My mother would not let me feel sorry for myself; she had high expectations. There isn't anybody including me who thought I would be surgeon general of the United States or health commissioner of the state of New York during September 11.

I made it in spite of the odds. It wasn't easy and I have the scars to prove it. Being first is never easy. I intended to be a good role model always doing the right thing. Nothing is impossible if you really want to get there. Keep going. Trust your gut. Don't let anybody hold you back. If I could do it, so can you.

Has there been an obstacle in your life that has been what you would call a "life-defining" event? How did you handle it?

Nephrologist Dr. Antonia C. Novello, the 14th U.S. surgeon general, was the first female and first Hispanic U.S. surgeon general. Her memoir, written with Jill S. Tietjen, is *Duty Calls: Lessons Learned From an Unexpected Life of Service.*

CHOOSE TO VOLUNTEER
Diana Karczmarczyk

It's now your choice to volunteer in your community, and it will be one of the greatest decisions you will make.

Students are often required to volunteer. The more hours, the better. Volunteer for anything, as long as you meet the requirement. I want you to know that volunteering is now your choice, a choice I highly recommend.

I have volunteered in many ways and in many places. I have volunteered locally, in my state, and at the national level. I have volunteered remotely and in person. I have volunteered for one-time events and for commitments that have spanned over years. I have volunteered in spaces that align with my profession or because the opportunity just brought me joy. I always choose with my heart how I want to spend my time and be a part of my community in a meaningful way.

I recommend that you also choose to volunteer because it may:

- Teach you skills that no classroom can teach you
- Give you the opportunity to meet people you may otherwise never meet
- Provide you with a space to share your gifts and talents in a meaningful way
- Feel really good to give back to your community
- Make a difference in the lives of others

Most important, I recommend volunteering because it will help you feel like you belong. Belonging to your community, no matter how you define community, is an invaluable gift you can give yourself. It reminds you that you are needed, that you matter and that you alone can make an important impact.

One of my favorite quotes about volunteering comes from Albert Schweitzer. He said, "I don't know what your destiny will be, but one thing I do know: the only ones among you who will be really happy are those who have sought and found how to serve."

What kinds of volunteering might interest you? How might volunteering fit within your overall life goals? Where could you turn to learn about volunteering opportunities that might work for you?

Diana Karczmarczyk is a Master Certified Health Education Specialist and holds an MPH degree in public health with a focus on community health education and a PhD in education with a minor in public health and a specialization in international education.

THE POWER OF CIVIC AND COMMUNITY ENGAGEMENT
Jay Fisette

Building a healthy community is not a spectator sport.

No person is an island. My life is much richer for having been actively engaged in my community. I moved to Washington, D.C., to pursue a public sector job and landed next door in Arlington County, Virginia. After studying international affairs, I pivoted to the local arena, thinking I could be a bigger fish in a smaller pond and have more satisfaction. Although my work path was difficult at times, I allowed my interests and passions to guide me.

I ran the neighborhood yard sale, helped pass a human rights ordinance and served on the boards of senior housing, arts and health-care organizations. My volunteer work led directly to the first job I loved, running a human services nonprofit, exposing me to the broader community and further options.

The more I explored Arlington, the more comfortable and connected I felt. I realized its values aligned with mine and that being gay was not an obstacle for further engagement. In fact, it helped motivate me as my coming-out process taught me the importance of being honest and having a seat at the table.

Ultimately, I was elected to the county board and served for 20 years, including 5 years as chairman ("mayor"). I met everyone, walked the streets and planned for the future. I learned you can't make everyone happy, yet found most are respectful if you explain your thinking. When you like your job, you blossom and people see it.

The experience of exploring and serving my community has given me purpose beyond myself and grounded us in our home. Many friends relocate when they retire. We decided that Arlington will be our primary residence until we die. It is familiar and comfortable, yet vibrant. We have contributed to our community and helped shape it, as it has shaped us.

On a larger scale, sustaining a healthy democracy is also not a spectator sport. Democracy thrives when people engage. It withers when people become apathetic and step back. Many take it for granted, yet history shows how fragile it is.

You don't need to run for office as I did. Simply volunteering can suffice. Volunteers always agree they get more than they give. As Marian Wright Edelman said, "Service is the rent we pay for living." It all starts in your community. Do your part. It feels good.

How are you connected to your community? What volunteer activity would give you joy and satisfaction?

Jay Fisette was born in New York City, raised in Pittsburgh's suburbs, landed in Arlington, Virginia, and became Virginia's first openly gay elected official. Jay and husband, Bob, have been together for 41 years.

OVERCOMING THE ODDS
BY FINDING JOY IN SERVING OTHERS

Stacy Titleman

Genuine self-worth can come from helpful mentors and quality experiences of service.

Little did I know that having a nonconventional childhood and upbringing would be the best thing that ever happened to me. If only I had known back then what I know now, I could have avoided many pitfalls and the low self-worth I experienced, especially during my teenage and young adult years. Now, with social media, I know the pressures are even worse! Please do not measure yourself against anyone else's social media posts. A post is just that – a post. Nothing else or even not necessarily reality.

As children, especially girls, our self-worth heavily relies on our parents showing us love – most important, unconditional love. My childhood wasn't easy. My parents divorced when I was five; my father was absent; my mother had a revolving door of boyfriends and married several times. Furthermore, she struggled with drugs and drug dealing (thankfully, she is now living a happy, healthy life). We moved around frequently and lived in relative poverty. There was little stability, and I often felt like I didn't matter to either of my parents. For me, life felt like Darwinism at its core – survival of the fittest.

If I could go back in time and offer advice to my younger self, it would be to seek a place that gives you a sense of belonging. Don't try to find it in the wrong places or through misguided actions that provide only temporary or even artificial self-worth. Places and people who want to help are out there, I promise. For instance, getting involved in community service and volunteer work can bring much-needed joy, personal purpose and a sense of belonging. As a young adult, this type of guidance would have been exactly what I needed. Instead, I found myself searching in all the wrong places for attention, which only further damaged my self-worth.

Some great places to start are in school, local charities or religious organizations.

Whether it's a local nonprofit or community service through your school, by serving others, you will find your self-worth, belonging, purpose and an entire community of wonderful and caring people. It'll be the best decision you've ever made. It will change your life.

Identify specific meaningful ways you can serve others locally or beyond.

Stacy Titleman's greatest purpose in life is her family. She is a proud mother of two beautiful children and wife to an amazing husband. She is a successful business executive living in South Florida, who enjoys spending her free time decompressing outdoors and appreciating the little things in life.

CREATING A RIPPLE EFFECT
Tammy Lee

Creativity helps identify ways to promote an important cause with ripple effects.

After our son Dylan died and three of his organs were successfully donated and transplanted, we sought to learn how to make a difference in the community by spreading the word and telling Dylan's story. Giving life to others through organ donation is a personal decision, but without donors, hope is lost for more than 100,000 people waiting on a hero. The gift of life creates its own ripple effect lasting far into the future.

As a business owner, we had a brand-new truck coming and wanted to do something to honor Dylan and spread the message of the importance of being an organ donor. We partnered with the OurLegacy organization, Donate Life Florida, Advent Health and the county tax office to achieve our vision. We wrapped our sanitation truck with the message to say yes to the heart on your driver's license and save lives. We unveiled the truck at the hospital where Dylan gave life to three others, thus providing each one with hope for more time.

FIGURE 8.3

Tammy and Ken Lee unveiling the new truck wrap at the local DMV honoring their Donor Hero son Dylan for saving 3 lives.

We took the truck to the "GR8 to DON8" annual event that supports donor families. People took pictures of the truck, hanging off the back of the truck and posting images and messages on social media. This was not your normal advertising, but sometimes you have to think outside the box.

Dylan's legacy has brought us to a path we never thought we would be. A purple truck adorned with the town characters goes to Give Kids the World Village monthly so the kids can touch it, work the back or get up in the driver seat and honk that big horn. The smiles on their faces and the joy it brings is priceless.

Since Dylan's nickname was "Turtle", we have put a turtle on each truck to represent our donor hero, as well as the Donate Life logo to continue to spread awareness. We continue to honor Dylan's legacy with more memories and more ripples, not knowing where they might lead.

What acts of unselfishness and kindness can you commit to doing?

Tammy Lee is a donor mom whose motto is "Live life . . . Give hope." She and her husband, Ken, own and operate Celebration Sanitation in Florida, and provide broad community awareness locally and beyond.

THE VALUE OF MENTORSHIP IN YOUR JOURNEY
Philip Wilkerson III

Having a mentor can provide extremely valuable guidance and support.

You may feel like you have the world at your fingertips – full of energy, creativity and ambition. But let me tell you, no matter how much you know now, there is always more to learn. Life is a great teacher, but mentorship can accelerate your growth in ways that are invaluable.

Mentorship has been a transformative part of my own personal and professional development. Looking back, I know that the guidance I've received from mentors has shaped who I am today. And although your journey may feel uniquely yours, the truth is that others have walked paths similar to the one you're on. So the sooner you connect with someone who is a few steps ahead, the sooner you will grow and thrive.

It's not a sign of weakness to seek help or advice from someone more experienced. In fact, it's a sign of wisdom. And it's a sign of strength. Many of the things you aspire to do have already been done in some form or fashion. Find those who are living the life you want to lead – those who are doing the things you aim to do – and learn from them. Ask them how they did it, and what they can share about their journey.

At the same time, understand this: As a mentee, you bring something powerful to the table, too. Your unique life experiences, fresh perspective and energy can offer valuable insights even to someone who has years of experience. Mentorship is a two-way relationship. It's reciprocal, and it can change the lives of both parties.

As someone who mentors others, I've learned so much from my mentees. Their innovative ideas, new skills and fresh approaches have reinvigorate my own work and remind me why I am so committed to guiding others. Many mentors will tell you they feel a great sense of pride in seeing their mentees succeed and grow. There's no greater legacy than helping others rise.

So my advice is simple: Find a mentor and find one early. Whether that's a supervisor, a colleague in another department, someone from a professional association, a graduate from your college, trade school or high school, or even someone on a professional networking website, seek them out. Don't hesitate. And most important, learn from them.

What steps can you take in the very near future to find a mentor?

Philip Linwood Wilkerson III is an employer engagement consultant at George Mason University's Career Services. In 2024, he was nominated as the National Association of Colleges and Employers' "Mentor of the Year" and was named to "Forty under Forty" for the northern Virginia area.

JUST SAY YES!
Gerri Taylor

You can learn and grow so much as you take on new responsibilities.

My father said always do what you LOVE and know that "there is no such word as CAN'T in the dictionary"! He and my mother, through their example, always encouraged me to go further. When my mother decided to return to work after being a stay-at-home mom, my father encouraged her to go for the top job based on her work experience and her commitment to excellence. She was a bit uneasy, having been out of the workforce for some years, but applied, interviewed and became the administrative secretary to the town's mayor, working with top local, regional and federal leaders. With his encouragement, she reached for the top, loved her work and received many accolades. My dad also took tons of courses to increase his knowledge about building codes and became the beloved building inspector for the town after a long career building homes.

Every step of my career was characterized by that same attitude. When asked to take on additional responsibilities, I always said yes and loved the new challenges, grew and learned more about myself each step of the way. I was a clinical nurse practitioner, loved my patients and said I would NEVER go into management. However, when asked to become a director, then an assistant dean, then an associate dean – all with more and more responsibilities – I found I loved each new challenge and each one gave me new enthusiasm for my work and life. I found I could still see patients clinically but also loved working with staff, developing high-quality, well-functioning teams and ultimately managing a high-quality health, counseling and wellness center that provided outstanding care for thousands of students.

When asked to be the program planner for a large annual national meeting, the cochair of a national task force and the president of organizations, I was at first hesitant but said yes, stretched myself and again found immense satisfaction in each new venture. I learned so much, loved the experiences and met many wonderful people who have become solid long-term friends and colleagues.

So my advice to you is, when you think you just cannot take on any more responsibilities but a part of you is pulled to a new role, just say yes and you will grow in ways you never imagined!

Think of a situation where you were asked to take on new responsibilities. How did you feel? What held you back? What can you learn from your decision?

Gerri Taylor is a board-certified Adult Nurse Practitioner and the former Director and Associate Dean of Health, Counseling and Wellness at Bentley University.

IT'S CALLED THE SERVICE FOR A REASON
Matt Sanders

We can't control when we're called on, but
we can control how we respond.

Nearly every vacation I took during my military career was canceled or interrupted to help support the mission, but that's what I signed up for: to serve.

Not every military member is in a combat situation where they might have to give their life for their country, but every service member sacrifices their everyday lives by forgoing often underappreciated privileges like where they live, what they wear and how they spend their time on – AND OFF – the clock.

On one occasion, the week leading up to the Fourth of July weekend was busier than normal because members of my unit were deployed. It was 5:30 p.m. on a Friday evening, and I was finally headed home, excited for the holiday weekend with my family. Just as I pulled into the driveway, I was notified that my deployed airman's spouse was found walking down the street, completely naked, drinking from two handles of liquor. It was recommended that I perform a wellness check.

I had a choice to make: (a) Enjoy my three-day weekend and check in on Tuesday or (b) Cancel my plans and check on my subordinate's family member.

When I arrived, the house was in shambles, the dogs were running loose and the spouse was clearly in an extremely drunken stupor. I called for medical attention, and while he was at the hospital, my supervisor and I cleaned the house and took care of the dogs. As things turned out, my airman's husband was nearing organ failure and would not have survived the weekend if someone had not intervened.

Had I chosen option A, he would have died, and my airman would have been called back from downrange, and someone else – likely with a family and plans of their own – would have then been deployed immediately to fill her spot. It wasn't what I had wanted to do with my long weekend; however, in my mind, I was literally being called to serve.

It's not just the ultimate sacrifice but also the everyday sacrifices that can make a difference and – literally – save lives. We don't have to like it, but it's what we've volunteered to do. That's why it's called "the service."

> *How would you respond in this scenario? How about other scenarios that you have experienced – what has your response been and how might you respond today?*

Matt Sanders served four years active duty in the U.S. Air Force as public affairs officer, base spokesperson and two-time commendation medal award winner and was honorably discharged as a captain (0–3).

COMMON PURPOSE
Mark Weber

Incorporating a common purpose approach results in both greater productivity and greater satisfaction.

It is often difficult to see progress at work, in a career and with life overall as day-to-day frustrations compound and our collective desire for instant gratification gets in the way of the time and effort needed to achieve big, bold goals. Yet, we push forward through the fits, starts, reversals and daily drama.

Creating common purpose among colleagues and friends helps with reaching our goals. Specifically, this approach encourages open and honest discussions about the audience for engagement, the intended impact and actual results, thus helping provide a proper perspective on ever changing priorities, new requirements and surprises.

The success of this common purpose approach is built on the premise that everyone involved is doing the best they can with the information and skills they have. So if the desired results are not being achieved, try something different. Share the results. Own decisions. Ask questions. Take risks. Celebrate those who bring failure forward. Wasting time and resources by continuing to do things that don't produce the positive impact desired is not okay.

And most important when changing things up, it is critical to involve the people who want change in creating the change. With data, shared decision-making and ownership, the results can turn out so much better and last longer!

Aligning people around a common purpose in rapidly evolving and increasingly noisy environments takes time and effort. Sure, celebrate short-term gains, but do not get lost in short-term distractions. Think about the long-term investment of time, energy and resources needed to achieve big, bold goals. We all have a finite amount of time, energy and resources in this world. Are the big bold goals aligned with your personal passions? Does the effort give you more energy than it takes?

Getting stuff done is the easy part (there are time-tested strategies for almost every scenario). However, only you know if the day-to-day stuff you are doing is the stuff you are willing to do over time to achieve progress toward purpose.

Identify ways you can use a common purpose approach with various parts of your life – work, service, relationships, studies, group activities, community events and more.

Mark Weber enjoys riding slow trains to nowhere and just getting stuff done.

FINDING MEANING THROUGH SERVICE
Joan W. Quinlan

Engaging in serving others can reap wonderful rewards for so many.

Since my teenager years (volunteering at local hospitals and at church) and as an adult (serving on the boards of and serving nonprofit organizations and facilitating support and growth groups), I have received so much in return for what I gave. I've found meaning where I didn't think I would. And as a federal civil servant, my career brought me immense satisfaction in knowing our work helped prevent injuries and deaths.

As Mahatma Gandhi said, "The best way to find yourself is to lose yourself in the service of others. When we serve, we step beyond our own needs to help others and weave a fabric of binding support and trust." Volunteering can provide a profound sense of purpose and fulfillment, knowing your efforts contribute to greater good. Your acts can usually inspire others, creating a ripple effect that can lead to meaningful change – both for the community and/or yourself by fostering a culture of empathy and mutual respect.

Acts can:
- bring people together, creating bonds and a sense of belonging.
- provide a way for us to grow personally, professionally and emotionally.
- challenge us, teach new skills and see life through different perspectives.
- help us understand others' struggles, promoting empathy and compassion.
- improve mental health by providing a sense of purpose and fulfillment, which can lead to greater happiness and reduced stress.

One does not have to have a career in service as I did. There are so many ways to be of assistance. Perhaps help serving the hungry occasionally, volunteering at an organization with interests like yours, helping a sick neighbor or friend . . . even just smiling at those you see every day or holding the door open for someone. Helping to serve is like the proverbial pebble in the pond – you may not always see the ripple effects of your efforts. If you are not already volunteering, ask what might be holding you back.

What are your goals, aspirations, values and strengths? Do you have a special gift or talent to share?

Joan W. Quinlan, M.A., CTLC, is a highly experienced advocate for public health problem prevention and holistic living. She spent almost three decades at the U.S. Department of Transportation and the U.S. Department of Health and Human Services developing and managing alcohol and other drug prevention programs, which included policy, program and research efforts.

FOLLOW YOUR HEART!
Gary Kreps

Get involved with issues or concerns of greatest personal importance.

As a longtime educator, researcher and author, I've found that it has been vitally important for me to work on projects that focus on heartfelt issues that mean a lot personally. These issues speak to my interests and concerns for health promotion, social justice and cultural sensitivity in modern life. I've tried to achieve these goals by promoting the use of personal and engaging communication strategies to build meaningful and cooperative relationships.

For example, I've worked on projects evaluating the effectiveness of communication programs, practices, media and campaigns for sharing relevant health information with at-risk and vulnerable populations who often need information and support. This has led me to design and refine the uses of evidence-based communication strategies, messaging and delivery systems to provide relevant, timely, accurate and compelling information for guiding important health decisions for health-care consumers and providers. My efforts have resulted in the development of new (and hopefully improved) health communication policies and procedures, training programs, support systems, health advocacy initiatives and the integrated use of both in-person and mediated communication channels for sharing relevant health information. This work has been tremendously gratifying for me because it has helped to enhance informed health decision-making, access to care and empowerment of health-care consumers to improve public well-being.

I encourage you to think about some of the key public issues that are most important for you personally. Think about how you can develop projects concerning these heartfelt issues for you. A good place to start might be to identify current problems of concern to you that are making life difficult in modern life. For example, some problems that come to my mind include current issues related to the spread of dangerous misinformation, growing levels of political polarization, acts of cultural insensitivity, incivility and bias, mistrust in science and unprecedented levels of violence in society. Think about some of the issues that you are most concerned about that you can examine with your work to help make contributions to modern life, Follow your heart!

What issues or concerns are most important to you now? How might you get involved – in the near future – to work on addressing these important issues?

Gary Kreps is a Distinguished University Professor and Director of the Center for Health and Risk Communication at George Mason University. He previously served as Founding Chief of the Health Communication and Informatics Research Branch at the National Cancer Institute.

PASS THE BATON

Joel Meier

Leave a legacy; give back.

No matter what you do in life, save wisely and give back to society in some way. The impact of those choices will not only improve the lives of others, but it will enlarge and enrich your life as well.

Within my profession, I gave and am still giving back in many ways through engagement in public and professional service. This ranges from voluntary involvements at the grassroots neighborhood and community levels to national professional organizations. I'd like to think that my service involvements have helped to leave this world in a better place.

Likewise, through philanthropy, you can provide financial support that touches people's lives in a very good way, and it is something that can last long after you are gone. For instance, my wife and I are repaying several long-standing "debts" to programs and mentors that have touched us deeply in various ways. As such, we now provide financial support to several conservation-related organizations and outdoor education programs that we appreciate and admire, as well as places where we went to school or where we worked. We provide program scholarships as well as financial support and endowments for faculty positions, knowing this "repayment" will result in advancements that rarely come along to institutions of higher learning. These endowment funds support salaries and research, professional travel, graduate assistance and other requirements of active scholars and teachers. Through our endowed gifts, these positions are funded in perpetuity, meaning they will continue well after we are gone.

When in a position to do so, give back to society in some meaningful way. Give back to people, places and programs you love. Embrace this opportunity and cherish the positive feedback you will get for doing so.

There are many ways to give back, such as volunteering your time, skills and energy to needy causes. This includes opportunities such as mentoring others who are starting in your field of employment, by serving on committees or holding offices in your professional organizations, by engaging in politics or making financial or philanthropic contributions where they count. When you are ready to give back to society, choose carefully for something that can utilize your skills, talents and financial resources so you can contribute to society in a significant way.

What programs or people have had a significant positive impact on you, and in what ways might you "repay" them for what they've done for you?

Joel Meier is Professor Emeritus and former Associate Dean of the University of Montana's College of Forestry and Conservation.

LIFE, SERVICE AND COMMUNITY
Norman F. Barnes Jr.

A life of gratitude and service brings rich rewards.

As I reflect on the valuable lessons that have defined my life, I am filled with a deep sense of gratitude for the path I have walked. Each experience has touched my heart, guiding me to a profound understanding of compassion and the importance of lifting those around us.

Reflecting on my days in a Boy Scout troop, I am overwhelmed by the warmth of lifelong community service. The treasured memories of forming lasting friendships while joyfully participating in holiday parades, engaging in neighborhood cleanups and extending our support to local food charities resonate deeply. Each act, infused with love and purpose, brought comfort to those in need. I hold dear the strength and unity we exhibited during challenging moments where we came together to provide support and hope.

The unwavering love of my family and the nurturing embrace of my church has profoundly shaped me. They instilled core values of service and community engagement that I cherish. Reflecting on the tumultuous 1960s – a time that tested our nation – I recall the emotional weight of the Vietnam War, the passionate cries for equality and the transformative Supreme Court decisions surrounding busing. These pivotal experiences were powerful reminders of our shared humanity, emphasized our urgent need for compassion and unity and provided essential lessons.

As an athlete who had the incredible honor of pursuing higher education, representing our nation as a U.S. Basketball team member in the Global South was a profound experience. It deeply enriched my spirit and enhanced my appreciation for the diversity and beauty of our world.

Years later, I felt a heartfelt calling to dedicate myself to public service. My journey began as a correctional rehabilitation counselor and recreation program supervisor, ultimately leading me to serve as a law enforcement officer. These times of significant transition for our nation allowed me to engage meaningfully with the challenges that arose, especially after the somber events of 9/11. My unwavering commitment to serve and uplift others has consistently guided me, helping me navigate struggles with empathy and resilience.

Today, I have embarked on a new chapter with an international consultancy dedicated to developing social infrastructure for the disadvantaged and underserved. My commitment to fostering hope and opportunity remains steadfast, drawing from the love and compassion that have shaped my life.

Where do you find nurturing and support in your life?

Norman F. Barnes Jr. is a global citizen and founder/CEO at N3 Global Solutions.

A LIFELONG EXPLORATION
Kaylee Fisher

Embracing the journey of discovery shapes a life of purpose and impact.

When you are growing up, your own little world is quite that – your world. It is filled with all the people, places and things you know and hopefully even cherish. The reality you find yourself in creates a worldview, for better or for worse. Every experience you have begins to mold how you engage with others, tie your shoes (wrap around or bunny ears) and predict what you are capable of accomplishing with your one lifetime.

There is a narrative that you begin to write about how your story should/ will go, with a minimal track record of proving yourself right. So what do you do with that?

Drop any sense of pride and explore.

Explore your strengths and weaknesses. Explore the world. Explore what inspires you.

Early in my youth, I started serving on international mission trips. From building houses in Mexico to serving special needs orphanages in Ukraine, I knew I just wanted to make a positive impact in this world. So I studied what I found most interesting – intercultural studies. I wasn't sure where my journey would take me, but I knew that wherever it was, I hoped that it would lead me to many corners of this world. So I started preparing.

Fast forward nearly a decade after that decision, I am now 27. I have traveled to 17 countries, engaged with 8 embassies and foreign ministries, raised $3+ million for nonprofits, and trained 100+ leaders globally.

All that to say, my little world has expanded quite a bit and has been an adventure that keeps on surprising me. It would be untruthful to leave out that my personal faith has been the cornerstone of my story. Therefore, I have no intention of claiming credit for my experiences thus far, but I do know that my exploration has only just begun.

Your worth is not determined by your accomplishments. Your impact is not limited to a job. Your path is not set in your predictions or goals. Perhaps there is so much more in store for you. Set out to be intentional with each day and the rest will take care of itself.

What measures to you use to determine your own worth?

Kaylee Fisher currently works as the Global Operations Director for the International Religious Freedom Roundtable on Capitol Hill, convening U.S. government, civil society and all faith groups, advocating for religious freedom for all. She has been an advocate in the nonprofit sector, championing the human rights of marginalized communities.

THE GREENFIELD EFFECT
Jim Kooler

*We have the power to shape the future for others
with our acts of encouragement.*

When my mom passed away, I had the responsibility of going through all her belongings and treasures. One box was filled with memorabilia from my childhood. My baby book, blanket, stuffed animal (his name was Tippy), pictures from birthday parties, school pictures and report cards.

The report cards tell a story of a very cooperative, rule-following, independent "fine boy" who was having problems reading and writing. It appears I was being socially promoted through elementary school because I was a pleasant happy child. Mrs. Greenfield, my third-grade teacher, noted my challenges: "Needs improvement in working out new words for himself" and "Needs improvement in writing legibly." Mrs. Greenfield invited me to come to class early and stay late to work on my reading and writing. I never knew I was remedial or had a problem; I thought I was special, getting some extra attention.

Mrs. Greenfield wrote on my report card that I improved my reading and that I needed to practice my cursive writing. Her last line was, "I have enjoyed working with Jimmy. You are raising a fine son."

I hope, in each of our lives, there was a Mrs. Greenfield who saw our potential, helped create a positive environment and charted a path for us to thrive. I did not recognize her contribution to my life until I was an adult and never had a chance to thank her.

Think about the Mrs. Greenfields in your life and consider reaching out to let them know what a difference they made.

I challenge you to become a Mrs. Greenfield, find the potential in others and help them grow. You may never get a thank-you, but you can become part of the Greenfield effect of quietly changing the world one person at a time!

Identify up to five people in your life today, and think of specific ways in which you can help them grow.

Jim Kooler, DrPH, has invested his career in promoting positive youth development and mentoring, helping engage young people to be champions for change in their communities, in their lives and the lives of others. He helped develop the Friday Night Live program, led the California Friday Night Live Partnership for 17 years, and led the California Mentor Initiative and the California Governor's Mentoring Partnership.

LEADING FROM THE BACK OF THE ROOM
Larry Lunsford

Some leaders are born, but many of the best leaders are made.

In my senior year in college, I ran for the president of my fraternity chapter and lost. I had been the vice president and assumed that I would win the presidency. I was deeply hurt and felt rejected by my brothers. Luckily and surprisingly, the individual who beat me took me aside in private afterward and told me that I was valuable to the chapter and to not drop out of involvement. Had he not had that conversation with me, I probably would have ceased involvement with the chapter because I was heavily involved on campus and could focus my efforts there instead of in the chapter.

I didn't need to be president or hold an office to be a leader in my chapter and on campus. I became editor of the chapter's alumni newsletter, cochair of the Homecoming Committee and chair of the Founder's Day celebration and assumed various other tasks. My efforts were recognized at the year-end spring formal when I was named Brother of the Year.

Leaders should recognize the talent of individuals who are diligent in attending meetings by appointing them to lead committees and undertake projects that contribute to success. Ask for volunteers. Everyone doesn't want to hold office or have a title. They want to be active and involved, but sometimes it takes encouragement. These individuals often become the best leaders.

As the philosopher Albert Schweitzer said, "Example is not the main thing in influencing others. It is the only thing."

In becoming a leader, consider the following:

1. Participate in activities in which you have an interest.
2. Volunteer when officers or leaders ask for volunteers.
3. Join committees or work on projects that interest you.
4. You do not have to be an officer or hold a title to be involved.

For each of these four points above, describe how each applies to you and what steps you can take to become a leader.

Larry Lunsford, Ph.D., spent 40 years in higher education and student personnel administration, including Vice President for Student Affairs, Emeritus, and Assistant Professor, College of Education. He assisted students in all aspects of their personal and professional development.

CONNECTION THROUGH SERVICE
Amara David

Human connection doesn't just have to be through our phones.

As an 18-year-old going through their first year of college, I know just how addictive social media and spending hours on a phone can be. It seems as if all my responsibilities and stresses of life dissipate when I get enthralled by the endless scroll of content a few inches from my face or messaging anyone at the touch of a finger.

However, instead of feeling relaxed or connected on my phone, I start feeling a deep sense of isolation. Human interaction is watered down to a cryptic text or a heart on Instagram, and I find myself yearning to be more social, even when I am supposedly "online."

To combat my isolation, I began to seek out opportunities to become more involved in my community. I started to meet new people and engage in meaningful service activities that offered me a space to decompress and ground myself.

I learned that the essence of service lies not in the size of the gesture but in the sincerity of its intention. From simply helping out teachers in school to volunteering for projects for those in the larger community, I realized that every moment spent serving others helps me in gaining a different perspective on my position in my community. I am not as powerless as I felt when I would scroll on my phone – I can, and do, spend my time creating positive change where it is needed most.

If I were to leave you with one piece of advice, it would be to immerse yourself in the community or communities you belong in and make them better than you found them. Inspire people to uplift one another so that you create a culture of kindness, generosity and respect. In doing so, you will notice that those negative feelings of isolation start to fade away. This is particularly true when you remember that there will always be a village for you to lean on. Not only will you connect with others, but you will likely discover a new part of yourself.

How can you put yourself out there so that you feel a sense of community offline?

Amara David (she/her/hers) is an 18-year-old from Guam, currently attending college in Hawai'i. She is interested in alleviating existing health-care disparities in the Pacific region and aspires to become a physician to serve the larger community.

PRINCIPLES THAT GUIDE YOU
Ronne Ostby

Careers and life can be guided by convictions of service and standards.

One of my mentors, whose life has exemplified service, often cites Benjamin Franklin, who is reported to have said "do well by doing good." A successful career *can* be one of benevolence. When I was 15, I read the following passage in my mom's *Reader's Digest*: "I shall pass through this world but once. Therefore, if there be any goodness I can do, or kindness I can show, let me do it now for I shall not pass this way again." At that time, I lived on a farm in North Dakota. I copied that quote onto a sticky note that stayed on the fridge for years. Although the paper faded, the words stayed with me.

I chose to attend a university where service to others was a focus of my education. I interned at an advertising agency and was immediately drawn more to the pro bono work than to the lucrative commercial accounts.

I moved to Washington, D.C., where the city and so many of its residents clearly lived to serve. I launched a successful and fulfilling career creating campaigns addressing topics ranging from suicide prevention to health inequities and from opioid overdose to COVID-19 vaccination.

While there, I helped care for the children of a Jewish family in exchange for rent-free living. They shared their tradition of mitzvahs and sitting shiva, and I adopted their conviction that one's life should serve the greater good.

A few years later, I began delivering groceries to a retired professor. I delivered his groceries for five years, with each visit incorporating a lecture in his tiny apartment. He taught me about religion, philosophy, history, and sociology. I learned about the gift of sharing knowledge and living with humility.

When I graduated with my master's, a professor encouraged me to write guiding principles for myself. This exercise – and the principles – have served me in powerful ways. Here are a few of mine: Underpromise and overdeliver; Volunteer for every opportunity; Ask questions; and Set the highest standard for myself and others.

Do you have principles that guide your actions today? Write them down and revisit them during times of challenge or success.

Ronne Ostby works as a consultant from Minot, North Dakota, after more than 25 years in Washington, D.C.

BE RESPONSIBLE FOR YOUR EXPERIENCE
Jacques Vauclain

There are many "right" paths.

Nobody can tell you what to do anymore. Only you are responsible for your own experience.

Through it all, here are some thoughts for you to consider:

Compete with yourself, not others. Although you will hopefully have many peers and mentors who help you set your bar high in life, do your best not to compete with them. One of my mentors taught me that the true measure of success is setting your personal bar high and working each day to be just a little bit better than the day before. If you can stack these days up over 5, 10, 20, 30 years, you will have developed into someone you will be proud of.

Cultivate relationships. You need to have people whom you trust to talk with when you are really down, facing adversity or having moments in life where you are afraid to talk it through but know you just should not keep it inside. Those relationships take time (usually in-person time), often involve shared experiences and require you to open your heart to develop the trust and vulnerability needed to share true friendship.

Remember that you have time. Please breathe and enjoy moments along the way. There are few decisions in life that cannot be "undone." I wish I had learned that earlier. If you surround yourself with people who care about you, believe in your abilities you have cultivated and have faith in those skills you have not yet developed, you will be okay over time. This was the toughest lesson for me to learn early in life. The word "yet" is often underused.

Be a citizen. As I was getting ready to change careers and start a family, another one of my mentors said to me, "Move somewhere you want to raise a family, become a citizen of the community and then find a job you love." In becoming a citizen, I have volunteered for several organizations, developed meaningful relationships I would not have had otherwise and hopefully made a positive impact on these organizations and people. It is true that you get more in return when you give of yourself to others.

> *How would you assess yourself on these four thoughts? How can you address the "yet" factor for each of these?*

Jacques Vauclain is a father of three who has been fortunate to visit 45 states, live in two countries and work in four complementary industries. He tells his kids to "work hard and have fun" and he strives to role model those words.

TRAVEL!
Hugh Gusterson

Travel broadens the mind; service deepens it.

I was a teenager in the United Kingdom in the 1970s. In those days, many students took a "gap year" between high school and college, and they didn't use it or their summer vacations to earn money because college tuition was free and the government gave a stipend to cover living expenses for poorer students (like me). I spent my gap year in Morocco in North Africa working (for $7 a week plus room and board) in a school for kids with polio. Some were in wheelchairs; most got around on crutches. Despite their disabilities, they went on hikes and played a kind of indoor soccer where you crawl at speed, dragging your paralyzed legs behind you. They taught me about joy, courage and determination. I don't know that I taught them anything except a few words of English (including a four-letter word I muttered under my breath, which they latched on to immediately!).

Summers back then were full of students traveling around, using astonishingly cheap rail passes that worked all across Europe. In 1978, a friend and I used a rail pass to travel through France, Italy, Yugoslavia, Hungary, Greece and Turkey (where we switched to buses). Along the way, we picked up a young French couple and a Japanese man with whom we traveled as a group. In Communist Hungary, a couple with whom we chatted at a restaurant took the five of us to stay at their home. In Turkey, a farmer, spotting us sleeping in his field, brought us breakfast. From this trip, I have memories and photos I treasure. But most of all, I have a now bone-deep appreciation for the kindness of strangers. And this early lesson in the beauty of different ways of life may explain why I became an anthropologist.

We're told that accumulating money is what matters. So untrue! What matters is respecting people in all their diversity and balancing the pursuit of your own well-being with service to others. This service could consist of any number of things: volunteering at an animal shelter (as my teenage daughter does), volunteering at a homeless shelter (as I did once a week when I was an undergraduate), going door to door for a peace group (as I did when I was a graduate student), joining neighbors for trash pickup days or taking your surplus food to a public food pantry instead of throwing it away (as my neighbor does). The time you "lose" will be more than repaid.

Where would you like to travel to and what kinds of people would you like to help? When you think of doing volunteer service, what kind of service calls your name?

Hugh Gusterson is Professor of Anthropology and Public Policy at the University of British Columbia. He grew up in the United Kingdom and lived in the United States after 1980.

RAISING THE VOICE OF THE CONSUMER
Nathan Monell

To improve service delivery, it is essential to make sure the voice of our constituency is heard.

As executive director of National PTA, my charge is to raise the voice of parents to improve the academic success and well-being of our nation's children. Most parents are motivated first to ensure their own child has the best opportunity to reach his/her potential. They soon recognize that none of our children live in a bubble. For my child to succeed, the child sitting next to him needs to succeed, and every level of decision-making from the local, to district, to state and national levels needs to be intentional and in sync for there to be success. The consumer voice is necessary at every level.

I first learned about the power of consumer voice when engaging the opinions and thoughts of individuals with serious and persistent mental illnesses who were moving from institutional care to live in the community with wraparound supports. It only made sense to ask them what worked for them to keep them healthy and productive without the guardrails of locked wards and closely managed medication supervision. The amazing part was how few of those individuals had ever been asked what works for them. Sometimes in our messianic zeal, we think we know best, but we do not. Beyond that, personal anecdotes humanize unfamiliar and confusing bureaucracy.

So raise the consumer's voice. Collect stories and share them widely. Sometimes all it takes is a heartfelt phrase. Here are two from my story bank.

> Misty Stenslie, my late colleague and friend who grew up in foster care and was never adopted, told this memory: "Ever since I learned the meaning of the word 'precious' in second grade, I always wanted to be that to somebody." She would also enclose a picture that she imagined resembled her as a child. She would offer, "If anyone had taken or kept any pictures of me from that age, this is what I think I would have looked like."

None of us can imagine our own children not being seen as precious or not having someone who cared enough to save their pictures. With those two phrases, Misty called us to be better, to do better. Her memory lives on.

What specific things can you do to make sure the voice of those you serve is heard?

Nathan Monell is a lifelong advocate dedicated to raising the voices of people living with serious and persistent mental illness, individuals and families impacted by HIV/AIDS, alumni of foster care, youth growing up in less affluent communities and parents of public school students.

A LIFE PURPOSE
Phil McCabe

Listening to others' voices and my own helped focus my life direction.

I experienced a life-changing event in October 1979: the first national march for gay rights in Washington, D.C. In D.C. that weekend, my mind expanded. There was the march, and there was also a rally and stage performances occurring all weekend. The speakers' messages were motivating and clear. Roughly 100,000 gay and lesbian people and their allies descended on the capital city from all across the United States to demand that their voices be heard. It was the first time I realized being gay was more than hanging in gay bars. Developing a positive gay identity became a priority.

It was during this time, the AIDS epidemic, that I found my life purpose. My professional career path became more evident. I found my voice, and I needed to use it. All around us, people were getting sick and dying who were much too young. Their lives were cut short by a disease that didn't have a cure and was often treated with fear and ignorance. I became an activist, community organizer, educator, trainer and grief counselor – some days, all rolled into one. As a community, we fought many battles and sometimes fought among ourselves out of frustration.

Today, I continue my life purpose. As an openly gay health education specialist for a university, I provide training on providing LGBTQ affirmative health care. LGBTQ individuals do not have to feel shame or deny aspects of themselves when seeking help. Providers need to know how to ask questions without doing more harm. Coming out is an act of courage, not a one-time event. It's about being visible, acknowledging your truth and finding your community. For many of us, **National Coming Out Day** (October 11) and **LGBTQ History Month** provide a moment to reflect on our journey and discovery into the depths of our sexual orientation or gender identity.

The sharing of intimate moments and lived experiences allows us all to enlighten others. Additionally, we are creating a willingness to be vulnerable and transparent. Coming out is a significant component of our lives. Our power is choosing to share with others who we are. We not only come out, but we also invite others to come in, see, hear, celebrate and learn from us.

What will comprise your life purpose? Write down key values, constructs, phrases or other words that will help guide you.

Philip T. McCabe, CSW, CAS, CDVC, DRCC, has over 40 years' experience as a community educator. He has been a health educator at Rutgers School of Public Health since 2000. As an openly queer professional, he proudly identifies as a social justice warrior.

HMM, THAT'S INTERESTING!
A.D.G.O.S AND GROWTH
Linda C. Hancock

Curiosity in the face of failure or regret is the key to reducing our anxiety and living a happier and more fulfilling life.

When have you learned the most in your life – the good times or the hard times? Most people will quickly say the hard times. All of us have them. We all mess up or do dumbass things. In reality, those times are just A.D.G.O.s, which stands for another darn growth opportunity.

The next time you or someone around you screws up, instead of rushing to harsh judgment, take a moment and get really curious. Practice saying, "Hmm, that's interesting. I wonder why I (or they) did that?" Whatever it was – making a hurtful post, getting blackout drunk, skipping an important class, losing a job, failing to use a condom – it served some purpose in the moment. By getting curious and being honest about what we or they really want, we are freed to live in a lighter way.

If we beat ourselves up over mistakes, it just leads to a spiral of anxiety or depression. A.D.G.O.s are in reality the secret to a great life. I've had a few big A.D.G.O.s in my life. Each one has been like a door that opened me up to change and gave me the power to use that mistake to help others. The only A.D.G.O. you can't learn from is suicide. Everything else is just an A.D.G.O. We don't just have them; we need them to be fully human and loving.

> *If there is something you did that is causing anxiety or depression, sit in silence for a few moments. Open to a space of kind curiosity. See what new insights arise. Then just do the next right thing.*

Linda C. Hancock, FNP, Ph.D., is a funny nurse practitioner with a doctorate in education. She has spent decades helping young adults deal with challenging health issues. Linda is a recovery ally and continues to serve others. See LindaGivesBack.com.

A SERVANT'S HEART

Tokeitha Wilson

Find ways to serve others with love and compassion.

A servant's heart is full of compassion, humility and love.
A servant may avoid recognition.
A servant may prefer to remain anonymous.
A servant's smile is priceless.

Every human heart has walls. Too often as humans, we build self-made walls that embody power, success and personal gain within our hearts. These self-made walls ensure we maintain a level of privacy, security or comfort. Serving others brings our hearts out of isolation. We depart from entitlement and arrive at a place of joy. By devoting our time to serving others, the landscape of our heart changes and the walls of selfishness start crumbling down.

In your lifetime, I hope that you will unlock the key to a servant's heart. Be intentional! Serve with love, compassion and humility. Don't look for recognition; someone will see you. Respect those whom you are serving. Every act of service doesn't need to be published on social media. I personally like to remain anonymous. Last and most important, always smile; a smile can brighten anyone's day. It's free to smile.

Love always,

Tokeitha

Identify at least three specific ways you can be of service to other individuals, groups, organizations and the larger community in meaningful ways.

Tokeitha Wilson is a public health executive who has influenced corporate and government infrastructure. She is a lover of sports and comedy, a mother to a musical genius and an aunt to three fur babies.

INSPIRATION THROUGH PERSPIRATION
Debbie DeLosa

Never underestimate the impact you can make.

You are capable of achieving much more than you think you can. This has certainly been my experience in volunteering with Habitat for Humanity. It started as a corporate-sponsored day of service. Even though I had no construction experience, it felt really good to work up a sweat while hammering some nails and being a part of providing a safe home for someone in need. I was hooked. The next year, my husband and I participated in the Care-A-Vanners program where volunteers with motor homes travel from around the country and meet to a build together; we call this "travel with a purpose."

One of our adventures brought us to Sullivan, Illinois. We were told that our team of 12 volunteers could fully "dry-in" the home in two weeks; this means all walls up, windows installed and the roof wrapped. My first reaction was that there was no way we could do that! But we were just there to help, so we said we should give it our best. After two weeks of hard work, perspiration, teamwork, learning how to use tools and having fun, we did it!

FIGURE 8.4
Debbie and her husband Joe are mid-way through the building of a home. Along with others, they are practicing their mantra: "Live Generously."

After a few years, we decided to go "all in" for an entire six-week build. Okay, that's crazy. Build an entire house with volunteers in six weeks? Yes, we did – with inspiration and perspiration! One of my favorite parts of the build is the opportunity to work side by side with the future homeowner, allowing me to better understand how this home will be life-changing for their family. As we say every morning, "Habitat's not a handout but a hand up!"

In reflecting on our Habitat journey, it's incredible to imagine that I would be able to help to give families a place they can call home. Beyond building, we have come to realize an unexpected impact on our family and friends. Although it was certainly not our initial intent, we have inspired others through our actions. Many have told us that they want to follow in our footsteps and make a difference.

I believe that everyone can become a role model and change the world!

What can you do to make a difference in the life of an individual or group?

After a rewarding career as a project manager leading diverse international teams for a large technology company, Debbie DeLosa retired and gets the most pleasure helping others achieve their dreams.

PREVENTION AND PUBLIC SERVICE
Rich Lucey Jr.

Build your legacy with purpose and intent.

For as long as I can remember, I dreamed of performing on Broadway, stemming from my days as a theater major in college.

But life's journey has many twists and turns. Instead of a stage on the Great White Way, my career has given me a different stage. This stage is one that allows me to speak on an issue I am passionate about – preventing drug use and misuse among college students. Interestingly enough, that is a topic I knew nothing about at the start of my career.

Once I had my college diploma in hand and a realization that pursuing a career in the theater probably wasn't going to provide a steady source of income, I took a job as secretary to the communications director of a government agency in my home state of New York. Through that job, I learned as much as I could about preventing alcohol and drug misuse, and after two short years, I was promoted to leading the agency's statewide prevention initiatives for colleges and universities.

I was excited at this new opportunity, but I also knew it was a tremendous responsibility, which filled me with apprehension and self-doubt. Trust me when I say that "imposter syndrome" is real, and I am not ashamed to say it has followed me throughout my career. However, over time, self-assurance in the subject matter, which was built on continual education and a refusal to be complacent, helped me overcome self-doubt (mostly, not completely).

Little did I know that my nine formative years in that role would lead me to opportunities in three federal government agencies over the next 25 years, resulting in my being recognized as a national leader in the prevention field. The passion I have for preventing alcohol and drug misuse didn't exist within me when I started my career. It was fueled and nurtured by the positive impacts achieved not only by my work but also by my colleagues around the nation.

As you embark on your professional journey, be purposeful about the steps you will take to advance your career. Be mindful that the courses of action you take are appropriate for you. The legacy you build will stand on its own merit because of the careful thought and intentionality you had along the way.

What steps are appropriate to consider now for you and your future career advancement?

Rich Lucey Jr. has over three decades of experience working to prevent alcohol and drug use and misuse among youth and young adults, especially college students. The views expressed in this piece are his alone and do not necessarily represent the views of the Drug Enforcement Administration, the United States Department of Justice or an officer or entity of the United States.

THE POWER OF GIVING BACK
Frank Ross

Share your gifts, create meaningful change and inspire others!

A commitment to volunteering and community service is something I carry from my own journey. I strive to pass it on to others, particularly young adults who are discovering their path and purpose in the world. Service is not just an act of kindness; it's a gift that shapes your character, expands your perspective and connects you to something greater.

We all have unique talents, passions and gifts. Whether it's time, skills, creativity or compassion, these gifts are meant to be shared. Volunteering allows you to do just that – it turns your abilities into meaningful action. It might be tutoring a younger student, organizing a food drive or lending a hand at a local shelter. Each act, no matter how small, strengthens your community. And in the process, you'll find that giving back often gives you something invaluable in return: a sense of fulfillment and belonging.

Reflection is key to understanding the impact of service. When we take time to think about why we help and what we've learned, we grow in empathy and purpose. After every experience, I ask myself questions like, "What did I learn? How did I contribute? What can I do next?" These reflections have shaped not just my career but also the person I strive to be.

Meaningful service also teaches us humility and gratitude. I've seen life from perspectives I might never have encountered otherwise. It's shown me the resilience of people facing challenges and the strength of a community coming together. These lessons are ones I hope my son will learn and carry forward, shaping his values and actions as he grows.

When we share our gifts, we build connections, create opportunities and leave a legacy of care and commitment. Together, we can make a difference, one act of service at a time.

I challenge you to discover a cause you're passionate about, use your talents to give back and take time to reflect on the difference you're making.

FIGURE 8.5

Dr. Ross and Butler University students volunteer at a local school-based urban farm. Photo Credit: Maria Diebolt.

Make a commitment to volunteer in the very near future. Then reflect on that experience and write your observations and feelings.

Frank E. Ross III, Ph.D., is a nationally recognized higher education leader dedicated to student well-being and success. He serves on the advisory board for the Clinton School of Public Service.

SHARING OUR GIFTS WITH OTHERS
M. Dolores Cimini

Use your gifts and talents to make the world better for others.

Each of us has unique gifts and talents, often hidden in plain sight, waiting to be shared. You might have the ability to solve problems creatively, bring joy with a sense of humor or uplift others through compassion and understanding. These gifts, when used in service to others, have the power to transform lives, build connections and create a ripple effect that can help change the world, one person at a time.

I learned this lesson early in life from my father. An immigrant from Italy without a formal education, he used his carpentry skills to transform ordinary blocks of wood into beautiful pieces of furniture and art that were enjoyed by many people who had the privilege to interact with him. But it wasn't his artistry alone that left a mark – it was the way he used it. Every piece he made, which was gifted to someone in need, whether it was a grieving neighbor or another immigrant entering the United States, made an impact on someone else. He didn't see his talent as something to keep to himself but as a means to comfort and uplift others. His example taught me that sharing our gifts, no matter how big or small, can bring purpose to our lives and hope to others.

Sometimes the hardest part of sharing our talents is recognizing them. We undervalue what we can offer, thinking it's insignificant or unworthy. But a kind word, a helping hand or a skill freely given can mean the world to someone else. The act of giving also benefits the giver, fostering fulfillment and a sense of connection.

Think of your talents as seeds. When planted in the soil of service, they grow into something far greater than you could achieve alone. By sharing your gifts, you encourage others to do the same, creating a legacy of generosity and kindness.

Identify one gift or talent you possess and find a way to share it with someone this week. Reflect on how the experience impacted you and the recipient.

M. Dolores Cimini, Ph.D., is a clinical psychologist and director of the Center for Behavioral Health Promotion and Applied Research at the University at Albany, State University of New York. Throughout her career, she has focused on supporting the health and well-being of college students and young adults through counseling, teaching, research and scholarship.

ASK WHAT, NOT WHY
Connie Kitchens

Reframing a situation by asking the proper questions
can be most helpful in providing a helpful path forward.

Many times, when things happen to us that seem negative, our natural inclination is to ask, "Why?" or "Why me?" Questions like these close the soul down. If you ask, "What?" or "What can I do?" it opens the heart up to inspiration and strengthening experiences.

When I was in my mid-20s, shortly after finishing my master's degree, I was at the college recreation center with a group of friends. I got called to the desk to receive a phone call (this was before cell phones, if you can even imagine that). I found out my sister-in-law, whom I was very close to, had died in an accident. She was pregnant with a third child and had a one-year-old and a three-and-a-half-year-old who now were without their mother. Nothing has ever hurt so deeply.

Of course, the questions of "why" kept going through my head. She was such an amazing person; why did she have to be taken, why, why, why? But as soon as I could breathe and think "what," "what could I do?" I knew almost instantly the answer. I was to move and live with my brother to help with his two kids until he could figure out his next steps. I took a leave of absence from my job and moved within a few weeks. I stayed with them for ten months.

Stepping into the caretaker role for the children definitely was hard at times, and some people questioned why I would do such a thing and give up the life I had. Family is important, and I didn't have any second thoughts about my decision.

Whenever the thoughts of "why" creep into your head and heart, turn it around and ask "what," "what can I do to make the situation different," "what can I do to . . ." This is an active statement that requires effort and positive thinking to create a positive energy.

> Think of a recent situation when you asked yourself "why," and reframe it with positive questions. What do you discover?

Connie Kitchens has a PhD in public health. Her 30-plus-year career has included program and grant management, assistant professor, and networker extraordinaire. She is passionate about being outdoors – gardening, hiking, paddleboarding, skiing – feeling the energy and rejuvenation from the beauty of the earth and sky.

MAKE YOURSELF USEFUL!

Suzanne Revell

*Volunteering your time and talents can result in amazing rewards –
for others and for yourself.*

Feeling bored or restless sometimes? My suggestion is to volunteer for a cause that captivates you. You will find that volunteer work opens doors that you would never even think of. It can lead to paid jobs, lifelong friends or even a career path.

At 23, having recently moved to New York City, I was experiencing a little bit of boredom in my first job there. I opened the Yellow Pages (there was no Google then) to find organizations that worked with children. I zeroed in on a well-established group that offered recreation services to people with disabilities (adults, as it turned out). After an interview and screening, I began, along with another volunteer, to lead groups of 15 or more people on Sunday afternoon trips to ball games, Broadway plays, movies, museums and more. We traveled by subway and had wacky adventures. Within weeks, the organization offered me a paid job.

A similar thing happened when I was handed a brochure on the street for a fledgling group that had a grant to help homeless people. I joined the group's "steering committee" and before long was working as an employee. When I left the organization to get a master's degree in social work, I served on the board of directors, eventually becoming chairperson. That group today is a large and respected service provider in the city.

By revealing your people skills, your reliability and your talents, you will make an impression on others and pave the pathway to a network of people who can make a difference in your life. Better yet, you will make a difference in other people's lives.

For me, volunteering led to a long and satisfying career in human services. I have worked and studied with people I consider the most interesting, salt-of-the-earth friends anyone could have. By exposing myself to the serendipity of brand-new people from all kinds of backgrounds, I piled on experiences that served me well.

I wish you, too, as much fun as I have had as a volunteer.

Identify some places and ways that would benefit from your talents and skills.

Suzanne Revell retired and maintains homes in New York and Montana. She still likes to serve on boards.

SERVICE TO OTHERS IS AN UNREALIZED DREAM
Ruth Esteban-Muir

Even difficult and uncertain situations can be overcome.

My life has not followed any traditional paths. Although I have had professional experiences contributing to small public changes and minor movements, I struggle to believe I could give valuable advice to anyone. Perhaps some may find a slice of my story helpful or at least interesting.

Early in my career, I was a young single parent, briefly homeless, who found myself in a professional job without a degree – just trying to make it in life. Fortunately, people were willing to open doors because they assumed my abilities reflected an academic degree.

It wasn't until much later, after working on many national-level efforts and building great relations, that I finally completed my master's degree – 24 years for my bachelor's degree and 16 more for my master's.

My biggest life lesson wasn't from education. After my parents' deaths, my son's near death experience, and my husband's battle with cancer, I realized the most important thing I could offer the world was to be present, to give my best to the people I love and who love me.

Facing retirement, I'm still trying to find my dream life. My parents struggled with being the typically tough Asian parents – and I was quite a disappointment because I was not a doctor, lawyer or engineer. Still, in the end, they would only ask if I was happy. They were happy being great-grandparents and believing I knew the president because I worked in Washington, D.C.

When you're on a plane, they tell you oxygen masks will deploy in an emergency and instruct passengers to put theirs on before helping others. Despite being a runner and cyclist, I was not in optimal health to donate an organ when my son was diagnosed with end-stage renal failure. It took a year to become a bridge donor, helping several people to receive kidneys. I learned I'm happiest when I help others, but I must first be mentally, physically and emotionally ready to do so. Maybe the ultimate dream life is being at my most optimal self for anything or anyone.

What parts of your life today help with you becoming the best you can be?

Ruth Esteban-Muir is a lifelong public servant who has created, led and contributed to local and national safety efforts and served on federal committees.

EFFECTIVE LEADERS SERVE
Rick Leichtweis

Highly functioning teams and organizations are led by servant leaders, increasing employee engagement, morale and productivity.

From the beginning of my career as a leader in the health-care industry, I did not fit in. I found the industry at the time being led using a top-down leadership style where C-suite executives made the decisions, set the agenda and directed managers to carry out the developed strategy. From the beginning, I struggled using this approach with my teams and quickly learned that going outside the established leadership protocol would have its consequences, and it did. I was miserable, and my staff felt unheard, ignored and devalued. Morale was concerning at best, and I was failing as a young leader. I then read Robert Greenleaf's essay, "The Servant as Leader," written in 1970. The essay changed my life and probably saved my career as a health-care leader.

A servant leader listens actively, supports growth and models desired skills and behaviors leading to an environment where everyone feels valued. In this journey, I found that not only was I elevating myself but also my team, creating a positive ripple effect inspiring a collective success. I was finally building a team, and the experience was intoxicating. For over 30 years, I have continued to learn how to serve my teams, lead by example and encourage staff to be transparent, brave and psychologically healthy.

In a challenging environment of behavioral health care, the use of servant leadership strategies allows leaders to share the stage in the celebration of successes as well as the disappointments. You are not alone in a servant leadership organization; instead, you are embraced by the strength and integrity of a highly functioning team. I tell my leaders often, "We are the orchestra in the pit, creating the foundation built on complex intricacies that allows our frontline team members to be the best they can be." When the team is successful, patient care improves, leading to better patient outcomes.

Servant leadership values and beliefs are not only effective with leaders, but they are also extremely powerful when applied to life. Consider the elements of servant leadership as you begin and continue your professional journey. "How can I help?" goes a very long way.

In what ways can you apply the elements of servant leadership, whether in a group where you are a member or with life in general?

Rick Leichtweis, Ph.D., has been a not-for-profit behavioral health-care leader, clinician and special educator for nearly four decades, providing mental health, substance use disorder treatment and special education services to children, adolescents and their families.

FROM ME TO WE
Robert Chapman

Completing good deeds is essential when promoting community.

An AA slogan says, "People do not care what you know until they know that you care." In an increasingly interconnected world, the essence of community and a commitment to service has never been more critical.

Communities, therefore, are essentially networks, connections of individuals. However, for a community to work efficiently, an infrastructure must exist to support it. This infrastructure comprises individuals and the services they provide to support and nurture one another.

Service to others is not just a duty but a privilege, a cornerstone of a fulfilling life. It transcends personal gain and taps into the more profound human need for connection and purpose. Acts of service, whether small or large, create a positive impact. Volunteering at a local shelter, mentoring young people or simply offering a listening ear can make a significant difference. Service cultivates empathy, compassion and a sense of responsibility toward others, but it also leads to personal growth and a deep sense of fulfillment.

A community that values service is one where members actively support one another, leading to a more resilient and cohesive society. Service-oriented communities tend to address challenges, innovate solutions and foster a culture of mutual respect and cooperation. Individuals in such communities experience greater fulfillment and purpose, knowing their contributions matter.

We were all placed on this earth to make a difference. However, the type of difference we make is up to us to determine. When we involve ourselves in the community, our actions today cannot help but shape the growth and resilience of our community tomorrow. An assignment:

> Commit to doing an anonymous good deed each day. Record this in a journal daily and review weekly, noting your thoughts following this weekly review. Note: Observed deeds remain good deeds but do not count as anonymous.

Seek opportunities to do a good deed. Repeat daily for a week using the guidelines noted above. Record in a journal how you feel when doing this. How does doing this affect how you look at your community?

Robert Chapman is a retired professor of behavioral health counseling from Drexel University. With 50 years of experience in behavioral health, he is particularly interested in preventing high-risk collegiate drinking.

REFLECTIONS ON LEADERSHIP
Sarah Van Orman

Lead to serve.

I sometimes reflect on why I end up in these situations. By that I mean, spending most of my professional life as a leader of people and organizations. Although I think it would be a lot simpler to step down or step back and get a job where my responsibilities lie with the task in front of me – rather than feeling responsible for the big picture and, more important, the people around me – I know that is not who I am.

My leadership journey in my early 20s as a camp director; it did not go well. I was very much in over my head and felt that I had failed most of the time. Despite that, after completing medical school and residency, I quickly was drawn back into leadership. I was prepared to be a good doctor, caring about my patients, providing good care and being a good colleague to those with whom I worked. Quickly, however, I couldn't help myself but to look around and imagine how we could redesign the system just a bit, offer a team member a bit more training or sometimes radically shift what we did to make it better for our patients and the team.

I was hooked. I have now spent almost 25 years as a physician leader, managing people and systems, rather than working with diseases. When I speak with newer professionals about leadership, I offer a few words of advice:

- *Consider how leadership fits into your goals and strengths.* Do it for intellectual and personal challenge and also for the ability to make a difference. Don't do it for power, money or because your peers are doing it.
- *Prepare to become a leader.* There are many different types of effective leaders, but all good leaders have taken time to know themselves and then actively develop their leadership skills. Good leadership requires great self-awareness.
- *Think about how you can lean into leadership.* Look for opportunities professionally and personally to try on a leadership role. Regardless of how successful you are, you will grow from the experience.
- *Leadership is most importantly about serving and empowering others.*

Actively reflect on how leadership fits into your personal and professional journey.

Sarah Van Orman, MD, MMM, FACHA, FACP, serves as Vice President and Chief Campus Health Officer, as well as Clinical Professor of Family Medicine and Division Head, College Health at the University of Southern California.

BECOME A MENTOR
Larry Robertson

Being a mentor has rich rewards – for all involved.

We all have those moments when we need personal or professional advice. I have been very fortunate to develop a team of mentors to do just that throughout my life. In fact, the value of finding the right team of role models is undeniable, and it is advice everyone will give you. However, I think that it is even more important to become a mentor yourself!

You may be wondering how can someone like you be a mentor? You are never too young or too inexperienced to help someone else grow. You can play a role in educating others. Challenge them to do what you have done. Look for opportunities to help younger people. Coach Little League. Support a Scout troop. Tutor. Volunteer.

In 1987, I became a peer adviser for first-year college students. I was so nervous and continually wondered what anyone could learn from me. One night, I was half-listening to the television when Minnie Pearl was awarded the Pioneer Award from the Academy of Country Music. I barely knew who this country music comedienne was, but her words stuck with me. She shared some advice that she had gotten: "Love 'em, and they will love you right back." These simple words changed my perspective, and I believe that this is exactly what good mentors need to remember.

Over the years, experience has proven:

- Respect them, and they will respect you back.
- Admit your mistakes, and they will admit theirs.
- Be a role model, and they will become one, too.
- Make a difference in their lives, and they will make a huge difference in yours.
- "Love 'em, and they will love you right back!"

It is an amazing gift to be a mentor. Start today!
Here are some action steps that can get you started:

1. Think about your mentors and what they have taught you.
2. What opportunities do you have to encourage others to do what you do?
3. Volunteer to work with younger people.
4. Challenge yourself to find ways to help others.

Think about each of the four action steps, and assess what would be appropriate for you at this point in your life.

Larry Robertson has spent decades working with college students at Longwood University and Virginia Tech.

GIVE BACK
Gerardo M. González

The value of giving to others can reap tremendous rewards for all.

It is said that it's better to give than to receive. In my life of service as an educator, I have found this adage to be true. Remember, "Do unto others . . ."

My family and I came to the United States as refugees from Cuba following the Castro revolution. My immigrant family was fortunate. America welcomed us with open arms. I was given the gift of a great education; I achieved something, and I can now give back to my adopted homeland and the world.

As an immigrant and a refugee, I experienced separation from extended family and friends, isolation, prejudice and many of the fears and anxieties common to those who are forced to leave their homeland. But with the support of my parents, friends, mentors and communities that embraced me, I was able to get an education, achieve a position of influence and leadership, meet the challenges of being different and give back to others. I'm proud of a letter I received from Ronald Reagan, the 40th president of the United States, commending me for the "fine contribution" I made to young people in my adopted homeland.

When I was given the opportunity to go back to my native Cuba as an ambassador for Indiana University where I served as Professor and Dean of Education for 15 years, I did not hesitate. I didn't go back with rancor for the painful memories or hatred in my heart. Instead, I wanted to make a positive difference – to help heal the wounds of the past and make things better for those who remained on the island as well as those who welcomed me with open arms across the Florida Straits. If my efforts help foster reconciliation and bring the people of both nations closer together through education, then, from my perspective, it's all worth it.

My family, including my children and their children, have benefited greatly from the freedom and opportunities America afforded us. Nothing would bring me greater joy than doing the same thing for others in need. If you achieve great things, you too will find that "it is better to give than to receive." Do your part. Ask yourself, what difference can I make? Give back in whatever way you can.

Think about people and events that have open doors for you. What can you do to give back?

Gerardo González, Ph.D., is Professor and Dean Emeritus of Education at Indiana University. Recognized as a leading founder of the peer education movement in America, in 2018, Indiana University Press published his memoir titled, *A Cuban Refugee's Journey to the American Dream: The Power of Education.*

MINDFUL SUCCESS:
BUILDING A LEGACY THROUGH SERVICE
Ariel Norris

*True fulfillment lies in creating a life centered on mindfulness,
connection and uplifting others.*

In business and in life, the most profound lessons often come from unexpected places. Growing up, I developed a heightened awareness of my surroundings, shaped by observing the dynamics and challenges in my environment. My early experiences included chaos and instability. However, these challenges taught me to prioritize meaningful relationships and to see success as an opportunity to serve rather than as a platform for self-interest. These lessons became the foundation for my personal and professional growth.

Building a successful business and life isn't just about strategy and hard work; it's about how you treat people. Every relationship matters, and the way you approach others – with kindness, respect and authenticity – determines how far you can go. Success is most fulfilling when it's shared. I have seen firsthand how focusing on genuine service and collaboration opens doors you never imagined.

Dale Carnegie once said, "Spend more time being interested than being interesting." This principle has guided my business and life journey, teaching me to listen, learn and approach every conversation with curiosity. Whether in team meetings, client interactions, networking opportunities or simply spending time with loved ones, showing genuine interest in others builds trust, unlocks opportunities and fosters mutual growth.

Over time, I've learned that success isn't about being the loudest voice in the room; it's about creating impact through thoughtful action and uplifting others as you rise. Just as those who believed in me supported my journey, I strive to pay it forward by creating opportunities for others to thrive.

In your next professional interaction, focus on listening 80% of the time and asking thoughtful questions to better understand the other person's goals.

Ariel Norris is the owner of Muse Street Marketing, a branding and marketing firm blending real-world connections with growth-driven strategies to create lasting, impactful success for businesses and communities alike.

LEADING IN SERVICE TO OTHERS
Ryan Travia

Servant leadership prioritizes well-being and growth as the key drivers to individual and, ultimately, organizational success.

Perhaps it stemmed from my upbringing as the eldest son of a schoolteacher and an investment manager who took great pride in providing for their family despite growing up poor. Or did living with my Italian grandmother (a career educator and longtime parochial school principal) during my youngest formative years nudge me in this direction? Was it my exposure to the Jesuits during my time at Boston College, their values grounded in service, "cura personalis" (care for the whole person) and a commitment to social justice and academic excellence? Responding to my vocational calling to be an educator and leading in service to others is as much a combination of all these variables as it was going through my own process of discernment.

Despite having earned three degrees in education (a bachelor's in elementary education/moderate special needs and human development, a master's in educational administration, and a doctorate in higher education management), I don't recall ever studying "servant leadership" as a concept. However, I strongly resonate with its focus on growing and developing people, with an emphasis on well-being. As Robert Greenleaf highlights in his book *What is Servant Leadership?*, this is accomplished by putting the needs of others first and helping them to perform to their highest potential.

Early in my career, I provided support to those affected by substance use/misuse and worked directly with peer educators, which remains both a hallmark and a highlight of my professional journey. My leadership was defined by (and very much remains) being student centered, striving to empower students with the knowledge and skills to make healthy, informed decisions and to develop as whole persons. As I advanced in my career, I began to mentor professionals who were now doing the direct service work, coaching and guiding them to effectively manage their teams in service to our students. Approaching your work with a genuine ethic of care for the members of your community will serve to advance the organization's overall well-being, producing more compassionate, dedicated individuals who share a commitment to the institution's success.

"The servant-leader is servant first. . . . It begins with the natural feeling that one wants to serve, to serve first." —Robert K. Greenleaf

In what ways does serving others make sense for your own life? In what ways can you put others' needs first – individually and with a group or organization?

Ryan Travia, Ed.D., is Associate Vice President for Student Success at Babson College, having previously held leadership roles at Harvard University and Dartmouth College. His career is dedicated to leading in service to others.

DO JUST ONE THING! VOLUNTEER FOR SOMETHING
Sherry Nelson

*Volunteering broadens your perspective, engages with
new people and makes a difference.*

Many of us hear about calls for volunteers in the community. Who can pass out flags along the parade route? Who could help walk dogs at the local animal shelter? Who will help pull weeds along Main Street? And we may think, "Somebody else will do it." Too often, we sit at home, oblivious to how stuff gets done in our own hometown. "Do just one thing" to leave your mark! You'll be surprised at the results.

Following my husband's death, I moved by myself to a rural, tourist community into what we had planned to be our dream retirement home. I didn't know anybody. Joining one group to promote conservation and Earth Week introduced me to a like-minded group; people in that group became friends. That was just the beginning.

Ten years ago, Cheboygan looked shabby with 27 vacant storefronts along Main Street – in contrast to the glorious lakes, rivers, trails and farmlands surrounding the town of about 5,000 citizens. Three friends who came over for coffee discussed the Main Street program, a nationwide initiative to revitalize rural downtowns. We lobbied our city council to join the program; we were denied. We had not yet developed the grassroots support the program required. The next time, we had 50 enthusiastic volunteers with us; the program was passed, although reluctantly.

Our first project was to install seasonal decor in every empty storefront window along Main Street. We had teams of volunteers washing windows, working with realtors for access to the properties that were for sale and collecting merchandise and decorations to project a festive atmosphere. The entire downtown looked vibrant. We made a difference.

Over the next two years, we grew to 350 volunteers, and leaders emerged and were elected to governance positions.

Cheboygan's Main Street looks dramatically different today than it did ten years ago. Investors have bought properties and have rebuilt and restored them. It all began when passionate volunteers who had vowed to make a difference.

What one thing can you do now to make a difference?

Sherry Nelson is a retired retail executive and newspaper business entrepreneur. She enjoys hiking the many trails nearby and volunteering.

THE JOY OF SERVING OTHERS
Donald Nichols

*In a complicated world, focusing on one person
can be extremely rewarding.*

Knocking on the door with little hope that there would be a response,
I continued knocking. Even though I had been here many times, I still had
hope that Mike would answer the knock. Like too many Vietnam veterans,
Mike suffered recurring bouts of post-traumatic stress disorder, and as his
therapist and friend, my attempts in assisting in his recovery over many years
had failed. Although I had tried every therapeutic intervention, none of them
worked. However, I refused to give up.

Mike was just one of the many thousands I had encountered in my work
as a psychotherapist during the 50 years of my career. Without bragging,
I used to say, "In five decades of working in this field, I have never had a dull
day!" People respond with some doubt since the research shows that many
Americans are not happy in their work and would change jobs if they could.

Psychology is one of the "helping professions" and is committed to serving
others as they navigate a challenging world. Although not every psychologist
is altruistic and committed to serving, the great majority have been influenced
by Gandhi's suggestion, "Find yourself by losing yourself in service to others."
As a humanistic psychologist, I am motivated by valuing every person, assisting
them in seeing their own value and helping them to move beyond personal
selfishness to make a positive impact in their work and personal lives. While
not being successful with everyone, the joy comes from seeing progress and
improvement in the lives of the ones who are moving forward.

The great benefit of a career serving others is that it can be done for a
lifetime. In our world of media dominance where countless hours are spent on
cell phones, the personal touch is still desired and effective. I see this as
I volunteer on the Navajo Nation in Arizona working among the "poorest of
the poor." No one there sees me as too old to function; I am honored as one
of the elders, and many benefit from my advice. And this gives me great joy!

*How do you derive purpose in your life? Are there things you can do to serve others
and find the joy that Gandhi suggests?*

Don Nichols is Professor Emeritus at Oakland Community College (Michigan),
a former Dean of Liberal Arts and Adjunct Professor at Madonna University
and the University of Windsor (Canada).

Conclusion
Reflection, Review and Action

Wrapping up a book like this is so different from most books. Simply put, *The Intentional Life* is based on a general flow with the seven thematic areas. This book is not like a novel that unfolds from the beginning and wraps up at the end. This book is not designed to be read straight through, as a traditional storyline does not exist. The book is meant to both share others' wisdom and be inspirational, providing the reader with the opportunity to be a bit more grounded and thoughtful as they move forward in their lives. By providing experiences and insights from hundreds of people of all ages, the book offers messages that may not have been heard elsewhere, particularly in a world filled with misinformation, generalizations and social media.

Further, two separate phrases in the subtitle speak volumes. The book is centered on "Crafting Your Legacy," which puts the responsibility on each individual to take others' background and recommendations and determine what works the best for them at this point in time. Through reading and reflecting on the various points of view and, further by engaging in discussions with others about different takeaways from individual or collective Legacy Letters, readers are likely to have greater grounding as they move forward. The other phrase in the subtitle – "One Day at a Time" – illustrates that this book is not designed to be read in a single setting. The intent is to review and absorb a single Legacy Letter each day of the year – just one page. Beyond that, the book is designed to be reviewed again and again, year after year. When the reader is reviewing a Legacy Letter for a second time, a year or two after the first time reading it, their life perspective will be different, because a full year or more will have passed. Growth is continual – or it can be, unless someone is stagnating. The opportunity exists to continue to grow and mature.

Of course, some readers will take a different approach to reviewing the Legacy Letters – like reading several Legacy Letters within a specific thematic area to address a current or emerging need. With this approach, the reader can reflect on different perspectives and insights on the same theme and determine what works well for their own lives.

DOI: 10.4324/9781003541080-9

Through the process of soliciting and compiling these, several insights can be offered. First, the interest in preparing something to share with others (even the writers' "younger self") was overwhelmingly strong. Colleagues and friends shared their thoughts readily. Second, many contributors reported that the "assignment" to them was difficult. They felt challenged, knowing they needed to dig deep within their own hearts and minds to share what they believed would be meaningful for others. Third, some Legacy Letter writers reported that their preparation of their contribution was transformational in their own lives; they asked themselves questions that they had not thought of in a meaningful way previously.

Further, while over two-thirds of the contributions were from people with whom a direct relationship existed, so much was learned that was not previously known. While some were high school friends with regular or sporadic contact over decades, and some were colleagues with close working relationships, so much was learned about a part of their lives that was not previously known. The question is why that was the case. Was it because they kept that hidden or did not want to or did not feel it was relevant or appropriate to share? Was it because those experiences were part of a period in their life where overlap didn't exist? Was it because more in-depth and personal queries were not pursued? Whatever the reason, the takeaway is that so much rich and heartfelt experience exists in the lives of those around us, and each of us can benefit from probing a bit more deeply, intently and compassionately.

With this book's framework around seven thematic areas, the focus is on helping individuals to have a life that is more focused and in directions desired by the reader. Will reading these and reflecting on the Legacy Letters provide a guarantee for a life that is sounder? No. No such guarantee exists. Are each of these seven thematic areas incorporated in a type of magic bullet? Of course not. Does the incorporation of the recommendations provided by writers promise results? No. These simply provide greater grounding and stronger foundations for the reader – should that choice be made – to be more focused and thoughtful with their lives.

To help wrap this up, six summative recommendations are offered. These help to pull together the wisdom and insights, the experiences and the challenges, of the over 300 contributors to this book. Through the 365 individual contributions, consider incorporating these as an overall framework for any future endeavor in life.

RECOMMENDATION #1: LISTEN

Life is a continuous, growth-oriented process. For young adults with the capacity to observe and absorb so much that surround them, it is important to continue to listen. Listen to the insights and experiences of others – both incorporated in this book as well as throughout life. The contributors for this book took a lot of time and effort to craft what they believed would be most helpful to young adults generally. They wanted to provide education and information and inspiration. Each person has a unique story – and the readers each have a unique story that is in the process of being written. The critical theme is that value CAN be added to that story. That's a choice that each individual has to make – what to be exposed to in terms of information sources and from which sources to draw motivation and inspiration. As this listening process occurs, it is important to process it, mull it over, and decide what to draw on and what to discard. The wisdom and insights shared by others are for the reader's consideration. Through listening, opportunities exist for individuals to become even more grounded and focused with their own lives, as they also listen to themselves as time moves on.

RECOMMENDATION #2: LEARN

Building on the process of listening to one's surroundings and influences, one also has the opportunity to learn from this listening process. Individuals can learn from others' experiences, both good and bad, and what is to emulated and what is to be avoided. Individuals can learn how to turn weaknesses into strengths, particularly if there is passion for a purpose. With the learning process, continual questions that can be asked are, "What was that experience supposed to teach me? What was I meant to learn?" Every day of one's life provides opportunities to live and listen and grow. Although someone may not know how to do things initially, they learn how by observing others and practicing helpful strategies. Through practice, they learn proficiency and gain confidence. The learning is based on blueprints and planning processes. Through learning, a view of creating a world that is more meaningful, healthier and productive – an aspirational perspective – can be attained.

RECOMMENDATION #3: REFLECT

While maintaining a listening posture and engaging in continual learning, the process of reflection on a regular basis is critical. Reflection includes a review of the content, from whatever source, that was observed and shared; reflection also includes a review of the processes used. Core questions focus on what makes sense, what information is valid, where can more be gathered, and what might be the implications of using that. Further, what are the applications relevant for each individual, starting with the basic belief that each individual has a legacy that lives within them. As individuals reflect on yesterday, today and tomorrow and reflect on dreams and aspirations, the acknowledgment is that each individual is responsible – and has the opportunity – for determining their own direction. Further, individual legacies are much like snowflakes: no two are the same. The reflection is based on what was learned when doing something, when talking with someone, when listening to some source, and when having an experience – reflect on what was learned from doing what was done, and acknowledge that current efforts may benefit from moving forward in some planful and constructive manner. The "now" is what matters, and the only way to address that is to show up for oneself and create one's own future.

RECOMMENDATION #4: PLAN

The background themes of listening and learning and reflecting are for naught if that's all they are. Although each one is vitally important, also essential is building on these foundations to make some plans for oneself. These plans can be general, like a vision or aspirational goal, or more specific with objectives and timelines. These plans can be fuzzy or more granular. Important, however, is starting with where one is and building on that. Strive to become more specific and focused as time goes on. Further, it is helpful to focus not just on what is the easiest to achieve; focus on something aspirational. For example, if one only picks the apples on a tree that are lowest and within reach, what could have been achieved if the reach had been extended or additional heights had been scaled? While perfection doesn't exist, that doesn't mean that it should be ignored. Imperfection is part of life and can be dealt with. Life is a series of transitions, including challenges and successes. Acknowledge that planning for one's life is a personal approach, much like a patchwork quilt where individuals do their own weaving. The planning is broader, for example, than just having a job – it encompasses goals and dreams. Attention is provided to complementing what is being done, to help individuals achieve the results they want. With planning, being more thoughtful and engaged will help with that goal attainment; again, it is not a guarantee but offers a greater likelihood of having the desired results.

RECOMMENDATION #5: CONNECT

Through the process of planning, important is the acknowledgment that this is not a matter of making it alone. It incorporates the acknowledgment that no one is a superperson, but they are, in fact, an "everyperson." As such, it is vital that the journey of crafting one's legacy be done with the involvement and support of others. Whether that is through collaboration, sharing, engagement, shared reflection or some other process, working with others is critical to achieving the desired end points. These connections may be family members or loved ones, they may involve mentors and mentees, they may be found in work or social settings and they may be found in various community settings in which they find themselves. The gift of shared stories is present, and these stories can be woven together to help enhance and solidify one's own journey. The journey of life planning and legacy development can be shared with others, by knowing them (listening) and caring about them. With these connections, one can start with what life can be imagined for oneself and what more do others imagine for oneself. One can learn a lot from others, so it is important to seek them out. Although the Legacy Letters and inspirational reflection pieces for each of these can be helpful, even more helpful will be conversations with others about the same Legacy Letters and reflections regarding applications and relevance for one's own life. With a final reflection about connections, consider how one wants to be remembered in the hearts of others.

RECOMMENDATION #6: AFFIRM

The final recommendation is that of affirming that a focus on one's own future, and ultimately one's legacy, is worthwhile. In response to the question "Why bother?" the focus is that each individual will benefit from doing something different. It is owed to themselves, their futures, their children, their friends, their communities and their world to be more thoughtful and a bit more organized in creating a healthy and safe future. If one is fully satisfied with the status quo, then the "Why bother?" question is irrelevant. However, the foundation of this book is that people, universally, are not satisfied with everything in their lives; they continue to strive and to produce, and they continue to exist and to survive. The thrust of this book is that by being a bit more thoughtful and planful and learning from others and growing from their experiences, then a brighter future is possible. Important is to both live in the present and live for the future and to be engaged – as actively as possible – in the creation of that future. The affirmation is also the belief that an individual's life is not based on who they were or are but who they are in the process of becoming. The affirmation comes from within, with the support and assistance of others (connect!). While challenges and disappointments and curveballs are thrown in almost everyone's life, the belief in oneself, and that internal confidence, will help sustain toward the future.

IN CLOSING

The Intentional Life is designed to inspire, to motivate, to ground and to share. *The Intentional Life* is designed to be a part of the thoughtful process of young adults as they take stock of their lives and determine the best ways forward. *The Intentional Life* is designed to help reduce, in some way, some of the uncertainty young adults face as they embark on their futures. *The Intentional Life* is designed to help round out the thinking and worldly perspectives of young adults, to broaden the scope of what they would like to achieve in their lives. *The Intentional Life* is prepared to help the reader think a bit differently and intentionally about their lives and how they are living their lives.

This book provides a framework, with its seven thematic areas, that complements and builds on several other theoretical constructs. It is not a road map per se, yet it does incorporate dozens of tools that may be useful and inspiring for the reader.

However, the value of the contents and processes embedded in *The Intentional Life* are only as good as the use to which they are put. The ways in which the contents of this book can be valuable is based on and limited by the diligence with which it is used. The intent is that human growth, and the development of a human's potential, is a slow and ongoing process – thus, the focus on "One Day at a Time." The results achieved will be based on the effort put into the process and the seriousness with which the reader takes the task, albeit the opportunity, to enrich their own life.

The power of the book, with its shared wisdom and insights, is with engaging in a process that is more planful, more intentional than what is typically used. Further, greater impact can be achieved by sharing the journey with others, embarking on some readings, reflections, discussions and applications with friends and colleagues along the way.

As outlined at the outset of this book, the word "intentional" in the book's title is designed to inspire greater self-reflection and awareness surrounding one's future. It does not mean that the envisioned outcome, once specified, will automatically be achieved. What it does mean is that one is more likely to achieve that outcome if it is envisioned and then plans are made to strive to achieve it. What it does mean is that the various decisions and opportunities along the way – such as whether to participate in some event, or whether to nourish a particular relationship, or whether to reflect and grow – can indeed be filled with greater intention so they contribute to the individual's actual needs and desires.

Each human on this earth has but one life. The question now is what to do with it and how to shape it. Individuals will continue to define or refine their goals and their strategies. Life is a process that continues to unfold.

Often, with a standard movie, two words appear on the screen at its conclusion: "The End." *The Intentional Life* is founded on a different phrase: "Not the End." The questions revolve around what steps each individual is willing to take and what footprints will be seen. The ultimate answer resides in the hearts and the actions of each person. Based on their actions and the legacy they leave, the continuity of life continues.

The foundations are laid. The inspiration is provided. The applications are plentiful. The choices abound. Individuals are encouraged to use their gifts in this moment and the next moment. The mandate is to get on with the future. This is the moment.

WHAT LEGACY DO YOU WANT TO LEAVE?

Consider your response from various perspectives, such as vocation, community, relationships, family.

FIGURE 9.1
Legacy Worksheet

THINK ABOUT THE LEGACY YOU WANT TO HAVE. WHAT CAN YOU DO SPECIFICALLY TO HELP YOU ACHIEVE THAT LEGACY?

Within 5 Years
Within 10 Years
Within 20 Years
Beyond 20 Years

FIGURE 9.2
Legacy Over Time

THINK OF THREE PEOPLE WHO MIGHT PREPARE A STATEMENT ABOUT YOUR LEGACY. HOW WOULD THE STATEMENTS READ?

From _____

From _____

From _____

FIGURE 9.3
Legacy From Others

WRITE A LETTER TO YOURSELF AS IF YOU WERE WRITING IT 20 YEARS FROM NOW. IN THAT LETTER, WRITE WHAT YOU BELIEVE YOUR LEGACY WILL BE.

FIGURE 9.4
Legacy Letter to Self

APPENDIX

RECOMMENDED CALENDAR FOR LEGACY LETTERS

Note: Please see "Using This Book" on pages 10-12 for suggestions regarding this calendar.

January

1	378	8	193	15	212	22	22	29	308
2	218	9	99	16	311	23	305	30	165
3	164	10	71	17	195	24	210	31	347
4	353	11	236	18	84	25	58		
5	48	12	294	19	231	26	349		
6	126	13	94	20	413	27	239		
7	247	14	409	21	169	28	122		

February

1	159	8	43	15	113	22	271
2	80	9	190	16	400	23	156
3	390	10	289	17	324	24	72
4	209	11	123	18	108	25	312
5	360	12	396	19	364	26	124
6	41	13	248	20	227	27	34
7	155	14	320	21	395	28	268

March

1	110	8	130	15	211	22	20	29	258
2	60	9	187	16	335	23	177	30	336
3	356	10	47	17	87	24	217	31	381
4	91	11	295	18	267	25	334		
5	232	12	252	19	362	26	62		
6	307	13	95	20	245	27	188		
7	405	14	393	21	161	28	144		

April

1	32	8	115	15	301	22	343	29	276
2	257	9	219	16	42	23	61	30	53
3	371	10	316	17	128	24	251		
4	379	11	369	18	216	25	394		
5	90	12	226	19	172	26	170		
6	331	13	414	20	411	27	134		
7	151	14	178	21	118	28	315		

May

1	35	8	136	15	214	22	167	29	254
2	160	9	157	16	291	23	350	30	194
3	230	10	125	17	181	24	81	31	38
4	318	11	330	18	83	25	229		
5	102	12	50	19	52	26	417		
6	408	13	348	20	326	27	45		
7	270	14	404	21	263	28	140		

June

1	264	8	309	15	69	22	192	29	131
2	186	9	121	16	185	23	387	30	384
3	21	10	321	17	327	24	89		
4	175	11	344	18	265	25	416		
5	345	12	391	19	120	26	234		
6	63	13	237	20	70	27	303		
7	256	14	92	21	290	28	49		

July

1	266	8	367	15	407	22	171	29	386
2	40	9	44	16	105	23	96	30	244
3	133	10	180	17	215	24	46	31	310
4	337	11	221	18	37	25	317		
5	25	12	297	19	82	26	363		
6	406	13	366	20	198	27	275		
7	98	14	168	21	260	28	200		

August

1	300	8	51	15	66	22	201	29	104
2	86	9	299	16	223	23	55	30	250
3	410	10	365	17	383	24	262	31	112
4	65	11	255	18	346	25	412		
5	179	12	328	19	23	26	182		
6	119	13	243	20	382	27	107		
7	277	14	139	21	293	28	174		

September

1	235	8	253	15	380	22	189	29	240
2	64	9	111	16	137	23	138	30	31
3	106	10	306	17	191	24	241		
4	351	11	18	18	56	25	325		
5	401	12	114	19	259	26	354		
6	176	13	242	20	127	27	397		
7	329	14	333	21	288	28	54		

October

1	261	8	313	15	249	22	103	29	196
2	57	9	361	16	319	23	19	30	225
3	93	10	183	17	233	24	154	31	352
4	392	11	33	18	129	25	385		
5	323	12	132	19	298	26	152		
6	402	13	388	20	370	27	143		
7	238	14	202	21	228	28	24		

November

1	28	8	398	15	135	22	142	29	403
2	116	9	220	16	67	23	199	30	163
3	158	10	292	17	278	24	224		
4	269	11	246	18	117	25	368		
5	286	12	85	19	36	26	141		
6	173	13	296	20	213	27	302		
7	29	14	359	21	377	28	39		

December

1	399	8	355	15	304	22	30	29	279
2	88	9	162	16	101	23	274	30	97
3	273	10	109	17	272	24	287	31	322
4	332	11	357	18	59	25	100		
5	153	12	314	19	166	26	358		
6	68	13	389	20	222	27	26		
7	415	14	27	21	197	28	184		

ABOUT THE AUTHOR

David S. Anderson, Ph.D., is Professor Emeritus of Education and Human Development at George Mason University, where he worked for 28 years; he served as Professor and Director of the Center for the Advancement of Public Health. Prior to that, he served as a college administrator at The Ohio State University, Radford University and Ohio University. He has managed hundreds of national state and local projects while teaching graduate and undergraduate classes. An active researcher and writer, he has decades-long research on college drug and alcohol issues, high school youth and community efforts. The focus of his work is on practical applications for youth, young adults, and leaders at the campus, community, state and national levels, and he continues with training, speaking and research. His most recent publication is *The Guide to the Eight Professional Competencies for Higher Education Substance Misuse Prevention* and includes eight hosted webinars (www. preventioncompetencies.org). His two most recent books are *Leading Campus Drug and Alcohol Abuse Prevention: Grounded Approaches for Student Impact* (coauthored with Thomas Hall; NASPA, 2021) and *Leadership in Drug and Alcohol Abuse Prevention: Insights from Long-Term Advocates* (Routledge, 2020). Other recent books include *Health and Safety Communication: A Practical Guide Forward* (with Richard Miller. 2017), *Wellness Issues for Higher Education* (2015) and *Further Wellness Issues for Higher Education* (2016). He orchestrates the College Drug and Alcohol Survey (formerly the College Alcohol Survey), a triennial survey on campus strategies addressing drug and alcohol misuse, done since 1979. In 2000, he received the Visionary Award from the U.S. Department of Education's Network. He serves on the U.S. Center for Substance Abuse Prevention's National Advisory Council and the Drug Enforcement Administration's Higher Education Workgroup. He remains active with research, writing, and consulting and has served as an active community leader in Celebration, Florida.

ABOUT THE COVER ART ILLUSTRATOR

Bruce MacPherson is a professional illustrator with over 40 years of experience preparing hand-drawn original art for magazines, books, museums and exhibits. His skill is developing concepts into visual representations to tell a story. With this cover art, Bruce was inspired by the lighting and colors of a path he walked in Tisbury, England, to use as inspiration for *The Intentional Life*.

INDEX

Note: Page numbers in *italics* refer to thematic chapters, legacy letters in chapters, and worksheets.

For Product Safety Concerns and Information please contact our EU
representative GPSR@taylorandfrancis.com
Taylor & Francis Verlag GmbH, Kaufingerstraße 24, 80331 München, Germany

www.ingramcontent.com/pod-product-compliance
Lightning Source LLC
Chambersburg PA
CBHW050555270326
41926CB00012B/2071